A WHORE'S PROFESSION

A WHORE'S PROFESSION

Notes and Essays

DAVID MAMET

faber and faber
LONDON · BOSTON

First published in Great Britain in 1994
by Faber and Faber Limited
3 Queen Square London WC1N 3AU

All rights reserved

Photoset by Parker Typesetting Service, Leicester
Printed in England by T. J. International Ltd, Padstow, Cornwall

© David Mamet, 1994

David Mamet is hereby identified as author of this work in
accordance with Section 77 of the Copyright, Designs and
Patents Act 1988.

Some Freaks © David Mamet, 1989
Writing in Restaurants © David Mamet, 1986
The Cabin © David Mamet, 1992
On Directing Film © David Mamet, 1991

Portions of *The Cabin* were originally published in the *Chicago Tribune*, *Harpers*,
HG, the *Los Angeles Times Magazine* and *The Traveler*.

'A National Dream-Life' and 'Against Amplification' first appeared in *The
Dramatists Guild Quarterly*; 'Radio Drama', 'Chicago', a portion of 'A Playwright
in Hollywood', and 'Address to the American Theater Critics Convention' in
Horizon; 'First Principles' in *Theatre* (Yale School of Drama); 'True Stories of
Bitches' in *Vanity Fair*, 'A Family Vacation' in *Vogue*; 'Oscars' in *Gentlemen's
Quarterly*; 'Pool Halls' (under the title 'American Icons') and 'Epitaph for Tennessee
Williams' in *Rolling Stone*; a portion of 'Things I Have Learned Playing Poker on the
Hill' in *The New York Times Magazine*; 'Concerning *The Water Engine*' in *The
New York Daily News*; and 'Realism' in *New York Arts Journal*. 'Notes for a
Catalogue for Raymond Saunders' was published by the Stephen Wirtz Gallery,
San Francisco.

'The Decoration of Jewish Houses' first appeared in *Penthouse*; 'A Plain Brown
Wrapper' in *Tikkun*;' 'Women' in *New York Woman*; 'Conventional Warfare' in
Esquire; 'The Laurel Crown' as 'In Losing, a Boxer Won' in *The New York Times*;
'Stanislavsky and the Bearer Bonds' in *Lincoln Center Theatre Company Magazine*;
'A Party for Mickey Mouse' and 'In the Company of Men' in *Playboy*; 'Film is a
Collaborative Business' in *American Film Magazine*; 'Practical Pistol Competition'
in *Sports Illustrated*; 'Encased by Technology' in *Interview*; and 'Kryptonite' in
Boston Review. *A Practical Handbook for the Actor* by Melissa Bruder, et al., with
an introduction by Mr Mamet is published by Vintage Books.

A CIP record is available from the British Library

ISBN 978-0-571-17076-0

6 8 10 9 7 5

Like jewels in a crown,
the precious stones glittered
in the Queen's round metal hat.

JACK HANDEY

Three apposite snippets in support: the first from the Bard, who has the Prince malign himself, in saying '. . . like a whore, unpack my heart with words'.

The second, attributed to Mrs. Patrick Campbell. Exiting her Theatre one night, she took shelter from the rain under the marquee. She found herself beside a streetwalker, and followed the girl's gaze to a carriage which held an upper-class girl and boy necking ferociously. Mrs. Campbell turned to her neighbor and sympathized: 'Another great profession ruined by Amateurs.'

The last from the streets of Chicago, the instruction, 'It isn't the men, it's the stairs.'

Best wishes. Thank you for your interest in my work.

D.M.

Contents

SOME FREAKS

ON DIRECTING FILM

THE CABIN

For My Sister
LYNN

Acknowledgements

I would like to thank Joni Evans and Julie Grau for their interest in and care of these essays; and I would like to thank my assistant, Harriet Voyt, for her lovely good nature and for her help with the preparation of this book.

Prologue:
Rutland Gate

I met Pat Buckley on my first trip to London. I had just turned thirty, and he was something over eighty.

We were walking near Parliament, and he gestured and said that his solicitors' offices were just nearby. I was shopping for a lawyer myself, and I asked him how long the folks over there had been his solicitors. 'For about a hundred twenty years,' he said.

He remembered, as a child, he said, being taken to see Queen Victoria. He had been at school with Lord Mountbatten; he was a man-about-town in the twenties. When the BBC did a retrospective on the Charleston in the seventies, Pat was remembered as a leading exponent of the dance, and he spoke about it and twenties London over the radio.

He had been in MI5 during the Second World War. He told this story: an MI5 officer friend of his had been traveling from London to Scotland by rail. The man was in a private compartment with his batman, when an enlisted man entered and said that there was another officer in the coach who somehow looked out of place. The MI5 man asked for the officer to be brought to his compartment, and he was.

The officer's papers were all in order, and there was nothing out of place about him, and nothing to excite suspicion. Nonetheless the man did not seem quite right.

'Take off your jacket,' the MI5 man asked, and the officer did so. He was then asked to take off his shirt and then his undershirt, under which were seen large red welts of the sort caused by a parachute harness. The man turned out to be a German spy who had parachuted into England that morning. He was tried and executed – 'lovely story,' Pat said, 'I could have dined out on it all throughout the War, but, of course, while the War was on, I couldn't tell it.'

I think he was himself the MI5 officer on the train.

I wonder what he did during the First World War, in which he must certainly have fought, but about which he would not speak.

I know that in the late twenties and thirties he wrote travel books, which were a favorite of Queen Mary – he showed me correspondence and a photograph she had autographed to him. He also toured America in that period, lecturing about Great Britain, and was a great success, it seems. He had several quite intimately inscribed photos of a very well-known film actress on his mantel.

We walked through Knightsbridge. He took me to a decorator's shop to show me some material. There was a very pretty young woman proprietor, and she treated him with great deference, and referred to him as Major Buckley.

We stopped at a storefront tailor where he was having his suits recut. They were of excellent manufacture, and quite old, and, as he was losing weight, he was having them made over from single- to double-breasted cut.

And at the tailor he showed me an innovation of which he was proud: he'd had the man sew a two-inch-diameter red felt circle over the label on the inside of the collar of his raincoat. Everyone in London had the same coat, he told me, and this made it a breeze to reclaim it from the coat-check room.

This seemed to me a terrific idea, and for years I have been meaning, and still mean, to do it to my coats.

We went back to his flat in Rutland Gate and he told me this:

A friend of a niece of his had come to visit London from the States. She came round to his flat, he made her some lunch, and, when she had left, he noticed that his wristwatch, which he had left on his dresser, was missing. He told me it was a Patek Philippe watch in platinum, that he had worn it for over fifty years, and that she had certainly taken it.

On my next trip to London five years later, Pat told me the story of the watch again, as if the theft had happened to him just the day before.

I was reading a posh British magazine the other day, and came across a real estate listing for a beautiful flat in Rutland Gate. It had several photos of the flat and listed the amenities, and, having visited there myself, I agreed with the description. One of the photos showed the mantel, and, on it, the photo of the very famous film star.

Well, we have no more Victorian gentlemen with us.

I would have liked to have known more about MI5, and the

Great War, and his affair with the film star.

I would have liked to have listened to him tell about the film community in the thirties, and whether it was in fact he who caught the German spy.

He was a gracious man, and good to talk to me. It occurs to me that he must have, consciously or not, told me the story of the Patek watch because he was worried that I might take something from him. I'd like to put another coloration on it, but if the reminiscence is going to have any worth it should, I think, be accurate.

This volume is, mainly, travel and reminiscence, and, if I am going to analyze the content accurately, I suppose it must mean that, I, too, am getting old.

Best wishes,
DAVID MAMET

The Rake

There was the incident of the rake and there was the incident of the school play, and it seems to me that they both took place at the round kitchen table.

The table was not in the kitchen proper, but in an area called the 'nook,' which held its claim to that small measure of charm by dint of a waist-high wall separating it from an adjacent area known as the living room.

All family meals were eaten in the nook. There was a dining room to the right, but, as in most rooms of that name at that time and in those surroundings, it was never used.

The round table was of wrought iron and topped with glass; it was noteworthy for that glass, for it was more than once and rather more than several times, I am inclined to think, that my stepfather would grow so angry as to bring some object down on the glass top, shattering it, thus giving us to know how we had forced him out of control.

And it seems that most times when he would shatter the table, as often as that might have been, he would cut some portion of himself on the glass, or that he or his wife, our mother, would cut their hands picking up the glass afterward, and that we children were to understand, and did understand, that these wounds were our fault.

So the table was associated in our minds with the notion of blood.

The house was in a brand-new housing development in the southern suburbs. The new community was built upon, and now bordered, the remains of what had once been a cornfield. When our new family moved in, there were but a few homes in the development completed, and a few more under construction. Most streets were mud, and boasted a house here or there, and many empty lots marked out by white stakes.

The house we lived in was the development's model home. The first time we had seen it, it had signs plastered on the front and throughout the interior telling of the various conveniences it contained. And it had a lawn, one of the only homes in the new community that did.

My stepfather was fond of the lawn, and he detailed me and my sister to care for it, and one fall afternoon we found ourselves assigned to rake the leaves.

Why this chore should have been so hated I cannot say, except that we children, and I especially, felt ourselves less than full members of this new, cobbled-together family, and disliked being assigned to the beautification of a home that we found unbeautiful in all respects, and for which we had neither natural affection nor a sense of proprietary interest.

We went to the new high school. We walked the mile down the open two-lane road on one side of which was the just-begun suburban community and on the other side of which was the cornfield.

The school was as new as the community, and still under construction for the first three years of its occupancy. One of its innovations was the notion that honesty would be engendered by the absence of security, so the lockers were designed and built both without locks and without the possibility of attaching locks. And there was the corresponding rash of thievery and many lectures about the same from the school administration, but it was difficult

to point with pride to any scholastic or community tradition supporting the suggestion that we, the students, pull together in this
new, utopian way. We were in school in an uncompleted building in
the midst of a mud field in the midst of a cornfield. Our various sports
teams were called the Spartans; and I played on those teams, which
were of a wretchedness consistent with their novelty.

Meanwhile, my sister interested herself in the drama society. The
year after I had left the school she obtained the lead in the school
play. It called for acting and singing, both of which she had talent for,
and it looked to be a signal triumph for her in her otherwise
unremarkable and unenjoyed school career.

On the night of the play's opening she sat down to dinner with our
mother and our stepfather. It may be that they ate a trifle early to
allow her to get to the school to enjoy the excitement of the opening
night. But however it was, my sister had no appetite, and she nibbled
a bit at her food, and then when she got up from the table to carry her
plate back to scrape it in the sink, my mother suggested that she sit
down, as she had not finished her food. My sister said she really had
no appetite, but my mother insisted that, as the meal had been
prepared, it would be good form to sit and eat it.

My sister sat down with the plate and pecked at her food and she
tried to eat a bit, and told my mother that, no, really, she possessed
no appetite whatsoever, and that was due, no doubt, not to the food,
but to her nervousness and excitement at the prospect of opening
night.

My mother, again, said that, as the food had been cooked, it had to
be eaten, and my sister tried and said that she could not; at which my
mother nodded. She then got up from the table and went to the
telephone and looked up the number and called the school and got
the drama teacher and identified herself and told him that her
daughter wouldn't be coming to school that night, that, no, she was
not ill, but that she would not be coming in. Yes, yes, she said, she
knew that her daughter had the lead in the play, and, yes, she was
aware that many children and teachers had worked hard for it,
et cetera, and so my sister did not play the lead in her school play. But
I was long gone, out of the house by that time, and well out of it. I
heard that story, and others like it, at the distance of twenty-five
years.

*

In the model house our rooms were separated from their room, the master bedroom, by a bathroom and a study. On some weekends I would go alone to visit my father in the city and my sister would stay and sometimes grow frightened or lonely in her part of the house. And once, in the period when my grandfather, then in his sixties, was living with us, she became alarmed at a noise she had heard in the night, or perhaps she just became lonely, and she went out of her room and down the hall, calling for my mother, or my stepfather, or my grandfather, but the house was dark, and no one answered.

And as she went farther down the hall, toward the living room, she heard voices, and she turned the corner, and saw a light coming from under the closed door in the master bedroom, and heard my stepfather crying and the sound of my mother sobbing. So my sister went up to the door, and she heard my stepfather talking to my grandfather and saying, 'Jack. Say the words. Just say the words . . .' And my grandfather, in his Eastern European accent, saying, with obvious pain and difficulty, 'No. No. I can't. Why are you making me do this? Why?' And the sound of my mother crying convulsively.

My sister opened the door, and she saw my grandfather sitting on the bed, and my stepfather standing by the closet and gesturing. On the floor of the closet she saw my mother, curled in a fetal position, moaning and crying and hugging herself. My stepfather was saying, 'Say the words. Just say the words.' And my grandfather was breathing fast and repeating, 'I can't. She knows how I feel about her. I can't.' And my stepfather said, 'Say the words, Jack. Please. Just say you love her.' At which my mother moaned louder. And my grandfather said, 'I can't.'

My sister pushed the door open farther and said – I don't know what she said, but she asked, I'm sure, for some reassurance or some explanation, and my stepfather turned around and saw her and picked up a hairbrush from a dresser that he passed as he walked toward her, and he hit her in the face and slammed the door on her. And she continued to hear 'Jack, say the words.'

She told me that on weekends when I was gone my stepfather ended every Sunday evening by hitting or beating her for some reason or other. He would come home from depositing his own kids back at their mother's house after their weekend visitation, and would settle down tired and angry, and, as a regular matter on those evenings, would find out some intolerable behavior on my sister's part and slap or hit or beat her.

Years later, at my mother's funeral, my sister spoke to our aunt, my mother's sister, who offered a footnote to this behavior. She said when they were young, my mother and my aunt and their parents lived in a small flat on the West Side. My grandfather was a salesman on the road from dawn on Monday until Friday night. Their family had a fiction, and that fiction, that article of faith, was that my mother was a naughty child. And each Friday, when he came home, his first question as he climbed the stairs was 'What has she done this week . . .?' At which my grandmother would tell him the terrible things that my mother had done, after which she, my mother, was beaten.

This was general knowledge in my family. The footnote concerned my grandfather's behavior later in the night. My aunt had a room of her own, and it adjoined her parents' room. And she related that each Friday, when the house had gone to bed, she, through the thin wall, heard my grandfather pleading for sex. 'Cookie, please.' And my grandmother responding, 'No, Jack.' 'Cookie, please.' 'No, Jack.' 'Cookie, please.'

And once my grandfather came home and asked, 'What has she done this week?' and I do not know, but I imagine that the response was not completed, and perhaps hardly begun; in any case, he reached and grabbed my mother by the back of the neck and hurled her down the stairs.

And once, in our house in the suburbs, there had been an outburst by my stepfather directed at my sister. And she had somehow prevailed. It was, I think, that he had the facts of the case wrong, and had accused her of the commission of something for which she had demonstrably had no opportunity, and she pointed this out to him with what I can imagine, given the circumstances, was an understandable, and, given my prejudice, a commendable degree of freedom. Thinking the incident closed, she went back to her room to study, and, a few moments later, he threw open her door, batted the book out of her hands, and picked her up and threw her against the far wall, where she struck the back of her neck on a shelf.

She was told, the next morning, that her pain, real or pretended, held no weight, and that she would have to go to school. She protested that she could not walk, or, if at all, only with the greatest of difficulty and in great pain; but she was dressed and did walk to school, where she fainted, and was brought home. For years she suffered various headaches; an X-ray taken twenty years later for an unrelated problem revealed that when he threw her against the shelf he had cracked her vertebrae.

When we left the house we left in good spirits. When we went out to dinner, it was an adventure, which was strange to me, looking back, because many of these dinners ended with my sister or myself being banished, sullen or in tears, from the restaurant, and told to wait in the car, as we were in disgrace.

These were the excursions that had ended due to her or my intolerable arrogance, as it was explained to us.

The happy trips were celebrated and capped with a joke. Here is the joke: my stepfather, my mother, my sister, and I would exit the restaurant, my stepfather and mother would walk to the car, telling us that they would pick us up. We children would stand by the restaurant entrance. They would drive up in the car, open the passenger door, and wait until my sister and I had started to get in. They would then drive away.

They would drive ten or fifteen feet and open the door again, and we would walk up again, and they would drive away again. They sometimes would drive around the block. But they would always come back, and by that time the four of us would be laughing in cama-raderie and appreciation of what, I believe, was our only family joke.

We were doing the lawn, my sister and I. I was raking, and she was stuffing the leaves into a bag. I loathed the job, and my muscles and my mind rebelled, and I was viciously angry, and my sister said something, and I turned and threw the rake at her and it hit her in the face.

The rake was split bamboo and metal, and a piece of metal caught her lip and cut her badly.

We were both terrified, and I was sick with guilt, and we ran into the house, my sister holding her hand to her mouth, and her mouth and her hand and the front of her dress covered in blood.

We ran into the kitchen, where my mother was cooking dinner, and my mother asked what happened.

Neither of us – myself out of guilt, of course, and my sister out of a desire to avert the terrible punishment she knew I would receive – would say what had occurred.

My mother pressed us, and neither of us would answer. She said that until one or the other answered, we would not go to the hospital; and so the family sat down to dinner, where my sister clutched a napkin to her face and the blood soaked the napkin and ran down onto her food, which she had to eat; and I also ate my food, and we cleared the table and went to the hospital.

I remember the walks home from school in the frigid winter, along the cornfield that was, for all its proximity to the city, part of the prairie. The winters were viciously cold. From the remove of years, I can see how the area might and may have been beautiful. One could have walked in the stubble of the cornfields, or hunted birds, or enjoyed any of a number of pleasures naturally occurring.

Memories of Chelsea

It was the winter before I married, and I lived alone in one floor of an old row house in New York's Chelsea. I was sick all winter with a lingering cold or flu, born, I think, at least in part, from loneliness. But I also enjoyed the solitude.

Every evening – I remember it as every evening, but it cannot actually have been – I took myself to dinner at a restaurant on Ninth Avenue, and sat by myself and read novels.

I read the entire works of Willa Cather, night after night. I would eat my breaded this or that, and linger on with coffee and several cigarettes until the restaurant closed.

I was making my living as a writer for the first time in my life. A young man in his late twenties in New York, involved in and very conscious of living a romance.

I remember one Sunday in October when I washed my windows.

My apartment had four windows, and I washed them at length on a cool, bright day, happy as I had ever been before or ever have been since.

I remember evenings in front of the fire. I had used a bearskin rug as a prop in a play of mine in Chicago, and the young woman who had lent the rug to the production later showed up in New York and made me a present of it. I'd lie on the rug in front of the fire and read, my head resting back on the head of the bear.

When I married, my wife supposed that I had made love to countless women on that bear rug, and suggested that I leave it behind. Which I did. I had made love to one woman on the rug – which story I'll tell later.

I adored that apartment. In the summer I'd sit home evenings, with a bottle of Pouilly-Fuissé, as cold as I could get it, and I'd drink and read. The wine was not expensive – this was just in advance of the vogue for white French wine – and I indulged myself.

In sum, I was self-sufficient. I was an independent young man of the world. I had an income and a future, and was beginning to have something of a name.

I was lonely on the weekends, and I remember various street fairs, cruising in search of the Woman of My Dreams, or, perhaps, for some other version of stability.

Weekdays I would go to the Chelsea YMCA and exercise, or I would go jog on the West Side Highway.

The elevated highway was awaiting demolition, and closed to traffic. I would jog from Twenty-third Street along the Hudson River, and, just across from the remaining passenger-ship terminals at Fifty-fourth, I would turn and jog back. On the run back I would occasionally race an ocean liner, just put out in the river and headed south. When they first started up I could keep pace with them for several hundred yards.

Chelsea was originally a community for the well-to-do in the shipping line. It was built for and housed ship chandlers, naval architects, captains, and others of a respectable middle-class station.

The great shipping piers spiked out into the Hudson on the west of Chelsea, two blocks from my apartment.

Ninety years before my tenure, the occupant of my house could have looked out of the kitchen window and seen that actual 'forest of masts and spars.'

The *Titanic*, had she docked, would have done so literally right down the street; and the reporters awaiting the survivors on the *Carpathia* drank at the bars right around the corner.

When I jogged south of the highway, I was alongside the huge deserted pier buildings, which had been appropriated for homosexual encounters and were the scene of much violence.

South of them I had a view of the Statue of Liberty, which I never saw without reciting some of Emma Lazarus's poem to pass the time and get myself a bit weepy. And I never saw the statue without feeling I was privileged to have such regular access.

Down on Eleventh Avenue was, and I hope still is, Madison Men's Shop, Melvin Madison, owner/proprietor.

I was lured into the shop by the very sturdy work clothes in the window, arranged alongside paraphernalia of the virtually defunct maritime trades – insignia, uniforms, and so on.

I became friendly with Melvin, and he allowed me to hang out in his shop, and we would chat about this and that and drink coffee.

The store had been under his command for many years. He had quite a bit of old, unpacked, unsold, excellent, hardy, and distinctive work clothes in stock. He had jackets and caps from the 1940s, pants and shoes of a durability unimaginable in today's manufacture.

I had once spent part of a summer working as a cook on one of the Great Lakes ore boats, so I was an actual – albeit surpassingly cadet – member of the Merchant Marine, and Mel would tell me stories of his life on the ships, and of his life in the neighborhood.

Some years previous to my residence in Chelsea, I had in fact spent a bit of time around the corner from Mel's shop, frequenting the hiring hall of the National Maritime Union, trying, unsuccessfully, to get out on a ship.

Mel and his store were a focus of both romance and comfort to the south of my apartment.

To the north was Chelsea Stationers, another neighborhood landmark. It was run and owned by Ken.

Ken, and his father before him, had been in the same spot for thirty years, and they, too, had old stock in the basement.

I'd buy old 1930s report covers with happy high-stepping footballers printed on them, old pens, and legal-looking blank books in which to write. And, as either Ken or I was usually in the process of getting off cigarettes, we would bum smokes off each other and talk about women and his adventures in his community-theater group in New Jersey.

The stationery store was the first stop on my daily walk home from the Y.

As I came out of the Y, I was facing the Chelsea Hotel, long touted as a New York City literary landmark.

The Chelsea had been home to Thomas Wolfe and Dylan Thomas and Brendan Behan, and other writers no doubt drawn by their tenure there. I had, on my first visit to New York, spent a few nights there myself – a very young man terrified by the squalor and violence and noise. The hotel embodied New York to me. Nothing in my middle-class Chicago experience had prepared me for that hotel. It was not that it was, as it was, beyond romanticizing, filthy and dangerous, but that, being such, it represented itself and was accepted as a cultural landmark, and a good choice for a serious artist looking for a room.

And everyone pointed out that Virgil Thompson still lived there.

I met Virgil Thompson around the corner from the hotel, at another of my regular stops on the trek back to my apartment from the Y. I met him at Dr. Herrmann's optometrical establishment.

Louis Herrmann was a fine eye doctor and, rest in peace, a true lover of the theater.

He was Bernard Herrmann's brother and, as a kid, had actually been with Bernard in the studios for Orson Welles's 'War of the Worlds' broadcast. I have never heard anyone speak more lovingly of another than Louis spoke of his brother Bernard.

He would reminisce about the Mercury Theatre, about Welles, about Bernard and Hitchcock; we would talk about the theater. Often his wife, Ruth, would be working in the office, and we would have coffee together.

He must have, at that time, been in his early sixties, and it was a revelation to me to see him with his wife, to see two people married thirty or forty years who were so obviously in love. He was a beautiful man.

Across the street from Louis was the shoe-repair store, where I would go for a shine.

That store figures prominently in my Chelsea mythology due to the interchange reported below.

I was out strolling one day with Shel Silverstein, whom I cite as my witness for the following improbable exchange.

I had broken a strap on my leather shoulder bag, and went into the shoe-repair store to have it fixed. The owner examined the bag at length, and shrugged. 'How much to fix it?' I said.

'That's gonna cost you twenty dollars,' he said.

'*Twenty dollars?*' I said. 'Just to fix one *strap* . . .?'

'Well I can't *get* to it,' he said. 'I can't reach it with the machine, I got to take the bag apart, do it by hand, take one man two, three hours, do that job.'

So I sighed. 'Oh, all right,' I said. 'When can I come back for it? Thursday? Friday . . .?'

'*Naaah*', he said. 'Go get a cup of coffee – come back ten, fifteen minutes.'

Down the street from the shoe-repair store was Kenny Fish.

Ken had a furniture store. He bought and restored and sold Grand Rapids oak. He was a superior craftsman, and he had good taste in what he bought. He was also a good companion and I spent many hours on my way back from the gym hanging out with Ken and playing gin. He was the worst gin player I have ever met, and my home, to this day, is spotted with heavy durable furniture I won off of Kenny.

(When I left the neighborhood, Ken was still in my debt for eighty dollars or so. I found him one day, driving a hansom cab at Sixth Avenue and Central Park South. He mentioned the long-standing debt, and I suggested that he and his horse take me up to the Dakota, and we would call it quits. I left him at Seventy-second Street and Central Park West, and have not seen him since.)

Next to Ken's store was Milton. He dealt in furniture and bric-a-brac, and went by the soubriquet of Captain Spaulding, perhaps because of the lyric, in the song of the same name, 'Did somebody call me *schnorrer* . . .?'

Below the captain was Charlie's Laundromat.

Charlie was always good for a smoke, or to cash a small check, or to hold or relay a message for the others of the neighborhood confraternity. He was a very nice and generous and accommodating man. His daughter, he told me, married Mark Rothko's son. And he once bought me a celebratory cup of coffee when the Rothko estate won a large judgment against some art dealer.

The block also housed Joe Rosenberg and his framing establishment. Joe framed many pictures for me, and gave me two important pieces of advice. He told me never to knock wood because (he had learned after fifty years of solecism) knocking wood was an appeal (through the True Cross) for the intercession of Jesus Christ. He also told me never to marry a non-Jewish girl.

After Joe and Charlie, I rounded the corner and was almost home. I turned down the residential block, nothing between me and the necessity of actually writing save the construction of instant coffee, and a reflection, perhaps, about Clement Clarke Moore ("Twas the Night Before Christmas') who at one time had lived next door.

(Anthony Perkins lived nearby, too. When I moved into my apartment I bought a clear shower-curtain liner and ordered a shower curtain to complement it. The curtain itself never arrived, so I lived with the clear liner, and that did the trick. I always wished, however, that the liner itself were enough of an oddity that someone would one day inquire why I had a clear shower curtain, and I could respond that I lived around the corner from Anthony Perkins. Well, now I have acquitted myself of it, and can get on with my life.)

In Chelsea I could look out of my living-room window and see the Empire State Building and reflect that other Chicagoans traveled 880 miles for the privilege. I could walk to the theater district or to the Village. I had a working fireplace and a pair of silver candlesticks that were the only things my grandparents brought with them out of Poland. I had a poster from the Barnum and Bailey Circus, and the bearskin rug I have spoken of before, and it is to that rug and an appurtenant misadventure connected thereto that I now refer.

To my lovely bachelor flat I had invited this very lovely young woman whom I mentioned earlier in conjunction with the bear rug. I had been pursuing her for some months, and apparently some blandishment or other worked its magic, for she finally said yes, she would come down to New York and spend the weekend with me.

She arrived in New York in the afternoon. I had promised to take her that evening to a performance of a play of mine uptown.

I took her from the station back to Chelsea, calculating that there was just enough time for some long-deferred and eagerly awaited sexual intercourse; but she said no, she'd have a bath if I didn't mind, and we could both have something to look forward to after the theater.

Well, fine. We went off, in due time, and saw the show. As the actors were taking their final bow, I hurried her through the lobby and out onto the street.

We were in the process of getting into a cab when I heard my name called, and made the mistake of turning around.

I had been called by X, an older actor, an acquaintance of mine.

He hurried up to me, his wife close behind him, told me how much he had enjoyed the show, thanked me for the tickets, and said I didn't need the cab, as he had driven down, and we could all go back in his car.

Go back? I said. Yes. And I remembered that I had, some long weeks previously, invited him and his wife to be my guests at the show, and they had extended to me their very kind invitation to join them in their home for an after-the-theater supper.

Well. My mind raced. I had to allow him to reciprocate my gift of the tickets, and I could not, I thought (having reasoned it out as closely as I could), be so discourteous as to stand him and his wife up.

So I introduced them to my young friend, explained that she had been traveling quite a long while and was exhausted from the journey, and that we really could not stay long at their house. 'Just a snack,' he assured me, 'and we'll send you on your way.'

We got to his house. He made us a drink, and then another. I less and less subtly hinted that if we were going to eat we *should* eat, as it was getting late and my friend was very *very* tired.

He finally rose and announced that, yes, it *was* time to eat, and that, in honor of my visit, *he himself* was going to cook. And he was going to cook matzoh brei.

Now, gentle reader, what is matzoh brei? It is fried matzoh.

It is matzoh (that crackerlike unleavened bread) that has been soaked in egg and milk, fried in grease, and served with syrup, sugar, butter, salt, jam or any combination of the above.

My mother, rest in peace, used to serve it on Sunday mornings. It is absolutely delicious, stupefyingly filling, and precisely the last thing one wants to eat at 11 P.M. before a scheduled night of love.

So I demurred. 'Don't put yourself out,' I said. And he said, 'Nonsense,' and cooked the matzoh brei.

He brought it out and served it heaping on my plate. And I had to eat it. Because, of course, it was an honor.

He was a Jewish Patriarch making a rare and ceremonial foray into the kitchen to cook a traditional Jewish dish to serve to me, a Young Jewish Lad, whom he had invited to his house because he was proud of me.

So I had to eat it.

I had that big, heaping plateful, and of course praised it to the skies, and so of course had to have another and a bit of a third. And I said, 'That was the most delicious matzoh brei I have ever eaten.'

And his wife said, '*You call that matzoh brei?*'

And *she* went into the kitchen.

And she called back that X and his family, in their ignorance, knew nothing of the nature and construction of the dish, and she started cooking her family's version of matzoh brei.

As I looked on, stupefied. I tried to leave, but X told us that we could not budge until I had made the comparison and told the world the truth.

So we sat there and waited while his wife cooked; and I had to eat as many plates of matzoh brei as I had before, and make the ceremonial declaration of the excellence of each recipe.

I finally extricated myself and my companion, as stuffed and as sleepy as I have ever been in my life.

In the cab she told me she liked the matzoh brei.

I waddled up the stairs to my apartment, the young woman behind me, and was young enough to engage in embraces to which, at that point, neither of us were much inclined.

That is the story of the bearskin rug, and of my Chelsea apartment. I would sit by the rear window at an oak-and-steel café table, and smoke cigarettes, and look at the row of gardens running between the backs of the houses on Nineteenth and Twentieth streets. They could well have been the gardens that inspired O. Henry's 'The Last Leaf.'

I had no television and, for the longest time, no telephone. I had a lot of books, and, for the first time in my life, a little money. It was a romantic time.

P.Q.

In 1965 I worked for several months at a roadside diner in Trois-Rivières, Province de Quebec, on the autoroute, halfway between Montreal and Quebec City. It was there that I learned to speak a little French. There were no tourists in the city. Just the natives and sailors off of the boats that had come down the St. Lawrence to the paper mills.

I lived there in the fall. The weather was cold and wet, and, because of the paper mills, the whole town smelled like the inside of a wet cardboard box.

The diner was right on the highway. My day there ran from 10 A.M., setting up, till 1 A.M., locking up, when I'd head the two miles back down Route 2 into the town proper.

It was twenty-seven years ago, which either is or is not a long time, but seems the impossibly distant past, when I remember that I would often hitch a ride back into town on what the proprietor, Roger Bellerive, assured me was the last horse-drawn milk truck on the continent. Occasionally, I'd hitched a ride back on the street sweeper.

I was young and lonely, and I remember a very potent Quebec potion called simply Alcool, a clear spirit of the white lightning variety, which I bought by the shot and the pint bottle; and a poster for the latest Elvis film, *L'Amour en quatrième vitesse*, which translation I found, ethnocentrist that I was, very dilute in French.

And there was a waitress co-worker of mine who invited me to cross the river and see her home several times. I was seventeen and she twenty-four. She told me that one had only to sleep with a Quebecoise three times in order to learn the language, but I didn't go, since she seemed, at twenty-four, vastly too old for me.

The sailors came in and ordered hamburgers and root beer, and I went home stinking of grease and the Ajax I used to scrub down the griddle.

That fall I left Trois-Rivières once, to attend Yom Kippur services in Montreal, eighty miles away.

I hitchhiked down the highway in a vicious snowstorm and found myself stranded some unknown miles short of Montreal, in the middle of the storm, in the middle of the night. There were no cars coming by. I walked to a motel back down the road. The office was locked, but one of the cabins was open, so I let myself in and shivered all night under my thin coat.

The next morning I made my way into Montreal. My dress-for-temple shoes were dissolving on my feet. I found the temple and was told I couldn't get in without a ticket, and I think I probably took a bus back to Trois-Rivières. As I write, I remember a phrase from the period: that the Quebecois were a minority in Canada, and that the English were a minority in Quebec, and that the Jews were a minority everywhere. In any case, I didn't get into the temple, but what would amuse a seventeen-year-old more than a feeling of righteous wrath and misunderstood religious fervor?

A year from the next summer, several college chums and I went north to find work at Montreal's Expo '67. We were told we couldn't work in Canada without a Canadian Social Security card, and we all bemoaned the nice fat jobs going begging until one day I walked over to the Social Security office and asked them for a card, and they gave me one and, as the Brits have it, 'Bob was my Uncle'.

I auditioned for and got a job as an 'acro dancer' with the Tibor Rudas Australian Living Screen.

Tibor's company was part of the Maurice Chevalier extravaganza, *Toutes voiles dehors!!!*, which played the Autostade at Expo '67.

The stage was in the middle of that stadium. Behind us was a drive-in-sized movie screen that was slashed vertically at intervals of one foot. A motion picture, a Parisian-street-scene drama, was projected on the screen, and at various points the cinematic characters would run toward the audience *out* of the movie and through the slits in the screen onto the stage before it.

I, as one of the acro dancers, portrayed a Parisian *apache* thug. On cue, I ran between the strips and onto the stage, where my confreres and I performed a rollicking dance, and, on cue, ran back into the screen, where our filmic doppelgängers continued the action.

At the end of the show, all of the extravaganza, which included the Barbadian Esso Triple-E Steel Band, and that's as far as my memory goes, joined Maurice Chevalier onstage and sang something or other.

I particularly remember the Esso, as they stayed in the Autostade night after night and drank Barbadian rum and partied, and on a few of those nights I was privileged to stay with them.

Expo was a treat if one worked there. The employee's pass got one straight into any of the exhibits without a wait; and, better, allowed one to stay on in the park after it had officially closed to the populace and metamorphosed into one big party.

I remember friends who, by the luck of the draw, got hired by the fair and assigned to sell programs at the main entrance of the brand-new metro — I was there on the metro's inaugural day, and stood in line and rode it. I think that is the only historical event in which I have participated. I once chatted with Howard Hughes, but I do not think that counts as 'of historical significance,' since it is, arguably, not important, and also since no one believes me.

In any case, friends were assigned, I say, to sell these programs at the entrance to the fair. The programs went for a buck, my friends got a 10 percent rake-off, and they were pulling down one thousand dollars, Canadian, a day. In 1967. I occasionally wonder what I would have done had I had that money at that age. I would, in my fantasies, have saved every cent and established my young self as a this or that. I would, perhaps, have bought a small business of some description and stayed in Canada. Who can say?

Well, I can say.

If I'd had that money as a nineteen-year-old, I'd have bought a car and a guitar and some clothes and partied myself into a liver condition. But I digress.

It seems that I was making three hundred or so a week at the Autostade, and was augmenting this with my stipend for work as Johannes Gutenberg.

Yes, if you went to Expo '67, the odds are good you saw me in the West German pavilion, dressed in a leather apron and running a replica of Gutenberg's press. There I churned out printed blackletter facsimiles of Gutenberg's fifteen-something-or-other Bible, and shrugged distractedly in response to questions in many tongues.

I lived in a hovel on Ste. Catherine Street with my fellow collegians, and we plotted the formation of a new Canadian theater company. Which company almost came into existence.

I think we did some few readings in our Ste. Catherine Street apartment. I cannot remember what we may have done, but it was probably something by Beckett or Pinter, the only two writers we deemed worthy of the name in 1967.

While wandering the fairgrounds early one morning before the starting bell, I met a Japanese man. He was lost, and in some pidgin amalgam, I found out where he wanted to go and took him there. He gave me a card that explained he was the manager-director of the next world's fair, which was to be in Osaka, and he indicated that I should come work for him.

That's the prologue to my Horatio Alger story, except that as the 1970 Osaka fair approached, I was poor and friendless in Chicago or some sodding where, and could not find the magic card. And to this *day* . . .

In 1969 I was back living in Montreal, acting in a theater company at McGill university and cheerfully starving. There was a workingman's café over near Simpson's department store that served a fresh fried trout and a short beer for one dollar, and I ate there every day, and hung around, and salted my beer to bring the foam back to it; and there was a famous and romantic bistro over on Mountain Street, the name of which I have forgotten.

I was terrible as Lenny in *The Homecoming*, and perhaps passable as the Dormouse in *Alice in Wonderland*. The theater company fell apart, I moved back to Chicago, where I wandered around looking for work, and never got to Japan.

I like the French Canadians. They have an indigenous culture and they're happy with it, they showed La Salle the way to Chicago, thus saving a million lawyers the ignominy of working on a Street with No Name, and they have always treated me more than fair.

The Watch

The Chicago in which I wanted to participate was a worker's town. It was, and, in my memory, is, the various districts and the jobs that I did there: factories out in Cicero or down in Blue Island – the Inland Steel plant in East Chicago; Yellow Cab Unit Thirteen on Halsted.

I grew up on Dreiser and Frank Norris and Sherwood Anderson, and I felt, following what I took to be their lead, that the bourgeoisie was not the fit subject of literature.

So the various jobs paid my rent, and showed me something of life, and they were irrefutable evidence of my escape from the literarily unworthy middle class. For not only was I a son of the middle class, I was, and perhaps I still am, the *ne plus ultra* of that breed: a Nice Jewish Boy. And, as that Nice Jewish Boy, I went to college.

I went to college in the East, at a countercultural institution, a year-round camp, really, where I and those of my class griped about the war and took ourselves quite seriously.

The college was in the very lovely midst of nowhere in New England. It was ten miles from the nearest town; those who did not possess either an auto or a good friend with an auto were under a *de facto* house arrest on the college grounds.

I did not have an auto. My father was the children of immigrants, born right off the boat. He had sent his first-born son, in effect, to finishing school, and it never would have occurred to him to compound this enormity by supplying that son with the sybaritic indulgence of a car.

Neither would it have occurred to me to expect the same. However, I had been told, from what seems to me to've been my earliest youth, that, on my graduation from college, I'd be given a convertible.

It was not any car that I'd receive, it was *the convertible*. How this notion got started, I don't know. But my grandmother said it, and my father said it, and I looked forward to it as a fixed point in my life.

Was it a bribe, was it to be a reward? I don't know. It was an out-of-character assurance on my father's part; for he was capable of generosity, and, indeed, on occasion, of real lavishness, but both, in my memory, were much more likely to stem from impulse than from a thought-out plan. However, he had promised it, and not only had the family heard it, but we joked about it and it became, it seemed, part of our family phrase book: e.g., 'Study hard, or you won't get into college, and then you know what you aren't going to get.'

So much that I forgot about it. It was nothing to long for, or even, truly, to anticipate. The one event would bring about the other, as retirement, the agreed-upon pension – not a subject for anticipation, or, even, on receipt, for gratitude, but the correct conclusion of an agreement.

It was my final year at college. Graduation was to come in May, and in the preceding November I would turn twenty-one. In three and a half years at college I had learned not a damned thing. I had no skills, nor demonstrable talents. Upon graduation I would be out in the world with no money, nor prospects, nor plan. Not only did I not care, I had given it no thought at all; and I believe I assumed that some happy force would intervene and allow me to spend the rest of my life in school.

Just before the Thanksgiving break my father called. He told me he was looking forward to my return to Chicago for the holiday. Now, this was news to me, as we had not discussed my coming to Chicago, and I'd made plans to spend the long weekend with friends in the East. But, no, he said, the holiday fell two days from my birthday, and it was important for him that I be back home.

I tried to beg off, and he persevered. He pressed me to come home, and told me that it was essential, as he *had* something for me. He was sending me a ticket, and I had to come.

Well. There I was. It was *the convertible*, and my father had remembered his promise, and was calling to tell me that he was about to make good on his pledge.

I left the phone booth smiling, and quite touched. I told my friends I would be flying to Chicago, but I would be driving back. I flew to O'Hare and took a bus downtown, and took a city bus to the North Side.

On the plane and on the buses I rehearsed both my gratitude and my surprise. Surprise, I knew, was difficult to counterfeit, and this

troubled me. I would hate to disappoint my father, or to give him
less than what he might consider his just due for the award of a
magnificent gift.

But no, I thought, no. The moment boded well to sweep us up in
sentiment free of hypocrisy on either of our parts. For was he not
the child of immigrants? And was he not raised in poverty, in the
Depression, by his mother, my beloved grandmother, and had we
not heard countless times, my sister and I, of their poverty, and our
ingratitude? And here before us was a ceremony of abundance . . . a
ceremony, finally, of manhood. It was my twenty-first birthday; I
was graduating from college.

I got off the Broadway bus, and walked down the side street,
rehearsing all the while, and there, across from his building, was the
car.

No. I had doubted. I realized that as I saw the car. No, I would
admit it. To my shame. I'd doubted him. How could I have
doubted? What other reason would he have had for his insistence,
his almost pleading that I come back home? Of course it was the
car; and I was ashamed I had doubted him. I looked at the car from
across the street.

It was a Volkswagen convertible. It was a tricked-out model
called the Super Beetle. It had outsized bubble skirts and wheels,
and it was painted with broad racing stripes. I seem to remember a
metallic black, with stripes of yellow and orange. I chuckled. I'm
not sure what sort of a vehicle I'd expected – perhaps I'd thought
he'd take me shopping, down on Western Avenue, and we'd be
buyers together, at the horse fair. I don't know what I expected
from him, but when I saw that Beetle, I was moved. It was, I
thought, a choice both touching and naïve. It seemed that he had
tried to put himself in the place of his son. It was as if he'd thought,
'What sort of car would the youth of today desire?' And there was
his answer, across the street.

I thought, No, that's not my style, and then reproached myself.
And I was worthy of reproach. For the gift was magnificent, and,
with the gift, his effort to understand me – *that* was the gift, the
magnificent gift. Rather than insist that I be like him, he'd tried to
make himself like me. And if my chums thought that the car was
somewhat obvious, well, they could go to hell. For I was not some
kid in the schoolyard who could be embarrassed by his parents; I

was a man, and the owner of a valuable possession. The car could take me to work, it could take me from one city to the next, and finally, my father'd given it to me.

As I walked close to it I saw the error of my momentary reluctance to appreciate its decoration. It was truly beautiful. That such a car would not have been my first choice spoke not to the defects of the car, but of my taste.

I remember the new car sticker on the window, and I remember thinking that my dad must have expected me to come into the building by the other door, or he wouldn't have left the gift out here so prominently. Or did he mean me to see it? That was my question, as I rode the elevator up.

He met me at the door. There was the table, laid out for a party in the living room beyond. Did he look wary? No. I wondered whether to say which route I had taken home, but, no, if he'd wanted to test me, he would ask. No. It was clear that I wasn't supposed to've seen the car.

But why would he have chanced my spotting it? Well, I thought, it's obvious. They'd delivered the car from the showroom, and he'd, carefully, as he did all things, instructed them on where it should be parked, and car salesman had failed him. I saw that this could present a problem: if we came out of the building on the side opposite from where the car was parked – if we began what he would, doubtless, refer to as a simple walk, and could not *find* the car (which, after all, would not be parked where he'd directed it should be), would it be my place to reveal I'd *seen* it?

No. For he'd be angry then, at the car salesman. It would be wiser to be ignorant, and not be part of that confluence which spoiled his surprise. I could steer our progress back into the building by the other door. Aha. Yes. That is what I'd do.

There was another possibility: that we would leave the building by the door *near* the car, and that he'd come across it in the unexpected place, and be off-guard. But that need not be feared, as, if I stayed oblivious to his confusion for the scantest second, he would realize the surprise would in one way be mitigated by the car's location. He would improvise, and say, 'Look here!' That he'd surely have words with the car dealership later was not my responsibility.

We sat down to dinner. My father, my stepmother, my half-siblings, and several aunts. After the meal my father made a speech about my becoming a man. He told the table how he'd, in effect, demanded my return as he had something to give me. Then he reached in the lapel pocket of his jacket, draped over the back of his chair, and brought out a small case. Yes, I thought, this is as it should be. There's the key.

Some further words were said. I took the case, and fought down an impulse to confess that I knew what it contained, et cetera, thus finessing the question of whether or not to feign surprise. I thanked him and opened the case, inside of which there was a watch.

I looked at the watch, and at the case beneath the watch, where the key would be found. There was no key. I understood that this gift would be in two parts, that *this* was the element of the trip that was the surprise. I'd underestimated my father. How could I have thought that he would let an opportunity for patriarchial drama drift by unexploited.

No mention had been made of the car. It was possible, though unlikely, that he thought I'd forgotten that the car was owing to me; but in *any* case, and even if, as was most likely, I had returned to Chicago expecting the car, such hopes would indeed be dashed before they would be realized. He would make me the present of the watch, and, then, the party would go on, and at some point, he'd say. 'Oh, by the way . . .' and draw my attention to the key, secreted in the lining of the watch case, or he'd suggest we go for a walk.

Once again, he would keep control. Well, that was as it should be, I thought. And a brand-new car – a car of *any* sort – was not the sort of present that should be given or accepted lightly, and if he chose to present the gift in his own way, it came not primarily from desire for control, but from a sense on his part of drama, which is to say, of what was fitting. I thought that was fine.

That I had, accidentally, discovered the real present parked outside was to my advantage. It allowed me to feign, no, not to feign, to *feel* true gratitude for the watch he had given me. For, in truth, it was magnificent.

It was an Illinois pocket watch. In a gold Hunter case. The case was covered with scrollwork, and, in a small crest, it had my initials. The back of the case had a small diamond set in it. There was a quite heavy gold chain. In all, it was a superb and an obviously quite expensive present.

I thanked him for it. He explained that it was a railroad watch, that is, a watch made to the stringent standards called for by the railroads in the last century. The railroads, in the days before the radio, relied exclusively upon the accuracy of the railroaders' watches to ensure safety. Yes. I understood. I admired the watch at length, and tried it in various of my pockets, and said that, had I known, I would have worn a vest.

As the party wound down, I excused myself from the table, and took the watch and the case into a back room, where I pried up the lining of the case, to find the key.

But there was no key, and there was, of course, no car; and, to one not emotionally involved, the presence of a convertible with a new car sticker on the street is not worthy of note.

I pawned the watch many times; and once I sold it outright to the pawnbroker under the El on Van Buren Street.

He was a man who knew my father, and, several years after I'd sold it, I ran into him and he asked if I'd like my watch back. I asked why such a fine watch had lain unsold in his store, and he said that he'd never put it out, he'd kept it for me, as he thought someday I'd like it back. So I redeemed it for what I had sold it for.

I wore it now and then, over the years, with a tuxedo; but, most of the time, it stayed in a box in my desk. I had it appraised at one point, and found it was, as it looked, valuable. Over the years I thought of selling it, but never did.

I had another fantasy. I thought, or *felt*, perhaps, that the watch was in fact a token in code from my father, and that the token would be redeemed after his death.

I thought that, *after his death*, at the reading of his will, it would be shown that he'd never forgotten the convertible, and that the watch was merely a test; that if I would *present* the watch to his executors – my continued possession of it a sign that I had never broken faith with him – I would receive a fitting legacy.

My father died a year ago, may he rest in peace.

Like him I have turned, I'm afraid, into something of a patriarch, and something of a burgher. Like him I am, I think, over fond of the few difficulties I enjoyed on my travels toward substantiality. Like him I will, doubtless, subject my children, in some degree, to my personality, and my affection for my youth.

I still have the watch, which I still don't like; and, several years ago I bought myself a convertible, which, I think, I never drive without enjoyment.

The Cabin

In the cabin I liked it so it really stank. I would get the smells on my hands and all over my clothes: gun oil and kerosene for the lamps, wood smoke from the stove, and the smell of cigars over all.

Inside, the cabin was filled with the signs of decay. The log walls were darkening, the floor was aging and nicked up, the wood in the wood box was checking. Most things showed the signs of use and age, and the smoke and the oil got into everything.

Once, when I'd been away for a while, I went out to the cabin on skis, and found it disappeared – all except a foot of chimney – behind a hummock of snow. I often saw the fox standing out in the field and occasionally I saw deer in the browse at the edge of the field.

I only saw the bear once, a sow and two cubs, at the pond below the field; but I saw tracks twice more, one winter in the flower beds around the house, and one spring on the pond ice just below the cabin field.

It was too early for signs of the bear that spring, because the snow was deep, and though we'd had a day or two of thaw, we were due for at least one more month of true cold, so the bear should have been asleep; and I worried a bit for my little girl playing around the house, and put a large-caliber pistol in the kitchen, on top of the cabinet with the glasses.

The pistol lay next to two large mustard-ware bowls and two maple-sugar molds. It was pushed to the back because the child had said it frightened her. I never told her it was there.

I took it, shoved behind my belt, when I walked in the woods.

It made me feel a bit overburdened and foolish, but I knew that black bears sometimes attacked; and, though I knew these attacks to be exceedingly rare, I fantasized about being the victim of one, and of dying unarmed in deference to a mocking voice that was, finally, just another aspect of my fantasy.

In any case, one day in early fall I was walking in the woods, practicing a silent walk in preparation for hunting season.

I moved very, very slowly, lifting one foot forward, and not transferring the weight until the forward foot was absolutely and silently placed.

When you move like that, time slows down. Just as when involved in a meditation, body and breathing fit themselves to the environment, and one becomes increasingly calm and aware.

I was moving slowly through the woods, glacially, almost, or so it seemed to me, when the hair on the back of my neck stood up, and I felt something in my head, in the back of my head. Something like a shock – the physical equivalent of an intuition – and I smelled this stench, very like a skunk, though not as unpleasant, a sharp smell. And I realized that my body had frozen, and that what I was smelling was a bear, very nearby.

I heard him then, a bit behind me and to the side, moving off through the woods; and I knew he was reacting to my reacting to him, as we react when we feel ourselves observed. After the bear moved off I left the woods.

The clean smell of the winter must be like a beautiful death – like a fall from a great height: complete exhilaration.

I remember that smell in the back of my nostrils – it smelled like a 'snap' – going to school on impossibly cold Chicago mornings, and I associate it with the smell of the woolen scarf wet from a runny nose and frozen to the face.

I think I was happy in those clothes because my mother was dressing me, touching me, and making me warm; and I think that must be how someone feels in the euphoria of freezing to death – that the woods are taking him home.

People say that the Indians venerated Vermont. That they worshiped, hunted, passed through, but did not make their homes there, because they held it as a sacred spot; and, indeed, many of my memories of Vermont are touched by both a joy of being alive and a consciousness of death.

Once, when I had pneumonia, I felt myself slipping into it; and, once, walking the land when I'd first bought it, carrying a survey

map and a compass, I got lost. It was February, and I was deep in
the woods. I had been walking quickly, and I was warm, but the
sun began to go down suddenly, and I stopped to get my bearings,
and I became chill.

I realized that I was turned around, and consulted my compass.
In a panic, I refused to believe what it said. It pointed one way to
the road, but my recollection and instinct pointed me the opposite
way, and so I thrashed around in the woods, my clothing wet and
cold, the cold seeping into my body as the sun went down, and, in
happy ending, stumbled, thankfully, and quite by accident, across
the road. And, in the case of the pneumonia, a friend called and
came over and took me, in my three-day delirium, to the hospital.

But one day, of course, there will be no accidental road or
antibiotic; and perhaps I delude myself, but I think that it will feel
somewhat familiar and, perhaps because of that, somewhat less
frightening, when that day comes. And there are times when I look
forward to it.

In the cabin was a dartboard. I would throw darts into it, and, if my
score surpassed a certain point, then I would say that something I'd
predicted would or would not come to pass – depending on the
agreement that I had made with the divining dartboard prior to my
throw.

But as I think back, I cannot remember what the event (for I
think it always an event of a certain type) I was divining about was
to be. It was, I think, something both good and improbable. And I
would link the ability of my subconscious to overcome both my
desire for the event and my lack of skill, with the likelihood of the
desired event. I would, in effect, pray for grace.

And I would pray for grace through the medium of solitaire,
which I would play by the hour to while away the working day. But
my target shooting, another beloved activity coming under the
general description of 'writing' – was another matter. It was always
a more serious concern, and success in it and failure both were my
own fault and no added burden on the Deity.

I would proclaim to anyone around me that I had to Go and
Work, and, having made the proclamation, would go off to the
cabin, happy with my happy fiction. To have to work never failed
to excuse me, or, so I thought, from any activity whatever.

Now: I leave for a moment the question of my feeling the need of an excuse, and address the question of superstition. I was so protective of my work, and so superstitious lest I draw the interrogation of the uninitiated and, so, anger the gods, that the only time I would refrain from the excuse of pressing work to extract me from an undesired situation was when I was actually working.

Otherwise, though – otherwise I would sit in my cabin and read or nap or throw darts or play solitaire or shoot targets; or I would smoke cigars and look out of the windows.

I would look out of the window and see the deer, or, on summer evening, see the beaver on the pond. I would look for the moose – I'd seen two moose up the road once, years ago, and others had seen them on my pond, and I felt that one day I would too. I'd watch the ducks; I'd look for the blue heron. The heron used to return for the summer once every two years. The animals, of course, were, like solitaire, a sign of grace; and grace increased somewhat with the rarity of their appearance. Although once I saw the mountain lion dart across the north road at dusk – like a fierce, muscular house cat five feet long – and it felt like something other than grace.

And twice in two days one summer, leaving the cabin just at dark, I heard dogs or coyotes in the woods tearing down a deer, and the sound of the deer barking, and the dogs chasing him back into the woods, and circling the cabin, and chasing back into the woods.

I would often sleep for a while at the end of the day, before I walked back to the house. Sometimes I would wake in a snowstorm. The cabin would be dark, the fire in the stove would be out finally – waking, you knew it first because you couldn't hear the hum of the fire, then you felt the cold – the wind would be pounding the west side of the cabin, coming up from the pond.

There is a calm that comes from the absence of electricity. I think the body recognizes and reacts to being encased in a structure through which electricity is flowing. I think the body, in some way, pulsates sympathetically with the electricity, and that the absence of electricity permits the reemergence of a natural calm.

This may just be my prejudice for the archiac, but I don't think so.

In any case, my cabin is heated with a turn-of-the century Glenwood parlor stove. It is a black iron box about three feet high, two and a half feet wide, and one and a half feet deep. It sits on a small base, which rests on chubby, foliated, bombé legs that lift it ten inches or so off the floor. It has small chromed fender and chromed knobs on its front-side loading doors. It possesses a top piece called, I believe, a 'victory,' which is meant to rise in Victorian uselessness in a sort of inverted cup-like affair. The victory is both black iron and chrome, and very impressive. I have stored it somewhere safe, and, I am sure, shall never remember where it is, let alone see it again.

The stove is both more beautiful and more useful without the ornament. It is now flat on top, and one can heat tea or burn wet socks on it, and the flat top is most useful for gauging the stove's temperature, and I refer to the different visual and auditory properties of spit on a hot stove and their application as a thermometer.

Light, when I infrequently stay past sunset, comes from various glass kerosene lamps and a few hammered-tin candle sconces. The combined smell and sound of the fire in the stove, the *thwicking* of the kerosene lamp, and the wind beating on the side wall excel all attempts to imagine it.

Next to my desk hang photographs of my four grand-parents, and notes for projects long done, and for projects never done and never to be done.

The desk is an old walnut rolltop – circa 1860 – with beautiful hand-carved pulls and a ratty green baize mat for writing surface. the mat is ink-stained and torn at all edges. The pigeonholes hold various memorabilia of my life and of the lives of others. Trinkets, in short.

On the desktop are several bottles of ink and a brass container made of an artillery shell and crudely engraved with the symbol of George V and the name H. STIMPSON, SOUVENIR DE LA GUERRE. I put paper clips in the box, and pens and pencils in an old Dundee marmalade container. There is a Winchester loading tool for the .38 Long cartridge, and a Colt model 1878 .45-caliber revolver, both of which function as paperweights. There is also a glass paperweight from the 1893 Columbian Exposition, and another in the shape of a horseshoe, made of pewter. The horseshoe has

surmounted on the apex a crest that reads FRENCH LICK SPRINGS
HOTEL: HOME OF 'PLUTO,' below which is written THE KEN-
TUCKY DERBY. Also on the desk is a small rock my daughter gave
me many years ago, and a ream of yellow paper.

It seems that I always have either too much or too little paper.
Either I am writing in a complete frenzy, and the ream has disappeared, or I have been staring at it for months, and it refuses to
diminish.

In the desk's various pigeonholes are various notepapers, a jade
pig a half-inch long, an unused pocketknife issued by the Knife
Collectors Association of America in 1985, a tape measure made
by the Otis Elevator Company as a promotional item around the
turn of the century, a medal the French government gave me for
translating a play some years back, some old postcards, a pair of
my eyeglasses, a blue Tiffany's box full of calling cards with my
name on them.

On the wall, near my grandparents, are handprints of my two
daughters, when each was aged one or so, a detective badge from
New York State, and another, from Chicago, numbered twenty-
six.

Stuck to the squared cedar logs of the cabin are notes and
memos, a small corkboard full of commemorative pin-back
buttons (Eugene Debs, Lindbergh, Roosevelt-Cox, Chicago
World's Fair of 1933, Fourth Youth Aliya, for a sampling).

There is a country-checked couch and, on it, a Pendleton blanket a friend gave me. There are two wood boxes, one for logs and
one for kindling. I filled them both years ago, and have left them
untouched since then, as I take my wood from the large pile out
on the covered porch.

On the porch are wind chimes made of hammered-out spoons
and forks. My daughter gave them to me several years back on
Father's Day. There is the skeleton and shell of a turtle placed on
one of the ends of a log that extends beyond the square.

Many of the impedimenta in the cabin were acquired in the area
at antique shops, yard sales, and auctions.

The best country auctions are the estate sales. Here the entire
contents of a home – usually house, barn, and out-buildings, are
taken out onto the lawn, a tent is set up, and the auctioneers

dispose of it all, treasures and junk, the personal and nonpersonal, the beautiful and the awkward, to the highest bidder.

We in the audience wonder at the tenacity and perversity that would drive the human being to accumulate so much. We see objects that speak of the tastes, needs, and follies of the collector, and feel ourselves, in our contemporary and personal insights and knowledge of the worth of things, superior to that person whose goods are out on the lawn.

Some things we will treasure because of their contemporary fashion, some because of their associations for us, and some out of love for or pride in our ability to intuit the associations of the former owner.

One day, probably not in my time, but perhaps it will be, the contents of my cabin will find their way out onto the lawn, and people will marvel over the folly or the prescience of the collector; and they'll come into the cabin and probably nod to themselves in appreciation of the workmanship, and they may look at the window that, as I write, lets in light over my left shoulder, and see the deep pencil mark at a slant across the sill, and written under it, 18 MAY.

I put the pencil mark there to show noon, on May 18, some year when I was sitting out here writing.

A Country Childhood

When I was a kid in Chicago, the country was YMCA camp. I remember the mess hall and sweating cold pitchers of milk; and I remember the kitchen boys, who were the stars of the camp community and granted every *droit de fou*, and when we were young we all wanted to grow up to be kitchen boys.

The camp was a paradise for a city kid. We had archery and riflery, and water sports off a complicated aluminum pier set out into a cold Michigan lake; and I remember several summers where my best friend, Lee, and I spent all our swimming time engaged in 'water wrestling,' which happy sport consisted of our attempts to drown each other.

And there were, of course, campfires, and references to the Native American in dance and crafts, and talent shows, and so on; but the distinctive feature of the camp was the trip.

We had three- and five- and twelve-day white-water canoe trips throughout Michigan, and one's status in the camp increased with age and consequent ability to take longer and more arduous trips.

I remember being in the coveted stern position of one of those heavy Grumman canoes, down on my knees, with the sand abrading my kneecaps, paddling away, with an eagle eye up ahead, and looking for the ducktails, which meant a rock in the water.

I remember the thrill of entering a race of rapids, which looked so complicated as to be incapable of navigation; and of thinking, at eleven or twelve years of age, probably for the first time in my life, Well, you are in charge – you'd better get an idea. I remember a trip where I wore my dad's World War II fiberboard helmet liner, which I had painted chrome yellow for some reason, and in which I felt, to use an expression of the period, neat. I was a gung-ho canoeist.

On the trip of the yellow helmet I pleaded with the counselor to let my canoe go last. I wanted the responsibility of being rearguard for the trip, chafing at the idea that grown-ups were following my progress and that, therefore, I was a child.

I resented the fellow's refusal to let my canoe go last. And paddled away in something of a huff and, later that day, broadsided a rock, and swamped, and got pinned between the canoe and the rock, and the fellow came along and saved me.

I lost the yellow helmet, and my pack and my sleeping bag, and, probably, one of the cute knives it was my privilege to carry to camp in those days.

We finally extracted the canoe. We borrowed paddles and made it to that day's campsite, where they told us that they knew we'd come to grief when they saw all our gear, accompanied by the yellow helmet, bobbing down the river.

I remember the eggs frying in bacon grease in the morning, and stick bread, and corn and potatoes cooked in ashes; and sassafras tea, which was advertised as, and did in fact taste something like, root beer that had been de-carbonated and altered so as to give one the runs.

On one trip we cooked those things for a week, camping in the dunes on Lake Michigan at what, I believe, was the Manistee National Forest, where the wind blew as hard and as continually as I have ever seen it. We spent the week inside our pup tents, except for the times we cooked. And sand got into everything, and we wondered if it were possible that the wind would never stop.

Once, on a hiking trip, I got lost. This trip was the feared 'survival hike,' which we all had to take at one point in our camp career, and when that point arrived, my cabin was told to assemble, wearing heavy clothes and carrying nothing.

On assembly, we were given one orange and one dollar each, and told to move out, that the trucks would come to reclaim us at the designated assembly point in twenty-four hours, and if we were not there when the trucks were there, the loss would be ours, as they would not wait.

So we moved out, and hiked, and when the sun went down, we ate our orange, and curled ourselves up, and got what sleep we could. I awoke very cold in the middle of the night, and looked around, and found that I was alone. There were no cabin-mates or counselors, just me in the middle of the night.

So I began to walk, and walked what must have been eight or ten miles, following the signs to our destination, which was Manistee, Michigan. I got to town, and found the beach, which was our pickup point. The sun was coming up, and there was a diner on the beach just about opening, and they sold me several doughnuts. I watched the sun come up, happy as I've ever been in my life. Then I fell asleep.

I woke to the counselor screaming at me. It was noon. The group had just arrived at the beach. They had been searching for me since they awoke, down the road, at dawn.

I think I must have, in my anxious state, half woken in the night, and walked down the road and fallen asleep again, and forgotten my waking; so that, when I woke again, I thought my comrades had deserted me, which is when I went off in search of them.

But all was well that ended well, and I suppose I was forgiven, for when the truck came to fetch us, we sat in the open back, singing all the twenty miles back to camp, and the counselor told me that he thought that I sang well.

I spent several years at that camp. When I became too old to come back as a camper, I vowed that I would apply for the post of kitchen boy, and, so, move on to the next stage of camp life.

They made it look like such fun, scrubbing out the pots and playing mainly water-based jokes on one and all, and no one immune to their antics. But for some reason that I have forgotten, I applied for a kitchen job at a different camp, and slaved the summer away with no rest and no fun, and nothing to ennoble the experience, save that I got to live in a trailer, and that I read *Atlas Shrugged*, and *The Fountainhead*, which, like the canoe trips, was a perfect experience for a preadolescent boy.

WFMT

I grew up on the WFMT voice. It was a male voice, and full of calm, reason, and – most important, I think – self-esteem. The voice seemed to say: 'This is the way we do things here. The music we play, the shows we air – we are proud of them. They reflect our vision of the world.'

That WFMT diction, which we, in acting school, called Middle Atlantic speech, those endless WFMT pauses, were (and still are) the sound of home to me. I would be traveling or living in the East and switch on the car radio and hear, 'And now . . . ' and it would be some local FM station rebroadcasting the Chicago Symphony Orchestra, and those two words would link me to home.

As a teenager, the big event of my week was listening to *The Midnight Special*. I would go over to my friend's house near the Midway in Hyde Park, and we teenagers would sit from the opening of Leadbelly singing 'The Midnight Special' through John Jacob Niles singing 'Lonesome Valley,' which, in those days, was followed by the sign-off. We would sit entranced.

The program *was* Chicago. It was the Chicago of the living culture of the mind. The Chicago of Hutchins, and the tradition of free thought: the Hyde Park tradition of Thorstein Veblen and Clarence Darrow, of Vachel Lindsay, of Dreiser.

The idea in the air was that culture was what we, the people, did.

The idea was – and is – that we were *surrounded* by culture. It was not alien to us. It was what the people did and thought and sang and wrote about. The idea was the particularly Chicagoan admixture of the populist and the intellectual. The model, the Hutchins model, the Chicago model of the European freethinker, was an autodidact: a man or woman who so loved the world around him or her that he or she was moved to investigate it further – either by creating works of art or by appreciating those works.

The very catholicity of the *Special* was instructive to us: blues, folk music, show tunes, and satire, as the lead-in has it. What better way to spend Saturday night, or one's life, for that matter?

Our heroes, we who grew up listening to the *Special*, were those with vast talent and audacity, and no respect: Shel Silverstein, Lord Buckley, Mike Nichols, Gibson and Camp, Studs Terkel . . .

We delighted in living in the same neighborhood in which Severn Darden first gave Professor Walter VanDer Vogelveider's 'Short Talk on the Universe,' in which he informed a theretofore ignorant world that, yes, fish think, but not fast enough. In the same neighborhood that housed the Compass Players, whose scions, Nichols and May, we would hear on the *Special* with regularity.

We would play at guessing which selection Ray Nordstrand or Norm Pelligrini, the program directors, would play next. Oh, he's just played Beyond the Fringe's cut of 'two miners,' next he'll most likely play Cisco Houston's 'Dark as a Dungeon,' or perhaps Pete Seeger's 'Miner's Life.' We played along, and were, if memory serves me, regularly correct in our guesses. It was our culture. We stayed up all night New Year's Eve with the *All-Night Special*, and called in our requests and comments. It was ours. Like the symphony, or the lions in front of the Art Institute, or the August sickness of the Cubs. WFMT was Chaliapin singing the 'Song of the Volga Boatman.' It was Ray Nordstrand saying, 'The time in Chicago is [*pause*] eleven [*pause*] fifteen [*interminable pause*] . . . a little later than usual' – one of the most bizarre utterances I have ever heard on the radio, and yet his reading rendered it perfectly comprehensible.

WFMT announcers, speaking of which, are the only people I have ever heard who have the capacity to read a phone number as if they were stating a philosophic proposition: I don't think I can do it justice in print, but you know what I'm talking about. They'd read

it as if it were a syllogism: that number is four seven *two* ['If *A*'] . . .
six three ['. . . and now I will conclude my argument'] nine [*short
pause*] four . . . ['Then *B*: QED'].

I once asked Norm Pelligrini how the station managed to train its
announcers, how it schooled them to the high level of recognizable
uniformity and clarity. He told me that the station didn't train the
announcers at all, that they 'just got the idea.'

WFMT meant listening to Studs and his humanism and enthusiasm and, finally, delighted *wonder* at the whole damn thing. Later on
in my life it meant going down to the studio and doing the show with
Studs – with him and me reading a part of some new play of mine,
and him always choosing the flashy role.

Most arts organizations decay and stink before they die. Most of
them have outlived their allotted span of days, their healthy usefulness, long before they are threatened by this or that encroachment.

Most arts organizations are short-lived.

WFMT has lived long and has served and continues to serve the
community in an essential way. It has persisted and grown.

I have been living outside of Chicago for many years, and can only
assume that keeping the station reflective of its directors' individual
and collective vision has not, at times, been easy or pleasant.

The station sounds to me today much as it did when I was a kid: a
voice saying, ' "*Culture*" is just that which we do. Here are some
things in our heritage which we enjoy, and we think you will enjoy
them, too.' It was and is a beautiful voice, a self-respecting voice, and
the voice of home.

Cold Toast

I once had a play running in the West End of London. The show, a
production with an American cast, was sold out and threatening a
very long run. I came over a few weeks into the run to visit and, I
suppose, to bask in the success of the play. I ran into one of the actors
on the street. 'Isn't it *great?*' I said. 'The damn thing's going to run
forever.'

'I'm going home next week,' he said. And there was a pause. 'The whole cast is going home next week.'

'Why?' I asked.

'Because,' he said, 'we're homesick.'

Well. They did go home. And I understood it completely.

I myself tend to get homesick in London. Because it is home and it is most definitely *not* home. For example, try as you will, you cannot remember the arcane rules of pub hours, and, thinking that you have finally figured it out, are forever going into a pub hoping for a drink and not to be again rebuffed, only to be greeted by a waitress looking you in the eye and proclaiming in what probably is not, but seems to be an air of paternalistic disappointment, 'Two-nineteen,' or some such, or whatever time it happens to be when you get into the pub and the pub has just closed, and you have no drink and are far away from home.

So, also, with the wrong-side-of-the-road. Tired, jet-lagged, usually dyspeptic from the constant balancing act of too much tea, too much liquor, not enough sleep, you are forever coming up to the intersection and thinking: Ah, yes, you only look the opposite way from the way you were *going* to look, and then ... Only to step off the curb and invariably be looking the wrong way – which, when coupled with the laudable directness of the London driver, can make life for the expatriate pedestrian no joke; and, in fact, a colleague of mine was most certainly killed on a London street as he stepped off looking the wrong way.

And why dyspeptic? Your stomach is out of whack from the time change, and what is there to eat?

In the States, and in a peripatetic business, one spends one's life eating restaurant and hotel food. After a few weeks in any one hotel, after a few years in all of the hotels, all restaurant and hotel food tastes the same. It tastes like 'food,' and food tastes like something to be gotten down so that one may have eaten it, and the best one can say of most of it is that it is (when it is) hot. My friend Greg Mosher and I, transported Chicagoans, spent years working in the New York theater. We were charmed by the compart-mentalization of New York, how, in this most materialistic and commercial of cities, whatever object one required, there was not only a store that sold it, but a district that housed many stores of that ilk. To wit: the fur district, the trimmings district, the flower district, et cetera. And Greg and I took to joking, whenever one or the other would require a particularly arcane item, for example, a shooting stick, 'Oh, get it in the shooting-stick district.' Or, to belabor the joke, as it was one we loved, cherishing habit at least as much as humor, the dental-floss district, or, for example, when at the dentist, 'I'm calling from the heart of the root-canal district.' We always referred to London as the cold-toast district. And we would remark to each other that in America, where anything new is good, and anything new and foreign is doubly good, never have we seen or could we imagine a sign that advertised BRITISH COOKING.

There are many many fine things about Great Britain, and London in particular. None of them are the cooking, and I don't think most Londoners could identify a vegetable with a gun to their head.

Greg was over in London directing a play of mine. He'd been there for some weeks. I came over, and we had breakfast; we met in the restaurant of the hotel, and I spied on the menu HOT BUTTERED TOAST, and grinned and turned the menu around to show Greg, who did not laugh. 'Let's order it,' I suggested merrily, but he did not laugh, and he did not laugh when the toast arrived, cold as earth, limp, and sodden. And the look in his eyes said, 'After a month, it is no longer funny.'

London and the States seem much the same, but they aren't. England is, of course, a different world. It has its own abundant courtesies and gentlenesses, but they are different from ours over here, and after a while, to us Murrcans, it gets wearisome, and we want to go home.

What do I do for comfort while I am there? I do as the Romans do and drink a lot of tea. I can't figure out when to get into those poncy pubs, but I adore the invitingness and accessibility of the various tea shoppes, and here follows a survey of comfortable and relaxed times drinking tea in London.

Embankment

I am walking down along the Embankment. I have slept much too late, because of the jet lag, and am betwixt and between. I am due at the theater in an hour and a half, not enough time to write or do anything serious, just enough time, I decide, to take a long walk. I walk from my hotel down Piccadilly, down to the mobs of Continental tourists at Piccadilly Circus, down past one of my favorite tea shoppes on a street I believe is called Haymarket, but I believe that because it houses a theatre called the Haymarket, so I am elaborating the trappings of my profession into a general rule, but so do we all.

I once had the most delicious afternoon in this shoppe, having been dreadfully jet-lagged – as, in fact, I am now – and was soothing myself with gallons of their tea hot beyond hot, not only the hottest beverage possible, but the hottest thing on earth. This tea did not grow cooler over time, as I sat outside in a very chill London afternoon, but stayed hot as it was, hot enough for Vulcan, and, if that can be true, cannot it be true that the tea, sitting out, actually grew hotter? Yes. It can. And I watched a Scandinavian couple at the table next to me on the street. They were very attentive to each other, and I was fond of them.

It seems to me that I also wrote something on that afternoon, and I probably was fond of what I'd written. In any case, I cherished this, my tea shoppe near the Haymarket Theatre, when I was disoriented, and cold, and knew no one, and had no idea what nuances of behavior meant in this strange land, and I was, in effect, as a ghost, who could see and not be seen because he was not there.

This day, though, I did not stop at this magic shoppe, for fear that it would not be the same; as, of course, it would not. Why, I thought, should I subject the current foreign couple or couples who would, no doubt, be there, to unfair comparison with my charmed Scandinavian pair in their leather jackets, who had, doubtless, retired to the north to pursue some incredibly romantic and important series of tasks?

I gave that shoppe a pass, and wandered in what I believed was the general direction of the Embankment, from which place I knew I could always turn to the left, and walk till I came to Waterloo Bridge, and then over the bridge to the theater.

I became disoriented, and found myself in front of some palace or other. There were two members of the Life Guards, up on their matched blacks. Imposing spectacle. These monsters in Hessian boots and plumed helmets, heads fifteen feet in the air, unmoving. What a magnificent thing, I thought. The one on the left gave a signal of some kind, and a foot soldier in the middle stamped, executed a right turn, and slow-marched over to the horsemen, where they held a stiff and military colloquy for a moment about what I assumed was girls.

The faces of the two were beautifully English, round and ruddy and open. The nature of their faces, and, in fact, their silhouettes in the plumed helmets, were identical to those of the London skinheads: choked, ruddy faces, spiked hair to increase height and refer to the equine and inspire something on the continuum from respect to terror. The skinheads and the Life Guards both proclaim, 'I am bigger than you, and I subscribe to a code so superior to yours as to enable me to commit any violence. You do not exist for me.'

I looked at these boys on their horses and was myself sufficiently awed by them as to find this thought springing into my mind: Yes, boys but we whopped your ass fairly roundly in 1778, then, *didn't* we . . . ?

And on that craven note of borrowed courage, I walked on and eventually discovered both the Embankment and a great hunger.

I had a half hour before the theater curtain, and I sat down at a café facing the Thames. Tourist buses from Germany and France were filling up at the curbside, the café was closing, and nobody wanted to serve me, so I got up after ten minutes and discovered a take-out tea shoppe next door, where I bought a tasteless apple confection of some sort, mostly paste. I wolfed it down gratefully, and walked down the Embankment, trying to clean the remnants of the sticky paste off my hands, and holding a piping-hot Styrofoam cup of tea. There was a sidewalk artist working on a pastel of a snake charmer. I heard or read somewhere that these men learned one scene by rote, and then went around drawing it on the sidewalk in chalk for the rest of their lives, the one picture that they knew.

I watched this man putting far-beyond-finishing touches on his snake charmer. The day was cold, there was pitifully little money in his hat, and he smoothed and resmoothed the border of his scene belligerently. I wanted to ask him if he knew only this one picture, but he radiated defiance. I threw some money in his hat and walked on. I felt a bit strange drinking on the street, a very un-British thing to do. The tea was wretched in any case, and tasted terribly of Styrofoam. I emptied the tea into the street, and threw the cup into a trash basket.

I walked past monuments on the Embankment, all to the dead. Not TO OUR HEROES, but to THE DEAD, the dead of the navy, of the air force. A lovely monument to the dead of the air force in the Great War, with a pathetic addendum engraved on the pedestal, homage to the dead of the Great War a scant twenty years later.

There was a beautiful sculpted group – a mother herding her children – from A GRATEFUL BELGIUM. Her neck seemed out-of-drawing, until seen from the side, where we got the benefit of her great solicitousness.

I climbed the stairs up from the embankment, at Waterloo Bridge. On the landing, someone had spray-painted I HATE ... And I climbed eagerly to see, as the view permitted me, what it was, in London, that one hated. I expected the traditional 'niggers,' or 'faggots,' or perhaps, 'kikes,' and was rather surprised to find THE POLICE.

Over Waterloo Bridge I went, and over to the National Theatre, and being some minutes early, to one of their great cafés for a cup of tea.

Camden Town

I am on a mission, to get my laundry done. I also want to go see all the old clothes in Camden Town.

It is a very rainy Saturday. I stuff my small clothes in my knapsack and set out for Camden Town by cab. The knapsack is a small black affair, and I have sewn onto it the patch of my partner's film company, Filmhaus. The patch has a cow staring at a camera, and the legend NEW YORK/MONTANA. The sack is full of soiled underthings, and the presence of this most mundane phenomenon reassures and encourages me as I venture out into Unknown London.

It is too cold and rainy to look at old clothes. The streets are mobbed with young people in Harley jackets, looking in at the stalls and shops, looking for that last perfect article of attire, that perfect suggestion which will complete them. I understand completely, and agree with Mr. Shaw that there is no peace in the world which surpasseth the peace of knowing that one is perfectly dressed.

These people on the street are all twenty years younger than I. I remember myself at their age, scrounging the thrift stores of Chicago, looking for the perfect leather jacket (then priced around five dollars if one got lucky at Goodwill Industries), the perfect Harris Tweed overcoat (twenty-five cents – that's right), the perfect barely worn white cotton shirt for a dime. That was our uniform in the sixties, as 'children of the sixties,' and well into the seventies as empowered by our profession of the theater to dress casually in all circumstances. And there I was, twenty years later, and still pursuing, in Camden Town, that vision of elegant tragedy first promulgated by Mr. Brando and James Dean. No, I tell a lie, and have committed that solecism of the nonprofessional – the actors just wore the clothes, the designer *created* the clothes. And, as I most certainly feel that when the time comes for me to write my theatrical memoirs, the world will be far past being able to print them, let alone appreciate them, I will share a memory of a dinner party in Cambridge, Massachusetts, 1988. The guest of honor was Lucinda Ballard, costume designer of *A Streetcar Named Desire, Cat on a Hot Tin Roof, The Sound of Music, Showboat, The Glass Menagerie*, and many other Broadway shows, and the creator of many American looks. I was her dinner partner, and asked her first, as, I am sure, many had done over the years, about Brando and his torn T-shirt in *A Streetcar Named Desire*. And she told me that it had come to her in a flash, that each T-shirt was hand-stitched to form to his torso, that each shirt was hand-dyed a washed-out pink, and that she personally distressed (that is, created artificial signs of wear) each shirt with a razor blade until she got the desired effect. So credit where credit is due. And here we were forty or so years after the fact (*Streetcar* opened on Broadway in 1947), longing for that grace of Brando, and seeking it in sainted relics. I was dressed like every Limey bloke on the high street in Camden Town. As they were younger than I, they were a bit more driven to get out in the rain and find themselves through clothing. Or perhaps I had just become over the hill and had given up. But give up for the day I had, and I found a Laundromat, and changed some pound coins for coins of ten shillings, and deciphered and employed machines to sell me soap, and got the laundry going, and felt quite proud of myself.

Down the side street was a shop that sold 'aeronautical models,' and I looked in the window at the lovely things; I so adored them as a kid – those balsa-wood gossamers, those 'thoughts,' which, powered by a gasoline engine the size of one's thumb, took to the air. I suppose 'planes' is the word I am looking for, and what American could walk through London without thinking of planes? No one who had ever been an American boy in the fifties, in any case.

I stopped in at the Penguin bookstore, always charmed to see the different formats and titles of the books. Books in our Benighted States are getting so regimented, aren't they? Fewer individually owned bookstores every year, less publication of the out-of-the-way or the questionable, and the benevolence of any present oligarchy must inevitably, must it not . . . oh well.

I bought a book by T. H. White, *The Goshawk*, a memoir of several months White spent in the English countryside in 1939, training a large hawk with the aid of only a three-hundred-year-old manual. I took the book around the corner to an Italian eatery – prices scribbled on slate on the walls, very much a 'lunchroom,' we would say in the U.S., or a 'luncheonette.' Many students inside, reading, talking, eating what looked like and proved to be good hot food. I had a pizza 'Neapolitan,' a designation the translation of which I cannot remember, but which I do remember was quite good. And I had, of course, a lot of dark hot tea, and the waitress suggested something for dessert that I could not understand, and no amount of repetition clarified it for me. After a pause, she averred: 'It's like a sponge,' and I decided to pass.

I bought a copy of *Time Out*, the nightlife magazine, and took it back to the Laundromat, where I put my clothes into the drier, then looked for something to do.

I found a film I wanted to see at the ICA, the Institute of Contemporary Art, that evening, and called my friends Dick and Laura, Americans who had just shown up most unexpectedly in London, and we planned to meet at the ICA in an hour.

I got a cab in the rain, and he took me down to the ICA on the mall. It took a bit to get there, and the cabbie kept circling, and eventually leaned back to explain, 'We seem to be caught in a one-way scheme,' so I got out, after asking directions, and walked under some rig that looked like the Brandenburg Gate, and arrived, in fifty yards, fairly wet, at the ICA.

I browsed in their bookstore, and looked at a bunch of Soviet paintings by Erik Bulatov. Very serious things they were, too, quite poster-presentational and dealing, it seemed, with life in Soviet society. How fine, I thought, to live in an environment in which it is not incumbent upon things to *mean* anything. And there were very serious and attractive young men and women in the ICA café, playing chess and looking at one another. They could not have been more skinny, or have smoked tobacco more beautifully. We do not have their like in my land anymore. I, of course, drank tea, although my teeth were floating; but, like driving cross-country, it is easier to continue than to stop. Dick and Laura showed up. We found that the film we wished was off, I had misread *Time Out*; and some Eastern European semianimated thing was showing. We were wet Americans and had had enough meaning for the day, and so trooped over to Leicester Square and bought tickets for a late showing of *Dangerous Liaisons*, and killed the time before the show by going to a French restaurant across from the Duke of York's Theatre and getting very very drunk, after which I believe we went to the film.

Islington

Much of my tourist career in London is spent waiting. I am out of sync with the life around me. Jet lag, sleeplessness, and cultural differences have unstuck me from any routine that could possibly be indigenous to the surroundings, and I spend a lot of time waiting for an event to occur, waiting to fall asleep, waiting for the city to come to life, waiting for friends to finish work. Today I am waiting in Islington. I don't know where much of anything in London is in relation to anything else, but since the taxi has not crossed the Thames, I suppose that Islington is to the north.

We drive through an area of antique shops, which disposes me kindly toward it. I love antique shops and antique districts, as they are, to my eye, a sign of healthy organic decay – usually of a lower-class district that has fallen on even harder times and is no longer capable of supporting its citizens, but offers very low rent to junk dealers. The junk dealers are supplanted by their high-rent artistic counterparts, and the antiques draw the adventuresome upper classes, who eventually gentrify the area with their very own abodes. A civilization eating and being eaten. Sounds good to me.

I am also, by nature and profession, a browser, and so feel very much at home in an area devoted to browsing. I have several hours to kill while friends finish a recording session in Islington.

I walk down the street and buy a FREE NELSON MANDELA button from a shop devoted to books and memorabilia supporting the ANC. I walk down the road through the midst of the antique stores in the high street, but they are all closed on this particular day.

Farther up the high street are stores selling 'retro' American clothing, and I mark down a tour of that enclave for the end of the day. But now I have found, one could hardly call it a tea shoppe – it is a hole-in-the-wall with four tables and an espresso machine in back. The radio is blaring, there are signs all over the walls about Irish events. Many of them refer to boxing. The woman behind the counter has an Irish accent so thick I cannot understand a single word she is saying, and no more can she understand me. I point to items on the menu, tea, minestrone soup, and toast. She nods.

I take a seat in the front of the place; sunlight is streaming over the road. Across the street is the Islington library. It is open today. I feel a great sense of security. Here are, in fact, two places in which I can write if I so choose. I have the T. H. White book in my bag, my notebook and pen and ink are in the bag, this Irish woman is about to bring me tea. The afternoon is, in effect, perfect. *Even should the tea shoppe be forced to close*, by some terrible mischance, I am free to go across the street and sit in what will certainly prove to be the most excellent library, and hang out there, a perfectly content man.

She brings the tea. It is the best tea I have ever had in my life. She brings the soup. It is red water with two noodles in it. I smell it, and it smells like the food in prison. I drink it anyway. The toast is actually hot, and buttery, and I have two orders. I start working on a poem about a dream I had the previous night.

The dream is one I have been having all my life. I am climbing a hill and, as I climb, the hill becomes steeper and steeper. I cannot walk another step. I have to make it up the hill, but I cannot climb. Why does the hill become increasingly steep? This is my recurring dream. I have had it hundreds of times. The night before, however, there was a change in the dream, the first change ever. I stopped halfway up the hill, and rested, and was joined by my stepmother and a beautiful naked young girl, who reclined on the grass and smiled at me.

The change in the dream is, to me, a great reprieve, and I am absorbed in writing for two hours. Drinking tea the while. When I look up, it is beginning to get dark in the high street, and I am almost late for my meeting.

I pay up and leave the little shoppe, and start off for the recording studio.

I can't resist stopping off at one of the used-clothing stores on the way. The gent behind the counter admires my leather jacket and asks where I bought it. (Vanson Leathers, Quincy, Massachusetts.) He asks what it cost and I tell him. I browse through his long-traveled American goods. He has a nice selection of stuff made by the Pendleton mills. I firmly believe that nothing in the world is better than an old wool Pendleton shirt that has been worn and loved and cared for and broken in over the years. Nothing is more comforting or more comfortable. The shirts he has on his rack are all these things, but they are too small. They are also cut on some strangely un-American pattern. The salesman tells me that they were a special order Pendleton did for Germany in the fifties. No, not for mine. And not for mine loden cloth. 'Thank you very much, I'm sure,' as they say here.

I hurry down the streets, armed with directions and a copy of *London A to Zed*, and find the recording studio, which is nestled in the back of an old church in a building that was probably the rectory.

The band is due to conclude recording at seven. But having lived my life in show business, I know better. I arrive at seven-fifteen and have my book to occupy me until they conclude their session at midnight, when we all go home.

Chelsea Farmers Market/
The Kings Road

Today I am meeting some actor friends for lunch. They are rehearsing on Old Church Street, 'down by the Embankment end.' So down I go to someplace called Pytet House. Inside everyone is smoking tobacco (very refreshing, as virtually all of us Yank theatrical types have given it up), and talking trash and history in order to avoid rehearsing the play.

The same the world over. I feel right at home, and settle back in the shadows. On the wall are paintings of the various houses on Old Church Street. I notice that the one supposedly next door to this Pytet House in which I now find myself was the home of George Eliot.

The actors muck about for the best part of an hour, and we all go off to lunch. I pass by the house where Eliot supposedly lived, but find neither the number indicated by the drawing nor a plaque commemorating her presence there; and how would I have known, I wondered, even *had* I found it, if it was the house of her unhappy marriage, or the house of her content cohabitation with Mr. Lewes? What a potential misstep you have been saved from, I thought – just think if you had waxed all sentimental over an abode in which your beloved Ms. Evans was miserable. We all troop off to the Chelsea Farmers Market, a surpassingly quaint collection of shops a couple of blocks away. We pass a palm reader, a perfumer, and then settle in a very good health-food restaurant, and we all have baked potatoes and tea and tell theatrical stories from two sides of the Atlantic and arrive back at the rehearsal hall ten minutes late. I am invited back to watch more rehearsal, but no, I have had enough Art for the day, and long for Life. I plead a previous engagement.

I hurry back to the palm reader. He sits me down and tells me my life story.

He tells me that these are the best years of my life. That I am in the process of changing everything that I believe in, that I feel frustrated, alone, frightened, and unsure, and what a wonderful thing this is. This period is wonderful, he explains, because God is protecting me. God is shielding me and preventing me from making a misstep. I try to go right. I cannot go right, I try to go left, I cannot go left. I will look back on this year, he says, as the luckiest year of my life.

I drink in this information so gratefully. He goes on for an hour. I know he is giving me a stock 'crossroads' reading; that he will give the same reading to virtually everyone who comes into his shop. I know that people come into his shop because and only because they find themselves at a crossroads. I know all these things, and I don't care. I drink it in. I pay him. I walk out of his shop, out of the

Chelsea Farmers Market, and I feel drained but good.

I walk down the Kings Road, past thousands of shops that all seem to be selling leather jackets.

I feel inspired to live through this year gratefully and, if I can, gracefully. I wander into Rylands stationery store and buy a new notebook, with the humble hope that I may write things in it that will be well done.

I am enchanted by the stationery store. I love office supplies. With their exception, everything in my line of work takes place in my head, which is to say, it is arguable whether it occurs at all. Office supplies are the only artifacts, and the choice of a pen or a notebook is a big deal to me. I discover very cunning medium-sized lined, bound notebooks. I suppress the urge to buy many (if I buy many I will feel taxed with filling them all, and I will become discouraged). I buy one and walk back out on the Kings Road.

I have a wretched cup of tea in some French patisserie-chain outlet. I find that I am exhausted – probably by my hour with the reader. I take a cab back to my hotel.

The Goshawk

That evening I go to the theater. And, after the theater I am alone.

In my hotel I take off my suit jacket and hang it neatly in the closet.

I set myself up at the desk in the hotel room. I prop my feet up on the desk and lean back. I am going to finish the T. H. White book.

This is one of the best books I have ever read in my life. The prose is hard and clear as a crystal. It is unsentimental, it is simply written, it is a delight and an inspiration. I read for several hours. I get up to open the French windows onto the street. It is now around two in the morning. I order tea and burnt toast from room service.

The tea arrives. It is the middle of the night. I am reading about the training of the goshawk. I am sharing Mr. White's experiences. I *myself* now want to capture and train a hawk. I want to live a simple and a pure life. I want to confine myself to the wind and the rain, and make the body and mind of a hawk the complete focus of my experience. However, I will gladly settle for sitting in this hotel room in London with my book and cup of tea.

The Truck Factory

I can't remember the exact year, but it was sometime in the mid-sixties. Either I was home from college or it was the last summer before I went away. I had a job at the truck factory.

I was living with my dad near the lake, and the truck factory was out near Cicero. I got there and back by riding with a couple of Swedish guys. I think I paid them a dollar a day, or it might have been a dollar a trip. In any case, halfway through the summer they decided to up the ante on me, and I remember the close and rather vicious expression on their faces when they informed me of the fare increase.

I started out my day around 5 A.M. It was still something other than unbearably hot on the street, and I remember running into the same paperboy every morning on Broadway around Addison, and thinking, as I nodded to him, what a beautiful place the world was. I smoked a cigarette at the bus stop on Addison, and waited for the bus.

The bus took me way the hell and gone out west, to the place where I would wait on the corner for my ride.

The two Swedish guys, picturesque and improbable as this seems, referred to me throughout the summer as 'The Rider.' I was The Rider. And I rode in the back. The car was a '55 Chevy in mint condition. They picked me up on Madison, and we rode at about thirty miles an hour out west to the factory. The ride burned me up every day, out and back. If they would have driven at the speed limit, I could have slept another half hour in the morning, I could have been home half an hour earlier and had a shower and a beer. The slowness of the ride seemed to me to be an expression of their hatred for the world.

We had to punch in before seven-thirty. It wasn't hard to do because we were always early. Another of the great moments in the day was that which came after punching in and before work. There was time for another cigarette and a cup of coffee from a vending truck. To this day I love those vending trucks with the quilted silver sides. I think everyone must.

I worked in the maintenance department, which meant that I

went where they sent me and did what they told me to do when I
got there. My favorite job of the summer was testing torque rods.
I am not sure what torque rods do, but I know that these torque
rods were around two and a half feet long and had a weld at each
of their ends, and that this batch had been welded incorrectly. So I
was placed in a corner of the factory with barrels of torque rods. I
took them, one by one, out of their barrel, first placed one and
then the next weld on an anvil, and whacked the welds with a
sledge hammer, in an effort to get the welds to part. I did that for
several days, and there was something about the rhythm of the job
– flipping the torque rod in the air to get to the weld on the other
side, whanging the thing – that was completely satisfying.

I spent a month about twenty feet above a concrete floor, ripping out an asbestos ceiling.

A hangarlike part of the truck factory was being renovated, and
I and a few others in the maintenance department were commissioned to get the ceiling down. We spent each day duck-walking
on two-by-six joists twenty feet up in the air, as I have said,
ripping the old ceiling out with pry bars. For many years I had less
than strong lungs, and fairly raspy breath, and I would like to
attribute those conditions to the month spent with the asbestos,
which seems to me a more dramatic story than twenty-five years
of tobacco.

There was another month spent with weed killer and a back-
pack spray canister. I roamed the outskirts of the factory, spraying
that which passed for grass. At one point I lost the nozzle for the
apparatus. I can't remember how or why, except that it was an act
of negligence on my part. I remember being bored, and thinking,
Oh, hell, I know I should do (a) with this nozzle, and it would be
just as easy to do (a) as to do otherwise, but I will do (b) because I
am bored, and perhaps this will make someone pay.

Soon after being transferred out of the weed job, I was called
before a tribunal of my superiors and asked what became of the
nozzle. I, of course, lied and told them I had no idea. I remember
that the tribunal went on for a godlessly long time, at the end of
which one of the senior men in the maintenance department said,
'Well, I *believe* him. I *believe* him, and that's that.' And I thought,
You dumb sonofabitch, of *course* I lost the nozzle. Everyone here
knows that except *you*. . . .

Why was the nozzle that important to them? I don't know. Why did they not just dock me whatever dollar or two it cost and be done with it? I don't know. I remember getting docked for various other things. I was docked for punching out early, for example, and for punching in late at the end of lunch.

Lunch was twenty minutes, whistle to whistle. When the whistle blew I was sodden with sweat and exhausted. Many days I would climb into the bunk of a sleeper cab and fall asleep. I remember them as the deepest sleeps of my life. I loved those sleeper cabs. I recall one of the factory hands gesturing to a matched pair of ready-to-roll tractors and telling me, 'Son, inside of a year, one of them is going to pay for the both. . . .' And when he told me, I wanted to be picking up those tractors, to be putting them out on the highway, and having one pay for the both inside of a year. I wanted to be sleeping in the back of the cab as the truck rolled down the highway. I can't imagine anyone who wouldn't.

One day they were digging a trench along the outside of the main factory building, and a couple of guys (I would like to say that they were from the maintenance department, but I don't know if that's true) were down in the trench; just before lunchtime, the trench fell in on them, and they died. I think I found out about it after lunch. I was most probably napping.

There was some sort of chemical factory on the far side of the truck factory, and when the wind blew toward us, which was much of the time, everything smelled as I think hell must smell. Inhuman, and contrived, and unhealthy beyond mistake.

What else happened that summer? I put a nail through the sole of my workshoe, and had to get a tetanus shot, and I limped for a week or so, and learned about steel-soled shoes.

I argued one long week with myself about taking a Friday off. The Monday was a holiday of some sort, and you were paid for it if you worked the two adjoining workdays. I had some important appointment and, of course, I didn't go in on Friday, and so lost the holiday pay, and am still upset about it twenty-five years later, and still do not know whether to be mad at myself for my weakness, or at the factory for coming up with such a good plan for ensuring attendance.

The trucks were made to order, and had a reputation for being top of the line.

I've seen them on the road in the Midwest or, infrequently, in the east, and invariably say to anybody in the car, 'You see that truck? I used to work there.'

In Vermont

The term that comes easiest to mind is *ghosts*, but the lights on the hill weren't ghosts, or, if they were, I am not sure what ghosts are; as, of course, I am not one. I can't say what they are, but I knew when I encountered them.

And the hill itself may have had something to do with it. Down at the bottom, near my house, there is the graveyard; and I was thinking about Annie's story on the night I passed it, coming home, and something pulled my coat.

I'd like to say that I 'felt something,' which is to say, some presence, but all I felt was the tug on my coat sleeve. I was walking dead on the crown of the road. The night was pitch dark, and I was on the crown to avoid any possibility of branches whipping my face. I was thinking of what Annie had said.

When she was young, she said, she lived in the white house, up the hill from my house, above the graveyard.

She was walking one day, when she was young, and all of a sudden there was a man by her side. On the lonely dirt road, in the country, and, all of a sudden, there was someone there.

She told me he was dressed oddly, in a fashion out of the past. And she said she felt frightened.

The man nodded and asked her name. She was young, and had been cautioned by her parents not to talk to strangers, so she didn't respond. He told her that his name was Anders.

She walked up to her farmhouse. Later that night she told her parents. They said that Anders had been the name of the hired man back in their grandparents' time; and it was of this that I was thinking when I walked in the crown of the road by the graveyard that night and something pulled on my coat sleeve.

Then there were the moving stars I'd seen, some fifteen miles from the town, and twenty-five years back.

One winter night, when I was young.

There were five or six of them in the sky. They looked like stars. They would be still for a while. Then they would move and group or cluster for a while, and dart, as if they were chasing one another from one side of the sky to the other.

Sometimes they would shoot across, sometimes they'd move slowly, to the other horizon, where they regrouped into various patterns. I was with several friends. We watched for a while, then telephoned the air-force base in Plattsburgh to report what we'd seen.

The fellow there thanked us. We asked if he had had other reports of the object, and he said no, he had not. We asked what he thought they might be, and he said he had no idea.

After I got home that night, up my hill, twenty-five years later, once again I saw the lights.

It was four in the morning. I was tired, I was alone in the house. I was brushing my teeth. I glanced out the window, and up the hill, up past the cemetery, past the white house, up the hill, up at the crest of the hill, or as they say, at the height of land, there was a light. It was a bright light, like truck-mounted beacons we would see at a film opening, or like an antiaircraft beacon, scanning the sky. As if it were describing a cone, whose point was on the ground. The shaft of light circled slowly. The beam was much stronger than truck-mounted klieg lights. And it was pure white.

On the ground, beyond the trees at the edge of the field, just at the top of the hill, was this beacon.

I nodded and, in my exhausted state, went on preparing for bed.

And then I asked myself what the light was, up the hill.

'Well, that's just . . .' I started to explain; and then I stopped, as I realized that I had no idea what it was, or what it possibly could be. I set myself to suggest a scenario that would put that light up the hill. I went back to the window, and it still was there, circling slowly.

I was fascinated by the white purity of the light, and I remember thinking that I'd never seen a light that white before. What could it be? It was a signal of some sort, but to whom and by whom?

And why would it be here, in the middle of the night, on a peaceful country road in Vermont?

One summer evening some years back, I had been sitting on the porch of this same house, looking, by chance, up the road at the white house, which was vacant at that time, and I saw a small fire burning below the barn.

I remember that I thought as I watched it, That's just a . . . and, when I could not discount it, I walked up the hill to find a rapidly spreading fire in the brush, now caught on the barn. I tried to get it out, but it had grown too big for me, so I ran back and called the village fire department.

They got the fire out, and I basked for some long time afterward in a self-awarded sentiment of rural neighborliness.

For, if I had not *seen* it, I thought, or *recognized* it, or investigated it, or acted upon it, the barn and the house would have burned.

And it was the memory of this feeling of neighborliness that moved me to decide to climb the hill to investigate the light.

For there was no one in the white house, and there was no one living in the house beyond it – the house across from the field from which the light was coming.

There was no one on the hill but me; and I must have felt that the light boded malevolence, or danger, for, when I redressed myself and started out of my house, I took a gun.

It was four in the morning of an early spring night as I opened my door, and I congratulated myself on my courage.

Many, I thought, would not venture that half-mile up the hill. Many would stay in their homes, I thought.

And I asked myself why they would do that; and I answered they would do that because the light meant great danger; and I became fearful. I went back in my house, closing the door softly, as one moves when one is a child and moving in the dark so as not to draw the notice of the evil creatures in the room.

I went back in my house, and looked out of the window, and saw the light was still there, up the hill.

I asked myself if I was content to live in ignorance of the nature of the light, and as much as I piqued myself with my cowardice, I found that I wasn't going to climb the hill.

I undressed and got into bed. Although my mind was busy, I fell asleep; and I awakened some time later to a great feeling of fear, and a brilliant, all-pervading white light pouring in my bedroom window, as if the source were down, just outside of my house.

And then I fell asleep again.

The next morning I asked everyone in town if they'd seen or heard anything, or if they could account for the lights I had seen; and they'd seen nothing, and could not explain it.

And down at the bottom of the old sugaring lane on my property, there is a dip in the land at the intersection of the lane with our dirt road, which marks the site of the town's earliest settlement two hundred years ago.

In any case, down the hill from my house, the land slopes to a depression at the bottom of what was the old lane. There was and remains something about the spot. I do not like it. I put a small compost pile there. It seemed fitting for a low, hidden, and somehow unpleasant spot.

Perhaps you've noticed spots like that. Not in the city, where the land is covered, but out in the country or the woods.

Perhaps you've felt the spots that are happy, and the spots that exude danger, as if they were sending the message, 'Ignore me at your peril. You should not be here.'

I put the small compost pile in the hollow at the bottom of the hill.

Up by my house, between the house and the cemetery, near the road, there was a swing set. And one afternoon I was pushing my daughter on the swing, and my eye went beyond her, down the hill, down to a form by the compost pile. It was the form of a man, and it was dead white, from head to foot.

I saw it for a second, then it disappeared.

I wondered if it had been conjured, somehow, out of my feelings of antipathy for the spot.

Some weeks later, it must have been at the end of summer, for there were apples on the trees, my daughter asked me to climb to get her an apple, which I did.

She took a bite, and told me that it was too early and the apple was sour, and she didn't want any more. 'What should I do with it?' she asked, and I told her to walk the fifty feet down to the compost pile.

'No,' she said, 'I don't want to go there. There's a monster that lives there.'

And there were people talking. Outside of various houses in the night. One summer, in a cottage at North Hero; one whole fall, back in the sixties, when I lived with friends in a rented trailer in the woods.

That fall there were two men talking outside all night, night after night, till one of us, left alone one night, called the state police. They searched and found nothing; and when we returned from our school vacations, or wherever we had been, we all said to one another, 'Oh, my God, you've heard it, too . . .?'

Like the old woman at the house outside of Newport.

A friend told me about the house on the lake, and I took it for a summer, and heard the old woman crying and scolding in the night, and went outside so many times to see her, but there was never anything there. Back in New York in the fall, the friend who'd suggested the house asked how the summer had gone. I told her it went well.

'Is the ghost still there?' she asked.

'Yes,' I told her, 'the ghost is still there.'

Music

I lived two terrible years as a smoker in Cambridge, Massachusetts. Not only was I a smoker, I was a smoker of cigars, and many of them.

I endured the polite signs in places of business and congress, and many impolite reproachful looks and stares of my liberal brethren – those looks that said, 'If I were less of a gentleperson, I would be looking at you in such a way as to let you know that your habit, which you must know is unhealthy, but from which you have not the will power to refrain, is as insulting and offensive to those around you as it is disgraceful to its practitioner.'

I become oh-so-tired of wondering whether my cigar smoking was going to elicit the above response, and spent a lot of time thinking about my prospective reply: should I be arrogant and ignore, arrogant and respond, courteous and beg pardon, et cetera.

This, of course, took the thrill out of cigar smoking. My liberal brethren had reduced me to a worried and cowering state on this one issue. I was upbraided in the park for smoking cigars; this park, which, previous to my correction, I had always thought of as 'outside.' And my last refuge was the lovely tobacco store on Mass Ave, where they let me sit up in the chess gallery and smoke their cigars while I worked – until this previously beloved resort became as a prison to me, and I stopped smoking.

I feel much better since I stopped. My clothes smell clean, my wind and general fitness are improved. I am, as any reformed person, aware of the benefits that this reform has wrought for the populace in general; and I find that I do object to smoking on planes, in restaurants, and in anyplace where the nonsmoker has no comfortable means of distance from the offensive object. I think and hope that I neither express nor feel the self-righteousness that I found so dreadful as its recipient, but I do admire the net result of those workers for a smoke-free world – the laws and improvements that they have wrought. It's not something I would have gone to court about, but I'm glad they did.

Now, however, I find it is my ox that is being gored; and though I fear that the quiddity of my objection opens me to ridicule, I am going to state it.

I am offended and upset by the universality of recorded music played in situations where the listener is powerless to escape.

I do not find it necessary that restaurateurs, business-people, and captains of transportation should elect to fill the arguably non-musical moments in my day with their notion of the correct theme.

I would prefer street sounds, general quiet, or the lovely rhythm of human conversation to music played in a restaurant. Why should the tastes of some restaurant 'consultant' predominate over my own predilection for silence?

I prefer the sounds of the gymnasium to the wretched throbbing of disco music, or whatever that phenomenon is called today. I do not like the time I spend weighing the rights of the restaurant against the rights of myself, the customer, each time I try to decide whether to ask that the music be turned off or lowered, or whether I should just leave. I spend a lot of my life in restaurants, on planes. I read in them, I write in them. Both activities are seriously curtailed by the presence of recorded music.

One might argue that said music is simply background, but it is not so for me.

I love music, I play music, I write music, and when it is being played I am unable to tune it out. I am listening to it against my will, distracted from my thoughts, my book, my work, and hating the choice, the fact, and the arrangement, of the music, and the arrogance of those who have subjected me to it. *Can it be* that those of a certain class cannot imbibe their alcohol or chew their food without hearing Ella Fitzgerald or Billie Holiday, that travelers would feel cheated if they did not hear the *Brandenburg Concerto* when the plane touched down, that others could not enjoy their shopping mall without 'By the Time I Get to Phoenix'?

I suggest that *no one* enjoys that music. That it is there because it is there, and that most people either do not notice it or have come to accept it as the correct background noise for the above activities.

I can do neither, and, though I know this confession brands me as an old maid, I feel I have a just beef, and you have just heard it.

I would not be so quixotic as to suggest that the courts are the proper venue for the settlement of that which even I, the offended, can barely envision as a dispute; but I suspect that there are others of a disposition similar to mine, and that perhaps somewhere we might have some redress.

Those of such mind might be thought of as neurasthenic individuals, but we might also be thought of as consumers – and, in that guise, perhaps we might gain consideration of an entrepreneur or two. If I saw a restaurant advertising 'good food, quiet surroundings,' I'd surely give it a try.

The Hotel Lincoln

I took down an old acting book the other day.

It was Richard Boleslavsky's *Acting: The First Six Lessons*, and, when I was a young acting student, it was beloved by me. The book was a fairly constant companion in the late sixties and seventies. It is an anecdotal and accessible rendering of Boleslavsky's understanding of that philosophy which, for want of better terminology, should probably be called the Stanislavsky System.

Here is why I took the book down: I was passing in front of my television, which, to my shame, was turned on. The television was advertising an upcoming showing of the film *Lives of a Bengal Lancer*. Well, I thought, I don't know the film, but I love the book. And I strove to prove to the television that my literacy predated the electronic. I scanned the bookcase for the *Lives*, and did not find it. I did, however, come across another book in the, I would think, limited sub-arcana of lancer memoirs, and this book was *Lances Up!*

Now, *Lances Up!* is by Richard Boleslavsky, and describes his career in the Polish Lancers at the beginning of the Great War. I had bought the book during the period when I frequented drama bookstores and because its author had been a member of the Moscow Art Theater – my youthful Camelot – and had written the excellent *Six Lessons*.

So, twenty years later, and involved in a rather pointless dialogue with a television set, my thoughts guided my hand to an old favorite book of mine, and I took it down from the shelf, and a rent receipt fell out of it.

It was a receipt for $170 for one month's rent at the Hotel Lincoln, which stood and stands at the southern end of Lincoln Avenue in Chicago.

I lived at the Lincoln off and on for various years of my youth, and I found it a paradise.

Let me tell you: when I first began staying there the rent was $135 a month, which included daily maid service, an answering service, a television set, and both the best view and the best location in Chicago.

The rooms looked out over Lincoln Park and the lake, and I thought the view much nicer than that afforded by Lake Shore Drive.

I had nothing but Clark Street between me and the park, while Lake Shore Drive had the vast concrete Outer Drive and constant noise and traffic. My room got the most beautiful of sunrises, and it was always clean when I came back at night. I believe I pitied the deluded gentry who paid fortunes for their apartments, and who did not realize that one required nothing more than shelter and solitude. Not only did my hotel room possess those, but it had

charm in the bargain. Elaine, the ancient telephone operator, somehow got into the habit of calling me up at eleven or twelve at night
and asking if I needed a cup of tea or anything. There was a
reported crap game down in the men's room, which I never found;
and there was the sound of the animals at night.

The animals lived in the Lincoln Park Zoo, which was pretty
much right across the street, and many times at night I'd hear the
lions or the seals.

The report of the crap game came from friends at Second City.

As a kid in high school I hung around Second City quite a bit. I
was friendly with the owners and their family, and was permitted to
frequent the joint. Later I worked there as a busboy, and occasionally I played piano for the kids' shows on the weekend.

In any case, in the early sixties, well before the time of the rent
receipt, I was exposed to *la vie bohème* as rendered by the actors at
Second City. The club was, at that time, half a block from the Hotel
Lincoln restaurant (which was not, I believe, called the Laff-In at
that juncture); and it was related to me that various illuminati of
the North Side lived in the Hotel Lincoln and ate and wrote and
schemed in the hotel restaurant, and shot craps in the men's room,
and, having been told these things, I remembered them. And when
it became time for me to go out into the world, I applied to the
hotel, and was rented a room.

I bought my first typewriter (an Olympia, for which I remember
paying two hundred dollars; it seemed like a lot of money for a
manual typewriter, but I've still got it, twenty-some years later, and
it still works fine) and paid a month in advance and lived at the
Hotel Lincoln. I went downstairs several times a day to the restaurant, now called the Laff-In, and sat in the same booths that had
once sheltered Burns and Shreiber, Fred Willard, and the great
Severn Darden. I received messages at the switchboard, and had
beautiful young women back up to my room. I went down to the
Laff-In in the middle of the night and had chicken soup with the
owner, Jeff, and talked about the world. I never went into the
hotel's bar, but did have a drink now and then with the proprietors
of the drugstore, behind the prescription counter.

I worked during those years at a day (or 'straight') job, and, in
one capacity or other, in the theater.

I sold land over the telephone for a while. The real estate office was way up north in Lincolnwood, and so I rode the length of Lincoln Avenue twice each day on the CTA bus, and it seemed significant to me that the long bus route began on the very corner where I lived. (And coming home at night, I could see the red-orange sign of the hotel from as far north, if memory serves, which it probably does not, as Addison Street.)

I worked as a waiter at a club just up Clark Street; and, during that period, I worked as a busboy in the final days of the London House.

I wrote plays in my notebook, sitting in the Laff-In; and wrote sitting on various benches in the park across the street.

I had just a few clothes and several theater books. Looking back, I think that I can say that I not only set out to but managed to emulate a model of the Life of a Chicago Writer.

I had guests at my house in Boston on the evening that I took down the Boleslavsky. One of the guests was a young actor. I started reminiscing with him and his friends about *my* early days in the theater, and told him, as, it seems, we middle-aged fogeys may do, how romantic and how cheap things had been in my day. I told him about the perfect life of charm and comfort lived for $170 a month, and brought out the book and receipt as if the fact of their existence would mitigate my garrulousness. He admired the book, and I made him a present of it, and inscribed it with his name and the wish that it would bring him much enjoyment and luck.

He asked if I meant him to have the receipt too. I hesitated a moment. The receipt had just become precious to me. It was an absolute relic of an earlier day of my life. I wanted the receipt. But what did the receipt signify? That I had, in fact, lived through those times in which I had lived? Who would doubt it, and, equally, to whom could it be important? It could be important only to me, and I knew the truth of it already. So I told the actor that, of course, I meant him to have the receipt, too; because I wanted to be part of the succession through Boleslavsky to Stanislavsky and the Moscow Art Theater, and I was flattered that the young man wanted to make the tradition continue to himself through me.

The Shooting Auction

I took the train out of Union Station in Chicago, and went south. I was going to meet a man I had known only over the phone. He ran an auction house for firearms. I'd bought several pieces from him, and sold a piece or two as well.

The last auction had in it a .45-caliber Colt pistol of mine. I'd had the gun extensively reworked and tuned for shooting competition. But business had taken me away from practice, so I decided to clean out my gun cabinet and sent it down to the auction house.

The pistol and the modification had run me well over a thousand dollars, but the auction was a place to find a bargain; I would be lucky to get eight hundred for the gun.

After the auction the proprietor phoned and told me that he was extremely sorry, but that my gun had only fetched $275. He was surprised and apologetic, and offered to waive his commission, but I told him, no, that I'd profited as a buyer at the auction, and that I knew the rules of the game, and that the pistol had fetched what the market thought it was worth, that he should deduct his commission and send me a check.

He then invited me down to his place in southern Illinois to see the operation, pick up the check, and do a little shooting at his range.

I was flattered by the invitation, which was, I knew, offered partly by way of apology for what he considered my disappointment at the auction price. I am not a gregarious person, and, further, wouldn't have wanted the man to feel beholden to me; but my experience of the shooting sports was of an exceedingly friendly and hospitable fraternity. My acquaintance with the owner of the auction had grown over the time of our business dealings. He seemed a friendly man, and his invitation to come down south and do a little shooting was very much in the fairly universally, in my experience, friendly style of the shooting world. His offer caught me in between projects, and a trip and some shooting sounded like a very good idea, so I got on the train and rode south.

He and his friend met me at the station, and we went to his friend's house. The man had a large collection of American shot-guns. There were perhaps eighty of them displayed horizontally on every wall of his gun room. On a table in the center of the room was a scale-model steamboat he had made. The damn thing was about two feet end to end and fashioned completely out of brass. I was told that it was detail-correct down to the smallest fittings and gauges and that it operated perfectly.

This seemed a bit obsessive, and I found myself repressing an impulse to question the infinite completion of the model. 'But surely,' I wanted to say, 'it can't have *every* gauge and fitting of the original . . .' But I held my tongue, although I found the intricacy of the model aggressive, and I admired his collection of arms.

One of his prizes was a German drilling, a double shotgun with a rifle barrel underneath. The guns are, I understand, popular in Europe, but I had never seen one. And its oddity was accentuated by various features fitted into the stock that would change the point-of-aim when the shooter changed from shotgun to rifle. The drilling had a comb-and-cheek piece that popped out of the stock when a button was pushed, and it was very well made and very German and I admired it no end.

The door to the friend's gun room was taken from a bank vault. Walking in his hallway, one opened a door to what could have been a linen closet, and found, beyond it, the massive steel vault door.

The two men gathered and advertised their guns each month in an old-fashioned hand-drawn brochure. I collected the brochures and bid on a few of the guns, and I sent some in to be sold, including, as I've said, the Colt .45 automatic.

The two men were to drive me out to their club. We went south through very flat farm country, over the blacktop road. In a while the land became slightly rolling and more wooded. We went off on a side road and then through a stretch of woods to the shooting club.

The club, I was told, was a rather exclusive affair and drew membership from all over the Midwest. Admittance had been closed for some long time, and new membership opportunities tended to devolve almost exclusively upon the family and friends of the old members.

Additionally, to apply, one must have spent, I was told, ninety days 'under canvas.' I had never heard the expression before, and thought it somewhat overly picturesque, until I reflected that my reluctance to embrace it was probably founded on both envy and ignorance of the situation it described; and to the world that would have need to refer to the phenomenon, the phrase was not only apt, but, to the contrary of my suspicions of its prettiness, direct and businesslike in the extreme.

As we drove through the club's long driveway – we have all, I think, had that experience of first exposure to a secluded and exclusive spot, in which the drive from the barred gate to the main buildings seems interminable – I was pointed out the house of the gamekeeper.

We drove past it, and over the various streams and past the small lake of the shooting-club preserve. I was told names of the streams and how the ice fishing took place and the ponds were stocked, and how the wives of the sportsmen prepared this or that traditional dinner on its appointed date.

We drove to a small cabin and parked. The cabin was furnished with a few long tables and a wooden chair or two. Around the walls were lockers and shelving.

My companions signed into a log book and took some targets from a bin, and we went outside, out beyond the cabin, where there was a hundred-yard rifle range.

The owner's friend took the targets and walked the hundred yards down to the butts. The owner and I went back around to the car and opened the trunk and took out several rifles, ear protectors, and a canvas shooting bag.

We took the lot over to a shooting table back at the firing line, and laid out the rifles, side by side. The man took a sandbag from the shooting gear and pointed to one of the rifles and asked me if I'd go first.

We saw the other man hoist up the targets, down at the end of the range. I waited, with that schematic shooting courtesy which always has in it just that little bit of 'show,' for him to return and move well back of the firing line before I prepared to shoot.

The rifle was some very quick and flat-shooting thing. A 220 Swift or something. A varmint rifle. I took the sandbag, whacked it down on the table in front of me, and pounded a valley into it with the edge of my hand. I opened the bolt of the rifle and laid the stock in the sandbag groove. The man gave me five rounds of ammunition, and I took them and put then next to the sandbag. I sat down in the metal chair and pulled it up to the shooting table.

I asked him if it was all right to dry-fire the piece and he said it was. I got down behind the rifle and looked through the scope. The eye relief was good for me, and it brought the target right up close. I got myself into a good shooting position, my left arm across my chest and the hand hugging the right shoulder; I closed the bolt and took aim at the target. I took a deep breath. In and slowly out; then in and half out, until the crosshairs rested exactly on the bottom center of the bull's-eye, and I squeezed the trigger, which broke clean at what felt like around three and a half pounds. I opened the bolt, looked up from the rifle, and loaded the five rounds down into the magazine. 'Well, I guess I'm going to shoot here,' I said. The two men nodded and stepped farther back from the firing line.

I put four shots into the target, and they felt so good that I got a bit nervous and pulled the fifth shot slightly. 'Flyer!' I called out after the last shot, and immediately felt foolish, as if anything in the world depended upon the consistency of my shooting.

I opened the bolt, and one of the men said I had shot very well. But I couldn't get over my last shot, and compounded my feelings of gaucherie by going on about it. 'No,' I said. 'Last shot's way off. Way off.'

We walked down to the butts and pulled the target down, and it showed four shots in a one-inch group just right of center at the bottom of the bull, and the fifth shot three quarters of an inch below and to the right of the group.

This was good shooting, even with the flyer, and both honesty – I was shooting rather above my head – and courtesy required that I shut up about it and let the next man shoot. But I just couldn't seem to keep quiet, and I kept going on about how the rifle 'felt,' and what a good rifle it was, and how I pulled the last shot. I felt like a fool and knew that my chat sounded false to the other men.

We put up some fresh targets and went back to the firing line, and shot some of the other rifles, but I was all over the target and couldn't get any of them to group.

I told the men I had to catch a 4 P.M. train back to Chicago. They asked me to stay on and shoot more, but I said I had to go.

We drove back through the farm country, into the town, and to the auction house. The owner showed me around his operation – how the good pieces were separated from the lesser ones, how they were all cleaned and logged and photographed. I walked through the aisles and looked at the various items in the bins.

It was about time to leave for the station. We were back in his office, drinking coffee and making our farewells. I admired a good-looking pistol in a box on a shelf.

'That one's mine,' the owner said. 'Picked up for a song. I stole it for two hundred fifty dollars.'

I picked up the pistol to admire it, and saw it was the one I'd sent him to be sold.

Wabash Avenue

Wabash Avenue ran under the El.

The significant part was eight blocks long. It ran from Randolph Street on the north to Van Buren on the south.

Wabash was the backside of Michigan Avenue.

Michigan was show. Fronted on the park, it looked out on statuary, the Art Institute, and the lake. It was a grand white-stone European vision. Michigan Avenue was old Chicago money patting itself on the back.

Wabash, running parallel, was, to me, a truer Chicago. The street was always dark. It ran underneath the El; the sun never hit Wabash Avenue. It was always noisy. It was a masculine street. It was a business street. As a kid I'd hang out on the fourth floor of Marshall Field's store for men on Wabash and Washington. That was a store for a young kid to be in.

The fourth floor had a Kodiak bear to greet you as you got off the elevator. The bear had been shot by one of the customers and donated to the store; and I always wondered what kind of man would shoot such a bear and then keep it anywhere other than in his living room. I still wonder.

In any case, it was on its hind legs and *looming* over you as you got off. Ten, twelve feet in the air. There were other animals and heads and fish displayed throughout the floor, but the bear was *it* in my book.

Over on the right was the gun section. You had to pass through the fishing rods to get to them, but it was a short walk.

Over on the left they kept the clothing. I don't remember much about the clothing on the fourth floor. I remember the hats on two.

My usual rounds took me from the fourth floor down the stairs to two. They had the most magnificent assortment of hats I have ever seen in my life.

Every summer I would try on countless straw boaters before deciding that neither the times nor my personality would support my sporting one. One summer I actually bought one, but I don't remember wearing it.

I also remember buying a beret or two over the years from the second floor. Very romantic. Not the $150 extra-selected Panamas – a true fortune in the early sixties; not the sable or marten trappers' hats, so beautiful I didn't even feel fit to ask to try them on; no, I bought a beret once or twice over the years, and wore it out of the store, feeling myself the creditable and up-to-the-minute rendition of a serious young man with artistic aspirations.

The ground floor of the store was haberdashery. I have looked that word up many times over the years, as every time I see it I am puzzled by its derivation. I am going to look it up once again. I see my dictionary tells me it comes from the Middle English, *haber-dassherie*, and it becomes clear to me I need a new or auxiliary dictionary.

In any case, I always felt the word was silly. Further, it was associated in my mind, of course, with Harry Truman, a man whom I did not associate with relaxed elegance. Neither endowment, however, lessened my affection for the first floor, which was the Hermès and Charvet's of Chicago Man, they had a fine line of goods in there – their like may still exist, but I haven't seen it.

I remember the most beautiful shirts and socks and underwear and belts and suspenders and leather goods. Truman Capote had said it of Tiffany's; 'Nothing very bad could happen to you there.'

The store was always deliciously cool in the summertime, and warm in the winter, on those very cold and very dark nights, when you would have to go out of that haven and fight your way through the people on Wabash who were trying to fight their way through

you and get home just like you. And the lucky ones were going on the
El, where at least they had a bit of shelter, and you were usually going
on the bus, and had to stand on Washington Street, exposed to that
cold, which is worse than any I've ever felt anywhere else.

And what is there about the El? I don't know. I notice that in
almost every thriller made in Chicago in the last few years, there is a
chase sequence involving the El, and someone riding on top of the El.
Well, the El is, of course, romantic, but why would anyone want to
ride on top? I always loved it, as it took you out of the cold. I never
lived near the El, and always wished that I did.

I remember the El outside the practice studios at Lyon and Healy's.
I used to while away many hours at the rate, if memory serves, of one
dollar per, in the small piano rooms there. I always requested one on
the Wabash side, facing the El. That was my Tin Pan Alley – just me
and a pack of cigarettes playing the piano in the closet-sized room . . .
the El thundering by outside of the fourth-floor window.

They were great people at Lyon and Healy's. In fact, as I think
about it, I don't remember any salespeople on Wabash who were
other than great to me. I spent untold hours in the shops, fingering
the stuff, questioning the clerks, making only the most minimal
purchases, and those rarely. They let me play all the guitars at Lyon
and Healy's, and across the street at Prager and Ritter's.

The salespeople at Abercrombie and Fitch told me about all the
custom knives in the first-floor cases. The first major sporting
purchase of my life was made there. After much deliberation, and
after much saving, I bought a Randall #5 bird-and-trout knife out of
the case at Abercrombie's.

It cost fifty-five dollars. It was, and still is, advertised as the knife
that Francis Gary Powers was carrying when his U2 was shot down
over Russia. I don't know why, but that seemed, and still rather
seems, a legitimate endorsement. I suppose that was what Wabash
Avenue was to me – a very romantic street. It had the weight of
seriously romantic endeavors – hunting, music, dress, reading. I got
my first credit card from Kroch's and Brentano's bookstore. I was, I
believe, seventeen years old, and they gave me a credit card.

I discovered literature in their basement paperback section. I
discovered contemporary writing on the first floor. The salespeople
would order books for me, then would look the other way while I stood
at the rack and read that week's new book. I felt like a member there.

What a different world. I remember the salesman at Iwan Ries tobacco store schooling me in the niceties of tobacco smoking as they sold me my first pipe – delighted to be passing on a tradition. I remember buying English Oval cigarettes there. I loved the box and the shape. Someone told me that you were supposed to squeeze them to recompress them into a round shape, but I never did this, and if it was the right thing to do, I didn't want to know. They tasted, to me, of powder and the very exotic – much more so than the heavier Balkan Sobranies, which, it must be admitted, came in the best package anything has ever come in – that small, flat white metal tin, which held ten cigarettes; or, later, a couple of bills and a driver's license, vitamins – it occurs to me that, even at the time, one knew that there were not really a hell of a lot of things that the Sobranie case was perfectly suited to accommodate – but what promise it offered.

That was Wabash Avenue. They were glad to see you smoke, glad to see you enjoy yourself, glad to help you do it, and delighted that they could earn their living by assisting you. I suppose it was the end of Chicago as the Merchant to the Frontier.

What am I forgetting? Up at the top, at Wacker, is the statuary group of General Washington, and somebody else, and significantly, to me, a Mr. Solomon – if memory serves – who is there inscribed as a merchant supporter of the Continental Cause. Away down the other end of Wabash were the main garages and offices of the Yellow Cab Company, where I had one or two interesting encounters during my days as a cabdriver, but the *real* Wabash ran just for those eight or nine blocks under the El.

Various Sports in Sight of the Highlands

I try to pop over to Scotland for a little golf once every forty-three years.

As there exists both religious theory and folk belief to the effect that, should one scorn someone or something in this life, in the life to come one will *become* that thing; so, in my introduction to golf, did I reap what I had sown.

For I had spent some time – as who could escape it – watching folks devoted to golf in that same way and with that same devotion others give to cats or the First Amendment, or to other sports and articles capable both of use and of receiving devotional fervor.

I had watched these folks and wondered. As a child, I spent far too much time in a new suburb of Chicago, which suburb's only claim to fame was that it bordered a golf course of, I believe, national distinction. And one summer, some *première-classe* golf contest was held there and neighbors of mine made a lot of money renting out space in a cornfield to those who had come to watch the golf.

And I had, of course, putted through the windmill, and into the mouth of the gorilla at those carny spots named 'Putt 'n' Grin,' and so on, on too-hot midwestern evenings.

As to golf itself, however, I was as innocent as the babe unborn is held to be under some of the more lenient of religious persuasions; and I had come to Scotland to learn.

I approached my first lesson with this attitude: how craven it would be to wish to excel at a sport the clothing of whose participants I had laughed at for so many years. And, as it turned out, I was not in any danger at all of so excelling.

I was welcomed at a beautiful resort devoted to sport, and put into the care of an excellent teacher, who showed me the position of the feet, of the hands, of the head and knees, and of the shoulders. I was shown how to relax the shoulders through raising the chin; and how the angle of the ball was sure to depend on the position of the club as it came to the ball, and how that was assured of depending on the angle of the backswing.

My excellent teacher broke it down section by section, and I was sweating with the effort of it all after a few minutes.

It reminded me hugely of the hook. My boxing coach said, of that other worthy mystery, 'Yeah, you try and try, and one day, next week, next month, *sometime*, one day, "Dawn over Marble Head."' Well, in time the hook began to make sense; and I, as I say, see the similarity in the golf swing.

In both, it seems to me, the hands and arms are along for the ride, and the legs and waist are doing the yeoman work; so the acquisition of both the hook and the golf swing must be a process of breaking it down, and learning the components by rote over lengthy periods during which one has nothing better to do.

This whole idea was fine with me, but I had been allotted only two half-hour lessons with the instructor, after which I was to play nine rounds with the resort's golf pro. At the end of my first half hour I had only progressed as far as missing the ball completely whilst concentrating on the movements of my arms and torso; and my second and last bout of tuition boded fair to consist of missing the ball while employing my entire frame.

Well, I consoled myself, what is golf anyway?

Nothing, I reflected, short of some bastard amalgam of billiards and hiking.

It was, I said in my fit of pique, guilty of falling into that category of most despicable of activities, something that would 'ruin the drape.' My preferred leisure hours of the last forty years have consisted of playing the piano or playing poker, a signal desideratum consonant to the two that they do not ruin the drape.

In neither the playing of the piano nor the playing of cards do we find the necessity of carrying around weighty, bulky, or awkward objects that would deform the clean and flowing lines of the nifty clothing elected by nature as appropriate to the pursuit of such endeavours. One cannot say the same of golf.

Yes, I understand that one is theoretically empowered to subdue the energy of human or mechanical caddies to carry one's golf clubs, but this seems to me an unattractive alternative for two reasons.

First, I think that there must be those times when one must carry the clubs some small way – even if that way is as limited as from the baggage carousel to the car – and this would ruin the drape.

Yes, you might say, but could one not simply point the golf clubs out to a porter and have him or her carry them that offending distance?

Yes, I reply, one could; but this would put one afoul of that which I feel is the second serious disqualification of the sport: it seems to me that a whole big bunch of time and space has to be put aside to play golf.

My hero, Thorstein Veblen, wrote in *The Theory of the Leisure Class* that the lawn, as we know it, is nothing more or less than the attempt to re-create a field that has been munched down by sheep – thus conferring upon its owners the status of gentlemen and -women farmers. Well, when I got up to Scotland, his point was driven home. My approach to the resort was through a vale called Glen Devon.

The car left Edinburgh and climbed higher and higher through green fields and country lanes until the land fell away on the left side and there was one of the most magnificent views it has ever been my pleasure to see.

I saw a steep mountain valley and, climbing away up the far side, sheep dotted on the hill, untold miles of intersecting stone walls, grass grazed down to look like the finest and most cared-for lawn, which had, on scant reflecting, and with homage to Mr. Veblen, been mowed down to resemble this vale.

And I looked out at the golf course, on which such obvious and loving care had been expended; and, to my untutored eye, it looked identical to the sheep-shorn little hills beyond it. But it was Coco Chanel, I think, who said that there are two good reasons to buy anything, because it is very cheap or because it is very expensive.

And I thought that, for myself, an indulgence in golf spoke too much of what Mr. Veblen called 'conspicuous consumption,' of both land and energy.

Now, I am no one to talk, for I am sure that I defy all but the most hardened and deluded golfers to have spent more on their clubs than I have spent flogging an obviously beaten pair of eights. And I am proud to have spent that most precious of commodities, my youth, mured in an area that, human nature being what it is, I have come to identify as the esthetically correct venue for sport: a small and smoky room.

So, go in peace, you golfers. Go your way and I will go mine. I returned for that lesson which was to unify in sport the higher and lower portions of my body, and, I think, learned a thing or two, and, I must say, looked forward to my meeting with the golf pro and our round of golf.

But it was raining hard that day, and the pro and I never got to play.

I spent a most pleasant half hour sitting with him in his office. I asked him about the birds I had seen on the golf course, and if, in his experience, they ever came to grief.

He told me that over the years he had knocked down a bird or two, and that, in his youth, he had even taken the odd one back home and cooked it.

He explained that a golf ball can be moving at upward of 120 miles an hour, and that these things happen. He told me that once, in fact, he downed a sheep.

Well, that was good enough for me. I unbuttoned my coat and relaxed, and we had a real good chat about sport, and hustling, and betting, and what a fine world it was to allow one to make a living doing what one loved.

I could have spent the day there, but he was a man with work to do, so I excused myself, and thanked him for his time, and moved on.

The rain continued to come down and the resort liaison asked if I would like to essay one of the other activities in the tuition and the practice of which they are famed.

I acceded and went in the rain to their shooting school, where, under the tutelage of another excellent instructor, I delighted in breaking several black clay pigeons, and returned after a while, wet and cold and glowing, to the shooting lodge, looking for a short drink of Scotch and feeling like a real sporting gent.

The rain was letting up a wee bit, and the golfers were preparing to play. Not my sport, as I have pointed out, but the people who pursue it certainly are serious, and as I looked at them teeing up in the rain I reflected that any leisure endeavor which can be pursued to the point of monomania is worthy of respect, and I was warmed by both the Scotch and my own generosity.

My House

In my younger days in New York everyone I knew lived in a walk-up apartment building, and I didn't know anyone who lived below the fifth floor.

At least that is the way my memory has colored it.

I remember the industrial wire spools that served as coffee tables, and the stolen bricks and boards out of which everyone constructed bookcases. There were red-and-yellow Indian bedspreads on the wall, and everyone had Milton Glaser's poster of a Medusa-haired Bob Dylan displayed.

That was how the counterculture looked in Greenwich Village in the sixties. We considered ourselves evolved beyond the need for material comfort, and looked back on a previous generation's candle-in-the-Chianti bottle as laughable affectation.

We children of the middle class were playing proletariat, and, in the process, teaching ourselves the rules of that most bourgeois of games: the Decoration of Houses.

The game, as we learned it, was scored on cost, provenance, integrity of the scheme, and class loyalty.

Now, in those days, status was awarded to the least costly article, and, as for provenance, those articles that were stolen ranked highest, followed immediately by those that had been discarded, with those that had been merely borrowed ranking a weak third.

Objects were capable of being included in the *ensemble* if they were the result of or made reference to the Struggle for a Better World; and points were given to the more geographically or politically esoteric items.

I look around my living room today and see that, of course, none of the rules have changed. They stand just as Thorstein Veblen described them a hundred years ago. The wish for comfort and the display of status contend with and inform each other in the decoration of the living place, and I'm still pretending.

Now, however, I am faking a long-term membership in a different class.

I live in an old row house in Boston.

The house is in an area called the South End, specifically in that section called the Eight Streets. These streets are lined with near-identical bow-front brick row houses, built in the 1870s as part of a housing development and intended as single-family residences. The panic of 1873 wounded the real estate market, and the row houses were, in the main, partitioned and rented out by the room.

My house, the local historical association tells me, is one of the few that were not partitioned. Consequently, it retains most of the architectural detail with which it was adorned a hundred and some years ago. It has beautiful mahogany banisters and intricate newel posts, the stairwell and the rooms on the parlor floor have ornate plaster molding, there are pocket doors with etched glass – the house was built with new mass-construction techniques that enabled the newly bourgeois to suggest to themselves that they were living like the rich.

I bought the house and thought to enjoy the benefits of restoring it to a Victorian grandeur that it most probably never enjoyed. I recalled the lessons of the sixties, and obtained the services of a decorator, who, in this case, was not a security-lax construction company, but a very talented Englishwoman named Susan Reddick.

Now, if fashion is an attempt by the middle class to co-opt tragedy, home decor is a claim to history.

I grew up on the South Side of Chicago, surrounded by sofas wrapped in thick clear plastic. My parents and the parents of all my friends were the children of immigrants, and they started their American dream homes with no artifacts and without a clue, so, naturally, that history to which I laid claim was late-Victorian arts and crafts.

That is the era which I am pretending bore and endorsed me – a time which was genteel yet earthy, Victorian in its respect for the proprieties, yet linked through its respect for craft to the eternal household requirement for utility and the expression of that truth in pottery and textiles. What a crock, eh?

But that is whom I am pretending to be, a latter-day William Morris, who suggested that a man should be able to compose an epic poem and weave a tapestry at the same time.

And that is the fantasy which my house probably expresses.

There are a lot of fabrics woven on a hand loom by a neighbor in Vermont, some nice examples of American art pottery, and rooms painted in various unusual colors, and applied with several arcane techniques of stippling, striation, and what may, or at least should, be called dappling.

My wife and I are very comfortable here. We spend a lot of time lounging on overstuffed furniture and reading or writing or talking in our own two-person Bloomsbury salon.

It is, as we would have said in Chicago, a real nice house.

Seventy-First and Jeffery

The area from Seventy-first Street north to the park was, in my youth, a Jewish neighborhood.

My grandmother took me shopping and spoke in what could have been Yiddish, Polish, or Russian to several of the shopkeepers on Seventy-first Street. She even knew one or two of them from the Old Country, which was the town of Hrubieszów, on the Russian-Polish border. We lived on Euclid Avenue in a brick house.

There was a policeman, or guard, hired by some sort of block or neighborhood association, and his name was Tex. He patrolled the street with two stag-handled revolvers on his belt, one worn butt forward and the other worn butt to the rear. He would stop and chat at length with us kids.

We spent as much time as possible out in the street. The manhole covers did duty as second base and home plate, or the two end zones, as the season demanded.

We would stay out far past dark in the summertime chasing one another around the neighborhood in what we called a 'bike chase,' which, if memory serves, was some version of the war game the New Yorkers called 'ringalevio.'

We went looking for lost golf balls at the city's Jackson Park course, four blocks to the north; and would trek in the park all the way over to the lake, where we'd look over at the South Shore Country Club.

The country club was, our parents told us, restricted, which meant closed to Jews. It was more a mysterious than a disturbing landmark. It held down the southeastern corner of my world.

Coming back west down Seventy-first Street, we passed the Shoreland Delicatessen, and the next oasis following was J. Leslie Rosenblum, 'Every Inch a Drugstore.'

Rosenblum's was, to me, a place from a different world. I found the style of the name foreign and distinctly un-Jewish in spite of the surname. The store itself was, if I may, the Apollonian counterbalance to the Ashkenazic Dionysia of the Shoreland. Rosenblum's was close and somewhat dark and quiet.

Its claim to my attention was a soda fountain, which smelled of chocolate and various syrups and that indefinable rich coolness coming off the marble, which, I fear, must remain unknown to subsequent generations. My dad took me there for Chicago's famous chocolate phosphate.

I would like to conclude the gastronomic tour of South Shore with mention of the Francheezie. That *ne plus ultra* of comestibles was the product of the Peter Pan restaurant, then situated on the corner of Seventy-first and Jeffery Boulevard, the crossroads of South Shore. The Francheezie was a hot dog split down the middle, filled with cheese, and wrapped in bacon, and, to be round, it was good.

The other spots of note to my young mind were the two movie theaters, the Hamilton to the east and the Jeffery to the west of Jeffery Boulevard. The latter was a block and a half from my house.

On Saturdays I'd take my quarter and get over to the movie house. The cartoons started, I believe, at 9 A.M., and there were so many of them. The figure I remember is '100 cartoons.'

At seven minutes per, I calculate that they would occupy almost twelve hours, and that can't be right; but I prefer my memory to my reason. In any case, there were sufficient cartoons to keep the kids in the movie theater until past dark on Saturday, and that was where we stayed.

The Jeffery and the Hamilton both boasted large blue dimly lit domes set into their ceilings, and my young mind would many times try to reason what their use might be. I found them slightly Arabic, and forty years later, can almost recall the fantasies I had gazing at them. I believe one of the domes had stars, and the other did not.

We had lemonade stands in the summer, and we trick-or-treated in the fall to the smell of the leaves burning in everyone's yard.

I remember fistfights at Parkside School, and the smell of blood in my nose as I got beaten up by the friend of a friend, for some remark I'd made for which I think I deserved to get beaten up.

Years later, I lived up on the North Side.

I drove a yellow cab out of Unit 13, on Belmont and Halsted, and I got a fare to a deserted area, where I got a knife put to my throat and my receipts stolen.

The fellow took the money and ran off. I lit a cigarette and sat in the cab for a while, then drove off to look for a cop. I told the cop what had happened, and suggested that if he wanted to pursue the robber, I would come and help him, as the man couldn't be too far away.

He nodded and started taking down information. I told him my name, and he asked if I was related to the people who used to live in South Shore; and it turned out he'd bought our house. We talked about the house for a while, and what it had been like, and how it had changed; and we both agreed that the robber would be long gone.

I drove off in the cab, and that was my last connection with the old neighborhood.

Cannes

Somebody told me this story. It was, he said, the quintessential experience of Cannes. He went the year Paul Schrader brought his film *Mishima*, and as part of some presentation, an actor on the stage, dressed in a kimono, knelt and went through the motions of ritual suicide. As the audience filed from the auditorium, they were greeted by a double row of eight-foot-high Care Bears passing out candy and leaflets advertising *Care Bears Movie II*.

Similarly, in my own story, there I was in the Grand Hôtel du Cap, surely the most beautiful hostelry on earth. We were having a celebratory lunch following the opening of our movie *Homicide*. Many members of the U.S. press were invited to the hotel by Ed Pressman, one of the film's producers. Ed stood and made a toast. He pointed out that it was perhaps something more than ironic that we were celebrating the premiere of a movie by Jews and about Jews in the building that had housed the Nazi headquarters for the Riviera during World War II.

Is this more or less ironic than the Care Bears? After three days in Cannes I cannot tell.

After a sleepy arrival at the Nice airport, my fiancée, Miss

Pidgeon, and I are gradually whisked to the Carlton Hotel, said transport's progress attenuated by the ministrations of a well-meaning group I could only take to be the festival's officialdom, who met us at the airport and insisted on our transportation in state, which insistence would have been rather more appreciated if they could have found the car, but there's a price for everything.

We got to what probably isn't referred to as 'down-town Cannes' and there was the Carlton, a grand Victorian, foursquare edifice that would have looked right at home in Brighton, save for two things; it was in actual good repair, and it was tarted-out road to roof with bill-boards advertising films and stars, most of which no one had ever heard of. So in we go. Someone informs me that the thing to have is a suite on the sea side. I ask for a suite on the sea side, and am informed that they have been booked years in advance, and that I should only live so long and prosper as the time in which I am not going to have a suite on the sea side. So we go up to the room and go to sleep, and then it is the next day.

I decide to break a several-years'-long avoidance of coffee, so I have one cup and then another and then several more, and we go out onto the beach to have a good time.

I have been informed that bare-breasted women walk the beach at Cannes, their favorite pet a leashed pig. (I tell the story to a Vietnam-veteran friend of mine on my return and he says, 'Oh. Those potbellied Asian pigs. We used to shoot 'em for sport. I should have brought them back under my shirt – I hear they fetch a thousand dollars.') But I saw no pigs. I did see the bare-breasted women, and it all seemed quite civilized to me. Also I saw many people walking dogs. Many had French poodles, which seemed a bit 'on the nose,' but what are you going to do?

I also saw a lot of the kind of off-brand mutts that appear only in dog books and paintings of Italian royalty, and I saw women of a certain age bringing their dogs to work. The dogs ranged in size downward from the small-medium to the ludicrous category. I saw one dog that was of a breed so small that I think the owner explained to me that she had to have two of them, as one was not large enough to hold all the organs. But my French is by no means perfect, and it is possible I misunderstood.

Dawned the next day, Wednesday, and Miss Pidgeon and I repaired to the beach, I say, there to sit and bask away our jet lag.

She was garbed in a classic one-piece maillot, and I had on jeans and a T-shirt, hoping to hide the physique I had worked so assiduously to acquire all winter.

Next to us was a French couple. I engaged them in conversation, and they told me they adored film, that their lucky number was eight, and that they had come down to Cannes when they heard that this was the forty-fourth film festival, said digits being combinable into eight, and here they were.

He was in the fur and leather business, and he told me that fur had had it, and that he feared that leather wasn't very far behind. I asked him if this was because of a certain growing sympathy for animals, and he said that a conjunction of that regrettable development and the inscrutable wave motion of fashion had 'put paid' to his life's work, but that he was branching out into fibers, and that I shouldn't worry.

'Why is it,' I asked, 'that, *ici-bas*, we give our fullest sympathy to them little rodents out of whom we make the furs, but are not so vehemently inclined toward their bovine brethren from whom we fashion the hides?' And well may you believe that that drained to oblivion the high school French to which I wasn't even paying attention thirty years ago. In response to my query, he shrugged. He shrugged and I nodded sagely, and no one has ever felt more Continental than I did at that instant. We spent the day on the beach, and lunched at the Terrace Café there, and listened to the peddlers hawking sunglasses and various pornographic materials, and had a fine old time all day.

Down went the sun. The film producers arrived and we all walked to the Festival Hall to do a sound check on the movie.

We walked down the Croisette, which I believe is the name of the main beach. The producers bought ice cream cones. Out in the harbor were several billionaires' yachts. All of us wondered if such people could be happy, and individually decided that they could not, and felt very pleased with ourselves.

We got to the hall, and after a predictable runaround looking for the right person to accept our credentials, we were admitted. Now, this hall seats around twenty-five hundred people, I think. It is vast. There is no end to it. Each of its dimensions is larger than all the others combined. I am introduced to various officials of the festival, and to the representative of Dolby Sound. I have never understood what the Dolby process does, but I am sure it is something important. The film's producers tell me that we have to stay only for a few minutes, to make sure that 'things' are in order. I nod. The festival functionaries chat among themselves, and the fellow sitting next to me explains that I have a direct line to the projectionist should I want to communicate anything to him. I rack my brain. What, I think, might I conceivably want to say to the projectionist? I am capable of remembering that the film might be out of focus, and there my mind stops. I also cannot remember the French for 'focus,' which is, given the damnable unpredictability of their corrupt tongue, most likely 'focus.'

So I sit there holding the phone, while various preparations are made for the screening.

The producers and the Dolby man have stopped chatting. Evidently *un ange passé*. I decide to fill the gap. 'What's the throw?' I say. This is the one question I know how to ask about an actual movie theater. The *throw* is the distance from the projector to the screen, and what it affects, and what throw is desirable, I could not tell you with a gun to my head. So I do not listen too closely to the response, the lights go out, and the film begins.

There are about ten of us in this hall built for twenty-five hundred. The film is preceded by two rather garish video logos for companies that, I think, coughed up part of the European money to finance the project. The festival functionary asks me if I want the logos in or out. I confer with my producers. They say to leave it in as a mark of respect. So be it.

The film looks great, but I can't hear a word of it. There are hurried conversations. It turns out that the stereo recording is on the widest speakers, and that the hall is so big we are getting an echo effect. The sound is then switched onto the middle two speakers, and it sounds a bit better.

I think the film looks dark. I ask the functionary and he tells me some technical info about how a film has to look darker on a screen that big, because if the projector lamps were turned up higher, something or other would happen. 'Well, if *that*'s the case,' I tell him, '*fine*.' I'm supposed to watch only a few minutes of the film. But I have invited my Parisian friends from the beach, and I do not want to disappoint them, so we all stay through the whole film.

The film is over. I expect the festival people to be weeping copiously or ritually rending their garments or something by way of encouragement; but my hopes, it seems, are too high, and they shake my hand and say they enjoyed the film and wish me well.

We all walk back along the Croisette. There are many people out walking around and looking in the windows of the very posh shops. Many of the people have dogs.

The drivers speed viciously. The hotel room has no air-conditioning. These are my reflections as I fall into a jet-lagged sleep. When I awake it has become Thursday, the day of the opening of the festival, which festival will be opened by the screening of my film.

My schedule for Thursday looked like this: interviews in the morning, then a trip to the Festival Hall for a press conference and a session with photographers, then more interviews, then the official festival opening screening, and then a party given by Jack Lang, the cultural minister of France. A full day.

I looked forward to doing all of my interviews on the beach, but when I awoke, it was pissing down rain, and so it was going to be interviews in the hotel room.

I said a prayer that I wouldn't make a fool of myself during my meetings with the press. I hadn't done any interviews for the last several years, and felt much better for it.

When I stopped talking to the press, I began to see the publicity process from an interesting remove – a bit like the fellow who has turned teetotal, and goes to the cocktail party and wonders why everyone is behaving in such an odd fashion and what they find so amusing in one another.

The publicity process had come to seem to me a good example of jolly mutual exploitation, and not unlike my memories of the climate of sexual promiscuity in the turbulent sixties – something that also seemed a good idea at the time.

In the publicity process the subject and the interlocutor both pretend to be disinterested. The interviewee is constrained to adopt some version of a humble demeanor ('Who *me* ...?'), and the interviewer poses as an honest seeker after truth – either for his own edification or on behalf of his readership.

In truth, the subject is trying to flog his wares, his ideas, or himself, and the journalist is – usually – hoping to 'catch him out,' as it 'makes better copy.' And I can't say that I blame the journalist.

Which, if we're looking for a villain, leaves the subject, which, in my case, was myself, which is why I stopped doing interviews. For it did seem to me to be two overweening ids – the Chorus Girl and the Producer; and the Chorus Girl said, 'I am going to bed with you because I am taken with your kindness and your generosity – two qualities I find attractive in a man'; and the Producer said, 'I respect your honesty and your integrity in going to bed with a man old enough to be your uncle, and, further, I am impressed with your fortitude in withstanding the sure-to-come barbs of those deluded souls who might just say that you are going to bed with me just to get the part, and, in *spite* of them, I am going to give you the part, which I was going to do anyway.'

And then we have the superego of the Bellhop, who says, 'Oh, *please* . . . Whyn't'cha just hop in the sack and get *on* with it.'

So I said a prayer that I would not make a fool of myself, and reminded myself of the supposed benefits of publicity, and went forth. I talked to a couple of journalists in the morning and then went over for the press conference.

Hundreds of thousands of journalists, so it seemed to me, had just been shown the film in a special press screening, and they were arrayed in a conference hall. The producers of the film and Miss Pidgeon and I were ushered into the conference hall and onto a stage. Many photographers took pictures, we were introduced by Henri Behar, the moderator and translator, and the press conference began.

People asked me questions, and I responded to them. People took pictures, the press conference ended, and we were ushered along by a nice burly Frenchman whom I took to be the director of security. We went through various passages of the Festival Hall, flanked by the burly man's myrmidons, who were all wearing madras jackets reminiscent of the fifties.

We ended up on a terrace at the side of the Festival Hall. There were, arrayed on bleachers on the terrace, three hundred photographers popping off pictures. Flashbulbs kept going off, and people were screaming at me to look at them.

I would turn to look at them, and people from whom I had turned away would begin screaming that perhaps I should look back in their direction. This went on for the longest time. Twice I waved good-bye to the photographers and made as if to leave, and twice I was rebuffed by the festival officials, who indicated that they'd 'be the judge of that.'

Finally it was determined that all had gone correctly, and that the photographers on the bleachers were done.

My party was then directed to turn around, which we did, and found another hundred photographers on another terrace some fifty feet away, and then it was their turn and they took pictures for a while. Finally we were allowed to leave. A car drove us back to the Carlton, and I suggested to the driver that he have his wheels aligned, but he politely remonstrated that the offending oscillation was caused by myself, who was shaking like that which we in Vermont have come to know as 'a leaf.'

And I talked to some more journalists that afternoon, and then it was time to prepare for the big night.

Which of us has not confronted that tuxedo? Yes, our loved one is in the bathroom, engaged in god knows what procession of ritual preparations, and oblivious to all else. There is a spiritual apartheid between the bathroom and the bedroom. The usual connubial cospiritedness that informs the happy home has ceased. One is alone.

I'd bought a new tuxedo, and was about to don it for the first time. The clothier suggested that I let out the waist a half-inch. I declined, as the waist fit right fine, I thought, and told him so. He suggested that as I was going to wear the tux with suspenders, rather than with a belt, I would be more comfy having the waist a bit looser. I knew, or thought I knew, that he was only being kind to me – and that, if I assented, he would let the waist an inch and a half and leave me, in my delusion, to believe he had let it out merely the promised half-inch – all of the above suspicions being justified by his use of slimming mirrors in his store.

So I told him not to let out the waist, and I started getting into the tux, and it fit *just fine* and rather loose around the waist, so I felt superior to my clothier, and then I thought that he had probably let the waist out *anyway*, and I suppressed an impulse to take the pants off and hunt for marks of the same.

Yes, my mind was racing.

I got into my tux by stages. There was a cunning little arrangement whereby the front of the stiff-front shirt was meant to attach itself through the inside of the fly of the pants, so as to keep the shirt nice 'n' neat and prevent its riding up. I finally got the arrangement to work, and then could not straighten up, so I redid it and got the bow tie tied and the whole nine yards and looked in the mirror and thought I looked pretty good.

Miss Pidgeon had bedecked herself in a stunning, very tight sequined dress and put on high-heeled shoes, and I lost my self-conscious vanity for a moment while I understood myself to be quite the luckiest man alive.

Down we went, we two fashion plates.

We went down into the lobby, and there were a load of paparazzi, and they took our picture.

One of the festival functionaries took us out the back door, where it was still pissing down rain, and escorted us into one of the festival cars.

We made our way down the main drag at a footslogging pace. There were gendarmes with their cinematogenic kepis at the intersections, and there were two solid walls of folks from the hotel down to the Festival Hall, all along the blocked-off street. When we came abreast of the festival, the line of traffic halted completely. We stopped for several minutes at a time, and then inched forward a car length.

Ahead of us, at some unknown distance, cars were stopping to disgorge their precious cargo at the foot of the ceremonial red carpet of the Festival Hall.

We were in an overarching tunnel of people. They pressed up against the car, and the two sides seemed to reach over the top of the car and meet in the middle. People were popping flashbulbs and pounding on the car, and put their faces up against the windows.

They asked one another who it was in the car and, I must say, displayed rather good humor when they realized they did not recognize us.

We inched forward. The driver asked us to check to see if the rear doors were locked. This frightened me a bit.

I'd been to the Oscars twice, and thought them rather smashingly pagan, but this festival could give them Cards and Spades; the onlookers at the Oscars were just bored and vicious Americans like me, but *these* folks were interested in 'film.'

We arrived at our destination – the end of the red carpet. The doors were opened and we stood out under an insufficient canopy while it rained like a cow pissing on a flat rock, as they have it in Vermont.

We were held back from our ceremonial entrance as various Continental celebrities went forward to the delight of the crowd. Then it came to be our turn. Up we went. Out from under the canopy and into the rain for fair. People took our pictures. I think the staircase was lined by double rows of someone or other.

I think that, after the fact, I was told there were trumpeters in Napoleonic livery, but I don't remember it.

I remember the gendarmes, who were all very young and very fit and stood quite still, with their hands clasped behind their back in parade rest, and they were very impressive. And I remember the troop of plainclothes bodyguards, who had changed their madras jackets to white-and-gray seersucker, and who looked very dap.

We went up the wide staircase of the Festival Hall (one of my film's producers likened the hall to the library of some midwestern university with a little too much money); up, I say, we went, and into the foyer and through that foyer into the vast auditorium. We were ushered to our seats.

On the stage, Geraldine Chaplin was speaking to the compere, a very relaxed and distinguished heavyset man in his sixties.

They called Roman Polanski up from the audience and introduced him as the chief judge of the festival this year, and he called the subordinate judges up, and they joined him on the stage.

I didn't know who many of them were, and my attention wandered. One of my film's producers introduced me to several of the Japanese backers of the movie, and we bowed and shook hands. Robert Mitchum was called out onstage, and he came flanked by two of his sons, and, in his quality of Prestigious Representative of World Cinema, he declared the festival open.

The compere asked for our, the audience's, forbearance, as the television equipment that had been obtruding on the stage was removed.

We, in the audience, chatted among ourselves for a while. Then the lights dimmed and the audience hushed.

We were shown a trailer for Polanski's *The Fearless Vampire Killers*, which was a nice historical touch; and then we were shown a trailer for *Citizen Kane*, which trailer starts and finishes with Orson Welles's trademark 'Mercury Theatre of the Air' logo:

Limbo. A man's voice calls for a microphone. The mike swings in on a boom. A man's hand adjusts it, then retires from the shot. The voice (Welles) speaks, introducing the project we are about to see.

This trademark appears at the end of the Mercury films, too. Welles reiterates various facts, the casting of the film and other information, and the mike swings away and into limbo.

I've always thought that this trademark is one of the most classy things in the world. It fills me with both delight and envy each time I see it. I find myself not only impressed, but *regressed*, and the ultimate laurel of my youth escapes my open lips: 'Cool.'

Rest in peace, Mr. Welles, and I wish I had been privileged to know you.

And so we quieted down, and they showed my film.

My film was preceded by the 'computer art' video logo of the festival. We see various free-floating steps, as if they are a staircase without the risers. We see that the steps are under water. The 'camera' rises up the steps, and the steps emerge from the water and into the air. The steps keep rising through the air, and into the dark starry firmament. The top step tilts to the camera, and reveals, embossed, the palm-leaf colophon of the festival. This golden palm leaf takes leave of the step, which sinks away. It is then joined by various typography that tells us what we are looking at, and then it is over. I hate computers. I think they are the tool of the devil. In any case, they then showed my movie.

It was the first time I'd seen the film with a real audience.

I saw it for six months on the screen of a Steenbeck editing machine – this screen is about the size of a paperback book. During the editing process, I saw it a couple of times in a screening room with an audience of thirty or so handpicked folks.

Now here we are. The screen is 180 feet across, and there are twenty-five hundred folks like myself – jaded, blasé, anxious, and demanding – looking at my film.

Well, it did real good. Various people said various things about it afterward, but twenty-five hundred people paid attention for one hour and forty-two, and the film reflects my intentions as completely as I knew how to express them at that time, and it holds their attention, which indicates to me that, at least on a technical level, I did my job adequately well, and, beyond that, everything is with the gods.

Now, this whole issue of popular reception is a curious thing. I've been staging my work, plays and films, for twenty-some years. During that time I have striven to come to terms with the phenomena of popular and critical reception.

Popular reception is the easier to become comfortable with. I started out writing plays for my own theater company, and my relation to the audience was fairly clear – if one did one's job well, they paid attention, if not, then not. If it was funny, they laughed, if it was sad, they cried; if it was *not* funny, they did *not* laugh, and a person who persisted in the asseveration that his work was funny in opposition to the view of the audience might have a career in philosophy, but was not long for show business.

When the audience got *out* of the theater, another set of circumstances demanded recognition and understanding: the audience that perhaps *did* laugh and cry, might say, of the piece as a whole: 'I didn't get it,' or 'I didn't like it.'

In theatrical environment, the audience signals this disaffection by staying away; if their presence at the play is paying your rent, you then starve.

So it is necessary to be very conscious of the audience, and work, I think, to help them understand your intention.

It is also necessary to learn to still the rancor that their lack of approval might create, and learn to evaluate this rancor and to respond to their opinion in one of two ways. One may respond to their disapproval either by saying (a) I see that I have not done my job sufficiently well – let me reexamine my work, and see if I could make it clearer; or (b) I, on reflection, think that my work is as clear as I can possibly make it, and I will resist the temptation to mutilate my work to please the audience.

If the work is paying the rent, one is, I think, fairly immune to the seductiveness of alternative (b), which goes under the name of Arrogance.

Dealing with critical reception is a bit more difficult – I think that critics are generally a bunch of unfortunates, and should be ashamed of themselves. Now, does this mean that I am philosophically immune to the desire for their praise? You may have already guessed the answer, which is no.

I have tried, over the years, to wean myself from this desire. I have repeated, fervently and oft, the wise words of Epictetus, who said: 'Do you seek the good opinion of these people? Are they not the same people who, you told me yesterday, are frauds and imbeciles? Do you then seek the good opinion of frauds and imbeciles?'

Well, I guess I do. I'm trying not to.

For a few years I didn't read reviews.

Most of us in the hurly-burly world of the stage tell one another that we don't read reviews, and we all pretend to believe one another. But, for whatever it's worth, for a couple of years I didn't read reviews, and was a much better man for it.

Now the reductio ad absurdum of the artist-critic *combat* is the juried competition.

It contains the worst elements of critical autocracy and committee compromise.

What *can* it mean that one film or actor or play is better than all the rest, and that we may rest assured of its distinction because of the imprimatur of a 'group of folks'? What can that mean? Well, it doesn't mean *anything*. Unless, of course, you win.

And that's why I had fallen off the ladder and brought my film to Cannes, and that's why I was sitting there, whore that I am, watching my movie with twenty-five hundred people dressed in what used to be called 'formal wear.'

The film ended, and they hit the general area of my seat with lights, and the audience applauded. (One reviewer, whose work I am aware of through having read it, said that the audience gave the film a standing ovation. My memory runs to the contrary, but . . .)

I stood up and wondered whether to ask Miss Pidgeon to take a bow with me. I sat back down, the audience applauded some more, and I stood up again, all the time wondering if I should ask her to stand with me. I was of two minds about it. I sat down again. They turned the lights off. I should have asked her to stand with me. My party was ushered out of the main hall and into the foyer. There we were placed in a human square formed by gendarmes. These gendarmes, about fifteen on a side, stood with their backs to us and kept us separated from a group, the audience, who had no interest in us whatsoever.

The plainclothes bodyguards, who had changed their jackets again, and now sported very nice reddish plaid affairs, escorted us out some side way of the festival and down to the harborside, where a huge tent had been erected.

We walked under various marquees, whipped by rain. The marquees were near to blowing away, and it was cold.

We went down into the tent, where there appeared to be seating for seven or eight hundred.

We were shown our table, and sat down. I had vowed, for reasons of general health, not to drink anything during the trip, but conceived an existential desire to nullify that vow, and I asked anyone who would listen if they knew where I could get a stiff double shot of something. Everyone said I was out of luck, but waiters started bringing wine to the table, and I started drinking it.

Jack Lang, the cultural minister of France, was seated down the table. My producer had given me a commemorative trinket from our movie, to present to him, but I never got around to it. Robert Mitchum was also at the table, and I went over and said how pleased I was to meet him, and he nodded.

I was seated between Miss Pidgeon and my good friend and agent, Howard.

Down at our end of the table were also a French movie star and his friend, who was a director of opera. This movie star was very taken with the film, and talked about it at length, and made me feel very good.

We sat around talking and drinking wine. The waiters brought the food, which was very French, and magnificent, and piping hot, which last was, I thought, quite a feat for a meal for eight hundred people in a tent in the rain.

Men I took to be producers began roaming from table to table and standing in the narrow and impossibly crowded aisles. Many of these men smoked cigars.

An African singer was introduced, and went up on the stage and played some very beautiful music on a native stringed instrument, and sang in accompaniment.

The atmosphere either became or appeared very smoky, and I felt a certain, dare I say, orgiastic undertone growing in the tent. We Levitical priests had performed our ceremony and retired into the tabernacle, which for the unanointed to approach was death, and we had taken our girdles off.

What strange, what wild and unforeseeable revelry would ensue as the evening continued its inevitable progress toward the dawn? With which of the young starlets would the producers retire?

What magnificent diversion, fresh from the opium dens of Indo-Chine would the sophisticates elect and practice?

Would they gash one another's flesh and drink one another's blood?

Would they play liar's poker for the souls of the yet unborn? Would they hug and kiss . . . ?

Well, I can't tell you, 'cause I'm not much of a party-goer, and I and Miss Pidgeon went home.

We said good-bye to the movie star and the opera director, who were a lovely pair of people, and quite a welcome bit of friendship and show-business hospitality, and we went out into the rain, which I have described before, and the wind, which I shall limn as an 'enraged monster, whipping now this way and now that.'

The bodyguards – I know you will not believe me – had changed their jackets once again and now sported white piqué affairs, and they helped us down the line of now-deserted marquees, and into a car, which took us back to the hotel.

Miss Pidgeon and I got into our bathrobes, and sat around dissecting the evening's events.

The phone rang. It was our friend Brigitte. She was down in the lobby, and had been missing us at each stage of the evening's festivities. We invited her up. She said that she was in the company of several members of our film's production-distribution team. We invited them up, too. Up they came.

There was a rather splendid bottle of champagne in the room, sent by an agent friend, with a well-wishing note that concluded: 'Today Cannes, Tomorrow the World, then the Creative Artists Agency.'

Brigitte and the crew previously described sat on the floor, and the men loosened their bow ties and took off their jackets and smoked cigars. We drank the champagne, and emptied the minibar, and Brigitte took pictures of Miss Pidgeon and myself sitting on our bed in our bathrobes.

The next morning, Friday, Miss Pidgeon and I awoke. The room smelled of cigar smoke.

We decided to enshrine the events of the last wee hours in our collective memory as 'the night of the penguins.' We went down for coffee.

That Friday noon found us at the Hôtel du Cap, in the space that, the producer told me, had been Nazi headquarters for southern France.

We had our lunch and talked in an open and friendly fashion with many journalists, most of whom would probably, thinking of their responsibility to their readership, turn around and cut us to shreds; but it was a lovely lunch.

That afternoon was spent chatting with various groups of international press, and I don't remember what we did that evening.

The next day was warm and clear, a beautiful day to sit out on the beach, looking at the harbor. But our plans were otherwise.

Brigitte was taking Miss Pidgeon's picture, and I had a couple of hours to kill. I walked down the Croisette, by the Festival Hall, which area was now, of course, deserted.

Down by the city hall I found a flea market, and I was in heaven for a half hour or so.

I bought a pot-metal barrette depicting a rooster, to bring back for my assistant, Harriet.

I bought a beautiful ceramic water jug in the shape of a crow, and bearing the legend HÔTEL DU CORBEAU.

I walked back to the hotel and bought commemorative T-shirts and trinkets for children and friends.

The concessionaire was a very old and very polite man. He took a great deal of time with me, opening each plastic-wrapped T-shirt to display the difference between the French idea of medium and their idea of large. He offered me several mints, and I took them. At the conclusion of the transaction a middle-aged woman, to whom this man deferred, entered the shop with her French poodle and walked behind the counter. This woman paid scant attention to the old man, who reiterated the details of our transaction. He showed the woman my bill, which he was in the process of preparing.

She acknowledged him hardly at all, and told me the total price, and I paid her and took my souvenirs. On my way out of the store, the man gave me another small packet of mints, and I thanked him.

Miss Pidgeon and I drove back to the airport in Nice.

The Buttons on the Board

First, I should like to speak of the Topperweins.

Ad and his wife, Plinky Topperwein, were trick-shot artists. They played vaudeville, and toured also for the Winchester Repeating Arms Company, whose products they used and promoted.

I was once at an auction in New York to benefit the arms-and-armor collection of the Metropolitan Museum of Art. Among the many beautiful and belligerophiliant items put up for sale there was the trunk of the Topperweins.

It contained many of their playbills and posters; it contained several of their hats and other articles of clothing; it contained two model-63 Winchester .22 pump rifles, one of which was guaranteed to be one of the battery with which Ad shot forty-three thousand two-inch wooden cubes out of the air. It contained, as if all this were insufficient, several of the copper 'rifle portraits' that Plinky and Ad shot as part of their various demonstrations.

These portraits were two-by-three-foot thin copper sheets that, in the demonstration, were put at a distance from the shooter, and on which he or she inscribed, by means of the .22 Long Rifle cartridge, a portrait of (to choose from their repertoire) George Washington, an Indian chief, a turkey, Abraham Lincoln, and so on.

I had heard much of these copper sheets, but, prior to the auction, the only one I had ever seen was in the shop of a celebrated gunsmith in Louisiana, which portrait was definitely not for sale.

So I sat amazed as, one after another, beautiful Edwardian artifacts came out of the trunk; mementos of shooting, and show business, and, in short, the dream material of 'another time'; and, for some reason I couldn't tell you, I did not bid on the trunk.

I think I was one of the only people in the audience who knew of the Topperweins (my knowledge coming more from the show business than from the shooting side of my experience), so the bidding did not go very high. The trunk went cheap, and somebody else bought it.

What would it have meant, I ask myself – as perhaps many of

you who are collectors of this and that do; what would it have meant to have possessed that trunk, that trinket, that connection to another time, or that suggestion to ourselves or others of another aspect of ourselves; what would it mean, and why is the longing for the unobtainable worse than the transmutation of the unobtainable into the everyday? (For, my reluctance to bid on the trunk was, finally, a refusal to contribute to the transmutation.)

In any case, some years later I saw, in a tray at an antiques show, a pin-back button, one inch across, promoting the Topperweins, and I bought it. The button bears a photograph of the two. She is a bluff and bulky-looking individual in a white shirt and black tie. She has a large mouth and dark hair. He is standing next to her in a dark suit. He has a thick mustache, and looks to be the passive one of the pair. Both wear large-brimmed hats, his blocked in the 'trooper' fashion.

The button reads THE WONDERFUL TOPPERWEINS. WHO ALWAYS SHOOT WINCHESTER GUNS AND CARTRIDGES.

Inside the button's back is the maker's mark: WHITEHEAD AND HOAG COMPANY (BUTTONS, BADGES, NOVELTIES, AND SIGNS), NEWARK, NEW JERSEY.

Whitehead and Hoag invented and patented the pin-back button in the 1890s. This mode of advertisement caught on immediately, and was soon used to promote any and everything thought remotely promotable. Politicians, comic strips, newspaper give-aways, religion, temperance, fraternal associations, and every article of merchandise and every service of that period can be found advertised on pin-back buttons.

Over the years I have collected, displayed, traded, and hoarded buttons. I have worn them and given them away as jewelry; I have even commissioned some.

Since I became attracted to the form, I have always stuck them in the wall or molding or bulletin board near any writing desk that I was using over any extended period.

Now, the above sentence displays a strained circumlocution for and reveals an inability to employ the term *office*. It is, perhaps, that inability or refusal to face the indignity of self-knowledge which has led me, over the years, to adorn my workplace with what, to me, are the artifacts of romance.

I do not want to be at the desk. I want to be at a place and in a time alluded to by these mementos. And, further than a *creed*, my *assertion*, while in my office at my desk, is 'anywhere but here.'

The buttons are not mere reminders, they are survivors, the archeological artifacts of the dream kingdom where, if and when I am doing my job effectively, I spend what I suppose must be called my working hours.

Stuck in the corkboard, directly in front of me as I write, is a six-point metal star that looks to be nickel over iron or steel. It is embossed APACHE POLICE, SAN CARLOS, ARIZ., and has a small brass head of an American Indian in feather headdress brazed into its center. The badge seems to have seen a lot of wear and use. Directly to the right is a small cloisonné pin in blue, with a large white cross in the center. Sailing out of the cross is a black-and-red ocean liner, and below, in gold, is written AMERICAN RELIEF SHIP FOR SPAIN. To the right again is a half-inch-diameter celluloid button with a girl's face on it.

The button's back informs us that it was, again, made by the Whitehead and Hoag Company, and that they, in this case, are advertising Perfection cigarettes. This girl's picture, it seems, was one of a series depicting types of feminine beauty that one could obtain and examine at leisure through the purchase of the Perfection brand.

The girl on the button is dark honey-blond, with correspondingly blue eyes, rosy cheeks, a bee-stung mouth, and a mole on the left side of her lip. She is placid and rather expressionless, I think; and her face is full and somewhat heavy, and childlike, and very much in line with the fin-de-siècle American notion of beauty. Perfect, heavy, regular, and docile – the picture would not, today, be recognizable as an attempt to depict feminine allurements.

And we would find the picture on the adjacent button odd by contemporary standards. It shows a happy Boy Scout in his campaign hat and red neckerchief. His white face beams boldly out from the blue background, smiling a wide, delighted, and unreserved smile. A linen ribbon is affixed to the button's back and reads CAMPOREE – 1935.

And, next to him is a rare employee's badge from the 1933 World's Fair, the Chicago Century of Progress Exposition, which may give a clue to the boy's expression.

That World's Fair was the most recent celebration of the final subjugation of the material world. It was the apotheosis of the notion of technology as grace. The innocent, happy, and overall *hopeful* Boy Scout was blessed to live on the very verge of that time for which his forefathers had striven: the future.

The deliberate, laudable, and serious rectitude of the Victorian Age had vanished in the unaccountable appearance of the First World War and the madness of the twenties, but society was once again on track and all of a mind; and the noble though outmoded notion of duty had been supplanted by the more perfect ideal of progress.

For what was the girl going to do, but court and marry, and give birth to and raise children? And why should she not be placid – for, if introspection and anxiety and anger were a part (as, of course they were) of her life, they were not a part of her age's ideal of beauty, as they are in our age.

To the left of the Apache police star is a metal-plant identification badge. It is stamped EBALOY. ROCKFORD, IL. FOUNDARIES INC. And numbered 708. It is a sandwich: two layers of metal, between which the employee's photo was to have been put, so as to be visible through a window in the badge's front. The photo it carries now is not of the original employee; it is a snapshot cut out of a proof sheet of 35-mm black-and-white film.

Even on the proof sheet, the photographic quality is extraordinarily good. We see a man and woman with their arms around each other, smiling at the camera. They both have on short leather jackets and sunglasses and baseball caps. They are standing on what seems to be a wharf or a pier. Behind them we see the water of a harbor, and a small fishing boat tied up to a pier opposite.

We can see that the woman is very beautiful. She has long dark hair, a lovely smile. She is very slender and graceful.

Sometime, eventually, this button will be destroyed. Sometime, it is likely, before it vanishes, someone will look at it and wonder who the man and woman could have been; and perhaps that person will make up stories about them. For, there they are, very little different from the Topperweins, woman on the left, man on the right, a head taller; two couples smiling at the camera, and what can they have been thinking that day, and who were they?

*

A foot or so off to the right on the bulletin board is Dwight
Eisenhower's picture on a cheap piece of tin. It says I LIKE IKE, and
has the five stars of his army rank below the photograph.

And there's the union button I picked out of the gutter – a
crimson rectangle that reads, STANDING WITH THE UNION. I
SUPPORT THE HARVARD UNION OF CLERICAL AND TECHNICAL
WORKERS. And I remember finding it. It was a rainy day in Cambridge, Massachusetts. And there had been quite a bit of agitation
and, I think, bad feeling – on both sides of an issue that had to do, I
believe, with the right of Harvard employees to organize, or to
strike, or to do something that they, as a group, desired and another
group opposed.

In any case, when I saw it I thought the STANDING WITH THE
UNION button rather unusual, as it was a rectangle, standing the
long-way up. I thought it rather clunky and unbeautiful. But I
looked down at it, in the rain, in the gutter, and I thought that I
would add it to my collection. But no, I thought, you didn't
appreciate the button when you saw it displayed legitimately on the
clothing of the antagonists, how could you be so greedy as to covet
it now, in the gutter? I castigated myself with the accusation of
having a taste for trash, rather than a clean and legitimate nostalgia. So I walked on down the street for a while, and then I turned
around and came back and picked up the button.

For it had not been sufficiently removed from me to endow it with
any of the totemic power of a romantic article, and to enshrine it
myself, without the intervening purification of a mercantile transaction, felt like a Gnostic leap of faith, and it made me uncomfortable.

But, nonetheless, I took it back, and stuck it in the bulletin board
in my office, off to one side. And as the months and then the year or
so passed since its acquisition – as I removed buttons from the
board to wear them, or to give them away, or just to change the
design, I moved the Harvard button into a more and more prominent position; and comforted myself with the twin notions that it
was being cleansed by time, and that someday, with my dissolution,
it would be completely purified.

WRITING IN RESTAURANTS

Acknowledgements

I would like to acknowledge several people who encouraged me to write prose, helped teach me to write better, and appreciated my work sufficiently to publish it or to help me get it published: Mr. Andy Potok; Richard Christiansen of the *Chicago Tribune*; Otis Guernsey of the *Dramatists Guild Quarterly*; Wayne Lawson of *Vanity Fair*; Dawn Seferian of Viking Penguin; and my agent, Andrew Wylie.

Preface

Some Russian filmmaker, Eisenstein, or Pudovkin, or Evreinov, wrote that the preeminence of the Soviet directors in the late 1920s was due to this: at the beginning of their careers they had no film. The World War and the Revolution stopped imports of film stock, so all the young filmmakers could do was sit about and theorize for five years, which is what they did.

I spent my twentieth year at the Neighborhood Playhouse School of the Theatre in New York. At the Playhouse we were exposed to, drilled in, and inculcated with the idea of a *unified aesthetic of theater*; that is, a theater whose every aspect (design, performance, lighting, rehearsal procedures, dramaturgy) was subordinated to the Idea of the Play. We were taught that the purpose of the play was to bring to the stage, through the medium of the actors, the life of the human soul.

The awesome technical and spiritual problems posed by a dedication to those ideas fascinated me. How, I wondered, can an actor overcome his self-consciousness while performing in front of people he desperately wants to please; how can the director understand a complex play and communicate his understanding to the actors in simple, physically actable directions; how can the playwright devote himself to the through-action of the play without having his dialogue become tendentious?

These essentially Eastern problems fascinated me no end, and I thought about them constantly. I recognized my state, years later, reading Abraham Cahan's *The Imported Bridegroom*. Reading this book I discovered in myself the racial type of the lapsed Talmudist. In theatrical musings I had, for the first time in my life, discovered a task which I adored, and to which dedication was the exact opposite of drudgery.

In this state of happy student I was a brother to the Soviet filmmakers who had the empty cameras – I was being trained as an actor, but it was a task for which I lacked both disposition and (more important) the discipline to which, perhaps, talent might have enticed me.

What was I to do, then, with my love of theory and lack of outlet? I took the usual path: I became a teacher. At the tender age of twenty-two I became a vehement, possessed teacher of acting.

As a practical laboratory for my Mandarin aesthetic interests, I began directing my students in plays, then I began writing plays for them to do, and that is how I came the long way around the barn to playwriting.

The following pieces reflect, I think, a continuing concern, and, more important, a never-flagging fascination with the two ideas I discovered as a student: (1) every aspect of the production should reflect the idea of the play; (2) the purpose of the play is to bring to the stage the life of the soul.

It is possible that I have – both in the pieces regarding the Theater, and in those treating things which are assuredly none of my business – lapsed at times into dogmatism – I hope it's not the case, and don't think it is, but you may. My makeup today is the same as it was eighteen years ago, essentially that of an unsure student who has finally discovered an idea in which he can believe, and who feels unless he clutches and dedicates himself to that idea, he will be lost.

D.M.
December 18, 1985

I
WRITING IN RESTAURANTS

Capture-the-flag, Monotheism, and the
Techniques of Arbitration

In Chicago's traffic court there is a room set aside for silver-suited lawyers. They sit there all day long, smoking and discussing who got caught, and defendants who wish to cop a plea go to the lawyers' room to shop for an attorney.

There the lawyers sit and, casually, anxiously, they watch the door their clients will come through. They look just like kids waiting for the captain to choose them for his team of Kick-the-Can.

We all were lawyers in the schoolyard. We were concerned with property and honor, and correct application of the magical power of words.

In the narration or recapitulation of serious matters our peers were never said to have 'said' things, but to have 'gone' things; we ten- and twelve-year-olds thereby recognizing a *statement* as an *action*. (He goes, 'Get over to your side of the line, or you're out,' and I go, 'I am on my side of the line – it runs from the bench to the water fountain.')

Our schoolyard code of honor recognized words as magical and powerful unto themselves, and it was every bit as pompous and self-satisfied in the recognition of its magic as is the copyright code or a liquidated damages clause. It was the language of games, the language of an endeavor which is, in its essence, make-believe – the language of American Business:

ME: I'm goin' down the Shoreland for a phos, I don' wan' Gussie comin' with.
TOM: Why not?
ME: We're playin' ball the *schoolyard* . . . ?
TOM: Football, baseball?
ME: *Baseball.*
TOM: Yeah . . .

ME: We lost the ball.

TOM: Whose ball?

ME: (*Pause*) *Gussie's*.

TOM: Yeah.

ME: So he goes he ain't going home until we're paying him we lost the ball, he's gonna call my ma.

TOM: Where did you lose it?

ME: On the roof. So I go, 'Look, you never called it, Gussie.'

TOM: He din *call* it?

ME: *No!* What's what I'm *tellin*' you. He goes 'I called it.' I go, 'No, you didn't, Gussie. No. You never called it, no. If you said 'chips' we woulda heard it, and you never called it. No.' I ast the other guys, his own team, huh? Maurice goes, 'I don't think you called it, Gus.' I go, 'Look here, your own man, Gussie, huh?' He says that didn' mean a thing. His own man . . .

TOM: Yeah.

ME: I tell him, 'I ain't trine a hock the ball off you, Gus; you called '*chips*,' I'd pay for it right now. It's not the money . . . '

TOM: . . . no . . .

ME: '. . . and you know times that *I* have loss my ball, and you ass Mike or anybody.' Huh?

TOM: Yeah.

ME: 'Or we're up in Jackson Park I got my headlight broke. I didn't say a word acause I din' say 'chips.' (*Pause*) And I have to say you never said it, too.'

TOM: So what he say?

ME: He goes I'm trine a cheat him out his ball. I tell him I will go up there and get it Monday. I would *like* to pay him back . . .

TOM: Uh-huh . . .

ME: I'll go up there and *get* it . . .

TOM: Yeah . . .

ME: But when he didn't *call* it, I can't pay him back. He knows this isn't fair.

TOM: Yeah.

ME: And I *tole* him that this isn't fair. He *called* it, we would all of played a little carefuller.

This is, no doubt, a somewhat romanticized, but, I feel, essentially accurate rendition of one of our schoolyard negotiations circa 1959;

and it differs only in the minutest particulars, the diction, and not at all in spirit, from most adult formal and informal contract negotiations.

Thorstein Veblen said that the more that jargon and technical language is involved in an endeavor, the more we may assume that the endeavor is essentially make-believe.

As in Law, Commerce, Warfare. There we were in Vietnam; there we were in Jackson Park.

'Olley Olley Ocean Free' was our South Side Chicago version of the cry which ends a game of tag. I think the phrase frightened us as children.

We knew that an afternoon of kick-the-can or capture-the-flag could only be positively terminated by the adjuration 'Olleyolleyoceanfree,' but none of us had one idea what the words *themselves* meant. We only knew they had magical power to cast off the restrictions of the game (to loose us from our vows) and let us go to dinner. (The 'free' was clearly pertinent, and the 'olley' could, by a stretch, be accepted as a rhythmic aid; but what, in the name of God, did the 'ocean' mean?)

The Schoolboy Universe was not corrupted by the written word, and was ruled by the powers of sounds: Cheater's Proof, Sucker's Walk, Rubber Balls, and Liquor. Our language had weight and meaning to the extent to which it was rhythmic and pleasant, and its power came from a juxtaposition of sounds in a world in which we were overtly pantheists.

'American Eagle' was the binding incantation in matters of barter. It was uttered at the completion of a trade by the party who felt that he had got the better of the deal, and it meant that the agreement could not be reneged upon.

The ultimate oath in matters of honor not covered by the rules of sport or commerce was 'My Jewish Word of Honor.' For example:

MAURICE: Tommy Lentz said that your sister was a whore.
ME: You swear?
MAURICE: Yeah.
ME: Swear to God?
MAURICE: Yeah.
ME: Jewish Word of Honor?
MAURICE: Yeah. (*Pause*)

ME: Say it.
MAURICE: I just *said* I said it.
ME: Say it.
MAURICE: I don't want to say 'Your sister is a whore.'
ME: Just say he said it.
MAURICE: Tommy Lentz, My Jewish Word of Honor, said your
sister was a whore.

Which meant that it was so. Until that day when one discovered
it was possible to swear falsely, and that there was, finally, *no*
magic force of words capable of assuring the truth in oneself or in
others, and so became adult and very serious and monotheistic in
one hard moment.

The other morning a man came into the McBurney YMCA to
run. He was told that the running track was closed until noon. He
was inspired with rage that he had made a long trip to the Y and
now could not run, and he was berating one of the office personnel
for not putting up a sign yesterday which would have informed him
that he could not run that day till noon. He wanted the clerk to say
a word or phrase of explanation or apology which would have the
power to have put a sign up the day before.

In his anger he had reverted to a universe where words were
clearly magic, in which all things were possessed of spirit, and
where anything was possible.

A National Dream-Life

We respond to a drama to that extent to which it corresponds to
our dream life.

The life of the play is the life of the unconscious, the protagonist
represents ourselves, and the main action of the play constitutes the
subject of the dream or myth. It is not the theme of the play to
which we respond, but the *action* – the through-action of the
protagonist, and the attendant support of the secondary characters,
this support lent through their congruent actions.

The play is a quest for a solution.

As in our dreams, the law of psychic economy operates. In dreams we do not seek answers which our conscious (rational) mind is capable of supplying, we seek answers to those questions which the conscious mind is incompetent to deal with. So with the drama, if the question posed is one which can be answered rationally, e.g.: how does one fix a car, should white people be nice to black people, are the physically handicapped entitled to our respect, our enjoyment of the drama is incomplete – we feel diverted but not fulfilled. Only if the question posed is one whose complexity and depth renders it unsusceptible to rational examination does the dramatic treatment seem to us appropriate, and the dramatic solution become enlightening.

Ecclesiastes 9:12. 'For man also knoweth not his time: as the fishes that are taken in an evil net, and as the birds that are caught in a snare; so are the sons of man snared in an evil time when it falleth suddenly upon them.' The solution – which is to say solution which will enable us to function happily in the midst of rational uncertainty to a personal and seemingly unresolvable psychological problem – is the dream; the solution to a seemingly unresolvable social (ethic) problem is the drama (poem). For the sine qua non of both the dream and the drama is the suspension of rational restrictions in aid of happiness.

The American theater, acting as a collective mentality, operates in much the same way as the unconscious of the individual in the choice of topics worthy of treatment, and in the choice of treatment *of* those topics. Election by the playwright of theme, action, and so on, the extent to which the plays growing out of those elections are deemed acceptable by producers, and the choice of actors and designers are made artistically (which is to say *unconsciously*) and are based, however they may be rationalized ex post facto, on considerations which approximate those which determine the individual's choice of dream material: 'Does examination of this idea, of this action, seem to offer a solution to an unconscious confusion of mine at the present time?*

---

*The objection that this assertion does not take into consideration purely venal motives on the part of the producers, authors, and so on can be answered by the proposition that in an election which is apparently *completely* economic, the

Surely individual instances of choices may not adhere to, or may even serve to mitigate against, this process, but taking the progress of the play from its inception in the unconscious of the playwright to its presentation before the public as a whole, and as a *community endeavor*, the process of collective choice is the predominant and overriding force. Through it, the artistic community (subconsciously) elects and forms our national dreams.

To the greatest extent we, in an evil time, which is to say a time in which we do not wish to examine ourselves and our unhappiness; we, in the body of the artistic community, elect dream material (plays) which cater to a very low level of fantasy. We cast ourselves (for in the writing and the production and the patronage of plays we cannot but identify with the protagonist) in dreams of wish fulfillment. These dreams – even and, perhaps, especially those which seem the most conservative and bourgeois – seem to offer solutions to our concerns based on the idea that the concerns *themselves* do not exist, that they are only temporary aberrations of an essentially benign universe, or (and here is, perhaps, the hidden delusional postulate in our election of the happy-ending comedy-drama) of a universe which is positively *responsive* at that point at which our individual worthinesses (or inabilities, as it amounts to the same thing) are brought to its attentions. We leave the theater after such plays as smug as after a satisfying daydream. Our prejudices have been assuaged, and we have been reassured that nothing is wrong, but we are, finally, no happier.

In a less evil time we are more capable as an artistic community of creating and ratifying plays (in electing for the subject of our dreams) questions concerning deeper uncertainties. We all dream each night, but at some times we are reluctant to remember our dreams; just so we, as a collective artistic unity, create poetic (theatrical) dreams, but at some times we are reluctant to remember (stage, accept, support . . .) them. Many times the true nature of our

---

producer does not ask the question 'Will this play offer a solution?' of *himself* but posits an imaginary individual called the Middle-Class Theatergoer and asks, if only subconsciously, 'Will this play offer a solution to or "please" such a person?' But the Middle-Class Theatergoer exists only in the producer's mind, and the concerns and desires of this chimera come from nowhere but the producer's own subconscious.

dreams is hidden from us: and just so in the Theater, the dramas elected and staged may represent an attempt at diversion or denial of our dream life. These instances may correspond, in terms of psychic economy, to a national period of inner-directedness and a hypochondriacal concern in the theater with the impedimenta of our lives (realism); or a complete and angry denial of the existence of all nonsuperficial concerns ('experimental theater').

A dramatic experience concerned with the mundane may inform but it cannot release; and one concerned essentially with the *aesthetic politics* of its creators may divert or anger, but it cannot enlighten.

As we move into a time when we as a nation once again can sense the possibility of a rational self-esteem, the theater both heralds and promotes the possibility of the greatest benefit of the reasoned self-view, an individual contentment born of balance. This possibility, at the moment, seems to exist in our national mentality and in our national theater. Freud said, 'The only way to forget is to remember,' and a subscription to this belief – this wish to cleanse and renew – can be seen in the current renewed interest in and reawakening of the poetic drama; and this reawakening is our national wish to remember our dreams.

Radio Drama

Sunday nights we would go visiting. Coming home we'd play the car radio. It was dark and we'd be rolling through the prairies outside of Chicago. CBS 'Suspense' would be on the air, or 'Yours Truly, Johnny Dollar – the Man with the Million-Dollar Expense Account.' And the trip home always ended too soon; we'd stay in the car until my dad kicked us out – we wanted to hear how the story ended; we wanted the trip to be endless – rolling through the prairies and listening to the intimate voices.

But we went into the house.

It never occurred to us to turn on the radio when we got in. We were the very first television generation. My dad was proud of the television, and we grew up considering the radio déclassé – it was used for information or background but not for entertainment.

We grew up with the slogans, overheard from our parents and their friends, enigmatic catchwords of their youth: 'Boston Blackie, enemy to those who *make* him an enemy, friend to those who *have* no friends.' 'Who knows what evil lurks in the hearts of men? The *Shadow* do ...' (That wonderful apocryphal transposition.) '*Gang*busters ...!' 'Can a young girl from Ohio find happiness ...' Et cetera.

I had written a piece called 'The Water Engine.' It was set in 1933 Chicago, during the Century of Progress Exposition, and concerned a young man who invented an engine which ran solely on water.

I wrote it as a short story, and it was rejected by many publications. I wrote it as a movie treatment and it was rejected by various studios. I threw it in the wastebasket and, later that day, someone introduced me to Howard Gelman, who was the producer of Earplay, an outfit which commissions, produces, and distributes radio drama to the National Public Radio network.

Howard knew my playwriting from Chicago. He asked me if I wanted to write for the radio, and I said yes, went home, and got 'The Water Engine' out of the wastebasket.

Earplay has since produced other plays of mine: *Reunion, A Sermon*, and *Prairie Du Chien*. And writing for radio I learned a lot about playwriting.

Bruno Bettelheim, in *The Uses of Enchantment*, writes that the fairy tale (and, similarly, the Drama) has the capacity to calm, to incite, to assuage, finally, to *affect*, because we listen to it nonjudgmentally – we identify *sub*consciously (noncritically) with the protagonist.

We are allowed to do this, he tells us, because the protagonist and, indeed, the situations are uncharacterized aside from their most essential elements.

When we are told, for example, that a Handsome Prince went into a wood, we realize that *we* are that Handsome Prince. As soon as the prince is characterized, 'A Handsome Blond Prince with a twinkle in his eye, and just the hint of a mustache on his upper lip ...' and if we lack that color hair, twinkle, and so on, we say, 'What an interesting prince. Of course, he is unlike anyone *I* know ...' and we begin to listen to the story as a *critic* rather than as a *participant*.

The essential task of the drama (as of the fairy tale) is to offer a solution to a problem which is nonsusceptible to reason. To be effective, the drama must induce us to suspend our rational judgment, and to follow the *internal* logic of the piece, so that our *pleasure* (our 'cure') is the release at the end of the story. We enjoy the happiness of being a participant in the process of *solution*, rather than the intellectual achievement of having observed the process of construction.

And the best model for this drama is The Story around the Campfire.

We hear '... a windswept moor' and immediately supply the perfect imaginary moor. And the moor we supply is not perfect 'in general,' but perfect according to our subconscious understanding of the significance of the moor *to the story*.

This is why radio is a great training ground for dramatists. More than any other dramatic medium it teaches the writer to concentrate on the essentials, because it throws into immediate relief that to *characterize* the people or scene is to take time from the story – to weaken the story. Working for radio, I learned the way *all* great drama works: by leaving the *endowment* of characters, place, and especially action up to the audience. Only by eschewing the desire to *characterize* can one begin to understand the model of the perfect play.

The model of the perfect play is the dirty joke.

'Two guys go into a farmhouse. An old woman is stirring a pot of soup.'

What does the woman look like? What state is the farmhouse in? Why is she stirring soup? It is absolutely not important. The dirty-joke teller is tending toward a punch line and we know that he or she is only going to tell us the elements which direct our attention *toward* that punch line, so we listen attentively and gratefully.

Good drama has no stage directions. It is the interaction of the characters' objectives expressed *solely* through what they *say* to each other – not through what the author says *about* them. The better the play, the better it will fare on the radio. Put *Streetcar, Waiting for Godot, Long Day's Journey, Lear* on the radio, and what do you miss? Nothing.

Our enjoyment is *increased* by the absence of the merely descriptive. (A note here, as long as I have the forum, to beginning playwrights. A lesson from radio: don't write stage directions. If it is not apparent what the character is trying to accomplish by saying the line, telling us *how* the character said it, or whether or not she moved to the couch isn't going to aid the case. We might understand better what the character *means* but we aren't particularly going to *care*.)

In *An Actor Prepares*, Stanislavsky is asked by a student actor how, faced with all the myriad choices open to an actor onstage, Stanislavsky always manages to make the correct choice, a choice which puts forward the play. He responds that once on a Volga steamer he approached the captain and asked how, when faced with the myriad decisions involved in navigating such a dangerous river, the captain always managed to make the correct choice. The captain, he tells us, replied, 'I stick to the channel.' So, Stan tells the student, 'Stick to the channel and you cannot be wrong. The choices that you make will not be 'in general,' but in aid of the story, and, so, they must be correct.'

Writing for radio forces you and *teaches* you to stick to the channel, which is to say, the *story*. The *story* is all there is to the theater – the rest is just packaging, and that is the lesson of radio.

Stan Freberg, a fiendishly inventive writer, once did a radio commercial for radio advertising, a dialogue between a television and a radio ad exec. The radio exec says, 'Here's my ad: You take Lake Michigan and drain it. Bombers of the Royal Canadian Air Force fly over, laden with whipped cream. They drop the whipped cream in the lake until the lake is full. A huge helicopter circles Chicago carrying a forty-five-ton cherry and drops it on the top of the whipped cream, as the tops of the Chicago skyscrapers explode and paint the evening sky with fireworks from horizon to horizon. Do that on TV.'

Broadway theater by no means withstanding, the best production is the *least* production. The best production takes place in the mind of the beholder.

We, as audience, are much better off with a sign that says A BLASTED HEATH, than with all the brilliant cinematography in the world. To say 'brilliant cinematography' is to say, 'He made the trains run on time.'

Witness the rather fascistic trend in cinema in the last decade.

Q. How'd you like the movie?

A. Fantastic cinemotography.

Yeah, but so what? Hitler had fantastic cinematography. The question we have ceased to ask is, 'What was the fantastic or brilliant cinematography in *aid* of?'

As 'fantastic cinematography' has been the death of the American film, 'production' has been the death of the American theater.

'Production' or 'production values' is code for *forsaking the story*. 'Production values' is a term invented by what used to be called 'angels' when they were in the theater to meet members of the chorus, and who are now called producers, and God *knows* why they are in the theater.

Writing for the radio teaches there is no such thing as 'production values.' The phrase means 'Pour money on it,' and it has been the ruin of television, movies, and the professional stage. It is The Triumph of the General – The Celebration of Nothing to Say.

If Mount St. Helens could fit in a theater some producer would suggest teaming it with Anthony Hopkins and doing *Huey. That* is 'production values.'

But radio drama, God bless it, needs inventive actors, an inventive sound-effects person, and a good script. You can produce it for next to nothing. The writer and the actor can both practice and perfect their trade away from the counter-vailing influence of producers, critics, and money; and if it doesn't work they can do another one just as simply and cheaply without ruining either their career or a large hunk of risk capital which might have meant an addition to the house in Larchmont.

Martin Esselin helped reinvent the British drama as head of BBC Radio Drama after World War II by commissioning Pinter, Joe Orton, and others. He helped re-create a national theater by *enfranchising creative talent*. In the same way Howard Gelman of Earplay, in commissioning Wendy Wasserstein, Terry Curtis Fox, Romulus Linney, Lanford Wilson, and so on, is supporting the American theater in the best way: by encouraging freedom of thought – by hiring the writers and letting them be free.

We live in oppressive times. We have, as a nation, become our own thought police; but instead of calling the process by which we limit our expression of dissent and wonder 'censorship,' we call it 'concern for commercial viability.'

Whatever we call it, it *is* censorship. It is curtailment of freedom of speech and of imagination, and, as Tolstoy says, this oppression, as usual, is committed in the name of public tranquillity.

How different is saying, 'It would create public unrest,' from saying, 'It's not going to sell. They aren't going to *buy* it'?

It's hard to find a Great American Play on Broadway. It's getting too expensive to produce. To mount a three-character, one-set drama costs around $750,000, and the people with the money aren't going to put it up to enjoy a *succès d'estime*. They're putting it up in the hopes it is going to *make* money, which means they are doing everything in their power to appeal to the *widest possible* audience, which makes it difficult for a play to be produced that *questions, investigates*, and so, probably, *disturbs*.

Similarly with the movies. They aren't administered by Miss Dove, but by people interested solely in making a buck on the buck they have put out. And television people who put out a news special on nuns being trampled to death by elephants would turn it into a series if the viewer response were great enough. These media (and we might as well include publishing) have, in an introverted time, become self-censoring – and they refer to the process not as thought policing but as cost accounting.

But radio is inexpensive to produce. God bless it – the essential nature of the form is that it *suffers immediately* from the addition of production values, just as would a dirty joke (when you introduce the Farmer's Daughter you don't put your hair in braids to illustrate). Radio drama can be produced by anybody with a microphone and a tape recorder. The time is auspicious for a rebirth of American Theater, and radio would be a good place to look for it to happen.

A Tradition of the Theater as Art

We are told the theater is always dying. And it's true, and, rather than being decried, it should be understood. The theater is an expression of our dream life – of our unconscious aspirations.

It responds to that which is best, most troubled, most visionary in our society. As the society changes, the theater changes.

Our workers in the theater – actors, writers, directors, teachers – are drawn to it not out of intellectual predilection, but from *necessity*. We are driven into the theater by our need to express – our need to answer the questions of our lives – the questions of the time in which we live. Of this moment.

The theatrical artist serves the same function in society that dreams do in our subconscious life – the subconscious life of the individual. We are elected to supply the dreams of the body politic – we are the dream makers of the society.

What we act out, design, write, springs not from meaningless individual fancy, but from the soul of the times – that soul both observed by and expressed *in* the artist.

The artist is the advance explorer of the societal consciousness. As such, many times his first reports are disbelieved.

Later those reports may be acclaimed and then, perhaps, enshrined, which is to say sterilized – deemed descriptive not of an outward reality, but of the curious and idiosyncratic mental state of the artist. Later still the reports, and the artist, may be discarded as so commonplace as to be useless.

It is not the theater which is dying, but men and women – society. And as it dies a new group of explorers, artists, arises whose reports are disregarded, then enshrined, then disregarded.

The theater is always dying because artistic inspiration cannot be instilled – it can only be nurtured.

Most theatrical institutions survive creatively only for one generation. When the necessity which gave rise to them is gone, all that is left is the shell. The codification of a vision – which is no vision at all.

The artistic urge – the urge to create – becomes the institutional urge – the urge to *preserve*. The two are antithetical.

What can be preserved? What can be communicated from one generation to the next?

Philosophy. Morality. Aesthetics.

These can be expressed in technique, in those skills which enable the artist to respond truthfully, fully, lovingly to whatever he or she wishes to express.

These skills – the skills of the theater – cannot be communicated intellectually. They must be learned firsthand in long practice under the tutelage of someone who learned them firsthand. They must be learned from an artist.

The skills of the theater must be learned in practice with, and in emulation of, those capable of employing them.

This is what can and must be passed from one generation to the next. Technique – a knowledge of how to translate inchoate desire into clean action – into action capable of communicating itself to the audience.

This technique, this care, this love of precision, of cleanliness, this love of the theater, is the best way, for it is love of the *audience* – of that which *unites* the actor and the house: a desire to share something which they know to be true.

Without technique, which is to say without philosophy, acting cannot be art. And if it cannot be art, we are in serious trouble.

We live in an illiterate country. The mass media – the commercial theatre included – pander to the low and the lowest of the low in the human experience. They, finally, debase us through the sheer weight of their mindlessness.

Every reiteration of the idea that *nothing matters* debases the human spirit.

Every reiteration of the idea that there is no drama in modern life, there is only dramatization, that there is no tragedy, there is only unexplained misfortune, debases us. It denies what we know to be true. In denying what we know, we are as a nation which cannot remember its dreams – like an unhappy person who cannot remember his dreams and so denies that he *does* dream, and denies that there are such things as dreams.

We are destroying ourselves by accepting our unhappiness.

We are destroying ourselves by endorsing an acceptance of oblivion in television, motion pictures, and the stage.

Who is going to speak up? Who is going to speak for the American spirit? For the human spirit?

Who is capable of being heard? Of being accepted? Of being believed? Only that person who speaks without ulterior motives, without hope of gain, without even the desire to *change*, with only the desire to *create*: The artist. The actor. The strong, trained actor dedicated to the idea that the theater is the place we go to hear the truth, and equipped with the technical capacity to speak simply and clearly.

If we expect the actor, the theatrical artist, to have the strength to say no to television, to say no to that which debases, and to say yes to the stage – to that stage which is the proponent of the life of the soul – that actor is going to have to be trained, and endorsed, *concretely* for his efforts.

People cannot be expected to put aside even the meager comfort of financial success and critical acclaim (or the even more meager – and more widespread – comfort of the *hope* of those) unless they can be *shown* something *better*.

We must support each other *concretely* in the quest for artistic knowledge, in the struggle to create.

We must support each other in the things we say, in the things we choose to produce, in the things we choose to attend, in the things we choose to endow.

Only active choices on our parts will take theater, *true* theater, noncommercial theater, out of the realm of *good works*, and place it in the realm of art – an art whose benefits will cheer us, and will warm us, and will care for us, and elevate our soul out of these sorry times.

We have the opportunity now to *create* a new theater – and to endorse a *tradition* in theater, a tradition of true creation.

There is a story that a student once came to Evgeny Vakhtangov, an actor of the Moscow Art Theatre who founded his own studio to direct and to teach, and said, 'Vakhtangov, you work so hard and with so little reward. You should have your own theater.'

Vakhtangov replied, 'You know who had his own theater? Anton Chekhov.'

'Yes,' the student said, 'Chekhov had the Art Theatre, the Moscow Art Theatre.'

'No,' said Vakhtangov, 'I mean that Chekhov had his *own* theater. The Theater which he carried in his heart, and which he alone saw.'

Sanford Meisner's greatness is that for fifty years he has been training and preparing people to work in a theater which he alone saw – which existed only in his heart.

The results of his efforts are seen in the fact of the Neighborhood Playhouse School, the work of his students, and in the beginning of the Playhouse Repertory Company.

Many of us are here tonight in partial fulfillment of a debt to Mr.

Meisner and more, importantly, to the same tradition to which he owes a debt – the tradition of Theater as Art.

The tradition of the theater as the place we can go to hear the truth.

First Principles

The proclamation and repetition of first principles is a constant feature of life in our democracy. Active adherence to these principles, however, has always been considered un-American.

We recipients of the boon of liberty have always been ready, when faced with discomfort, to discard any and all first principles of liberty, and, further, to indict those who do not freely join with us in happily arrogating those principles.

Freedom of speech, religion, and sexual preference are tolerated only until their exercise is found offensive, at which point those freedoms are haughtily revoked – and we hear, 'Yes, but the framers of the Constitution,' or Christ, or Lincoln, or whatever saint we are choosing to invoke in our support, 'surely didn't envision an instance as extreme as *this*.'

We tolerate and repeat the teachings of Christ, but explain that the injunction against murder surely cannot be construed to apply to *war*, and that against theft does not apply to *commerce*. We sanctify the Constitution of the United States, but explain that freedom of choice is meant to apply to all except women, racial minorities, homosexuals, the poor, opponents of the government, and those with whose ideas we disagree.

The Theater also has its First Principles – principles which make our presentations honest, moral, and, coincidentally, moving, funny, and worth the time and money of the audience.

Most of us are acquainted with these theatrical rules, which subjugate all aspects of the production to the *idea* of the play, and cause all elements to adhere to and *express* that idea forcefully, fully, without desire for praise or fear of censure. But, in the first moment of difficulty with our work we, many times, assure ourselves that principles of unity, simplicity, and honesty are well and good under normal circumstances, but we surely cannot be meant to apply them under the extraordinary pressures of actually working on a play.

We discard our first principles at the moment they cause us unpleasantness – when they might send the author back for another draft, or the piece back for another week or month of rehearsal, or cause the director to work on a scene until it is finished, or cause a producer to say, 'You know, on reflection this piece is garbage. I think it would be better for all concerned if we didn't put it on.'

... Yes, but we have seats to fill, we have to get on to the next act, we have a deadline to meet.

If we act as if the Aristotelian Unities, the philosophy of Stanislavsky, or Brecht, or Shaw, were effete musings, and intended for some ideal theater, and not applicable to our own work, we are declining the responsibility for *creating* that ideal theater.

Every time an actor deviates from the through-line of a piece (that is, the first principle of the piece) for whatever reason – to gain praise, or out of laziness, or because he hasn't taken the time to discover how that one difficult moment actually *expresses* the through-line, he creates in himself the habit of moral turpitude; and the *play*, which is a strict lesson in ethics, is given the lie.

Every time the author leaves in a piece of nonessential prose (beautiful though it may be), he weakens the structure of the play, and, again, the audience learns *this* lesson: no one is taking responsibility: theater people are prepared to *espouse* a moral act, but not to *commit* it.

When we deviate from first principles we communicate to the audience a lesson in cowardice. This lesson is of as great a magnitude as our subversion of the Constitution by involvement in Vietnam, in Ford's pardon of Nixon, in the persecution of the Rosenbergs, in the reinstatement of the death penalty. They are all lessons in cowardice, and each begets cowardice.

Alternatively, the theater affords an opportunity uniquely suited for communicating and inspiring ethical behaviour: the audience is given the possibility of seeing live people onstage carrying out an action based on first principles (these principles being the objectives of the play's protagonists) and carrying this action to its full conclusion.

The audience then participates at a celebration of the idea that Intention A begets Result B. The audience imbibes that lesson as regards the given circumstances of the play, and they *also* receive the lesson as regards the standards of production, writing, acting, design and direction.

If theatrical workers are seen *not* to have the courage of their convictions (which is to say, the courage to relegate every aspect of production to the laws of theatrical action, economy, and, specifically, the requirements of the superobjective of the play), the audience, once again, learns a lesson in moral cowardice, and we add to the burden of their lives. We add to their loneliness.

Each time we try to subordinate all we do to the necessity of bringing to life simply and completely the intention of the play, we give the audience an experience which enlightens and frees them: the experience of witnessing their fellow human beings saying, 'Nothing will sway me, nothing will divert me, nothing will dilute my intention of achieving what I have sworn to achieve': in technical terms, 'My Objective'; in general terms, my 'goal,' my 'desire,' my 'responsibility.'

The theatrical repetition of this lesson can and *will* in time help teach that it is possible and *pleasant* to substitute action for inaction, courage for cowardice, humanity for selfishness.

If we hold to those first principles of action and beauty and economy which we know to be true, and hold to them in *all* things – choice of plays, method of actor training, writing, advertising, promotion – we can *uniquely* speak to our fellow citizens.

In a morally bankrupt time we can help to change the habit of coercive and frightened action and substitute for it the habit of trust, self-reliance, and cooperation.

If we are true to our ideals we can help to form an ideal society – a society based on and adhering to ethical first principles – not by *preaching* about it, but by *creating* it each night in front of the audience – by showing how it works. In action.

Stanislavsky and the American Bicentennial

There is a homily popularly attributed to the Chinese to the effect that the time one spends fishing is not deducted from one's life span. The may or may not be true of fishing (I for one am not at all loath to believe in a universe ruled by aesthetically pleasing ideas rather than immutable laws) but it is certainly not true of the theater. The time one spends in a theater – whether as spectator or as worker – is deducted from one's total allotment, and this is what Stanislavsky had in mind when he said, 'Play well, or play badly, but play truly.'

Stanislavsky recognized that the Theater is a part of one's total life experience, that it is an environment wherein human beings interact (where they breathe together, the actors and the audience), and that not only the physical and psychological, but also the *ethical* laws of life on the stage are no different than those on the street. The theater is not an imitation of anything, it is real theater.

Stanislavsky's art, his humanism, his great gift to world theater, was the recognition that on the stage, just as in the office or the supermarket or the school, human beings must concern themselves with the truth of the individual moment, and recognize and ratify their coconspirators' existence and desire.

Tolstoy was the major philosophical influence on Stanislavsky, and Tolstoy's dictum 'If you cannot deal with Human Beings with love, you must not deal with them at all' is the *a priori* of the work of Stanislavsky and his colleagues and his students and their students.

Stanislavsky's ideas, basically philosophic rather than technical, are generally known as the Stanislavsky System, and posit the theater primarily as a place of recognition and ratification. Implicit in the Stanislavsky System is the idea that human beings are infinitely perfectible, and always strive to do good – to the limit of their ability and according to their best lights. (This concept is embodied in the technical sphere in the idea of *objective*.)

The theater must be a place where mutual recognition of this desire can take place. The artist must avow humanity in him- or herself, and also in the audience. (Many theatrical artisans have an incorrect or incomplete, but in any case, unhappy, understanding of the relationship between themselves and the audience. The misunderstanding exists for many unfortunate reasons, not the least of which is the general low esteem in which the theatrical artisan is held and learns to hold him or herself.)

In the theater we must strive to recognize and to ratify the universality of our desires and our fears as human beings. If we continue to shove them under the rug – our anxieties and also our joys – if we continue to lose a basis for comparison (and, with it, a rational self-image), we will continue to live in an unhappy land.

'Play well, or play badly, but play truly.' Try as one might, one cannot escape the temporal exigencies; all the polish in the world will not mitigate the fact of Death or the reality of a mutable universe. You can't make it so pretty that it goes away, all you can do is live the moment fully and *avow* the finite and fleeting nature of consciousness.

The theater is not a place where one should go to forget, but rather a place where one should go to remember.

Just as the act of making love can and should be made a spiritual act by an avowal of the transient nature of the body, just so the theatrical experience must be an *adoration* of the *evanescent*, a celebration of the transient nature of individual life (and, perhaps, through this, a glimpse at some less-transient realities).

The magic moments, the beautiful moments in the theater always come from a desire on the part of artist *and* audience to live in the moment – to *commit* themselves to time.

Kafka wrote that one always has the alternative of ignoring and choosing not to participate in the sufferings of others, but that in so doing one commits oneself to the only suffering that one could have avoided.

We live in an unhappy nation. As a people we are burdened with a terrible self-image. As a theatrical worker, I perceive that one way to alleviate the moral pall and the jejune supersophistication of our lives is by theatrical celebration of those things which bind us together.

I, personally, had a very rewarding week last week. I finally went to see *Three Women* at Victory Gardens, and *Our Town* at the Goodman, and I left each feeling much better than when I went in. I thought: isn't it the truth: people are born, love, hate, are frightened and happy, grow old and die. We as audience and we as artists must work to bring about a theater, an American Theater, which will be a celebration of these things.

An Unhappy Family

In the American Theater *status* – the ability to extract deference from others – is automatically conferred on the basis of a set hierarchy – on the basis of *job title*.

The actor is manipulated and controlled by the director, who is similarly in thrall to the producer. The unquestioned acceptance of this 'Great Chain of Being' is based on the fiction that it is 'good for the production.' But any reasonable person in the theater sees this is seldom the case, and so the conscious acceptance of this hierarchy ('It's good for the production and I better shut up or I'll lose my job') is coupled with a deep, deep anger.

Those down the chain seem to have two choices: they may accept an idealized version of those over them: ('I don't know or like what they're up to, but – on the basis of their credits and their position – I can only assume that they are right and I am wrong'); or they may rebel, fume, gossip, and plot – much as if those in control were their parents – which is precisely what this relationship recapitulates . . . that of the child to the parent.

This paternalistic pattern in the theater infantilizes the actors, so they feel compelled to please rather than to create, to rebel rather than to explore, to perform rather than to express.

As in the parent-child relationship, the motive for control in the theater is always stated as The Good of the Child. 'I, as producer, director, must *ignore* your questions about the worth of this piece of blocking/piece of direction/piece of dramaturgy. My word is law, it is for your own good to obey unthinkingly, and if you begin to doubt and question me, the havoc you cause will destroy all the good I am trying to do for you and your colleagues.'

In the family, as in the theater, the urge to control only benefits the controller. Blind obedience saves him the onerous duty of examining his preconceptions, his *own* wisdom, and, finally, *his own worth*.

The desire to manipulate, to treat one's colleagues as servants, reveals a deep sense of personal worthlessness: as if one's personal thoughts, choices, and insights could not bear reflection, let alone a reasoned mutual examination.

Members of a healthy theater/family treat each other with respect and love; and those who know better *do* better, knowing that those who love them will strive to emulate them.

In a meritocracy, status and the power to direct the actions of others would, at least, be won by demonstration of excellence and *some* form of communal assent. But in *our* theater, in *our* unhappy family, those who come in 'last,' who come in 'at the bottom' – the actors – are subject to the unreasoned, unloving, and frightened whims of those in (financial) power over them. They are the new baby born to oppressed parents who *finally* have someone to control.

In both situations the recipient of this control is made to fear for his livelihood – for his very life – if he does not obey unquestioningly, and so is robbed of his dignity.

This unreasoned commercial hierarchy of actor-director-producer has drained the theater of its most powerful force: the phenomenal strength and generosity of the actor; and, as in any situation of unhappy tryanny, the oppressed must free the oppressor.

Some Thoughts on Writing in Restaurants

In a restaurant one is both observed and unobserved. Joy and sorrow can be displayed and observed 'unwittingly,' the writer scowling naively and the diners wondering. What the *hell* is he doing? Then, again, the writer may be *truly* unobserved, which affects not a jot the scourge of popular opinion on his overactive mind.

Couples play out scenes in restaurants. The ritual of acting out and displaying changes in one's state before the tribe has disappeared, but the urge lives on; and the ritual of dissolution of the affaire in a

restaurant is strong and compelling now when the marriage ceremony has become an empty form.

One might say the urge to participate in the ritual is almost
irresistible because it cures, cleanses, and assures. The man stands
in a restaurant and testifies before his peers (and what better place
to locate them than in a restaurant?). 'I'm *trying* and I call on you
all to witness me. I am not bad, but good; for I would not dissolve
this union without your blessing.' He is the carny operator riding
solo on the carousel to dissolve his union, the Indian squaw putting
her husband's moccasins outside the tepee.

True ritual evolves spontaneously in and among those with a
community of interests. As the Fourth of July, Christmas, and
Chanukah no longer meet our needs and we begin to celebrate them
with a *mauvaise honte*, the rituals of screaming at an unpopular
choice of the Academy Awards, of shrieking disbelief when your
guy catches the long one in the end zone become stronger – for the
involuntary 'Goddamn that man can throw' is just 'Allah Akbar,' in
twentieth-century urban clothing. Deny them as we may, we still
need the gods.

'Is God dead?' and 'Why are there no real movies anymore?' are
pretty much the same question. They both mean that our symbols
and our myths have failed us – that we have begun to take them
literally, and so judge them wanting.

In taking those questions as anything more than rhetorical, it is
as if we are saying, 'I am going to stay up all night and *prove* to you
that no white-haired man is going to come down the chimney.'

We want to see movie stars' genitals on-screen and to be assured
that 'they did their own stunts.' We are asking Christ to throw
himself down from the building.

When we demand a rational and immediately practical translation of rituals, we deny their unconscious purpose and power; we,
in effect, reject our own power to solve problems – to deal with the
abstract. So doing, we are forced to ignore those problems incapable of immediate, rational solutions. As these are the problems
most important in our life, by denying their existence we create
deep personal and communal anxiety.

Most of our communal anxiety is treated in the low level (low
level because it is not cathartic but analgesic – it does not cleanse,
but merely puts off) ritual of television.

Television is the whipping boy elected to suffer our emotions; it is the husband in the African tribe who undergoes the labour pains, as to have the wife undergo them would be too debilitating.

So television ritualizes our disapproval (of the Polish government), our grief (at the memorial anniversary of Dr. King, or Robert Kennedy), and our joy (when Billie finds her Lost Dog). None of these subjects actually has the power to elicit the emotions television supposes to treat, so its supposed *treatment* of them is nothing other than nostalgia for the capacity to be involved.

But the writer elects himself to suffer the emotions society disavows; the act of creation, no less than the final production, when suffered in public gives to the lone creator the satisfaction of fulfilling a place in society.

Policemen so cherish their status as keepers of the peace and protectors of the public that they have occasionally been known to beat to death those citizens or groups who question that status.

The urge to support each other's social position has atrophied, much as architecture has degenerated in a time of buildings too large for reference to the human scale. Where the individual cannot compare himself to the group, he cannot compare his achievements to the achievements of the group.

As the Victorians assiduously expunged reference to sex, so we expunge direct reference to that which *we* desire most, which is love and a sense of belonging.

The writer sits at a two-top near the window in the restaurant. The sound of traffic just might mimic a mother's heartbeat and the Muzak plays love songs the true meaning of which can be simply found by replacing the word 'you' every time it appears in the lyrics, with the word 'I.'

Through these manufactured perverted songs and their counterparts in television, movies, and publishing, we express love much as we express chagrin: over those things which cannot reciprocate and, further, over those things whose acceptability *as a love object* is absolutely incontrovertibly safe: we have ritualized the expression of love and limited its objects to other men's wives (in country music); the past and the future (in movies); and in television, puppets.

Movie stars have idiosyncrasies. They exist on screen and off; they are subject, on screen and off, to the same unacceptable urges that confront us all, so they have been replaced in the public estimation by Miss Piggy, E. T., the Muppets – constructions incapable of spontaneity and so of inspiration – a ritualized celebration of (what greater example?) the Absence of Will as a laudable state.

Some tribe in the future, far in the future, might find a pistol, perhaps the world's last pistol, and one hundred rounds of ammunition. The priests of that tribe, in tribute to the unknown, might invent a holiday and fire one bullet each year as a link to the unknown. After ninety years, it isn't difficult to imagine that a new bull might be put forth that shots were to be fired only every *hundred* years, at the expiration of which time the something extraordinary might be foreseen to occur.

And perhaps at the expiration of nine hundred years a new bull might go forth to the effect that the last round never was to be expended – that the tribe would choose to worship *potentiality* in their artifacts rather than uselessness.

But *our* tribe has fired the last round and our only link to the possibility of powers greater than ourselves is the useless gun, the essential element we no longer possess. And since our priests have fired off that last round, they have expended any possible link to the past, as such a memory would surely cause us pain. Therefore, our dead rituals are rituals of denial. They concern not potential but *lack*, and express contempt – contempt, mainly for ourselves, and for our urge to celebrate.

Let's look elsewhere. Not in the shul and in the church; their time has passed – though it will come again. The human urge to celebrate, which is to say the reemergence of religion, the reemergence of the involuntary, and that which tends toward release and reaffirmation, will be seen to reassert itself in the profane, commonplace, and pagan aspects of our lives, in the scorn heaped on the Academy Awards committee that we cannot dare attribute rightfully to *government*; the ritual suggestion of sodomy in 'take this job and shove it'; the ritual of the fire department's dog; the writer in the restaurant; the adopted southern accent of airline pilots; the exclamation of awe at the long run up the middle. These unproclaimed but operative rituals are meager, but they are close to all we have of spiritual community – they have replaced the awe of the sacrament, which itself replaced the miracle of rebirth from the dead.

II
EXUVIAL MAGIC

Exuvial Magic:
An Essay Concerning Fashion

The pursuit of Fashion is the attempt of the middle class to co-opt tragedy.

In adopting the clothing, speech, and personal habits of those in straitened, dangerous, or pitiful circumstances, the middle class seeks to have what it feels to be the exigent and nonequivocal experiences had by those it emulates.

In progressing from an emulation of the *romantic* to an emulation of the *tragic*, the middle class unconsciously avows not only the aridity of its lifestyle, but the complete failure of its fantasies, and of its very ability to fantasize.

We dress in the denim of the farm worker and the prisoner of the state, the olive drab and khaki of the field soldier, the gray and blue of the Chinese laborer, the beaten leather jackets of the breadline.

The white world tries to emulate the black world; the straight world takes its fashions straight from gay society. The gay world, in its preoccupation with the *chic* of the banal, of the *passé*, of *gaucherie*, emulates those elements of the America it considers tragic – the clothing of the 1950s. So with black emulation and exaggeration of the fashion of suburbia – the Cadillac El Dorado, the color-coordinated shirt and tie and suit.

In contemporary plastic art much attention is paid to the artist capable of making a completely obtuse statement. The middle class sneers at the analytical and exults the occult. The very fact of something being beyond the experience of the middle class is sufficient to ratify that something in its eyes. In pursuing the tragic we gainsay our own too-sad intelligence, our increasingly worthless common sense, in favor of that which is beyond our experience and, therefore, *possibly* productive.

Our preoccupation with personalities – particularly the personalities of artists – is another manifestation of our frantic search for nonequivocal experience. The product of the artist has become less important than the *fact* of the artist. We wish to absorb this person. We wish to devour someone who has experienced the tragic. In our society this person is much more important than anything he might create.

We are like warriors of old who, upon vanquishing our opponent, must rip the warm heart from his body and immediately eat it, and thus absorb his strength. The eating of the heart is a very real attempt to understand. The adoption of the tragic as fashionable is the same attempt to understand through imitative magic. 'What,' we ask, '*is* it that gives these people – our opponents – strength?' Additionally, we know that only by taking on the most private characteristics of those we fear can we be assured of having unconditionally subdued them.

The *chic* of the summer dress of the last several years – baggy pants, bowling shirts, socks and sandals, Hawaiian shirts, sun visors – seems to have been an unconscious recognition of the generation of the fifties as a time of great confusion, fear, and national self-loathing; as a time of tragedy. So the middle class comes to recognize the tragic in itself.

We might regularly scrutinize fashion magazines, to see what class or group is being envied, and who lies in danger of becoming understood, and to what extent we members of the middle class have come to recognize ourselves.

True Stories of Bitches

The bitchiest person I know is my sister. She lives in Des Plaines, Illinois – which she refers to as 'The City of Destiny.'

One evening in said city we were out drowning our sorrows at a delicatessen, and I said of my pastrami sandwich, 'How can we eat this food? This is *heart*-attack food . . . how can we eat this?'

'Listen,' she remonstrated, 'it gave six million Jews the strength to resist Hitler.'

And there you have the difference between talent and genius. In a few impromptu words, my sister managed to malign me, the pastrami, restaurant goers of like tastes, and six million innocent victims.

Why? Because I ate a pastrami sandwich? Not exactly, as she, too, was eating a similar sandwich. All of the above incurred my sister's wrath because I had the bad taste to express an opinion.

'You are a fool,' she was saying, 'you are a fool to be eating food you disapprove of. Your inability to rule your life according to your perceptions is an unfortunate trait and, doubtless, it was in some wise responsible for the murder of the European Jewry. They, although they unfortunately couldn't be here to defend themselves, were most likely equally foolish in submitting by degrees to a deathlike oppression – much as you submit to that sandwich – and I am a fool for sitting here with you.'

When we were younger, my sister put my stepsister up to calling me on the phone and pretending to be a friend of a friend from college who was smitten with me and would like to meet me for a drink. An affable chap, I acquiesced, and heard, and still hear twenty years later, the giggles of the two girls over the phone.

Often, when speaking of completely unrelated topics, my sister will ask if I remember the time I invited my own step-sister out for a drink; and then, honor being what it is, I riposte by asking if she remembers the time her boyfriend drowned in the bathtub. His death was elevated from the unfortunate to the remarkable by the fact that he drowned in the bathtub while testing out his new scuba gear; and reference to his passing tends to cap the argument, as being the ne plus ultra of response, which is to say, bitchiness. Similarly, in husband-and-wife arguments, or, as they are generally known, 'marriage,' the ultimate response the man feels is, of course, physical violence. People can say what they will, we men think, but if I get pushed just one little step further, why I might, I might just _____(FILL IN THE BLANK) because she seems to have forgotten that I'm stronger than her.

And there you have the *raison d'être* of bitchiness and its identification as a feminine tactic. We've all got to have an ace in the hole when dealing with those who are stronger.

My wife, in the whirlwind early years of our marriage, disapproved of my playing poker. Looking back, it occurs to me that she felt I should have found her exclusive company sufficient, and indeed I would have, but she didn't play poker.

Many times she would resort to a cunning and wily ruse to lure me back home from my game. She would call, for example, and say that she was down the road at the filling station, as she had forgotten the keys to the house, and would I please come home. She once called me to ask me to come home because she was scared. 'Why are you scared?' I asked. 'Because there's a bat in the toilet,' she said.

Man that I am, I resisted her blandishments, and, on arrival home, found that there was indeed a bat in the toilet. It was a rather junior bat and had folded its wings and gone to sleep on the floor behind the bathtub, and so I nodded my head and said, 'Well . . .'

Speaking of which: once my wife called and spoke to me thus: 'Why don't you come home? Why don't you leave that silly game and come home to a woman who loves you?' If my memory serves me, her voice became somewhat husky at this point, and lower in pitch, and she said. 'You know I can't sleep unless you come home.' Well, I hung up the phone and I thought. I looked at my stack of chips and, as I seemed to be winning, I said to my companions, 'Fellas, I'm sorry, but I have to go home.'

I went home, I entered my house humming to myself, and sprinted up the stairs, loosening my clothing. My wife was fast asleep. I rubbed the small of her back. 'Wake up, honey,' I said or some such. 'Mffff,' she said, 'Sleeping.' I paused. 'Yes, but,' I said, 'you said come home, 'cause you couldn't sleep if I'm not here.' 'Well, you're *here*,' she said and went back to sleep.

So you see what I mean.

The culmination of which came one night when I had come home from the game quite late, and with less money than I went out with. My wife, at this point, was awake and took it up with me, my playing poker. Things escalated, as things do, and finally she shouted, 'All right, if it's so important to you, just *leave*. Just leave, and never come back.'

'All right,' I said. And she stormed out and I got out my suitcase and started throwing versatile items of clothing into it. Boys, my mind was racing: I was free at last. I would play poker every night, and smoke cigars right in the house. I would look up all of those New York gals who understand what 'freedom' means, I would live in Cheap Hotels. She came back in the room, 'And take the kid,' she said, and thrust our sleeping two-year-old daughter at me and walked out. There it is again: I thought I was winning. I thought I had won, and what was I left with? A very difficult form of behavior to negotiate with, that is, 'I don't understand the *rules*, but I'm so nutsy that I might do anything . . .'

I put the kid back to sleep and meditated that no one forced me to get married.

A further story of me and my wife:

One night by the fire she asked me, 'Who was the most famous person that you ever slept with?' I was stunned. My wife is a genteel and sensitive woman, and that question, even in the protected intimacy of marriage, seemed crass and invasive. 'Oh, honey,' I said, 'ha-ha-ha,' and went back to my reading. 'Who was the most famous person you ever slept with?' she repeated. I asked if I looked like the type who'd kiss and tell, and she said, yes, I did. After some bantering – me truly on the defensive, as I couldn't figure out what prompted this out-of-character question – I hit on a response: 'Okay,' I said, 'who was the most famous person *you* ever slept with?' She responded instantly with a name. There now I have you, I thought, 'Him?' I said. 'Him??? *He* was the most famous person that you ever slept with? You slept with *him*? That lox . . . are you *joking*? Ha-ha-ha!' And limitless was my mirth for some minutes, as I expounded on her lack of taste and choice.

When I'd run down, she said, 'All right, now your turn: who is the most famous person *you've* ever slept with?' There was a slight pause, I lowered my eyes, and said demurely, 'All right, I slept with_____.' There was a moment's silence and my wife said, 'Who . . .?' As Tolstoy tell us: mediocrity sees nothing higher than itself, but talent recognizes genius instantly. People say that Bruce Lee was killed by the Touch of Death, a martial technique so occult and so advanced its adepts, with a simple touch to an unspecified part of the body, can reverse the vital mechanism and bring about death within twenty-four hours.

My mother knew and would do the usual required dressage of forgetting the names of girls of whom she did not approve, complaining that I had missed events whose existence she had neglected to inform me of, and so on. But she had one technique which, even though I was its victim, filled me with admiration.

It was in a period of my life when I was doing a lot of traveling – commuting between New York, California, and our home in Vermont.

On my stops in Chicago, we would have a fine dinner at my mother's house, and discuss the lives of various members of the family who were fortuitously not present; for example, my sister and her boyfriend who had gone to both Davy Jones and Kohler of Kohler simultaneously, and so on.

After dinner as I rose to leave, my mother would do the modern equivalent of 'take a little something for the train.' She would present me with a token to be taken home to commemorate the odd intervening birthday or anniversary. This was a charming habit of a charming woman and my joy in the gift was dissipated only by the fact that I was invariably traveling light and in the midst of a flying visit to five cities, and the gift was invariably a Staffordshire serving platter. So there I was. Evening after evening. On the sidewalk outside her house – my go-getter shoulder bag with a notebook and a toothbrush and a spare pair of socks, and my arms endeavouring to protect this three-foot confection of spun porcelain.

Now, you couldn't *check* it, you couldn't carry it on the plane unless you held it in your lap, and *then* it was odds on to break. The most intelligent course would be, of course, to throw it in the trash, but HOW COULD ONE ACT LIKE THAT TO ONE'S MOTHER? And so, lashed to this fragile anchor, one thought about one's mother for the length of the trip. What did one think? *Surely* she must know . . . *surely* she could have sent home a nice antique pillbox . . . *surely* some part of her must know I'm going to have to dedicate my life to this monstrosity, and let alone 'Put it in the closet, we'll take it out when she comes over,' I would have to encase the damn thing in glass to try to prohibit it from shattering spontaneously.

It occurs to me that the three prime examples of bitchiness are three of the four women closest to me (the fourth being my daughter, who is too young and partakes of too much of my forthright nature ever to be a bitch). So I would, for a moment, speak like a member of the 'helping professions,' and suggest that people can't be bitchy to us unless we let them be close to us. This is a splendid theory and would hold water unless one had ever tried to complete a transaction in a New York bank.

I once spent about an hour in line at a New York bank waiting to make a deposit. When my turn finally came, I handed the teller my savings passbook and a check for twenty-five hundred dollars, meant for deposit. The teller credited the money to my passbook, then returned the passbook along with twenty-five hundred dollars in cash.

As I am a well-brought-up individual, my cupidity was inched out by my fear of being caught, and I said to the teller: 'Excuse me . . .?' to which she responded 'You've had your turn, if you want another transaction, go to the back of the line.' I stepped aside and meditated on how much sharper than *anything* it is to do business with a New York bank, and *again* my fear of capture came to the fore. I got in the somewhat shorter line which led to the bank officers. After about a half hour it came my turn, and I explained the situation to a vice president. She nodded, took the twenty-five hundred and began and *ended* her speech of thanks with the simple 'Well, what are *you* waiting for?'

And speaking of the Capital of Bitchiness:

I was walking down the street on a beautiful New York day, hurrying to a business meeting. I had on a sports coat as I thought I would comport myself in a deferential manner. I was not wearing a tie because I do not own a tie.

Passing Bendel's, I thought I would improve the few moments before my business meeting by buying a tie, so completing my 'professional drag,' and, in the very act of the transaction, becoming one with the mercantile society around me.

I went into the men's boutique section and smiled approvingly at the well-turned-out young woman in charge.

Ingenuously, I said, 'Hi. I got dressed up for a business meeting. I put on a special outfit, and it occurs to me that I should have a tie. Which tie do you think I should choose to go with this outfit?' The young woman looked at me for a moment and responded, 'Get a new outfit.'

Yes, I admire it: the ability to spew those pungent periods right on the spur — the bile of a wasted life tempering the steel of a vicious disposition . . . for the world is full of cruelty, and how can we cease being cruel if we are *not* cruel?

Once in the midst of a particularly bad day I was having lunch at a crowded eatery. I was asked to share a table with a pretty woman in a proclaimedly unpleasant mood.

Being by profession, experience, and inclination suspicious and not a bit paranoid, I took her truculent silence personally. On arising to pay the check I nodded at my accidental table partner and said, 'Nice chatting with you.' She looked up and said, 'My best friend died today,' to which I responded, 'Hey, Bitch, I didn't kill her . . .' Laugh if you will, cry if you must, but I like to think, like bitches everywhere, that my quick and elegant rejoinder raised that woman from the morass of her legitimate personal problems, and enmired her in mine.

Notes for a Catalogue for Raymond Saunders

My shoulder bag broke and I took it to the shoe repair shop.

The cobbler looked at it and said that it would cost me ten dollars to have the strap repaired. I protested this seemed rather high.

He told me that it could not be fixed by machine and would take at least an hour of hand-work.

All right, I said, when should I come back, next week?

No, he said, go get a cup of coffee, come back in ten or fifteen minutes.

I had the bag in Louisiana, where I'd gone to meet an old gunfighter.

I asked him if he'd like a cigar. No, he said, I only want to know what's in the bag.

I saw that he thought the bag suspect, and explained that I had my notebooks and pens in it. Next week, back East, I realized he thought this *more* suspect. Today I see in the New York *Times* that ultra-fashionable men have taken to wearing skirts.

I always like to look at the title first. Like the rest I was brought up saying that I had a five-year-old child at home who could do as well, and also wondered, 'Yes, but would he show me he can adequately draw a horse?'

I always wanted to see the horse first. What does that mean? Finally I have to tell myself it means that I am not judging the art and not even judging the artist but am judging myself.

Whence this idea that the purpose of painting is to allow the viewer to exercise judgment?

People always ask me where I get my ideas. I always tell them that I *think* of them. There seems to be a great confusion about the purpose of technique, and most of us, raised in states which begin with a vowel, unconsciously agree that the purpose of technique is to free the viewer from the onerous responsibility of experiencing anything.

A well-drawn dog is better than a badly drawn lion.

Also we confuse 'I like it' with 'It is very realistic.'

If we like it we say, 'Yes, that's very true.' And so our judgment of techniques becomes a peremptory challenge for that which we do not like.

Alfred Hitchcock. Doesn't that just capture the essence of A. Hitchcock. 'Yes, but it doesn't really *look* like that . . .' 'Yes, but it's a play.'

I once wrote a movie about Lawyers, who wrote in droves to say that real lawyers don't behave that way. Someone was guilty. 'What in the world does this nonsense have to do with *me* . . .?'

In a world we find terrifying, we ratify that which doesn't threaten us.

Wishing things would go away.

It is all right for an orchid to look like female genitalia, but may be objectionable for someone to call attention to that similarity . . .

Why do fat adolescent girls have bandages on their calves?

How is it you always know when a salesperson is about to shortchange you?

Why is it that everyone knows that people tend to touch their nose when they lie but that we do not act on that information?

What does it mean that someone 'has suffered enough,' and why should we take their own word for it? Does it not seem that if someone has the gall to presume that this suggestion might forestall further grief that they have *not* suffered enough?

I have a friend who wanted to construct and market a down-filled Hawaiian shirt. *Does* this not render Tristan Tzara and the fur-lined teacup rather woosy?

Why is it that, stopped for a supposed traffic infraction, we can not *help* ourselves from saying, 'What seems to be the trouble, Officer?' Would it make any difference if we said something else?'

Don Marquis said that the ultimate reconciliation of the Doctrine of Free Will and of Predestination was that we were free to do whatever we chose and whatever we chose to do would be wrong.

Judge says: Mr. X, can you account for your behavior?

Guy says: Judge, as a child I played the violin. The other children shunned me, but I followed my star and I studied every day.

A group of toughs called Legs O'Donnel and the Dead Man's Lot gang put out word that if they ever caught me on their turf that they would beat me silly.

So I stayed away from Dead Man's Lot.

One winter evening I was hurrying home. I'd studied late and knew my mother would be worried, so I, timorously, took the shortcut across Dead Man's Lot.

Halfway across I looked up and there was O'Donnel and his gang. He said that they were going to beat me. I felt, if I was to get a beating I would take it for that in which I believed. So I took out my violin and played. I played as I had never played before, and when I finished I looked up, prepared to take my medicine.

And I found I was alone.

Many years later I was taking a cab through midtown and, passing by the Artists' Entrance of Lincoln Center I saw several men who looked familiar.

I asked the cabbie if he knew who those men were, and he told me they were the Juilliard String Quartet.

I paid off the cab and stepped out on the sidewalk. I stared at them.

The Juilliard String Quartet were no other than Legs O'Donnel and the Dead Man's Lot gang.

It became clear to me that my playing for them on that cold December night had turned them from a certain life of crime and had inspired them to become the most accomplished string musicians in the world.

I drew nearer them and I saw recognition come into their faces.

And they beat the shit out of me.

Rudolph Arnheim suggests we have difficulty perceiving true harmony in art as we are so seldom exposed to true harmony in our daily life.

We are becoming incapable of recognizing the harmonious and so begin to doubt that it exists.

What does it mean that we have eschewed the traditional tests of art, of conduct, of accomplishment in all forms?

Is it accidental that movies are worse than ever? and country songs – that last bastion of traditional free expression – increasingly make reference in their lyrics to the title of other country songs?

Every year the number of public places which do not broadcast music dwindles, and the quality of that music dwindles, too. We hear it in elevators, on airplanes, in lobbies, on the telephone. What is the purpose of this music? To delight? To express? It does neither. To soothe? I cannot find it soothing. I can only be enraged by it.

The question, it seems to me, is not what the Impresario thought he was selling when he put music in elevators, or what the Consumer thought he was buying.

The question, it seems to me, is what is the real meaning of the transaction.

And it seems to me that, in re: elevator music, we all – sellers, buyers, and victims, conspire to limit thought. Why?

Because those thoughts which might come in moments of response are too frightening.

Our concerns with Corporate Takeovers, with Homosexuality, and Nuclear Power, with the Dissolution of the Family – taken singly each of these topics seems both significant and insoluble. Taken conjointly they seem to me to indicate a sort of social elevator music – a concern with the symptomatic rather than with the substantive.

I think these issues are a screen which prevents us from looking at ourselves.

We accept the degeneration which seems to be the order of the day ... in our health, in our social institutions, in our environment, in the World Situation.

Our poetry does not rhyme, our doctors cannot cure, our politicians cannot represent, our artists cannot explain.

It seems to me obvious that we are in line for a great and fast-approaching catastrophe of some sort and that nothing will avert it; that these symptoms are unimportant in themselves and are only the inescapable forewarnings of that which is to come.

As a deeply diseased body seeks to throw off its imbalance through the skin, the glands, the digestive system, so these frightening financial, nuclear, sexual, geophysical declines are only healthy symptoms of a diseased world experimenting in an attempt to bring itself back to health.

A countryside suffused with hope peopled by animals and schooled in thought had by the roadside one small tree which said:
The queen saw her chance and she took the chance to quit
She packed her bags and fled
She lives in Southern France
A bear lies in her bed.
The rose inside the luggage she had brought is withered
She has tied the bags with rope
The rope is frayed
The windowsill is scarred where she has lowered it.

Decadence

A vogue or fashion is nothing other than the irresistible expression of a profound longing. This expression has the power to affect society-at-large because it is unconscious and symbolic.

A fashion may seem to be the creation of one mind or will, but that will must be ratified by many: the producers, the critics, the media – *by the popular mind acting as one*, in short. The power of fashion is the power of the collective unconscious ratifying a collectively held wish.

The popularity of disaster movies, for example, expresses a collective perception of a world threatened by irresistible and unforseen forces which *nevertheless are thwarted at the last moment*. Their thinly veiled symbolic meaning might be translated thus: We are innocent of wrongdoing. We are attacked by unforeseeable forces come to harm us. We are, thus, innocent even of negligence. Though those forces are insuperable, *chance* will come to our aid and we shall emerge victorious. 'Our own innocence (or know-nothingism) is our own most powerful weapon; and there is no lesson to be learned from this nearly escaped disaster, as it could not have been foreseen and it could not happen again'.

The popularity of slice-and-dice, young-girl-murdered-by-an-ax movies expresses a psychotic misogyny – a hatred of women and a hatred of sex. They symbolize, and our ratification of them symbolizes what the ax murderer symbolizes: a wish to be castrated: to be relieved of the burden of sexuality.

We are in the midst of a vogue for the truly decadent in art – for that which is destructive rather than regenerative, self-referential rather than outward-looking, elitist rather than popular. This decadent art is elitist because it cannot stand on its merits as a work of personal creation. Instead it appeals to a prejudice or predilection held mutually with the audience.

This appeal is political, and stems from the political urge, which is the urge to control the actions of others. It is in direct opposition to the artistic urge, which is to express oneself regardless of consequences. I cite 'performance art,' 'women's writing,' and, on the less-offensive end of the scale, 'nonbooks' – 'The_____Handbook,' etc. – which are not books at all, but badges proclaiming a position.

Plays which deal with the unassailable investigate nothing and express nothing save the desire to investigate nothing.

It is incontrovertible that deaf people are people, too; that homosexuals are people, too; that it is unfortunate to be deprived of a full happy life by illness or accident; that it is sobering to grow old.

These events, illness, homosexuality, accident, aging, birth defects, equally befall the Good and the Bad invididual. They are not the result of conscious choice and so do not bear on the character of the individual. They are not the fit subject of drama, as they do not deal with the human capacity for choice. Rather than uniting the audience in a universal experience, they are invidious. They split the audience into two camps: those who like the play and those who hate homosexuals (deaf people, old people, paraplegics, etc.)

Fashion in clothing is also the expression of a wish. It is the wish to co-opt the experience – the tragedy, the joy, the mobility – of that group being emulated. Military garments express the desire to be regimented; miniskirts expressed the wish to be without responsibility – to be considered as infants; the current punk fashion, in its comment on the fifties, is an indictment of the aridity of our parents' era.

In both the haute couture and street fashion we see the torn, the ragged, the baggy, the drab.

In musical videos, time and time again, battered children move jerkily, stare bleakly, standing in scenes of rubble. The videos portray a fantasy of autism. They stage our view of ourselves as abused children – abandoned, beaten, so imbued with rage that we are incapable of movement, as if the slightest movement would unleash an anger so uncontrollable that it would destroy us, those around us, and the world. This fantasy of autism masks overpowering anger, as does our acceptance and ratification of the nonbook, the nonplay, the photorealist painting.

And so art, the social purpose of which is to *create*, has been pressed into service as a *censor*, whose purpose is to *control*. We are left with this spectrum of expression: the Radical, which seeks to destroy (blank canvases, graffiti art); the Liberal, which seeks to reform (plays, books, films about homosexuality, feminism – works about *conditions* rather than about *character*); the Conservative, which seeks to lull, to distract, to sentimentalize (E.T., the Muppets); the Fascist, which seeks to control and manipulate (Walt Disney World, Up with People).

This spectrum of our National Mentality, this one-party system, is not a conspiracy, but a *trend*. The trend expresses our deep wish to deny. The trend silences ferment, stills inquiry, and, at no point, allows the purpose of true art, the purpose of which is to *create*.

The absence of the urge to create is decadence.

A Family Vacation

My people have always been anxious about traveling. I think this dates back to the Babylonian Exile. In any case, when I was growing up, the smallest move was attended by fear, puttering, and various manifestations of nerves. My father and mother would fight, we would invariably get lost, we would miss meals, bedtimes, and destinations entirely.

My parents' fears took many convenient forms: fear of polio, of contamination from drinking fountains, of drowning from swimming too close on the heels of eating . . . all of these were just handy guises for the severest xenophobia, which I saw all around me as a child, in my home and my friends' homes.

Looking back, the fear of the strange that I saw around me is understandable, and I am only half kidding in referring to it as a cultural trait. My parents and the parents of my friends were one short generation removed from The Pale of Settlement in Russo-Poland: and to *their* parents the shortest trip away from home offered real possibilities of real trouble: difficulty of obtaining food acceptable to their religious laws, of confusion as to the local customs, of persecution and murder itself.

So this was the jolly burden which my parents inherited from their parents and passed down to me; and seventy years removed from the Cossacks I was still unable to take a vacation.

On our honeymoon, my wife and I went to Paris and I spent two days curled up on the bed. Yes, you will say, correctly, that probably had something to do with getting married – but isn't that a journey of a sort as well?

The above specious observation to the contrary notwithstanding, in eight years of marriage, and based on our informative experiences on the honeymoon, we have not really had a vacation.

But this year it occurred to both of us that we were not going to live forever, that our daughter was not forever going to stay a fascinating, loving, three-year-old, and that on our respective deathbeds we were going to be unlikely to say, 'I'm glad I advanced my career in 1986.'

So my wife, speaking not for herself, but for the Group, signed us up to take a vacation. A model husband, I, of course, agreed and congratulated her on her decision, knowing that as the time came to leave, I could find some pull of work that kept me at home, or at the very best, feign sickness, and failing that, I could actually *become* sick.

The last being a tactic I'd employed before and to advantage: '*You* girls go away, don't worry about me, go and refresh yourselves,' and then they'd go, and I could stretch out over the whole bed and smoke cigars in the living room.

But this time it was not to be. And, as the day set for departure drew near, I told my wife that I was heartbroken, but I could not accompany them; to which she replied that she had checked my datebook, and I had nothing scheduled for the week in question save a haircut appointment, which she had canceled for me; and that she had already told the kid how Daddy was going to come down for a week and 'not work.'

Well, I fought a holding action on the rectitude of her having unilaterally canceled my haircut appointment, and on the collateral issue of my well-known inability to enjoy myself when my hair is too long. To which arguments my wife responded, 'Tough,' and off we went to fun and frolic in the Caribbean surf.

On the way to the airport, the cabbie asked us why we were going to vacation on an island which was currently being decimated by a hurricane. I thought, Aha! The cavalry arrives. But my wife said, 'We're going down there to find out, and if it has not passed we'll just come home, and that's what we're going to do.' We prepared to get on the plane.

I explained to my wife that on the plane going down I was going to have to do research, and she said, 'Fine.' My research consisted of reading the galleys of a detective novel someone wanted to make into a movie, and my enjoyment of it would have been increased if she had resisted, but she did not. So I struggled through the book. My daughter watched *Romancing the Stone*, and my wife colored in the kid's coloring book for three and a half hours.

At the island we found that the hurricane had indeed passed, so I scowled and we went off to our hotel. We got to the hotel, and I braced for what the Semitic Traveler will of course recognize as the interlude of: I am here, I am paying good money, everything is wrong. Change everything immediately and make it different or I am going to die.

The bellman put the bags in the room, I open the doors to the patio beyond which was the sand beach and the Caribbean, and a football landed with a huge 'plop' in the water outside.

Fine, I thought, here I'm paying good money for some peace and quiet, and some overly American jock who can't leave home without his props is going to ruin my vacation.

Then as I watched, the football opened its wings and revealed itself to be a pelican which had just dived for a fish.

Okay, I thought, I'll try. And I did try. I changed into my suit and sat on the beach. I thought about Somerset Maugham and his sea stories. I thought about Joseph Conrad. I picked up a seashell and thought how very Victorian it looked, and wondered at the Multiplicity of Nature.

The sun went down, we put the baby to bed, and my wife and I went to dinner. We sat in a beautiful restaurant, hanging out on a cliff over the beach. There was a 'popping' sound below, like far-off fireworks. I looked and saw the sound was made by the undertow, dragging the stones behind it. I said, 'The stones on the beach being dragged sound like far-off fireworks.' My wife said nothing. I said, 'It occurs to me that the teaching of literature is completely *wrong*. Now: here we have a lovely simile – but the point is not the *simile* . . . the point is not the writer's knack at making a *comparison* – the point is the *stone*!'

My wife said, 'Why don't you take a vacation?'

Well, I had another drink, then I had *another* drink, then we went back to our room and we fell asleep, and I slept for eighteen hours on each of the next two days, and on the third day I wasn't thinking about Joseph Conrad anymore.

My daughter asked me to come out and make 'flour,' and rather than responding 'Just a minute' I went out and made flour. Making flour consisted of pouring sand into a palm leaf, and I was surprised to find it just as enjoyable as (and certainly more productive than) a business lunch at the Russian Tea Room.

The punch line was that we had a grand old time. We swam and went waterskiing, we had breakfast on the patio. The baby went naked on the beach for a week with a strand of beads around her neck, and her hair got bleached and streaked.

Some good friends were vacationing on a neighboring island, and they came over for a day and we all got drunk and went skinny-dipping in the moonlight; my daughter and I bounded on a trampoline a couple of hours every day; and all in all, it was the trip of a lifetime.

I thought: we are Urban people, and the Urban solution to most any problem is to do more: to find something new to eat in order to lose weight; to add a sound in order to relax; to upgrade your living arrangements in order to be comfortable; to buy more, to eat more, to do more business. Here, on the island, we had nothing to do. Everything had been taken away but the purely natural.

We got tired as the sun went down, and active when it rose; we were treated to the rhythm of the surf all day; the heat and the salt renewed our bodies.

We found that rather than achieving peace by the addition of a *new idea* (quality time, marital togetherness, responsibility), we naturally removed the noise and distractions of a too-busy life, and so had *no need* of a new idea. We found that a more basic idea sufficed: the unity of the family.

I did leave the island two days earlier than they, as I had to be in Los Angeles on business. As I got on the plane, I harbored a small secret joy at my forthcoming return to the addiction of busy life: I would have meetings and talk on the phone and lounge across the bed and smoke cigars in the hotel room.

I waved from the plane window and put my writer hat back on, and several thoughts occurred to me. The first was of Thorstein Veblen, who said that nobody traveling on a business trip would ever have been missed if he did not arrive. And I said to myself, you know, that's true.

And I thought Hippocrates, and his hospital on the island of Cos, where the sick were treated to a peaceful view, and warm winds, and the regenerative rhythm of the surf – to a place where man could be healed because the natural order was allowed to reassert itself; and I missed my family, and was very grateful for the week that we spent with each other on the beach.

Semantic Chickens

In our motion-picture theaters big black scary monsters interfere with white starlets.

Huge and persistent sharks devour tugboats.

Things burn, crumble, and/or are inundated with unpleasant amounts of water.

These are our world-destruction dreams. There is, in our dream life, no certainty. We objectify our insecurity and self-loathing in the form of outside forces endeavoring to punish us.

They may not know what we have done, but *we* do.

We turn on our television and we see one show after another glorifying our law-enforcement agencies.

We are an open book.

We propitiate those forces we elect to stave off, those who would take our electric ranges from out of our kitchenette.

We pay homage to the medical profession, glorifying them as superbeings capable of not only *understanding* the diseases of both the sick and worried, but of *caring* about them.

Surely we must be safe from terrors both of corporeal and social malefactors. The Cop on the Beat and the Doc in the ER protect us. Zeus is great.

Our tenuous monotheism disappears in the face of our great insecurities, and we live once again overtly in an animistic universe surrounded by superbeings.

There is no surety. What is the use of discrimination in a world where anything can happen?

Our magazines are full of photographs of naked men and women. Our pulp literature is the same tale told over and over again: the world is ending, only one man or woman (a spy, or a soldier, or a news reporter, or an ordinary citizen) possesses the ability to save it.

They tromp through the book and get laid and get hit on the head and save the world at the end and then they go home.

What are we telling ourselves through this popular culture?

Why are we, as a nation, and in the persons and through the abilities of our artists, constantly ending the world?

This is my question. Certainly, it indicates a great abiding and inchoate anger.

As Mr. Chayefsky told us so brilliantly in *Network*, we would like to say, 'We are mad as hell, and we aren't going to take it anymore.'

But we are going to take it, and we do take it, and we have a great amount of trouble expressing it because we don't trust words. Our anger is so great we can only blurt and stammer. Our semantic chickens have come to roost.

We have bought so many things labeled *improved* which were

only repackaged that we no longer believe that something *may*, in fact, be improved.

We have watched our constitutional government suborned by petty, hateful men and women sworn to obey the law, and we have heard them characterize their crimes as actions taken in the public interest. Consequently we have come to doubt that it is *possible* to act in the public interest.

My generation grew up in a time when constant vicious aggression publicly avowed came to be the norm of our foreign policy. We had changed the name of the Department of War to the Department of Defense, and went about making war continually and calling it defense until today we doubt if there *is* such a thing as defense, or if, in fact, the real meaning of defense is not 'aggression.'

We have come to accept all sorts of semantic inversions, just as George Orwell told us we would.

And now, overcome by information, decimated by anger and feeling completely impotent, we feel unequipped to do other than submit to whatever next atrocity chooses to take stage, be it another psychopathic public official or a giant ape.

But I wonder if this is necessary. I wonder how we can eliminate the boogeyperson from beneath the bed.

We are so ruled by magic. We have ceased to believe in logic. The cause to which we attribute so many effects is, thinly masked, our own inadequacy.

We take refuge in mumbo jumbo, in the Snake Oil of the Seventies, in escapism.

But the people must have what they want. If the people want trash, they will *have* trash. Trash at the movies, trash on stage, trash in the bookstore, trash in Office, trash at the supermarkets.

What can we do to overcome this habit of saying, in effect, things are not what they seem to be, but what we are told that they are?

A good first step might be to turn off the television sets.

(On a more serious note, after the catyclysm, be it giant ape or flash flood or tongue of newt or whatever, there will be no more television, neither will there – for a while – be a motion-picture 'industry.' There will be only human beings and the human urge to dramatize. There will be theater, and those who will be in the 'know' will be those who have sharpened their sensibilities through preholocaust attendance, so get out more.)

Another good idea would be to go to the theater when you feel the need of diversion. The theater, in the main, uses live personnel, and one can go backstage afterward and tell the actors and actresses and the director and writer, if they are around, that what you saw did not make sense, and recommend that they fix it.

For just as the purpose of the motion picture is the gradual revelation of the human genitalia, and the purpose of television is the support of several manufactories of small arms in Connecticut, just so the purpose of the theater is the making of sense.

To become very parochial, the purpose of the theater, as Stanislavsky said, is to bring to light the life of the human soul; and the theater, essentially and even today, possesses this potential. Alone among community institutions the theater possesses the power to differentiate between truth and garbage. We do not always acquit ourselves of our responsibility to the limits of our power, but we have the power. There are live people on stage and live people in the audience, and if the words and the actions do not come out even, everybody knows it – we may not always admit it, but we always know it. We have no helicopter shots, we have no EKGs, we have no press secretaries. We do not have to sell soap.

Perhaps if we went to the theater more we might learn to regain our faith in words. If we went and watched and listened and made some demands.

My premise is that things do mean things; that there is a way things *are* irrespective of the way we *say* things are, and if there isn't, we might as well act as if there were. 'And that's how it is on this bitch of an earth.'

Chicago

Chicago's literary history truly begins around the turn of the century with Alderman Bathhouse John Coughlin, coruler (with Hinky Dink Kenna) of the First Ward, Chicago's Downtown.

From Coughlin's 'Ode to a Bathtub':

Some find enjoyment in travel, others in Kodaking views.
Some take to automobiling in order themselves to amuse.
But for me there is only one pleasure, although you can call me a
  dub—
There's nothing to my mind can equal a plunge in a porcelain tub.

Fifty years later the ward found another champion in Richard J.
Daley – he is gone but he will never be forgotten – the man who
said, 'The police of the City of Chicago are not there to create
disorder, but to preserve the existing disorder.' Let it also be noted
that a previous mayor, Big Bill Thompson, once threatened to
punch the King of England in the nose, an un-Chicagoan sentiment,
as we have always been kind to visitors.

Hedda Gabler had its world premiere in Chicago, as Ibsen
couldn't get anybody to produce it at home. Ten blocks away and
twenty years later Al Capone ruled the city from his headquarters in
the Lexington Hotel.

J. J. Johnston, a Chicago actor, told me Al's wife was an Italian
girl, and that she was never accepted by her husband's family until
the day of his funeral. Overcome by grief she stood by the grave and
proclaimed, 'Al created an empire on earth, and he will build
another one in heaven.' After which she was accepted into the fold.

Dreiser worked on Wabash Avenue downtown, and he used to
eat at the Berghof Restaurant. Every time we went from the Goodman Theater over to the Berghof for lunch, I wondered if this was
the restaurant Hurstwood was managing when he met Sister Carrie. And when we rehearsed plays in the Fine Arts Building on
Michigan Avenue, I wondered if the woman practicing *sol-fe* could
have run into Lucy Gayheart (or at least Willa Cather) in the old
iron elevator.

(The woman was there when I started studying piano in 1951,
and she was there when we were rehearsing *Native Son* in 1980. I
see no reason she shouldn't have been there trying to hit that same
goddamned note in 1905.)

We have some strange local mythology.

Nobody makes gangster jokes or thinks of the city as particularly
violent (which it isn't). Yet we do make police jokes and take pride
in considering the force *haimishly* corrupt (which it isn't). And we

take *great* pride in our excellent fire department.

Robert Quinn, fire commissioner till just lately, was an old friend and crony of Mayor Daley. Their association went back to the days of the Hamburger Athletic Club in Bridgeport – Chicago's equivalent to having been there in the Oriente Mountains. So Quinn was fire commissioner forever.

In 1978 there was a furor because Quinn, rather than purchasing efficient, van-type paramedic ambulances, was still contracting for the old-fashioned low-slung Cadillacs. Interviewed on television news, he said, 'I think when the people of the City of Chicago do go, they want to go in *style*.' This caused something of a commotion, and the next night Quinn called a news conference to defend himself and explained, 'What I *meant* was the People of Chicago, when they *go*, they want to go in *style*.'

God bless our journalists. Carl Sandburg once wrote film reviews for the *Daily News* (Chicago's greatest newspaper – eight years now demised, and may it rest forever in peace and in our memories). Dreiser was a drama critic in town; Hecht and MacArthur worked for City News Service; Nelson Algren was a reporter, as was Vachel Lindsay, our finest poet Midwesterner.

Lindsay was writing of Bryan's campaign visit to Springfield, Illinois, but he might as well have been writing of Chicago:

> She wore in her hair a brave prairie rose.
> Her Gold friends cut her, for that was not the pose.
> No Gibson Girl would wear it in that fresh way.
> But we were fairy Democrats, and this was our day.

In our beloved Windville we curse the cold and revel in being the most senseless spot in North America to spend the winter in. But the air feels new, and all things still seem possible, as they did to Willa Cather and Sherwood Anderson and Willard Motley and Hemingway and Frank Norris and Saul Bellow and all the other Chicago writers who – when speaking of Home – finally wrote the same story. It was and is a story of possibility, because the idea in the air is that the West is beginning, and that life is capable of being both understood and enjoyed.

Those writers exhorted us, as did their philosophical confrere Alderman Hinky Dink Kenna – Bathhouse John's partner in crime:

'Whatever the endeavor, make of it a lollopalooza.'

With thanks to Chicago historians
MARK JACOBS and KENAN HEISE.

On Paul Ickovic's Photographs

I have always felt that people look on me as an outcast – that the simple request for a cup of coffee elicits a slight tightening around the eyes.

I have always felt like an outsider; and I am sure that the suspicion that I perceive is the suspicion that I provoke by my great longing to *belong*.

I would like to live a life free of constant self-examination – a life which may be ruled by the processes of guilt, remorse, hope, and anxiety, but one in which those processes themselves are not foremost in the mind.

I would like to belong to a world dedicated to creating, preserving, achieving, or simply getting by. But the world of the outsider, in which I have chosen to live, and in which I have trained myself to live, is based on none of those things. It is based on observation.

The habit of constant *acute* awareness can be seen in animals with no recourse, with no option to fight, with no margin for error. It is the habit of one completely dependent on the vagaries and good will of his environment. It is the habit of the young child. Historically, it is the habit of the Jew.

As the children of immigrant Jews, we are spurred in our need to observe by the memory of old humiliations, of old indignities. We are spurred by the learned and enforced pleasures of isolation and reflection.

Trained to live by our wit, to live on margin – trained not to assimilate, we have found useless the virtues of compromise with our environment. And so our lives are a fierce attempt to find an aspect of the world that is not open to interpretation.

True to our past, we live and work with an inherited, observed, and accepted vision of personal futility, and of the beauty of the world.

A Playwright in Hollywood

I am a playwright, which is to say that what I have done with most of my time for most of my adult life is sit by myself, talk to myself, and write the conversation down.

This year I was hired to write a screenplay, and what had been – for better and worse – the most private of occupations became a collaborative endeavor.

I have never been much good as a team player or employee, and it was difficult for me to adjust to a situation where 'because I say so' was insufficient explanation.

When you write for the stage you retain the copyright. The work is *yours* and no one can change a word without your permission. When you write for the screen you are a *laborer* hired to turn out a product, and that product can be altered at the whim of those who employ you.

When the meaning of the script is unclear in the theater, the actors and director usually assume that the author knew what he or she was doing, and they reapply themselves to understanding the script.

In the movies if the meaning and the worth of the script is not immediately obvious, everyone assumes the writer has failed.

That was the hard part of working in the movies; and if you have ever tried to explain why a joke you have just told actually *is* funny you know what I'm talking about.

One of the good things, on the other hand, about a year spent as an employee is that I received a lesson in consistency.

Most playwrights are acquainted with the basic rules of dramaturgy, and most of us – from time to time – cheat.

If the action of a character in one scene, for example, is to FLEE THE COUNTRY, we know that a good way to start would be by having him LEAVE THE ROOM. But most of us are loath to eliminate the moving 'Death of my Kitten' speech the hero utters on his exit.

The necessary progression is:

TANIA: Franz, the Army of the Reds is in the Village Square, and you must leave.
FRANZ: See you in Bucharest. (*He exits*)

But we lie to ourselves, hoping that no one will notice the interruption of the action, and the scene is written:

TANIA: Franz, the Army of the Reds is in the Village Square, and you must leave.
FRANZ: Leave? Leave? How *many* ways there are to leave! When I was young I had a kitten . . . (*etc.*)

'Yes,' we say, 'it's not consistent, but it sure is pretty. Why should I be bound by the rules of dramaturgy when no one knows them but me, and *my* understanding of them is by no means perfect?'

The rule in question here is Aristotle's notion of unity of action: in effect, that the play should be about only one thing, and that that thing should be *what the hero is trying to get*.

Unstinting application of this rule makes great plays because the only thing we, as audience, care about in the theater is WHAT HAPPENS NEXT?

All of us writers know this but few of us do it.

We don't do it because it is too difficult.

It is much easier to write great dialogue (which is a talent and not really very much of an exertion) than to write great plots. So we playwrights do the next best thing to writing great plots: we write *bad* plots. And then we fill up the empty spaces with verbiage. Or we assign interesting attributes to the characters so that the audience will care about them. (In the thirties a popular attribute was Great Wealth. In the fifties it was Lower-Class Background. In the seventies and the eighties it was Physical Handicap or Deformity.)

These attributes are super, but the only thing we want to know when our friends come back from the theater is, 'What's it about?' We do not ask, 'Are there heartwarming or compelling types involved who make me cry?'

Working in the movies taught me (for the moment, anyway) *to stick to the plot and not to cheat.*

Now we Americans have always considered Hollywood, at best, a sinkhole of depraved venality. And, of course, it is. It is not a Protective Monastery of Aesthetic Truth. It is a place where everything is incredibly expensive.

The movie is costing $100,000 a day to film. So it's not too bright to write a beautiful scene which impedes the plot, as, when the film is being cut and the editor has to get the turkey down from two hours fifteen minutes to two hours flat, the beautiful scene that impedes the plot is going to fall on the floor, and the writer has just wasted $100,000.

Hollywood's interest in economy took me back to early days in the theater.

When we put on plays in garages and in church basements everything used in the show was borrowed, stolen, or, as a last resort, purchased out of the cabdriving or waitressing wages of the company members.

This healthy relationship to financial necessity made for good theater because only that was put upon the stage which was unquestionably essential to the production.

Another instructive aspect of financial necessity which I rediscovered in the movies was an abiding concern for the audience.

In garage theater if you aren't funny they *don't come.*

This principle does not seem to be in force on Broadway, but it does apparently operate in the movies.

In an attempt to get the audience to buy their popcorn *before* the show, Bob Rafelson (*Postman's* director and my sponsor in Hollywood) quizzed me about my screenplay relentlessly, and what he asked was this: *can it be better?*

When people have been calling you an Artist for a number of years your personal acquaintance with this question can fall into desuetude.

My work in a collaborative situation where I could not say 'It's perfect. Act it' was a healthy tonic.

It reassured me about my ability to solve problems, and also about my ability to get along with people. The film's production people are pleased with themselves – not only do they have a good script, but they took a chance to get it; they have made a 'discovery.'

So that is my success story: someone felt it would be more rewarding to teach an artist a new technique than to attempt to induce a hack to be interesting, and everybody went home happy.

There is a *vast* amount of talent in this country's theater – in the small theaters of Chicago, Boston, New York, Louisville, and Seattle, especially. Theatrical artists in these and other cities are working. They are acting, designing, directing, and writing plays constantly. Because they live in an atmosphere fairly free of commercial pressure, they have no need either to withhold their skills from the marketplace to drive up the price, or to pander to mercantile aesthetics; so they are developing their skills, their point of view, and their talent.

Traditionally the movies industry has developed this talent by demonstrating to it how much better a Mercedes handles than a Chevy.

Collaborating with, rather than exploiting, this talent would make our Friday nights at the movies a lot more diverting.

It wouldn't be that difficult to do. It wouldn't even call for altruism on the part of the producers – just a little creative venality.

I have, personally, profited in several ways from my sojourn in Hollywood. I am going back to work on a new play with, I admit, a slight residual attitude of 'Who *knew*? We all thought they were summer camps'; and I look forward to doing another movie.

Oscars

We live in a world ruined by Reason.

If you take the faith out of Religion, you have a wasted Sunday morning. If you take the belief out of Law, all you have is litigation. And if you take the Ritual out of celebration, all you have is Presidents' Day.

Presidents' Day is a bastard amalgamation of the birthdays of George Washington and Abe Lincoln. Where once we had two distinct and spontaneously created national rituals, all we have is an extra day of leisure.

Each of these two presidential celebrations arose for a reason. One celebrated our own espousal of the virtues of dull honesty; one mourned the passing of a great soul.

But no paper cutout silhouettes are made for Presidents' Day, and no addresses are memorized and delivered, and no more is the bizarre story of the cherry tree retold. Reason has been applied and our Rich Uncle has awarded us another day off in the interest of increased productivity.

We do not arise from Presidents' Day refreshed; and we do not ask, as we ask at Passover, 'Why is this night different from all other nights?' It isn't.

If you apply Reason to the Wake you might say, 'Why bother, he's dead *anyway*.' But the naturally evolved use of Abe Lincoln's birthday was a reminder that there are qualities which we may strive to emulate which are both excellent and lovely. And now the celebration of Abe's birthday is no more.

As we have lost our barbershops and pool halls, our cousins clubs and fraternal organizations, so we have forsworn our rejuvenating rituals.

Only two legitimate national holidays remain. By 'legitimate' holidays, I mean this: holidays with a specific, naturally evolved meaning, the celebrations of which we find refreshing and correct, and in the celebration of which we, as a People, are united. Those holidays are the Super Bowl and the Academy Awards.

The Super Bowl, it seems to me, is a celebration of our national love of invidious comparison. We Americans love to find out if A is better than B, for – having located them on the Great Chain of Being – we are permitted to find points of goodness in both. To show fealty to the one and compassion to the other.

Having come the long way around the barn: what of the Oscars? I have enjoyed, looked forward to, and watched them for over thirty years. I have participated in them twice: once as a nominee, and once as backstage wife. In all capacities, I have found them fascinating and refreshing – different, distinct, different from all other days, delineating a set period – a true ritual whose meaning and forms have arisen from a mutual cultural necessity.

It is the physical and emotional exigencies of a ritual which reveal – much more than the verbal formula – the ritual's true meaning.

It is not written, but it is generally understood that the groom is supposed to be nervous and to wonder if he has lost the ring. He is buoyed up by the calm of the best man, who *himself* is somewhat anxious lest he lose the ring. So, as the close male friendship is partially dissolved in favor of marriage, the best man is consoled by being allowed both to share in the anxiety of his friend and to stand superior to his friend's display of emotion. The ritual eases parting through affirmation of the close tie and reassurance that the best man's life will continue in spite of his loss.

At the Oscars, we participants anxiously wonder: have I given the Academy the correct hotel address to which to deliver the tickets? Will they arrive in time? Should I put them in the safe? Will they be stolen? Do I really want another carafe of fresh orange juice, or am I just ordering it because the studio is paying for it and I want to punish them for subjecting me to this ordeal?

In the limousine, we cannot fathom why in the world we have left the hotel so early and what we will do with the extra time. As we approach the Pavillion, we wonder if we can possibly push through the traffic and arrive at all.

We find ourselves making stupid, predictable, and conventional remarks to those around us; *especially* to those in authority. And, childlike, we have broadened our definition of authority to include anyone who controls or directs us at the present moment: the limousine chauffeur, the desk clerk, the ticket taker. Reason has been suspended and we have regressed. We are no longer self-determined individuals, we have become children. In spite of ourselves, Ritual has evolved and enveloped us. We are once again part of the Tribe.

What do the Oscars mean? On some reflection, I think they mean this: they are a celebration of the power of the will of the people.

The Oscars demonstrate the will of the people to control and judge those they have elected to stand above them (much, perhaps, as in bygone days, an election celebrated the same).

The constituency of the moviemaker is the Entire Country. Everyone goes to the movies, and when we purchase a ticket, we make a sacrifice – a token but nonetheless real gesture of subservience. We make this gesture again in accepting the Movie Greats' enjoyment of their own prerogatives. When we read of their loves, their incomes, their foibles, their crimes, we shrug and smile, and, in so doing, we commit an act of subservience – we cede to others the ability to transgress the norms we have set up for ourselves.

At the Oscar ceremony, we, as people, compel those we have permitted into a privileged class to stand alone and hear the verdict. We, for one night, strip them of their privileges. And, just as in any court, the verdict itself is less important to the community than the power to summon. Just as at a court of law, the accused (the Oscar nominees) are compelled to hold themselves in a state of anxiety, nervous anticipation, and fear, and suffer the verdict passed on them.

Out in the audience, the Great, lured by the offer of a final laurel, hold themselves in fear of the unknown and are reduced to uttering magic incantations, to wit: 'It's an honor just to be nominated'; 'I knew I was going to lose'; 'Oh, why did I prepare a speech? I know that's going to blow it for me,' etc.

We, the American public convened as a tribe, see the faces of these muttering nominees. And we see that they are finally just mortal folks who must bear their losses stoically and be graceful in victory – just like us. We force the Great – just as they forced Caesar – to sue the Crown, and we see that, by Jove, they *do* sue for it. How about that?

The Oscars are a kind of Purim. We, at home – no less than the gawkers behind the police barricades – are there to make fun of the Rabbi: 'Oh, God, did you see her dress? ...' 'I heard he's gay ...' 'See how nervous he is ...' 'His movie was a bust and he's death at the box office ...' Why is she nervous? Doesn't she know she's never going to win?' We are united as a community in that most satisfying and unifying of social activities – gossip – the purpose of which is to define social norms. And, just as in another time we might have met around the cracker barrel, we are meeting around the TV to talk about them folks who live up on the hill. The Oscars are rather a beautiful ritual, I think. They celebrate both secrecy – devotion to tradition, and surprise – the healthy fear of God.

What would the Oscars be without the presence of the two men from Price Waterhouse? Every year their office as protectors of the faith erodes, and the traditional formula of the reading of the rules for balloting is made fun of. But, more important than the fact that it is mocked, is the fact that it is still there. The Oscars would not be quite right without Price Waterhouse. Why? Because those two ritualistically dumpy men assure us that – in spite of the vast rewards to be gained by irregularity – our interests as a people are being protected. There still may be a surprise winner, God and the Devil still exist.

The ritualistically awful quality of the entertainment seems to proclaim this: that the true purpose of the event is not the celebration of excellence, but the celebration of ordeal.

The traditional confusion, sarcasm, or stupidity of the Presenters is a disclaimer on their part of participation in the ordeal at hand ('Don't confuse me with tonight's potential victims. I am so far from their anxiety – as you see – that I don't even know what's going on here'). The presenters – lured by the offer of mass publicity – are also there to witness the power of the pageant and to educate themselves in the correct behavior of the victims.

When one is nominated for but passed over by the Academy Awards, one is told this: 'It's a great honor just to be nominated.' And, of course, it is, for it means that one has been tapped out as powerful, and, as such, elected to make a pledge to the people.

When the winner is revealed, he is expected to reveal himself – to be reduced to humility or confusion by the great honor done him. And, having left the podium, the winner is expected to display either giddy abandon or discernible ambition. Either one will do. Much as, among the four or five nominees, anyone will do.

And any winner will do. We'll cheer Our Side if they win, and we'll curse if we lose, they're both equally enjoyable. Also enjoyable is this: The Oscars are a final verdict. They have an end, and – much as Lent does – they mark the end of a period which now will begin anew. What a lovely ceremony, and how flattering that society has elected Motion Picture Art to be the backdrop for it.

The wake probably began as an attempt to capture a few last moments with the spirit of the departed. A more important function emerged – the comfort of the widow. This function is so important, so powerful (for it blesseth him that gives and him that takes) that it must be masked. Just so, the Oscars began as an in-house ceremony of appreciation. They have evolved into The Big Bar Mitzvah. Like that more senior ceremony, they command a demonstration of subservience to the will of the Tribe.

This once-a-year ritual obeisance to tribal will is as important for those inside the movie industry as it is for those outside.

Just as on that day in England, when the masters and the staff change clothes, it reminds the masters that there *is* a limit, and that God has not damned them for omnipotent power. On that day, the masters get, for a moment, to live in that envied state of being 'just folks.'

The moviemakers are made to stand review on television; and then cleansed, held for a moment between one period and the next. Forgiven, shriven, if you will, they all tromp off to the Governors' Ball at the Beverly Hilton Hotel. There they eat chicken and dance with each other's wives. Much as they might at an automobile awards banquet in Detroit. They have served the people and now they are entitled to be refreshed.

If I were of a hortatory bent, I would suggest we put the gossip and philosophy back into the courts of law, Bert Parks back into the Miss America Pageant, and strike off Presidents' Day from our too-sad calendar.

But as Spengler reminds us, we may not have chosen to live in this unfortunate time, but nobody asked us. As it is, I am thankful for the Oscars. As an American, I thoroughly enjoy the ritual. As a sometimes-member of the film industry, I am proud that my group has been chosen to stand as acolytes.

Pool Halls

The novel *The Hustler* is set in a Chicago poolroom called 'Benn-ingtons,' pool-shooting capital of the world.

The actual name of the Chicago poolroom was Bensinger's. The Bensinger family owned Brunswick Corporation. Brunswick held, and perhaps still holds, the copyright on the word 'pool,' which is a trademark name for pocket billiards, and I used to play pocket billiards at Bensinger's in Chicago.

The pool hall I played at was not quite the one immortalized in the novel. A postwar cleanup of Chicago's Downtown Area eradicated much of the demimonde living there, and the passing of the railroads took care of the rest.

When I was a habitué, Bensinger's had moved from Randolph

Street up to the North Side, and its sign said that it was called Clark and Diversey Billiards, but the clientele, of course, still called it Bensinger's.

The pool hall opened, if memory serves, at eleven o'clock in the morning. And that was a wonderful time to arrive, especially in the summer, when Chicago was hot. You'd come out of the glare and the concrete-trapped heat, down a long flight of stairs, and there you were in this dark cavern.

In the cavern were forty pool tables, six three-cushion-billiard tables, snooker tables, a separate exhibition room, a bar, and a short-order kitchen. So there you are. It's eleven o'clock of a hot morning, you walk through the louvered doors and are greeted by Bob Siegel, who either did or did not own the place. Bob had been a postman, and remembered everybody's name that he had ever met. So if you'd been there every day since the Downtown Days, or if you'd been in once ten years ago, when you came by he greeted you by name, and he'd say 'regular table?' and you'd say 'yes,' and he'd hand you the tray with the balls on it, and you'd say 'I'm going on sixteen,' or whatever table you were particularly enamored of in that period, and he'd nod, and you'd start off to your table.

Then – here comes the best part – you would say – over your shoulder – 'would you send *John* over with a cup of *coffee*, please?' and Bob would say 'sure thing.' So you walk back to table sixteen or table seventeen far in the back of the hall. Everything is brown, the light is brown, the tables are brown, the oak benches are brown, the air is brown but it's cool. And you arrange your book, or your hat, or your newspaper on the bench next to your table, and you turn on the light over the table, and you spill the balls out of the tray and onto the table with a jerk of the wrists; when you do it right, they hardly bounce at all, and they don't hurt the surface. Then you kind of fling the tray under the table and you sit down on the bench.

Now the thing is if you're going to have a cigarette before your coffee comes, and, of course, you are, and so you light your Camel, or your Lucky, maybe the pack's crumpled, and maybe it's the last cigarette from last night. You light it and you're in the Perfect Place.

People are supposed to gamble here, people are supposed to drink here, people are supposed to spend their days here in pursuit of skill, cunning, comradeship, and money. No one is supposed to be pompous here, or intrusive, or boring; no one will be held unaccountable for the bets they make, or the way that they comport themselves. But if they choose, they can choose to be left alone.

Well, there I am getting high on my first cigarette, or however it felt, getting cool down in the basement. There's the click of a couple of guys shooting pool back near the entrance. John brings my cup of coffee, and I say 'thank you.' He asks me if I want breakfast, and I tell him 'thank you, yes, a little later . . .'

Several years later, and in the last years of Mayor Daley's life, there was a pool hall called The Golden Eight Ball, down off Rush Street on Walton, and it had Muzak, and orange-yellow felt on the tables, and it was decorated. You could find businessmen there, and young couples on a fun date, and it lasted for a couple of years, and then it was gone.

Just as Bensinger's was gone. In the mid-seventies, the neighborhood got a tad too upscale, and all us warbabies needed somewhere to live, and so there went the neighborhood.

On Clark and Diversey where once an American could shoot pool for an hour in the summer and then dash across the street to the Parkway Cinema and catch a double feature at the before-twelve price of seventy-five cents (program changed thrice-weekly, hard to believe, but it's true), now there were candle stores, and restaurants with cunning names, and the beautiful 3,500-seat Century Movie Palace gutted to house a shopping mall.

Bensinger's moved again, down the street and up a flight of stairs over a record store. There were ten tables and Bob Siegel kept apologizing that they hadn't got the carpet in, so one had to stand on concrete all day long.

Bob, of course, never got the carpet in before the place got closed, a year or so later, and then there was nowhere to go.

Similarly in New York, on Eighth Avenue amid the girlie peep shows, you could walk down two flights into McGirr's Pool Hall and there the same setup, minus the bar and grill; and people were selling dope and people were selling stolen merchandise and booking horses over the telephone and shooting a little pool into the bargain, and, around 1980, they closed that one down, too; they opened on Seventy-ninth and Broadway in New York, which currently is a Rug Warehouse. My question is where are the pool halls? And the answer is they're gone.

There is one on the main street in Gloucester, Massachusetts, and I went in there one day and tipped the guy five dollars to disconnect the video games for one hour so I could shoot pool in peace. After the hour was up, he was pressured from the teenagers and he wouldn't renew my deal, so I packed up and left.

There used to be a pool hall in the airport in Detroit, which I thought was the most civilized accoutrement I could imagine for an airport, and very advanced. It may still be there. And there was a pool hall downstate Illinois where they took a lot of money from me while I was waiting for a train to get me out of downstate Illinois one time.

But, basically, I think we have to say they're gone.

The point was not to play pool. One can do that, to a certain extent, in the Family Billiard Centers one sees stuck now and then in the Concrete Suburbs. And dads go there to have some sort of fun with their progeny. But the point of the pool hall was not fun. The point of the pool hall was the intersection of two American Loves: the Game of Skill and the Short Con.

The denizens of the pool hall came in to practice their skill, and the transients were those upon which the skill was practiced.

So you had to be near a transient neighborhood; you had to be in a neighborhood in transition; you had to be near the railroad.

Well, I guess that America is gone. We no longer revere skill, and the short con of the pool hustle and the Murphy Man and the Fuller Brush Man. The short con, which flourished in a life lived on the street and among strangers, has been supplanted by the Big Con of a life with no excitement in it at all.

You see the clunky old elephant-legged pool tables from those old pool halls for sale from time to time, refinished, lovely leather puckɛtɔ, heautiful new felt; and you might have a fantasy of taking them and housing them sʋmɛplaɛɔ, ɔnd that's what happened to the Country-at-Large: we turned America into a Den. Whɛrɛ sɔuld you be more wonderfully alone than in those old pool halls? You could sit there all day and no one would bother you except the occasional guy come over to say 'shoot a game of eight-ball. Split the time?' and you'd say 'no,' thank God, and you could stay all day.

You could sit there and drink your coffee and go find the good House cue where you hid it up behind the ventilator (where you'd have to sort through the *other* House sticks that everyone *else* hid up behind the ventilator) and you'd shoot a little pool.

If you got hungry, you could raise your head and John would come over and you'd order breakfast and a *Daily News*, and maybe another pack of Camels.

Later you could amble to the bar, where they would have the Cubs (who played three blocks away) on the TV, and have a beer. Bob would call over 'time off, Dave?' and you'd say 'yeah, time off.'

One night in the Exhibition Room, Sr. Juan Navarro, billed as Billiards Champion of the World, ran any number of straight-rail billiards, shot left-handed, made a billiard shooting *from one table to the next*. One night at the joint on Seventy-ninth Street me and a friend got lured from a nine-ball game where we had beat the local hustler, and he got us into the backroom and involved in a crap game where he cleaned us out with Shapes. One night I beat a guy in eight-ball at a bar, and he paid up and later followed me out into the night, until I turned around and looked at him, and I could see that he was just confused.

The best times were the days – the late mornings and the afternoons away from the world in a pool hall. 'Let everything else revolve,' you would think, 'I've gone fishin'. I am nowhere to be found. I am nowhere. No one can find me here.'

Things I have Learned Playing Poker on the Hill

In twenty years of playing poker, I have seen very few poor losers.

Poker is a game of skill and chance. Playing poker is also a masculine ritual, and, most times, losers feel either sufficiently chagrined or sufficiently reflective to retire, if not with grace, at least with alacrity.

I have seen many poor winners. Most are eventually brought back to reality. The game itself will reveal to them that they are the victim of an essential error: they have attributed their success to divine intervention.

The poor winner is celebrating either God's good sense in sending him down lucky cards, or God's wisdom in making him, the lucky winner, technically superior to the others at the table. In the first case, the cards will eventually begin to even out and the player will lose; in the second case, both the Deity and the players will tire of being patronized. The Deity will respond how he may, but the players will either drop out of the game or improve. In either case the poor winner will lose, and pride, once again, will go before a fall.

Speaking of luck: is there such a thing as luck? Yes. There is such a thing as luck. There is such a thing as a *run of luck*. This is an instructive insight I have gained from poker – that all things have a rhythm, even the most seemingly inanimate of statistics.

Any mathematician will tell you that the cards at the poker table are distributed randomly, that we remember the remarkable and forget the mundane, and that 'luck' is an illusion.

Any poker player knows – to the contrary – that there are phenomenal runs of luck which defy any mathematical explanation – there are periods in which one cannot catch a hand, and periods in which one cannot *not* catch a hand, and that there *is* such a thing as absolute premonition of cards: the rock-bottom *surety* of what will happen next. These things happen in contravention of scientific wisdom and common sense. The poker player learns that sometimes both science and common sense are wrong; that the bumblebee *can* fly; that, perhaps, one should never trust an expert; that there are more things in heaven and earth than are dreamt of by those with an academic bent.

It is comforting to know that luck exists, that there is a time to push your luck and a time to gracefully retire, that all roads have a turning.

What do you do when you are pushing your luck beyond its limits? You must behave like a good philosopher and ask what axiom you must infer that you are acting under. Having determined that, you ask if this axiom, in the long run, will leave you a winner. (You are drawing to a flush. You have a 1-in-4½ chance. The pot is offering you money odds of 5 to 1. It seems a close thing, but if you did it all day, you must receive a 10 percent return.)

If the axiom which you are acting under is not designed to make you money, you may find that your real objective at the game is something else: you may be trying to prove yourself beloved of God. You then must ask yourself if – financially and emotionally – you can afford the potential rejection. For the first will certainly and the second will most probably ensue.

Poker is boring. If you sit down at the table to experience excitement, you will consciously and subconsciously do those things to make the game exciting; you will take long-odds chances and you will create emergencies. They will lose you money. If your aim, on the other hand, is to win money, you will watch the game and wait for the good cards, and play the odds-on chance, and, in the long run, you must be a winner. And when you do *not* win, you can still go home without mumbling, for, as Woodrow Wilson said: 'I would rather lose in a cause which will eventually prevail than triumph in a cause doomed to failure.' (I'll bet that most of you didn't even know he was a poker player.)

Playing poker you must treat each hand, as Epictetus says, as a visit to the Olympic Games, each hand offering you the chance to excel in your particular event – betting, checking, managing your money, observing the players, and, most often, waiting.

The poker players I admire most are indeed like that wise old owl who sat on the oak and who kept his mouth shut and his eyes on the action.

As for observation, Confucius said man cannot hide himself – look what he smiles at, look what he frowns at. The inability to hide is especially true of men under pressure, which is to say, gamblers. This is another reason for stoic and correct play.

When you are proud of having made the correct decision (that is, the decision which, in the long run, *must* eventually make you a winner), you are inclined to look forward to the results of that decision with some degree of impassivity. When you are so resolved, you become less fearful and more calm. You are less interested in yourself and more naturally interested in the other players: now *they* begin to reveal themselves. Is their nervousness feigned? Is their hand made already? Are they bluffing? These elections are impossible to make when you are afraid, but become easier the more content you are with your own actions. And, yes, sometimes you lose, but differences of opinion make both horse races and religious intolerance, and if you don't like to take a sporting chance, you don't have to play poker.

Poker will also reveal to the frank observer something else of import – it will teach him about his own nature.

Many bad players will not improve because they cannot bear self-knowledge. Finally, they cannot bear the notion that everything they do is done for a reason. The bad player will not deign to determine what he thinks by watching what he does. To do so might, and frequently would, reveal a need to be abused (in calling what must be a superior hand); a need to be loved (in staying for 'that one magic card'); a need to have Daddy relent (in trying to bluff out the obvious best hand); et cetera.

It is painful to observe this sort of thing about oneself. Many times we'd rather suffer on than fix it. It's not easy to face that, rather than playing cards in spite of our losses, we are playing cards because of them.

But poker is a game played among folks made equal by their money. Each player uses it to buy his time at the table, and, while there, is entitled to whatever kind and length of enjoyment that money will buy.

The pain of losing is diverting. So is the thrill of winning. Winning, however, is lonelier, as those you've taken money from are not likely to commiserate with you. Winning takes some getting used to.

Many of us, and most of us from time to time, try to escape a blunt fact which may not tally with our self-image. When we are depressed, we re-create the world around us to rationalize our mood. We are then likely to overlook or misinterpret happy circumstances. At the poker table, this can be expensive, for opportunity may knock, but it seldom nags. Which brings us to a crass thought many genteel players cannot grasp; poker is about money.

The ability of a poker player is judged solely by the difference between his stack when he sat down and his stack when he got up. The point is not to win the most hands, the point is not even to win in the most games. The point is to *win the most money.* This probably means playing less hands than the guy who has just come for the action; it means not giving your fellow players a break because you value their feelings; it means not giving some back at the end of the night because you feel embarrassed by winning; it means taking those steps and creating those habits of thought and action which, in the long run, must prevail.

The long run for me – to date – has been a period of twenty years.

One day in college I promoted myself from the dormitory game to the *big* poker game Up on the Hill in town.

After graduation I would, occasionally, come back to the area to visit. I told myself my visits were to renew friendships, to use the library, to see the leaves. But I was really coming back to play in the Hill game.

Last September one of the players pointed out that five of us at the table that night had been doing this for two decades.

As a group, we have all improved. Some of us have improved drastically. As the facts, the statistics, the tactics are known to all, and as we are men of equal intelligence, that improvement can be due to only one thing: to character, which, as I *finally* begin to improve a bit myself, I see that the game of poker is all about.

III
LIFE IN THE THEATER

Epitaph for Tennessee Williams

The theater is a beautiful life but a harsh business. Just as the price of gold represents the thousands of unproductive work-hours spent seeking it, artistic fame and remuneration – though awarded to the individual – represent society's debt to many.

That debt, though it may be paid quite gratefully, is rendered as a conditional trust rather than a perpetual freehold. It is subject to being withdrawn so that it may be awarded to another.

The pressure this creates to continually achieve makes play-writing a young man's game, for it is easily tolerated only by the inspired and naive – by those bursting with the joy of discovery and completely, unselfconsciously generous of that gift.

This generosity and superfluity of life compelled the public to Tennessee Williams's writing, and when his life and view of life became less immediately accessible, our gratitude was changed to distant reverence for a man whom we felt obliged – if we were to continue in our happy feelings toward him – to consider already dead.

His continued being and the fact of his later work disturbed our illusion; and we were embarrassed as our unease was hidden neither from ourselves nor from its subject, Tennessee. And we were piqued as he seemed neither to contest nor shun this attitude. He just kept writing.

We are a kind people living in a cruel time. We don't know how to show our love. This inability was the subject of his plays, the greatest dramatic poetry in the American language.

We thank him and we wish him, with love, the best we could have done and did not while he was alive. We wish him what he wished us; the peace that we all are seeking.

Regarding a Life in the Theater

Thorstein Veblen wrote that typesetters were given to alcoholism in the 1880s because they belonged to a profession which was mobile and unstable.

They would switch jobs often, as the need for their services arose in some other town or part of the country; and they *could* switch jobs often, as their skill was much in demand, and their equipment was their talent only.

They had no investment in machinery, stock, or goodwill, and moved as the need for employment or change arose.

In a new locale the typesetters would seek out their own kind. After a day of work they would congregate in pubs or restaurants near work and socialize.

The only means they had for displaying their worth to each other were *social* means: conviviality, liberality, wit, good nature.

So they drank and talked, and the excellent man was one who could drink much, buy many rounds, and talk interestingly of the exploits of himself and others in the confraternity. The typesetter had no goods. He could not display excellence through the splendor of his carriage or his home.

He had no history except that which he invented for himself and could substantiate through bluff or humor.

He traveled light and carried few clothes, and so could not impress others by his wardrobe.

He could only establish his excellence through his social habits.

So he drank a lot.

Excellence in the theater is the art of giving things away.

The excellent actor strives not to *fix*, to codify, but to *create* for the moment, freely, without pausing either to corroborate what he or she has done or to appreciate the creation.

(This is why theatrical still photographs are many times stiff and uninteresting – the player in them is not *acting*, which is what he or she is trained and, perhaps, born to do, but *posing* – *indicating feelings* – which is the opposite of acting.)

A life in the theater is a life spent giving things away.

It is a life mobile, unstable, unsure of employment, of acceptance.

The future of the actor is made uncertain not only by chance, but by necessity – *intentionally.*

Our problems – like the problems of any professional group – are unique.

Our theatrical drolleries, necessities, and peculiarities may be diverting to others, but they are fascinating to ourselves.

The question of who did what to *whom*, who forgot his lines, what the producer said to the propman, who got and lost what part to whom and *why* ('This is the *real* story. I was *there*') is the endless interesting inquiry.

We in the theater tell stories about and on ourselves and our colleagues, and these stories are exactly the same ones Aristophanes told to and on his friends. They are attributed to different personalities, but the stories are the same. The problems and the rewards are the same.

It is important to tell and retell stories, as the only real history of the ephemeral art is an oral history; everything fades very quickly, and the only surety is the word of someone who was there – who *talked* to someone who was there, who vouches for the fact that someone told him she had spoken to a woman who knew someone who was there.

It all goes very quickly, too.

Apprenticeship becomes rewarded with acceptance or rejection. This seems to happen overnight, and the event we have decided on as the turning point in a career was, looking back, quite probably not it at all.

A life in the theater is a life with the attention directed outward, and memory and the substantiation of others is very important.

We acquire skills through constant practice. They accrue in increments so small that we seem to be making no progress. We lose competence in the same way – taking for granted our hard-won habits and barely aware they are leaving us.

At the end of a performance, or the end of a season, the only creation the performer has left is him- or herself. This, and artifacts: clippings, programs.

Which is, perhaps, one reason we love stories.

'Do you remember . . .?' also must mean, '*I* remember. *Don't* I?'

At the Neighborhood Playhouse School of the Theatre, Sanford Meisner said, 'When you go into the professional world, at a stock

theater somewhere, backstage, you will meet an older actor –
someone who has been around awhile.

'He will tell you tales and anecdotes about life in the theater.

'He will speak to you about your performance and the performances of others, and he will generalize to you, based on his experience and his intuitions, about the laws of the stage. Ignore this
man.'

Not only do these people exist, but as one continues a theatrical
career, one has a tendency to turn into them. At least I find that I
do.

We certainly all need love. We all need diversion, and we need
friendship in a world whose limits of commitment (a most fierce
commitment) is most times the run of the play.

Camus says that the actor is a prime example of the Sisyphean
nature of life.

This is certainly true, and certainly not novel, and *additionally*
there is this: a life in the theater need not be an analogue to 'life.' It
is life.

It is the choice and calling of a substantial number of persons –
craftspersons and artists – and has been for a very long time.

My play, *A Life in the Theater*, is, though I may have led you to
believe otherwise, a comedy about this life.

It is an attempt to look with love at an institution we all love, The
Theater, and at the only component of that institution (about
whom our feelings are less simple), the men and women of the
theater – the world's heartiest mayflies, whom we elect and appoint
to live out our dreams upon the stage.

Concerning *The Water Engine*

We Americans know the real news never reaches the newspapers.
We know the interests it affects are much too powerful to allow
events which might disrupt the status quo to be truthfully reported
in the press.

We each have our own notion as to who, in fact, killed Kennedy,

and who killed Lincoln; as to what actually happened to the Lindbergh baby, or at the Bay of Pigs; as to how much Nixon actually
knew.

But we do not look to the press for ratification of our beliefs. We
believe gossip before we believe journalism, and we are much more
likely to accept as true the statement of the relative of the cabdriver
who heard Politician X say so-and-so in his cab than to accept the
politician's broadcast statements meant for our consumption.

We believe the word of a human being whom we can look in the
eye – however much his testimony rests on hearsay – before the
statements of a faceless press.

Myths and fables live on without advertising – without the
backing of high-powered interests – with no one profiting from
their retelling.

The only profit in the sharing of a myth is to those who participate as storytellers or as listeners, and this profit is the shared
experience itself, the *celebration* of the tale, and of its truth.

We believe that Edith Wilson ran the country in her husband's
name while he was comatose, and that she forged his signature to
documents of state; that we've had contact with intelligence from
foreign worlds, and that our government's suppressed the information; that, somewhere, someone's found a cure for cancer; that
Roosevelt let Lindbergh into Hauptmann's cell before the execu-
tion; that some governmental agency killed Martin Luther King.

These beliefs are part of our oral history. They are neither more
nor less true than those things which we read in the press.

They are, however, more steadfastly believed.

Our distrust of institutions is great and well founded.

We're always ready to believe the worst of them because we
know we'll never *know* the worst.

One of our hardiest and most beloved myths is that of *suppression by the government, or by an industrial pseudo-government*, of
discoveries or of inventions which could improve our lives.

We have all heard stories, told both as fact and as fiction, of the
light bulb which would not burn out, of runless stockings, of the
pill which made gasoline when dropped in water, of the cheap
patent drug which would cure the cold . . .

These myths of suppression ring true to us because we distrust
institutions.

We feel malevolence in their lack of accountability.

We cannot *talk* to them. Who *is* 'The Government'?
Who is 'Big Business'?

We feel these faceless monoliths can only wish us harm.

We cannot look them in the eye. They're not accountable, and in this lack of accountability we feel danger, we feel they're capable of anything, and we express this feeling in our myths.

Tolstoy wrote that the only time human beings treat each other without pity is when they have banded into institutions.

Buttressed by an institution, he said, we will perpetrate gross acts of cruelty and savagery and call it 'performance of our duty,' and feel absolutely no necessity of judging our own actions.

The code of an institution ratifies us in acting amorally, as any guilt which might arise out of our acts would be borne not by ourself, but shared out through the institution.

We have it somehow in our nature, Tolstoy wrote, to perform horrendous acts which we would never dream of as individuals, and think if they are done in the name of some larger group, a *state*, *a company*, *a team*, that these vile acts are somehow magically transformed, and become praiseworthy.

The Water Engine is an American fable about the common person and the institution.

It is set in Chicago during the Depression – in the second year of the Century of Progress Exposition, a celebration of technology.

The story starts like this: 'In September 1934, a young man in Chicago, Illinois, designed and built an engine which used distilled water as its only fuel.'

Decay:
Some thoughts for Actors

Theodore Spencer Memorial Lecture, Harvard, February 10, 1986

We live in a very confusing time.

Many simple words seem to have lost their meaning, and many simple processes are being called by new words.

In neologisms and circumlocutions we seek to deny the essentially finite nature of the terrifying processes to which these words refer.

We speak of *relationships* rather than *marriage*.

We speak of *parenting* instead of *raising a child*; of *defense* as if the goal of defense were not the *elimination* or *negation* of a threat, which threat, of course, being eliminated would do away with the necessity of defense.

We speak of *progress* and *growth* as we speak of parenting. As processes without an object. We are afraid to think of the results of what we do. We refer to growth in the economy, growth in the 'self,' growth in relationships, as if one could progress except toward a specific goal, or grow except to mature. Hence these terms, progress and growth, used in a sense of infinite expansion, deny the idea of *completion* and *rest*.

But what *grows* must, at some point, *cease* growing. And, following a period of maturity, must decay and die.

Decay is an inevitable part of life, and the attempt to deny the existence of death is evidence of either an immature or a disturbed understanding.

Things grow over time. We do not conceive and deliver in the same instant; we cannot take in and give out at the same time. There is a time to accumulate and there is a time to disperse, and the final disassembly is decay, which takes place so that new life may take place.

The study of natural growth and decay is the study of The Theater; and theatrical organisms: a career, a play, a season, an institution, grow and mature and decay and die according to the same rules which govern the growth and death of a plant or an animal. The organism grows toward a set point, and is shaped by the resistance it encounters on the way to its predetermined goal.

The ambitions which bring a group of young people together in an urge to buck the odds and start a new company will eventually shake that company apart, as the ambitions, *when one set of goals has been reached*, carry the individuals involved to new conquests and so on.

All plays are about decay. They are about the ends of a situation which has achieved itself fully, and the inevitable disorder which ensues until equilibrium is again established.

This is why the theater has always been essential to human psychic equilibrium. The theater exposes us to the notion of decay, to the necessity of change: in comedy to the tenuousness of our social state, in tragedy to the inevitability of death. It is a constant human need, to dramatize, and the question, Is the theater dead? is not a request for information, but the expression of a deep personal anxiety (as, 'Momma, are we going to have to move to a smaller apartment?'). 'Is the theater dead?' means, Am *I* dead?

The dramatists and the play strive to create order out of a disordered state. Their job is to observe and enact decay as it leads to its conclusion of *rest*, and offer the solace, the conclusion appropriate to that rest. (In fables or cautionary tales: 'So be careful what you do'; in melodrama, 'So be assured that your emotions are intact, and these bind you to the rest of the people in the theater.')

During a period of growth, disorder is caused by *lack of completion*; the organism, the play, the tree grows till it is complete. Having completed itself, the process is reversed and order can only be restored by disassembly of the organism.

When a society is *growing* (just as when a play is growing) all aspects of that society promote growth: the arts, the economy, religion (as in nineteenth-century America). When a society is *growing* those things appear and thrive which will make the organism strong, virile, happy, outward-directed – *seminal*, in short. And we have all had this experience when working on a new project: we do without sleep, people who will help us miraculously appear, we master new skills easily, people are glad to meet us . . .

When the society has achieved itself, all aspects of that society tend toward *disassembly*, toward reducing that society into its smallest component parts, so that rest can be achieved and those components can be employed in a new task.

When a society has achieved itself, has achieved its inscrutable purposes, it is not 'bad luck' but common sense that all aspects of the society promote war, waste, pollution, doubt, anxiety – those things will hasten decay. (The operation of this decay can be seen simply by looking at a small society, a theater company, or a business. It becomes successful, the members get ambitious, bickering ensues, previously close relationships degenerate, no one shares the same opinion, monied interests appear to offer the going concern large amounts to stop what it is doing [franchising, etc.].)

When we look at our large society today we see many problems – overcrowding, the risk of nuclear annihilation, the perversion of the work ethic, the disappearance of tradition, homosexuality, sexually transmitted diseases, divorce, the tenuousness of the economy – and we say, 'What bad luck that they are besetting us at once.'

Even taken individually these occurrences seem incomprehensible. Taken as a whole the contemplation of them can surely induce terror. What is happening here and why have all these things, coincidentally, beset us?

Like many things which seem insoluble as problems, these things can be viewed also as solutions. They are an attempt to find rest.

Consider friendship which has run its course. Out of nowhere, an incident flares up, something nonsensical, over which friends take sides, and which ultimately tears the friendship apart. The problems which beset us are an attempt of the universe to, by natural selection, if you will, discover that one thing which will bring about a state of rest.

The problems of the world, AIDS, cancer, nuclear war, pollution, are, finally, no more solvable than the problems of a tree which has borne fruit: the apples are overripe and they are falling – what can be done? The leaves, coincidentally, are falling, too, just at the time when they are needed most; and the tree, already weakened, is being weighted down with ice, and the very sap which might sustain the valiant fight to keep life in the tree is draining.

What can be done? What can be done about the problems which beset our life? *Nothing* can be done, and nothing needs to be done. Something *is* being done – the organism is preparing to rest.

We, as a culture, as a civilization, are at the point where the appropriate, the life-giving, task of the organism is to decay. Nothing will stop it, nothing *can* stop it, for it is the force of life, and the evidence is all around us. Listen to the music in train stations and on the telephone when someone puts you on hold. The problem is not someone or some group of people unilaterally deciding to plague you with bad music; the problem is a growing universal and concerted attempt to limit the time each of us is alone with his or her thoughts; it is the collective unconscious suggesting an act of mercy.

Now, how long will this tendency toward final rest take, this dissolution of the civilization? One day, one hour, perhaps, a year, a hundred years, certainly not more. And our civilization could dissolve, as people my age have known all their lives; it could happen at any time, and in one moment.

Where is the peace in this knowledge? Perhaps in this: as the Stoics said, either gods exist or they do not exist. If they exist, then, no doubt, things are unfolding as they should; if they do *not* exist, then why should we be reluctant to depart a world in which there are no gods?

And what about in the short view: most of you young people have more diverting and more appropriate things to do than burden yourselves with too much philosophy.

In the short view, life goes on, and there *is* a reason you are here; there is a reason our civilization grew, and there is a reason it is going to die – and those reasons are as unavailable to us as the reasons *we* were born and are going to die.

We need not fall victim to the liberal fallacy of assuming that because we can perceive a problem we are, de facto, not part of the problem. We are the problem, like the man driving home from the Hamptons on Sunday night and cursing the idiots who have caused the traffic jam. We are part of the process, the world is decaying rather rapidly, and there is *nothing* we can do about it.

Let's face it and look at it: how is our parochial world decaying? The theater has few new plays and most of them are bad. The critics seem to thwart originality and the expression of love at every turn;

television buys off the talented; the art of acting degenerates astoundingly each year.

You younger people in the theater might say: Where is the kind and generous producer? The insightful talent agent? The wise critic? Better stop looking for them and assume they don't exist. Today the job of the agent, the critic, the producer, is to *hasten decay*, and they are doing their job – the job the society has elected them to do is to *spread terror* and the eventual apathy which ensues when an individual is too afraid to look at the world around him. They are the music in the railroad station, and they represent our desire for rest.

You might say what of free will in all this, what about the will of the individual? But I don't believe it exists, and I believe all societies function according to the rules of natural selection and that those survive who serve the society's turn, much like people stranded when their bus has broken down. Their individual personalities are unimportant; the necessity of the moment *will* create the expert, the reasonable man, the brash bully, the clown, and so on.

Now, what about *your* job?

Most of you who decide to stay in the theater will become part of the maelstrom of commercials, television, the quest for fame and recognition. In this time of decay those things which society will reward with fame and recognition are bad acting, bad writing, choices which inhibit thought, reflection, and release; and these things will be called art.

Some of you are born, perhaps, to represent the opposing view – the minority opinion of someone who, for whatever reason, is not afraid to examine his state. Some of you, in spite of it all, are thrown up by destiny to attempt to bring order to the stage, to attempt to bring to the stage, as Stanislavsky put it, the life of the human soul.

Like Laocoön, you will garner quite a bit of suffering in your attempts to perform a task which you will be told does not even exist. Please try to keep in mind that the people who tell you that, who tell you you are dull and talentless and noncommercial, are doing *their* job; and also bear in mind that, in your obstinacy and dedication, you are doing *your* job.

If you strive to bring order to the stage, if you strive to recreate in yourself that lost art of acting, the lost art of stagecraft, that ten-thousand-year-old art which has disappeared, for the large part, within my lifetime, if you strive to teach yourself the lost art of storytelling, you are going to suffer, and, as you work and age, you may look around you and say, 'Why bother?' And the answer is you must bother if you are selected to bother, and if not, *then* not.

It is a very confusing world. So, as the Stoics say, we might all try to keep our principles few and simple, so that we may refer to them quickly. If you can keep in touch with natural processes, with yourself and your God, with the natural rudiments of your profession – the human necessity to tell and hear stories – with the natural process of growth and decay, then you can, I think, find peace, even in the theater.

Our civilization is convulsed and dying, and it has not yet gotten the message. It is sinking, but it has not sunk into complete barbarity, and I often think that nuclear war exists for no other reason than to spare us that indignity.

We might have wished these things not to be the case, but they are the case; and, for you young people, to quote Marcus Aurelius again: you receive a bad augury before a battle, *so what*? It's *still* your job to fight.

Those of you who are called to strive to bring a new theater, the theater of your generation, to the stage, are set down for a very exciting life.

You will be pulling against an increasingly strong current, and as you do so, you will reap the great and priceless reward of knowing yourself a truly mature man or woman – if, in the midst of the panic which surrounds you, and calls itself common sense, or commercial viability, you are doing your job simply and well.

If you are going to work in the true theater, that job is a great job in this time of final decay; that job is to bring to your fellows, through the medium of your understanding and skill, the possibility of communion with what is essential in us all: that we are born to die, that we strive and fail, that we live in ignorance of why we were placed here, and, that, in the midst of this we need to love and be loved, but we are afraid.

If you are blessed with intelligence you will find yourself in a constant battle between will and fear. Please know that this battle is exposure to the central aspect of drama: the battle between what you are called to do and what you would *rather* do. Exposure to this battle is an education in tragedy.

Your attempts to answer the question, 'What must I do?' may lead you to embrace and study both philosophy and technique; to learn to meditate and to learn to act, so that your personality and your work become one, and you fulfill your true purpose, your highest purpose, as a member of the theater. And that purpose is this and has *always* been this: to represent culture's need to address the question, How can I live in a world in which I am doomed to die?

Notes on *The Cherry Orchard*

When playing poker it is a good idea to determine what cards your opponents might hold. There are two ways to do this. One involves watching their idiosyncrasies – the way they hold their cards when bluffing as opposed to the way they hold them when they have a strong hand; their unconscious self-revelatory gestures; the way they play with their chips when unsure. This method of gathering information is called looking for 'tells.'

The other way to gather information is to analyze your opponent's hand according to what he *bets*.

These two methods are analogous – in the Theater – to a concern with *characterization*, and a concern with *action*; or, to put it a bit differently: a concern with the *way* a character does something and, on the other hand, the actual *thing that he does*.

I recently worked on an adaptation of *The Cherry Orchard*.

My newfound intimacy with the play led me to look past the quiddities of the characters and examine what it is that they are actually doing. I saw this:

The title is a flag of convenience. Nobody in the play gives a damn about the cherry orchard.

In the first act Lyubov returns. We are informed that her beloved estate is going to be sold unless someone acts quickly to avert this catastrophe.

She is told this by the rich Lopakhin. He then immediately tells her that he has a plan: cut down the cherry orchard, raze the house, and build tract housing for the summer people.

This solution would save (although alter) the estate.

Lopakhin keeps reiterating his offer throughout the play. Lyubov will not accept. Lopakhin finally buys the estate.

'Well,' one might say, 'one cannot save one's beloved cherry orchard by cutting it down.' That, of course, is true. But in the text other alternatives are offered.

Reference is made to the rich aunt in Yaroslavl ('who is so very rich'), and who adores Lyubov's daughter, Anya. A flying mendicant mission is proposed but never materializes. The point is not that this mission is viewed as a good bet – it isn't – but that, if the action of the protagonist (supposedly Lyubov) were to save the cherry orchard, she would vehemently pursue and grasp *any* possibility of help.

The more real hope of salvation is fortuitous marriage. Gaev, Lyubov's brother, enumerates the alternatives: inheriting money, begging from the rich aunt, marrying Anya off to a rich man.

The first is idle wishing, and we've struck off the second, but what about the third alternative?

There's nobody much around for Anya. But what about her stepsister, Varya?

Varya, Lyubov's adopted daughter, is not only nubile, she is *in love*. With whom is she in love? She is in love with the very wealthy Lopakhin.

Why, hell. If I wanted to save *my* cherry orchard, and *my* adopted daughter was in love (and we are told that her affections are by no means abhorrent to their recipient) with the richest man in town, what would *I* do? What would *you* do? It's the easy way out, the play ends in a half hour, and everybody gets to go home early.

But Lyubov does not press this point either, though she makes reference to it in every act. She does *not* press on to a happy marriage between Varya and Lopakhin. Nor, curiously, is this match ever mentioned as a solution for the problem of the cherry orchard. The problem of the botched courtship of Varya and Lopakhin exists only as one of a number of supposed subplots. (More of this later).

In the penultimate scene of the play, Lyubov, who is leaving her now-sold estate to return to Paris, attempts to tie up loose ends. She exhorts Lopakhin to propose to Varya, and he says he will. Left alone, Lopakhin loses his nerve and does not propose. Why does Lyubov, on learning this, not press her case? Why did she not do so sooner?

Even now, at the end of the play, if Lyubov *really* cared about the cherry orchard, she could save it from the ax. She could easily *force* Lopakhin to propose to Varya, and then get the bright idea that all of them could live on the estate as one happy family. And Lopakhin, who reveres her, would not refuse her.

But she does not do so. Is this from lack of inventiveness? No. It is from lack of concern. The cherry orchard is not her concern.

What about Lopakhin? Why is *he* cutting down the cherry orchard? He has been, from his youth, infatuated with Lyubov. She is a goddess to him, her estate is a fairyland to him, and his great desire in the play is to please her. (In fact, if one were to lapse into a psychological overview of the play at this point, one might say that the reason Lopakhin can't propose to Varya is that he is in love with Lyubov.)

Lopakhin buys the estate. For ninety thousand rubles, which means nothing to him. He then proceeds to cut down the trees, which he knows will upset his goddess, Lyubov, and to raze the manor house. His parents were slaves in that house; Lyubov grew up in the house; he doesn't need the money; why is he cutting down the trees? (Yes, yes, yes, we encounter halfhearted addenda in regard to future generations being won back to the land. But it doesn't wash. Why? If Lopakhin wanted to build a summer colony, he could build it anywhere. He could have built it without Lyubov's land and without her permission. If his objective were the building of summer homes and he were faced with two tracts, one where he had to cut down his idol's home, and one where he did not, which would he pick? Well, he has an infinite number of tracts. He can build anywhere he wants. Why cut down the trees and sadden his beloved idol? Having bought the estate he could easily let it sit, and, should the spirit move him subsequently, build his resort elsewhere.)

What, in effect, is going on here?

Nothing that has to do with trees.

The play is a series of scenes about sexuality, and, particularly, frustrated sexuality.

The play was inspired, most probably, by the scene in *Anna Karenina* between Kitty's friend Mlle Varenka and her gentleman companion Koznyeshev. The two of them, lonely, nice people, are brought together through the office of mutual friends. Each should marry, they are a perfect match. In one of the finest scenes in the book we are told that each knew the time had arrived, that it was Now or Never. They go for a walk, and Mr. Koznyeshev is about to propose when he is distracted by a question about mushrooms. And so the two nice people are doomed to loneliness.

If this description sounds familiar, it should. Chekhov, pregnant of his theme, lifted it shamelessly (and probably unconsciously) from Tolstoy and gave it to Lopakhin and Varya.

Not only do Lopakhin and Varya play out the scene, *everybody in the play plays out the same scene.*

Anya is in love with Pyotr Trofimov, the tutor of her late brother. Trofimov is in love with *her*, but is too repressed to make the first move. He, in fact, declares that he is above love, while, in a soliloquy, refers to Anya as 'My springtime, my dear Morning Sun.'

Yepihodov, the estate bookkeeper, is in love with Dunyasha, the chambermaid. He keeps trying to propose, but she thinks him a boor and will not hear him out. *She* is in love with Yasha, Lyubov's footman. Yasha seduces and abandons her, as he is in love with himself.

Lyubov herself is in love. She gave her fortune to her paramour and nursed him through three years of his sickness. He deserted her for a younger woman.

Now, *this* is the reason she has returned to the estate. It is purely coincidental that she returns just prior to the auction of the orchard. *Why* is it coincidental? Because, as we have seen, she doesn't come back to *save* it. If she wanted to she could. *Why does* she come back? What is the event that prompts her return? Her jilting. What is the event that prompts her to return again to Paris? The continual telegrams of her roué lover begging for forgiveness.

Why did Lyubov come home? To lick her wounds, to play for time, to figure out a new course for her life.

None of these is a theatrically compelling action. (The last comes closest, but it could be done in seclusion and does not require other

characters. As, indeed, the role of *Lyubov* is, essentially a mono-
logue – there's nothing she *wants* from anyone on stage.)

If Lyubov is doing nothing but these solitary, reflective acts, why
is she the protagonist of the play? She *isn't*.

The play has no protagonist. It has a couple of squad leaders. The
reason it has no protagonist is that it has no through-action. It has
one scene repeated by various couples.

To continue:

Lyubov's brother is Gaev. He is a perennial bachelor, and is
referred to several times in the text as an Old Lady. What does *he*
want? Not much of anything. Yes, he cries at the end when the
orchard is cut down. But he appears to be just as happy going to
work in the bank and playing caroms as he is lounging around the
Morning Room and playing caroms.

The other odd characters are Firs, the ancient butler, who is
happy the mistress has returned, and Simeonov-Pishchik, a poor
neighbor who is always looking on the bright side.

Pishchik, Firs, and Gaev are local color. They are all celibate and
seen as somewhat doddering in different degrees. And they are all
happy. Because they are not troubled by Sex. They are not involved
in the play's one and oft-repeated action: to consummate, clarify,
or rectify an unhappy sexual situation.

The cherry orchard and its imminent destruction is nothing other
than an effective dramatic device.

The play is not 'If you don't pay the mortgage I'll take your cow.'
It is 'Kiss me quick because I'm dying of cancer.'

The *obstacle* in the play does not grow out of, and does not even
refer to, the actions of the characters. The play works because it is a
compilation of brilliant scenes.

I would guess – judging from its similarity to many of his short
stories – that Chekhov wrote the scenes between the servant girl
Dunyasha and Yepihodov first. That perhaps sparked the idea of a
scene between Dunyasha and the man *she* loves, Yasha, a footman
just returned from Paris. Who did this fine footman return with?
The mistress. *Et ensuite.*

To continue this conceit: What did Chekhov do when he had two
hours' worth of scenes and thirteen characters running around a
country house? He had, as any playwright has, three choices. He
could shelve the material as brilliant sketches; he could *examine* the

material and attempt to discern any instriniscally dramatic through-action, and extrapolate the play out of *that*. Compare the structure of *The Cherry Orchard* with that of *The Seagull*. In *The Seagull*, the famous actress Arkadina wants to recapture her youth, which causes her to devote herself to a younger man and ignore the needs of her son, whose age is an affront to her pretensions of youth. He struggles to obtain her respect and the respect and love of Nina (another actress), who represents one split-off aspect of Arkadina's personality: her available sexuality. *The Seagull* is structured as a tragedy. At the end of the play the hero, Treplev, undergoes recognition of his state and reversal of his situation – he kills himself. What happens at the end of *The Cherry Orchard*? Everyone goes home – they go back to doing *exactly* what they were doing before the play began. You might say *The Cherry Orchard* is structured as a *farce*. That is the dramatic form to which it is closest. One might also say that it is close to a series of review sketches with a common theme, and, in fact, it is. The play is most closely related to, and is probably the first example of, the twentieth-century phenomenon of the revue-play ... the *theme* play, for example, *La Ronde*, *Truckline Cafe*, *Men in White*, *Detective Story*, *Waters of the Moon*, etc.

To return: Chekhov has thirteen people stuck in a summer house. He has a lot of brilliant scenes. His third alternative is to come up with a pretext which will keep all thirteen characters in the same place and *talking* to each other for a while. This is one of the dilemmas of the modern dramatist: 'Gosh, this material is *fantastic*. What can I do to just Keep the People in the House?'

One can have a piece of jewelry stolen. One can have a murder committed. One can have a snowstorm. One can have the car break down. One can have the Olde Estate due to be sold for debts in three weeks unless someone comes up with a good solution.

I picture this pretext occurring to Chekhov, and his saying, 'Naaaa, they'll never go for it.' I picture him watching rehearsals and *wincing* every time Lopakhin says (as he says frequently): 'Just remember, you have only three (two, one) weeks until the cherry orchard is to be sold.' Fine, he must have thought. That's real playwriting. One doesn't see Horatio coming out every five minutes and saying, 'Don't forget, Hamlet, your uncle killed your dad and now he's sleeping with your ma!'

Oh, no, he must have thought, I'll never get away with it. But he did, and left us a play we cherish.

Why do we cherish the play? Because it is about the struggle between the Old Values of the Russian aristocracy and their loosening grasp on power? I think not. For, finally, a play is about – and is *only* about – the actions of its characters. We, as audience, understand a play not in terms of the superficial idiosyncrasies or social *states* of its characters (which, finally, *separate* us from the play), but only in terms of the *action* the characters are trying to accomplish. Set Hamlet in Waukegan and it's still a great play.

The enduring draw of *The Cherry Orchard* is not that it is set in a dying Czarist Russia or that it has rich folks and poor folks. We are drawn to the play because it speaks to our *subconscious* – which is what a play should do. And we subconsciously perceive and enjoy the reiterated action of this reiterated scene: two people at odds – each trying to fulfill his or her frustrated sexuality.

Acting

We live in very selfish times. Nothing is given away free. Any impulse of creation or whimsy or iconoclasm which achieves general notice is immediately co-opted by risk capital, and its popularity – which arose from its generosity and freedom of thought – is made to serve the turn of financial extortion.

The successful workingman's café is franchised nationwide, and the charm of its artlessness wholesaled. The energy and invention of the bohemian quarter is transformed by promoters into the marketability of 'Artland.' The privacy of the remote seaside resort conducive to contemplation and renewal is sold piecemeal to millions of vacationers hungry for retreat who are willing to pay for a frantic, thronged pilgrimage to a spot where retreat was once possible.

It's not a very good time for the arts. And it is an especially *bad* time for the art of acting; for actors, as Hamlet told us, are 'the abstract and brief chronicles of their time.'

There are, of course, actors whose performances are hailed as great, because critics grade (as they must, in the absence of any aesthetic criteria) on the curve. But a comparison of that which contemporary journalism lauds as great acting with the great actors of the thirties and forties (Cary Grant, Garbo, Henry Fonda, James Stewart, etc.) shows how drastically we have lowered our standards.

We expect less of our actors today because we expect less of ourselves.

Our attention is limited; and in this time of fear and anxiety, our attention is devoted to ourselves, our feelings, our emotions, our immediate well-being. This makes for *very* bad acting, as the more our attention is focused on ourselves the less interesting we become – think of how many fascinating hypochondriacs you know.

The laws of attention which are true off stage are true *on* stage. The self-concerned person is a bore and the self-concerned *actor* is a bore. And whether the actor is saying, 'I must play this scene in order to be well thought of,' *or*, 'I must remember and re-create the time my puppy died in order to play this scene well,' makes no difference. In both cases his attention is self-centered, and in both cases his performance will tell us nothing we couldn't have learned more enjoyably in a library.

Acting, as any art, must be generous; the attention of the artist must be focused outward – not on what he is feeling, but on what he is trying to accomplish.

The *organic* actor must have generosity and courage – two attributes which our current national hypochondria render in low supply and even lower esteem. He must have the courage to say to his fellow actors on stage (and so to the audience): 'I am not concerned with influencing or *manipulating* you, I am not concerned with *nicety*. I am here on a mission and I *demand* you give me what I want.'

This actor brings to the stage *desire* rather than completion, *will* rather than emotion. His performance will be compared not to *art*, but to *life*; and when we leave the theater after his performance we will speak of *our life* rather than *his technique.*And the difference between this organic actor and the self-concerned performer is the difference between a wood fire and a fluorescent light.

In a Golden Age, that which delights us on the stage (that acting we would call 'art') would be the same things which delight us in our lives: simplicity, elegance, kindness, force – not that which is portrayed but that which allows us to infer; not the technical but the provocative. And in a Golden Age we would judge an actor's 'character' on stage the exact same way we judge it off stage: not by his protestations and assurances but by his determination, his constancy of purpose, his generosity – in effect, his 'goodness.'

But we don't live in a Golden Age, and the actor, the Brief Chronicle, is an expression of and a servant to his times.

We have demanded of him and received of him little other than this: a continual portrayal and repetition of the idea that nothing very much is happening around us, that we need not worry, and that it is absolutely correct that our actions should *not* be determined by our perceptions.

We have demanded of the actor that he repeat to us constantly that it is fine to laugh when not amused, to cry when not moved, to beam gratitude upon the unacceptable, to condone the unforgiveable, to express delight in the banal.

That most of today's acting is false and mechanical is no coincidence – it is a sign of our society's demanding that its priests repeat the catechism essential for our tenuous mental health: that nothing is happening, that nothing very bad or very good can befall us, that we are safe.

There are exceptions, of course. There are organic performances and organically directed productions and companies. But there aren't many. The actor works in a community, and the communal ideal of excellence is contagious and exigent.

Can we again ratify the Actor and the Theater which is organic rather than mechanical – which responds to our need to *love* rather than our need to *have*?

In this century the great and vital theaters (The Group in 1930s New York, Brecht's in 1920s Berlin, Staniolavsky's Art in 1900 Moscow, The Second City in 1960 Chicago) have emerged in response to, and signaling the end of, introverted, uncertain social periods.

For the moment, generous, organic acting can be seen occasionally in the theater (though seldom in the commercial theater), more regularly in film (generally in smaller roles), and most consistently as part of dance or opera, in performances given by those dedicated not to their *performances* but to the actions demanded by their material – in the work of Pavarotti or Baryshnikov, or Hildegarde Behrens, or Yuriko, or Fischer-Dieskau.

When, once again, actors are cherished and rewarded who bring to the stage or the screen generosity, desire, *organic life*, actions performed freely – without desire for reward or fear of either censure or misunderstanding – that will be one of the first signs that the tide of our introverted, unhappy time has turned and that we are once again eager and prepared to look at ourselves.

Realism

Most American theatrical workers are in thrall to the idea of *realism*. A very real urge to be truthful, to be *true*, constrains them to judge their efforts and actions against an inchoate, which is to say against an *unspecified* standard of reality.

That the standard is unspecified is important, as it thus becomes the explanation and excuse for any action or effort the artist feels disinclined to make. It becomes a peremptory challenge.

A necessary response to the artist who says 'It's not *true*' must be 'True to what?'

Stanislavsky and, more notably, Vakhtangov suggested that – that to which the artist must be *true* is the aesthetic integrity of the play.

This places a huge responsibility on the artist. He or she faced with this charge – to care for the *scenic truth* – can no longer take refuge in a blanket dismissal or *endorsement* of anything on the grounds of its being not realistic.

In general, each facet of every production must be weighed and understood solely on the basis of its interrelationship to the other elements; on its service or lack of service to the meaning, the *action* of the play.

A chair is not *per se* truthful or untruthful. That one may say, 'Yes, but it is a chair, an actual chair, people sit on it and I found it in a cafeteria, therefore it belongs in this play about a cafeteria,' is beside the point. Why was that *particular* chair chosen? Just as that particular chair said something about the cafeteria *in* the cafeteria (its concern for looks over comfort, for economy over durability, etc.), so that chair, on stage, will say something *about the play*; so the question is: What do you, the theatrical director, wish to say *about the play?*

What does the chair mean *in the play?* Does it symbolize power? Then have *that* chair. Abasement? Possession, and so on. Choose the correspondingly appropriate chair. One might say, 'Give it up, *it's just a chair* . . .' But, again , someone is going to *choose* it; shouldn't that someone *recognize* that he is consciously or unconsciously making a choice, and make the choice consciously, and in favor of an idea more specific to the play than the idea of 'reality.'

A conscious devotion to the *Idea* of a play is a concern for what Stanislavsky called the Scenic Truth, which is to say, the truth *in this particular scene.* The important difference between realism and truth, Scenic Truth, is the difference between acceptability and necessity, which is the difference between entertainment and Art.

So what if the play is set in a cafeteria? A cafeteria has no objective reality, as far as we artists are concerned. Our question is *why* is the play set in a cafeteria, what does it mean that the play is set in a cafeteria, and what *aspect* of this cafeteria is important *to the meaning of the play.* Having determined that, we may discard immediately all other aspects of the cafeteria and concentrate *only* on that which puts forward the meaning of the play. E.g.: if, in our particular play, the cafeteria means a place where the hero is always open to surveillance, the designer can build a set which reflects the idea: inability to hide. If the meaning of the cafeteria is a place where reflection and rest are possible, the designer's work can reflect *these* ideas. In neither case is the designer's first question: 'What does a cafeteria look like?' His first question is: 'What does it mean *in this instance?*' This is a concern for scenic truth

In devotion to this Scenic Truth the artist gives him- or herself a choice. In discarding the armor of realism he or she accepts the responsibility of making every choice in light of specific *meaning* – of making every choice assertive rather than protective. For, in this age, to make a 'realistic' choice, to assert that such and such a choice was made because it is, in fact, *as it is in life* is to say no more than that the choice was made in such a way as to avoid any potential criticism.

Everything which does not put forward the meaning of the play impedes the meaning of the play. To do too much or too little is to mitigate and weaken the meaning. The acting, the design, the direction should all consist only of that bare minimum necessary to put forward the action. Anything else is embellishment.

The problem of realism in design and its deleterious effects should be studied as a guide to the similar problem in acting. Actors for the last thirty years have been hiding in a ludicrously incorrect understanding of the Stanislavsky System and employing incorrectly understood jargon as an excuse for not acting.

Almost *never* are the teachings of Stanislavsky employed as an incitement; they are offered as an excuse – a substitute for action. The purpose of the system was, and is, to *free* the actor from extraneous considerations and permit him or her to turn all of his or her concentration to the objective, which is not 'this performance,' but the *meaning* of the play.

The notions of objective, activity, moment, beat, and so on are all devoted toward reducing the scene to a specific action which is true to the author's intention, and physically capable of being performed. The purpose of these concepts is to incite the actor to act. They all prod the actor to answer the one question which is capable of freeing him from self-consciousness and permitting him or her to become an artist: 'What am I doing?'

The purpose of the Stanislavsky system of thought was to permit the actor to freely give the truth, the highest truth, of him- or herself, to the ideas, to the words of the playwright. The system teaches specificity as a tool of release rather than constraint. To make the transition from realism to truth, from self-consciousness to creativity, the artist must learn how to be specific to *something greater than him- or herself* on different levels of abstraction: the meaning of the scene, the intention of the author, the thrust of the play. But never 'reality,' or 'truth,' in general.

That to which one must learn to be true is not one's vision of reality, which, by its very nature, will make the actor more self-conscious and less able to act, but to the *aspirations* central to the meaning of the play and expressed in the objectives of the characters.

All theater is about aspirations – it is about longing and the desire for answers – small theater concerns itself with small questions, and great theater with great. In any case, the question at stake is never the *comfort* of the artist.

To have this never-ceasing concern with one's personal comfort, with the 'naturalness' of the script, the blocking, the direction, the other actors, is to reduce every play to the *same* play – to a play about 'That which I am not prepared to do' or 'Those choices I will not make, and which I cannot be *forced* to make.'

And so what?

Let us cast aside concern of comfortability on stage. Why should one be comfortable acting Othello or St. Joan? The study of all theatrical artists should be action. *Movement.* A first test of all elements should be not 'Do I feel comfortable (i.e., *immobile*) when considering it?' but 'Do I feel *impelled*? Do I start to *move*? Does it make me want to *do* something?'

Actors are many times afraid of feeling foolish. We should teach each other to feel *power* rather than fear when faced with the necessity of choice, to seek out and enjoy, to feel the life-giving pleasure of the power of artistic choice.

Against Amplification

Let's be serious for a moment. If you are an actor and you can't make yourself heard in a thousand-seat house, you're doing something wrong – you should get off the stage and go home. Go back to voice class or wherever your instincts lead you, but get off the stage.

Dramatic works are meant to be *acted*. They concern themselves with commitment and its consequences.

They cannot be delivered conversationally and then amplified – that is not *drama*, that is *television*.

Any actor, producer, writer, or director who thinks that transistors and circuitry can fill the gap between the ability of the artist and the needs of the audience is degrading all concerned.

The correct, necessary, and only amplification needed in a theater is the commitment of the artist (and here I mean primarily the writer and the actor) – commitment sufficient, if the case is that they cannot be heard, to send the one back to the typewriter and the other back to the studio.

The writer who writes *behavior* rather than *drama*, of course, has a need of actors who are miked, because that writer's words are not going to awaken in the actor the *need to speak* – the need to be heard.

The actor who permits him- or herself to be miked on the dramatic stage is destroying both art and livelihood – destroying the profession in much the same way that television has, which says to the artist, 'It's sufficient for you just to get up there in front of the cameras and say the lines.'

The art of the theater is action. It is the study of commitment. The word is an act. To *say* the word in such a way as to make it heard and understood by all in the theater is a commitment – it is the highest art to see a human being out on a stage speaking to a thousand of his or her peers saying, 'These words which I am speaking are the *truth* – they are not an approximation of any kind. They are the God's truth, and I support them with my life,' which is what the actor does on stage.

Without this commitment, acting becomes prostitution and writing becomes advertising.

The electronic amplification of the live stage is yet another wretched expediency which benefits no one but the speculator.

The beautiful, trained human voice and its extrapolation, live music, are the most beautiful and perfect sounds we will ever hear. Let us not participate in eliminating, through laziness, this beauty from our lives.

Let us assume responsibility for putting something on the stage worth saying – something the actors will feel moved to speak with commitment and something the audience will feel moved to listen to. That, traditionally, has been the limit of our responsibility.

But I think that today we have a responsibility to oppose this sonic garbage in the theater, to oppose it every way we can.

We can specify in individual contracts that our plays are not to be amplified; we can bring a resolution to the council to decry and/or investigate positive means to reverse this trend; we can be vocal about it in public and in print – the audience could use some education on this score; they are being robbed and they don't know it.

I know some of you are thinking that I'm vastly overstating the case. I feel this issue, *far* beyond threatening the purity of the theater, threatens its very integrity.

Neil Simon said that the laugh track killed television comedy because the writers no longer needed to be funny.

Electronic amplification is killing and will kill the Broadway stage because the actors and the writers will no longer need to speak out.

Address to the American Theater Critics Convention

At the Tyrone Guthrie Theater, Minneapolis, Minnesota, August 25, 1978

If only the stage were as high and narrow as a tightrope, so that only those completely trained would dare to venture out on it.

— SANFORD MEISNER

The first task of the actor, the first lesson, and one of the hardest, is to learn to take criticism – to learn to view self-consciousness as a tool for *bettering* the self, rather than as a tool for *protecting* the self. Mastery of this lesson is essential if one is to learn to look dispassionately at what he or she has done.

One must look honestly at what one has done, and to compare it to what one was *trying* to do. To learn useful *mechanical* lessons from the comparison is difficult; many workers in the theater never learn to do it.

Not to know how to make this comparison is the mark of an amateur. It is the mark of a person to whom the theater is, finally, a diversion rather than a profession, and it is the mark of a person who wants the theater to give to *him* or *her*, but wants to give nothing in return.

One of the worst things that can befall a beginning, an untrained actor is to be ratified, to be praised for idiosyncrasies – for those things which, given time and technique might become strengths, but in the absence of these are no more than eccentricities.

If one has no ability or inclination to scrutinize what he or she does *in terms of greater goals*, to be ratified early can be, and usually is, stultifying.

It is especially stultifying when accompanied, as often happens, by blandishments to the effect that there is no such thing as technique; that there *is* no need to study; that the only way to learn is through doing; and that, finally, pursuit of good habits of work, that is, technique, and good habits of thought, that is, philosophy, are effete.

This advice to 'do what one does so well' causes a well-known inversion. It creates in the performer a necessary interest in 'know-nothingism,' and he or she comes to deny the very existence of both technique and of aesthetic. He or she becomes, in effect, a fascist, a complete egocentric who is the champion of 'doing what I feel,' 'saying what I feel,' 'writing what I feel.'

And the result is more or less harmful garbage.

The garbage is, of course, all the more harmful when it is the product of some incipient 'talent' on the part of the creator, as the talent will make the product a little bit more attractive, though no less unworthy. But there *is* such a thing as technique. And a career in the theater must have long-range technical and philosophic goals. And these cannot be egocentric goals.

Without these goals one does not have the strength or the distance for moment-to-moment honest self-criticism, and without this self-critique there is no improvement and there is no happiness.

Performers who lack the ability to criticize themselves, who take no responsibility for understanding *what it is that they do* and the moral and mechanical precepts to which they must adhere, are not happy. Not one.

They are confused by success and humiliated by failure, and they are always looking for someone either to kiss their ass or to hold their hand, and well they might, for they, naturally, have no faith in themselves and they are not happy. They make themselves unhappy by denying themselves the comfort of anything *greater* than themselves. They are sterile.

So with the performer in the theater, and so with you, the theatrical critics. If you do not learn your craft, the Theater, and its moral and practical precepts, if you do not make this your constant study, if you do not learn to judge yourselves against a standard of artistic perfection and amend your works day to day in light of that standard, you *must* be unhappy.

Just as with the performer. If you trust outside plaudits and support for your work, you are being controlled. Your life is not your own. Just as is evidenced in that sick moment when you have a deadline to make and not a thing in the world to say, and you think not *what must I say about that piece*, but *what would be acceptable*, or *witty*, or *nouveau*.

Many of you, as with performers, treat the theater as your personal beat – your personal amusement and nothing greater than a shooting mark which will enable you to display your expertise.

My question to you is this: Would you not be happier as a *part* of the theater?

If your answer (and it may be hidden in your secret heart) is yes, then treat the theater with love. We, as members of the community, have the right to demand this of an actor, or director, or writer, or designer, and we have the right to demand it of a critic, for, barring this, the critic in question is not *of the theater*, but is an exploiter, no matter what title he or she goes by.

Treat the theater with love and devotion sufficient to learn some of its rudimentary fiats.

Learn your craft and be part of the theater, for, while you are learning and striving to write better and to write more informedly and to write more in light of a standard of artistic perfection, you are as much a part of the theater as anyone else in it – now or in antiquity; and while you are *not* striving to improve and to write informedly and morally and to a purpose, you are a hack and a plaything of your advertisers.

Study acting; it is a fascinating study. If you are uneducated in its techniques, you are incapable of distinguishing good from bad – unless you are prepared to fall back on that old saw, 'I know what I like,' or, 'I write for the popular taste of my subscribers,' which is to say, 'for a hypothetical person dumber than I am'; and if that is what you are doing, you are in serious trouble and insulting yourself and the people who read your publication.

And I say to you: write for *yourself*, and be an artist.

Study theater history. Teach yourself some perspective, so that you are not at the mercy of the current *fad*, which is another levy of 'I know what I like.'

Study voice and movement – learn the difference between the beautiful and the attractive.

Learn to analyze a script the way a director should and almost none can.

Make *yourself* the expert, and let us lay to rest the critic as *weather vane* and reporter to the *public taste*, which is only a fiction in the minds of knaves.

Study the theater. Your friends will tell you you are making yourself foolish – that you are wasting your time and no one will appreciate the finer points in any case. And this is exactly what bad actors say to devoted actors.

Love the theater and learn about it and strive to improve it and create a *new* profession for yourselves. The profession of the 'theater critic' is debauched, but you don't have to be debauched.

Train yourself for a profession that *does not exist*. That is the mark of an *artist* – to create something which formerly existed only in his or her heart.

Observations of a Backstage Wife

Iceman is a science-fiction film which was released in the summer of 1984. It is about a group of research scientists in the Arctic who discover and revive a 20,000-year-old Neanderthal man they have found frozen in a glacier. It was filmed during the four months of February–May 1983 on locations in Churchill, Manitoba, and Stewart, British Columbia, and in studios in Vancouver, British Columbia. The film stars Tim Hutton and Lindsay Crouse. As Ms. Crouse's husband, I spent much of the shoot in Canada with the film, and was privileged to enjoy the companionship of the cast and crew and the courtesy of the production company.

On location we are isolated. We are like people whose bus has broken down – we are going to have to choose temporary roles and make the best of it for a while.

A traditional hierarchy of power controls most relationships in the entertainment industry, but that hierarchy holds its most powerful sway back at home. At home we are divided by craft-within-the-industry (the directors don't live next door to the technicians), by income, and by achievement. Here, on location, everyone's lumped together twenty-four hours a day for four months.

The recognition symbols which give us power at home don't do the trick up here ('Okay, that's *still* a Patek Philippe watch; I saw it yesterday. What else can you do?'). Most of the perquisites of money have been eliminated in towns in which there is nothing to buy.

Life on location is a Clean Slate. We have entered Tombstone Territory and, to a large extent, are free to invent identities for ourselves and for the group as a whole.

The cast and crew had just arrived on Hudson Bay, in Churchill, Manitoba. It was February, and constantly 40 to 50 degrees below zero.

My wife was staying at the Tundra Inn, and I called to see how she was doing. The friendly hotel operator said, 'They're all in the bar,' and put the phone down while she paged my wife. I heard much raucous laughter in the background; then my wife came to the phone. 'Well,' I said, 'what's it like up there?' There was a pause and then she said, 'It's like Film Camp.'

Professional Hierarchy

Joe Somer and Richard Monette are two of the featured actors in the movie. We are taking a several-hours' walk down a seemingly endless sandpit in the Portland Canal outside Stewart, British Columbia. We are taking this walk as there is absolutely nothing to do in this town.

Outside of the Alpine Motel, where half of the cast and crew is lodged, is a vacant lot full of mud. On the weekends, many inhabitants of Stewart drive their four-wheel-drive vehicles through and around the mud lot, hoping to get stuck and then become unstuck. If we had such vehicles we would, no doubt, join them. Having none, we complain about the noise they make and find our excitement where we can. This afternoon our excitement is a walk.

Monette avers that this is the only town in the world whose

cultural life would be improved by a nuclear war. 'I rather like it,' says Somer. 'Do come by for tea this afternoon, will you, I'm at the Edward . . .' 'In the Terrace or the Lounge?' asks Monette.

The 'Edward' is the King Edward Hotel, a rather basic cinder-block affair on the town's one short street.

And so we pass the time playing the dozens on the 'Edward' and Far Northern Life in general. Monette had created something of a cultural stir the day before by producing a copy of *Huck Finn* he found on a rack in the back of the town's shoe store. He announced the store had several copies left. All of them disappeared by that evening.

There is *nothing* to do in this town in which we are very much strangers, and bitching – if only for the moment – turns home-sickness and boredom into a sense of exclusivity.

When the thrill of dishing the 'Edward' wanes, Monette takes up the leitmotif of the helicopter. He is slated, when weather permits, to do a shot hanging out of the door of a helicopter airborne over the glacier.

In the shot a stuntman, dressed as the Neanderthal, hangs on the skid of the airborne helicopter. A second stuntman jumps from the plane and free-falls with a camera. He films the Neanderthal stuntman, who then loses his grip on the skid and falls while Monette leans out of the door and tries to save him.

Monette does not like flying, doesn't like the idea of helicopters, and doesn't like the fact that he has agreed to do the shot.

Joe Somer and I concur with all his reservations. It seems to us all that Monette's part of the shot should be played by a stuntman who has been both trained and rewarded for undertaking this kind of danger. Monette is neither, and is hiding his anxiety beneath a display of anxiety.

Somer suggests Monette go to the town pharmacist and explain that everyone back in his hometown has a toothache and could he please have eight million Percodans. As he is speaking, one of the film trucks pulls up and Warren Carr, the second assistant director, leans out and tells Monette to saddle up, as the weather has cleared and he is going for a helicopter ride.

We all drive back to the airstrip, where we watch Monette rehearse the shot (on the ground) with the stunt crew. At the airstrip, Norman Jewison, who with Patrick Palmer is producing the film, is consulting with the pilots. This is a very important, very expensive shot, and the producers are on hand to see that it goes well or to have been there if it goes badly.

Jewison nods to Monette who says, joking in earnest, that he hopes Jewison will remember this favor when casting his next film. Jewison, distracted by the logistics of the shot, smiles and moves on.

Jewison will almost certainly *not* remember Monette when casting his next film. This is no particular reflection on Norman Jewison – it is just the way things are in the Biz: a thing's worth is identical with its price, and Monette is doing the stunt as a favor.

So, amazingly, in spite of the recent Vic Morrow tragedy (the deaths of several actors, two of them children, in a helicopter accident while filming) and the great clamor it created in the trade press for strict adherence to industry safety codes; in spite of the fact that he *knows* that a producer will usually consider the granting of a favour a display of contemptible weakness, Monette will do the shot.

In Vaudeville Times, legitimate actors were known as the Harold and Arthurs. Monette, Crouse, Joe Somer, and I were very much Harold and Arthurs on location. We are from the East, and each came to the movies first having spent one or two decades working in the theater.

We are *specifically* conditioned to consider ourselves sub-servient to directors and producers: the director passes out the work and the producer hands out the paycheck. Most actors make a virtue of necessity and, being members of a profession which prizes gentility and courtesy, treat directors and producers with such. And it is good to know one's place.

Monette is a fine actor; he doesn't want to gum up the works. He is also a considerate man and has been asked a favor. Though scared stiff, he did the stunt.

Joe Somer and I left the airstrip and strolled over to the old, abandoned Empress Hotel, which is being used as our soundstage. At the Empress, we watch Fred Schepisi, the film's director, shooting a scene with Lindsay Crouse. He finishes the scene and shouts, generally, 'Where's Richard Monette?' Nobody on the set knows. 'He's up in a helicopter,' Somers says.

'Up in the helicopter,' says Schepisi. 'Isn't that *dangerous* . . .?'

Fun on Location

That evening Monette, safely returned, is celebrating his new-won wings with a lobster dinner at the Edward. He regales us with the story of his life in the clouds.

There were four men in the helicopter: Monette and the pilot in the cockpit proper, and Dar Robinson and Carl Loburn, the two stuntmen, in a separate compartment at the rear of the aircraft.

At the assigned altitude the two stuntmen walked out along the skid to the front of the plane. The cameraman jumped, free-falling and filming while the second stuntman (dressed as the Neanderthal), hung on to the skid. Monette, secured by two seat belts, leaned out of the open door attempting to 'save' the Neanderthal, who lost his grip and fell from the skid.

The stunt successfully completed, Monette closed the door and leaned happily back in his seat while the pilot flew him back to the airstrip. Several moments later, his happy reverie was broken by the sound of someone frantically banging on the outside of the helicopter window. Monette turned to see the face of a completely unknown individual leering at him from outside the helicopter. This person then waved bye bye, jumped from the skid, and free-fell to within a very scant number of feet from the ground, where he opened a parachute. This was a third member of the stunt team – a parachute packer – who came along unannounced and thought he would enliven everybody's day.

At night most of the company walked or bused the two miles across the American border into Hyder, Alaska, which looks like a derivative and not very effective student scenic design project: 'The Western Town, 1850.' Main Street has three bars, the border customs station (which was never manned), and a gift shop.

Group Identity

As a company, we were quite taken with souvenirs. They validate our travels and they fix us as a group. They are our uniforms. In Churchill, Manitoba, the company's location before Stewart ('Churchill: the Polar Bear Capital of the world. Our household pests are ten feet tall and weigh half a ton'), the local industry was fur and the company got off the plane from Churchill in wolf parkas, vests, hats, moose mukluks, and (John Lone, the Iceman himself) in a massive black bear parka. Lone quite literally stopped traffic on the street and he was known for the next few days as 'pom-pom.'

In Stewart the only article of native interest for sale is beaded belts. These cost three dollars and say ALASKA on them. One day after we have arrived, all of them are gone from the store.

In Vancouver, our uniforms came from Three Vets, the city's great army surplus store. Much of the actual cold-weather gear needed in the 40-below weather of Churchill was supplied by them, so the cast spent a lot of time there getting fitted out for the shoot.

One day Jim Tolkan, who plays one of the scientists, came back from his fitting wearing a Canadian Postal Service surplus leather jacket: 'Seventy bucks to the public, they gave it to me for fifty . . .' By the end of the week, most of the company had their Canadian Postal Service jackets.

Jim Tolkan doesn't induce you to look on the bright side, he *is* the bright side. He is the King of Hanging Out. His room in Vancouver was stuffed with souvenirs: fur-lined World War I flight goggles, old but mint-condition riding boots, handmade knives he found in an obscure corner of Vancouver. He is a fashion plate and could make a gunnysack look elegant. He is always having a good time. Everyone wants to wear what he is wearing. He is an actor of much experience on the road, and he turns every stop into a happy treasure hunt. He is, unfortunately, not with us in Stewart/Hyder.

At night in Hyder, one could lounge about the bar of the Sealaska Hotel shooting pool or playing video games ('Good to be back in the States') or go down to the Border pub and get Hyderized.

Hyderization is the consumption of a straight shot of a local white alcohol called Moon, which is about three billion proof. One stands between two metal handrails of the bar service station. The rails are twisted and gnarled – presumably by the gyrations of those communicants who have gone before. One is given, free, a shot glass of the aforesaid liquor and must down it in one gulp. Should it refuse to stay down or the drinker refuse to stay up, he or she must buy a round for the house.

One member of the cast was only seen evenings during our three weeks in Stewart. He was on call to shoot a standby scene. And it was evident that we had so much scheduled work to do that he was never going to get called. He didn't work the whole three weeks and, depressed and Hyderized, pub-crawled through the northern nights and slept out his days in the privacy of the Edward.

Monarchy

In Stewart, British Columbia, shooting took place on the glacier. There was a small but real danger of avalanche, and a watch was set up and evacuation procedures planned. There were not enough helicopters, of course, to take the whole crew off at once, and someone asked, in the event of an emergency, how we would evacuate the site. 'We'll evacuate in order of billing,' a crew member quipped, and everyone laughed. But, of course, we *would* evacuate in order of billing. The movie is built around the star, and with the ice coming down the mountain, all attention would turn unthinkingly to hustling him into the plane while droves of women and children – joining in the general anxiety for his safety – looked on. For the star of the film is not only an avatar to the audience, he is the Prince of the Movie. He stands for the movie, and so, like other princes, he stands for ourselves. One day in May, Tim Hutton was hurt by a rock falling on his foot. Work, of course, stopped while all looked on and then looked away in a hush. A thick anxiety spread over the set and rippled over to the production office, where calls were going out for ambulances, and over to the lunch truck, where people were talking in whispers. A man who didn't know what had happened came into the production office cracking a joke and was told to shut up: 'Don't you know what happened?'

The Film Industry is the American Monarchy: it is strict entailed succession and Horatio Alger in one. Except for the money manipulators and speculators on the top, it is a society built on work, achievement, and fealty to those in power.

At the lower levels one's superiors have the right either to bestow or to deny employment, and at the upper levels they have the right to ennoble, to elevate out of the realm of the workaday and into the realm of power: the star's boyfriend/girlfriend made a 'producer,' and so on. Also, as in any good monarchy, there is the American Element of Luck: who just *happened* to be there when the star got sick, the runaway carriage of the Daughter of a Wealthy Manufacturer saved by the Newsboy.

The Great Chain of Being

Several of us are dining out on Sunday. We are in the charge of John Lone who plays the Iceman, and Michael Westmore, the makeup artist. They have formed an ad hoc supper club. They seek out the culinary hotspots of Vancouver and share their finds with the rest. But Sunday evenings in Vancouver are usually spent at the Paradise, the *in* room of a larger Chinese restaurant. John orders for us all in Chinese. The dinner is magnificent. After dinner our conversation turns to film gossip. We all chuckle at the idea that Lana Turner was actually discovered on a stool at Schwab's, but we earnestly recount to each other how we know for a fact that Sly Stallone ('. . . and he *deserved* it!') was discovered tearing tickets at the Sutton Theatre in New York; or that Jessica Lange was found waiting tables at the Lion's Head pub on Sheridan Square; or that George Lucas got where he is on the basis of talent. ('Do you know how much money he makes in a *day*. . .? I have a friend who saw a check sitting on his desk . . .')

The other part of the conversation, of course, is *trashing*: 'You know who's a real _____?' And what both parts of this fugue add up to is Belowstairs Gossip. Though we would, at first, laugh the idea to scorn, what we are doing is 'talking about our betters.'

If there are those greater than ourselves in luck, if there are those lesser than ourselves in talent, if, in fact, *anyone* in the business can be fixed on a scale of luck, talent, achievement, success, then we can compare ourselves to that point on the scale and, in a quite real sense, *know our place*. We can then see that, moment to moment, life is very ordered, and that, within this structure, there is the possibility for change and advancement.

This feeling of *knowing one's place* is a good feeling, and mostly absent in our contemporary culture in which one generally compares oneself to one's peers with either vanity tinged with dread or envy tinged with dread.

At our various bull sessions, *everyone* says (with some surprise), 'You know, I kind of wish we were back in the old studio days.'

None of us really knows what those good old days were like, but we all long for order, and dream of that imaginary society which would make us feel secure.

Identity in Craft

Patrick Palmer says that one can usually identify a film worker's job by his or her appearance. Each job, as one might expect, attracts a person with the emotional and physical predisposition for that job – much in the way that people choose dogs they feel best exemplify their own personal strong suits.

In the film industry (as in the theater), this phenomenon is very pronounced. The makeup woman, the costume designer, and the still photographer (that person responsible for making a still-photographic record of the appearance and the action on the set) are always *very* attractive and special looking.

(Lorey Sebastian is our still photographer. She, out of the goodness of her heart, became our social director, organizing a cinematheque in her room every night in Vancouver, sight-seeing excursions, Crouse's surprise party, a Canadian Strip-O-Gram to celebrate the birthday of Don Levy, the unit publicist, etc.)

The sound recordist and the editor are usually introverted endomorphs – Dungeons and Dragons types. The producers (they seem to come in pairs) are always Mutt and Jeff: one is a smiler and one is a worrier. (On this film Jewison is the smiler.) The stuntmen are always good-looking and seem to behave in the extroverted way in which people assume that movie stars behave. The movie stars behave like wallflowers. The teamsters (the people who drive the film's cars, trucks, and station wagons) are usually potbellied, quiet, and kind

A Canadian Digression

One day I was sitting in one of our station wagons outside a film supply house in Vancouver. The teamster was waiting to pick up some equipment and we had some time to kill as the man he was to get it from was at lunch. He saw a young prostitute across the street looking for trade and proceeded to speak about her in some intricate detail: her habits, her personality, her history. I remained noncommittal as I didn't know what the correct response was. Obviously something between 'Everybody has to have a hobby' and 'Mmmm.'

Another prostitute came on the corner and the teamster began a similar rendition of *her* life story, personality, and attributes. They were joined by a third and on he went. There was a pause in the conversation; it was my turn to speak. Not wishing to appear a fool, and struck by his garrulousness (this was, after all, Canada), I said, rather tentatively, 'You sure seem to know a lot about these young women.' He explained that his wife ran a halfway house for them.

So my illusions about Canadians remained intact; although, curiously, the teenage hookers of Vancouver seem – to a transient – to be the most prominent cultural touchstone of this very Calvinist city. The cabdrivers point them out to you – much as in Chicago a quarter-century ago, one was driven through the ghetto as a tourist attraction. One reads about these hookers and proposed laws to deal with them in the local editorials constantly; the streets around our hotel are labyrinthine with random islands, malls, and round-abouts, and we are told this was done to cut down on the traffic of cruising johns. And on last Easter morning, many of the hookers dressed as Easter bunnies. This last impressed us all greatly as, professionally, we approve of any show of spirit: which is why we all loved the softball game.

Us and them

Patrick Palmer and Don Levy, our unit publicist, arranged the game with the Arts Club Theatre of Vancouver. We got to the park early and started warming up, and Patrick showed up with his clipboard, took notes on our performance, and assigned positions and batting order.

Jim VanWyck, first assistant director, played AAA ball with the Minnesota Twins farm team. *He* could have been the captain, but it was certainly more fun to see Patrick in his sweatsuit scribbling in his clipboard.

Palmer is a taciturn and somewhat forbidding man. Many thought he was a stick-in-the-mud and labeled him standoffish until it was discovered he started in the film business as a craft service-man – that person responsible for maintenance of the coffee urns and snacks on the set, at which point his stock shot up immediately. To the most extent in films, and completely in the theater, we all enter from the bottom.

How wonderful it was to be American at that softball game. We were cheering each other on and booing the bad calls, we were giving each other high five. Tech people the actors had only nodded to on the set were doing circus catches in the outfield and getting their day in court. The day was perfect, we were sweating, we were exercising, we were killing them, the sun was shining on the moun-tains across the Sound, and the best of all David Strathairn – who plays Dr. Singe, one of the surgeons who bring the Iceman back to life – had brought a small grapefruit, just the size of the softball, and lovingly painted it white.

In the top of the eighth, with the score 12–5 (us), the pitcher put the grapefruit over the plate in a perfect slow strike and the Arts Club batter sunk into a powerhouse swing and blasted that grape-fruit for all he was worth. The grapefruit exploded, spraying rind and juice and pulp in a halo I can still see, and the batter's mind turned to Jell-O. He started for first, he faltered, he blinked. The underpinnings of his world collapsed, and for a long three or four seconds he and the opposing team and all their fans and family, having been chastened by our athletic expertise, were reduced to awe and wonder by our thaumaturgy. It was, in short, a perfect moment. Perhaps, the pitcher said later that night, the one perfect moment of his life. All the next week, it kept cropping up in conversations at lunch: 'Boy, you missed it. You missed the *grapefruit . . .*'

Xenophobia

The softball game marked, more or less, the end of the shoot. Filming continued for three more weeks but everyone felt that the back of the long project had been broken.

People started talking about future plans, movies coming up, vacations, getting back to the comfort of *The New York Times*. We began trading stories about the unpleasantness of Canadians.

One crew member was asked to extinguish his cigar in a Vancouver poolroom as it offended the patrons; an actor was told to remove his baseball hat in the hotel racquetball club as it was in violation of the dress code. These incidents are discussed and rehashed for days. We all agree that the Canadian accent seems to be getting worse.

Now the Canadians of Vancouver are, for good and ill, a placid people. There is little or nothing offensive in them. We are projecting our xenophobia onto *them*. *We* want to go home. We feel the job is finished and we want to go home. We have spent four months away from our loved ones and possessions in 50-below weather, beyond the Last Black Post (as Fred and Ian would have it, or, alternative, 'in the wuup-wuup'). We have been eating hotel food for months in a city where people slavishly obey the traffic laws, and enough is enough.

(It seems to me that actors – quick to grasp and easy to worry – have about two speeds when it comes to talking about work: (1) 'I'm never going to work again,' and (2) 'I'm going to be stuck in this lousy play, soap opera, movie *forever . . .*')

Pride

In any case, the day before the softball game, we are shown the rough cut of the first half hour of the film. The company works six days a week, twelve to sixteen hours a day. Saturday night, the twelfth of May, Fred Schepisi, the director, announces that after dailies (the viewing of the previous day's developed footage) he will be showing a rough cut of the first half hour of the picture – that is, a rough-edited, trial assemblage of the film's first half hour.

The company is amazed and impressed. Most directors would not show a rough cut at this stage to anyone who did not have the contractual right to see it. It is always dangerous to show half-finished work to a child, as the proverb has it, and one never knows how wagging tongues might misinterpret (or *correctly* interpret) a rough-finished product. Many directors won't even let the actors see dailies. So the company as a whole and the actors especially take

Fred's gesture of showing the rough cut as a great compliment: he is, incontrovertibly, acknowledging *everyone* as having a share in the making of the movie.

So at the end of a ninety-hour workweek, we sit in part of a warehouse on the second floor of a building at Dominion Bridge (where much of the Golden Gate was built), sipping beers, waiting to see the rough cut.

First, we see the previous day's dailies. The scene shot the day before is one in which Tim Hutton, Lindsay, and the Iceman, John Lone, are in the Vivarium, a huge terrarium built to simulate tropical conditions in which the Neanderthal lived 20,000 years ago.

The Iceman, whom Tim, the anthropologist, has befriended, and with whom he learns to communicate, develops a passion for Lindsay, the doctor, and makes advances toward her. Tim intervenes and the Iceman concludes that she is Tim's woman. He then tries to barter with Tim for her and when Tim refuses, the Iceman realizes that he is all alone. He has no woman, he is in a foreign world, and he will never get home.

John Lone played the scene in a four-minute take – he is playing, basically, silently, with one or two grunts, and his acting is so pure, his intentions moment to moment completely unmistakable. Rather than playing the Iceman as a grunting gorilla, he gives his entire self to the scene, editing nothing, sparing himself nothing. We see how high the stakes are for him, and when he fails in his attempt to find companionship in an alien world, his realization is *devastating*.

After his take, there is silence and then *prolonged* loving applause. We are proud of him, we are proud to know him, and it is obvious that the movie is going to 'work.'

The magic of the moment is also, of course, informed by Fred's gesture of letting us see the rough cut; we have been permitted to apostrophize the film. It is our film, and it is a beautiful film.

The dailies continue with snippets of other scenes and, while they are going on, one by one, the principal actors go over to John and congratulate him – those who have not worked directly with him somewhat awed: 'Mother of mercy, that fellow can *act* . . .' He is very touched and somewhat overcome.

Every one of his days has started at five A.M. with several hours of makeup. He has spent twelve to sixteen hours a day made up, head and body, he has kept himself to himself and done a magnificent job, and the warehouse room is full of the idea that that work we have just seen embodies all that is best about ourselves as People in the Theater.

All of us in the movie have reached some sort of artistic middle age. Being middle-aged we are presented with a *new* task, which is to learn to accept ourselves. We're no longer struggling against casting agents, producers, script readers, and the Artistic Establishment. We have arrived, or it is clear that the way is open to us. And what we see before us is a life of hard work, difficult living conditions, not much glamour, not much leisure. A life in which we are going to have to give ourselves those rewards we would like to enjoy.

The Theater today can provide, at best, an intermittent living. Even to the most accomplished. We may long for the days when a writer, director, or actor could live in New York and work year to year on provocative material and experience financial security. *None* of those things is possible anymore. So the theatrical worker is torn: Yes, there is a play I would like to do, but it means two months in Chicago, or Seattle, at a minimum wage and away from my family. Just so with the movies. Fewer and fewer are made every year. They are made on bizarre locations. Many times one is among strangers, working without a common history or vocabulary. Much time is devoted during and after work to establishing credentials and good faith . . .

We have, effectively, been thrust back to the nineteenth century, to the days of touring companies and pickup casts, when the stage vehicle was built around the Star and the rest of the cast were not even given the script, but 'sides,' those lines which they said and the cues which preceded those lines. We are tritzing around the world eating a lot of Chinese food and spending many days saying, 'But, you see, I love you . . .' or 'Get the roast, oops! There's the doorbell.'

And many of us experience the malaise of feeling that somehow our life got lost, that the gods have punished us by answering our prayers. We will never get back to Kansas and we will never have the doorman at the studio or the doorman at the Barrymore Theatre nod to us and ask us about our children. We feel that we are becoming a bizarre diplomatic corps, never getting home,

cycled as soon as we start to Go Native, seeing old friends intermittently every half-decade or so . . .

This is perhaps a bit melodramatic, but there you are, and that's
the prejudice of *my* profession.

But Fred's invitation to see the rough cut and John Lone's work
in the take have turned us around, and we're all thinking, *I* know
what I'm missing, an interest in my work. That's why I got involved
in this whole business in the first place, I loved the work.' The
projectionist brings up the lights and starts changing the reels. Fred
makes the speech every director (stage or screen) makes when
showing something other than the absolutely finished product:
'What you are going to see is *rough*, we're still working on it, it
doesn't have the *music*, the *sound* isn't right, we're still working on
the editing, please keep this in mind.'

People run over to the card tables for some more pretzels or
carrot sticks or beer, the lights come down, and we start watching
the movie.

The movie is beautiful. It is lovingly shot; Ian seems to have made
even the shots of the machines simple and eloquent. It is simply and
gracefully edited. The whole film is pervaded by a sense of loss: the
blue-green colours of the huge ice block in which the Neanderthal is
found. Rondy Johnson's costumes that transform the ordinary
work clothes of the scientists; she has made the clothes, and so
helped make the people, very personal.

We are watching a film about real people. They are doing their
job, they are isolated in the Far North, forced to rely on each other.
We are watching a film about ourselves.

We *are* those people. We *were* those people in the Far North,
forced to rely on each other. And those quirks and idiosyncrasies
we see on the screen are not the weak formulations of actors trying
to 'create a character,' but, rather, the unknown and loved idiosyncrasies of people whom we know, and we are watching them doing
their job. We are seeing the true revelation of character: how people
react under pressure.

And as in any piece of art, the theme seems to have magically
asserted itself in all aspects of the work: it is a film about a good
man who isn't ever going to get home, and we are that good man.

Everybody is high on the film after the first half hour; then,
abruptly, the rough cut ends. We are as upset as if the projector

broke, but there is nothing more to see. That's as much as Billy and Fred have done. We want to see more. No one is unaware that this feeling and its expression are a traditional and expected compliment after seeing a rough cut, but, nevertheless, we are surprised and pleased to feel it.

Fred and Ian Baker are warmly congratulated by all. The whole company is standing around smiling at one another. 'Ladies and gentlemen,' says Fred, 'let's get Adrian.'

We go off to restaurants or bars or hotel rooms telling each other how brilliant John Lone is, Fred is, Billy is, Lindsay and Tim are, what a genius Ian is . . . telling each other how proud we are of ourselves as a group. And the next day is the softball game, and our pride is augmented by our trouncing of the Arts Club Theatre.

The final three weeks of filming are downhill.

It is over, Jim Tolkan is gone, Richard Monette finishes shooting a day early and shaves his beard. He is going to the Stratford Festival, where he will play seven classical leads. Patrick Palmer runs into him at lunch and asks where the beard is. Monette explains they finished his shot early and he is done with the film. 'We're paying you until tomorrow,' says Palmer, 'put it back.' Rondy Johnson, our costume designer, is retired, upset because several of the extra costumes for the last sequence have not yet been chosen. She has been let go, as money is getting very tight. The film is running close to the wire. A sign goes up at the lunch trailer: THE BREAKFAST BURRITOS ARE NOT FREE. IF YOU ARE NOT PRINCI-PAL CAST OR PRODUCTION STAFF, YOUR CHARGE IS $2.50. Horst Grandt, the propmaster, complains that his chewing gum has been eliminated from the craft service tables. Many people comment, 'Well, King, I guess this case is *closed*.'

A second softball game is scheduled. We are to play a Vancouver radio station. They have a regular team, they have their own uniforms, and they practice once a week. But our game is scheduled over the long weekend. It is Victoria Day in Canada and most of the station's team is on vacation out of town, so we are pitted against their B team, and we romp over them.

David Strathairn has brought another grapefruit, but, of course, it is not the same.

SOME FREAKS

Acknowledgements

I would like to thank my editor,
DAWN SEFERIAN,
and my assistant,
CATHERINE SHADDIX,
for their help with and enthusiasm
for this book.

Slavyansky Bazaar

An Introduction

In June, Eighteen Ninety-Seven, Constantin Stanislavsky and Vladimir Nemirovich-Danchenko, two gifted theatrical amateurs, met over coffee at the Moscow emporium Slavyansky Bazaar. They talked for eighteen hours, and found their views on life, on Theater, on Art complementary in the correct places and identical in the right places. They formed a marriage which gave birth to the Moscow Art Theatre, a home to classics and an inspiration to the new writers of their day.

The name Slavyansky Bazaar always was a talisman to me. It symbolized the Place Where Three Roads Meet, the mystic Conjunction of Opposites into the Whole, the possibility of True Love; and, on a less abstract plane, the gratification of the desire for ease, comfort, and companionship.

There, at the Slavyansky Bazaar, it seemed to me, were all the good things in life. There was good food, good conversation, alcohol and tobacco, the joy of mutual discovery, the feeling that the universe had a plan for one, and that one was setting about on that marvelous adventure filled with both the virile certainty of risk and danger, and the unspeakable comfort of ordination.

'*Yes*,' the men said to each other. '*Yes*. Isn't life like that ...?' And I held that picture as a beautiful dream, and have been privileged to partake of it from time to time.

I hope you enjoy these essays.

Some Freaks

A Talk to the Signet Society, Harvard University, December 11, 1988

It is traditional to dissuade those planning to pursue a career in the Fine Arts by pointing out to them how much more secure are positions in the other pursuits.

These other pursuits, it occurs to me after a score of years as a writer, have the reputation of being and, in fact, *are* more secure because work in them is not judged by utility; and, in fact, the pursuits themselves are capable of absorbing any number of apprentices because they have little or no final utility; and, so, unlike a career in the Fine Arts, the public can never be surfeited by either an overabundance of practitioners, or an overabundance of unqualified practitioners. These professions are, in the words, I believe, of Mr Veblen, a 'conspiracy against the Laity.' So, of course they are more secure, as there is one born every minute.

But the law of life is to do evil and good, to eat and be eaten, and the most supposedly innocuous good is, perhaps, also and occasionally violence in disguise.

What does it mean to be a member of the intelligentsia? It occurred to me one day that it is something akin to being the germ of a virus; that the intelligentsia, we 'fops,' are driven to seek out, to explore, to endorse, to, finally, be the first exploiters of certain aspects of the material world, that we, in our quality of avatars of fashion, are the first news of the co-option of the theretofore natural.

Which of us has not seen, heard of, and dreamt of emulating that artist, painter, writer, whatever, who quit the city and enjoyed the wild; who found rapture in the contemplation of that which the natives took for granted: beautiful views, clean water, deep woods, clear beaches, unspoiled native honesty or wit?

Well, we went there, and we *did* enjoy it, and we either wrote or painted it, or told our friends, or were discovered by those who trailed in the wake of free spirits like ourselves, so that all that remained of that beach, woods, or indigenous accent was just our depiction of it.

It was bound to happen anyway, of course, but it occurred to me that we were the disease; first speaking of that New Thing which, having been noticed, must, then, become Old.

We could not *stop* ourselves from doing it, from renovating that old house, that old Factory District, that old Basket, and, so, set fashion, and consigned the Timeless to the Round of Time, which is to say, to Death.

But at least we weren't Working in an Office All Day Long. No, we were working in an office all day long, and then carrying that office home with us in our heads for the evening and into the night, and driving our families crazy with the dreariness of our concerns for the hidden, for the exquisite. Who did we think we were?

And how useful was it, finally – as much as we, full of pride, looked at those who toiled and spun to no effect or purpose whatever other than the accumulation of Gold, or Status, or Power, or something Chimerical and Useless – when compared to the thrill we artists felt in our discoveries, or in the Populace's discovery of us. As Mr. Ginsberg wrote, 'Businessmen are Serious, Politicians are Serious, everybody's serious but *Me* . . .' And so we turned to anyone who suggested that our 'work' was merely a toy, and the flywheel of a great society spinning off excess steam, and weren't we *précieux*, children that we were, to assume that our work had a use. . . .

Though, of course, none of us did it because it had a use, we did it because, like the businessman, like the developer, we couldn't help ourselves.

Sometimes an individual is thrown up *who does not fit the norm*. One reads of the Indians of the Plains. And their magnificent society. Among the warrior race, a young boy, subject to visions, incapable of assimilating, of taking up the major burdens of the culture, of being a Man in the Culture, if you will, was given the option of becoming a Man by another, by a more solitary route, as a seer, or a sage, or Medicine Man, and so was exempted from the daily task of his brethren, and afforded a certain living, and a position in the society. And that Individual and Society as a whole benefited.

They benefited, perhaps, from his visions, and they benefited, perhaps most importantly, from the endorsement of the notion that *all* people born into the society are precious. What Is Worthwhile in a Society? I suppose it depends on how close, in time or space, one is to the phenomenon in question. Finally, pursuits, places, and people are made romantic, which is to say, irresistible, and are made to seem important in order to attract us to them as part of a plan *beyond the plan of reason.*

I was always confused by the verse 'Consider the Lilies of the Field, . . . they neither toil nor spin; and yet I say unto you that even Solomon in All his Glory, was not arrayed like one of these.'

And, over the years, when I would hear or think of that verse, it would seem to me specious – an indictment of *labor*, and *talent*, or perhaps, of the conjunction of the two, or of 'fortune.' And finally, the verse made no sense to me. It seemed to me 'weak,' and in praise of weakness.

I had not thought of that phrase for some time, I'd passed my fortieth year, and it came to my mind in conjunction with these thoughts, and I understood it for the first time. I had changed since last I thought of it, and I said, 'Of *course*, it *is* an indictment – a gentle indictment of the prideful love of labor or talent, for that pride neglects what, to the author of that phrase, is obvious, that both that labor and that talent, that ambition and that reward, are gifts of God.'

That the creation of these differing professions, these differing pursuits, different levels of achievement, of the chaos of competition, this, as in the arts, aesthetic Darwinism, taken to its logical extreme, becomes the opposite of the random view.

All professions, achievements, impulses, are thrown up to compete, to strive, to an end which is *not* chance, but is the effect of some Universal Will; and, to that end, all these efforts, of Solomon *and* the lilies of the field, are equal. It is not *given* us to know the worth of our impulses, or of our acts. To some, and, in some times, the acts the wisest have held to be the best are otherwise seen as heinous.

We are all held in the sway of a superior intelligence, and it is in the interests of that power that each of us finds his or her pursuits compelling.

It is in the interest of the Whole, and, I think, in the pursuits of something beyond the whole, that some are driven to pursue the arts, that some are driven to pursue power, or wealth, or solitude, or death.

I always felt proud, and not a little arrogant, that I was one of those freaks privileged to live in the world of the Arts. As I become older, I feel still happy, and quite privileged to be working in an area where I am happy; but I am, I hope, a bit less proud, and, increasingly, awed by the way the universe has been thoughtfully construed even to include a freak like me.

This is not to say I feel that I am devoid of talent, or that my work is devoid of worth; but that my *profession* of artistic vision arose, I think, not so much to express whatever 'individual' ideas I may have had or may have, but, rather, to accommodate and embrace a deviant personality which was not going to be employed elsewhere. *Much* like the growth of the computer, and computer-run business, *coincidentally* in time to accommodate a burgeoning work force which has nothing to do. This work force inherited an economic/business system and world built around and given birth to by a machine which does nothing but shuffle 'facts,' and these 'facts' give rise to an enterprise system infinitely expandable. And so more lost ones were subsumed in the burgeoning whole.

Whatever you choose or are called to do, apart from doing that which you may know in your heart to be wrong, and I wouldn't advise you to do that, I think that you and I *are* all those freaks, or *are* those lilies of the field, and it is not given us to know the time in which we live. We may think we are creating masterpieces (and, in fact, we may be) or we may think we are bent over our tatting frames like Victorian women doing our 'work'. In any case, we are this: A part of the surplus shriven by Mother Earth.

The Bible says God loves us all.

The Decoration of Jewish Houses

My parents were the children of Ashkenazi immigrants. In my childhood home, and in the homes of my friends of like extraction, there was a feeling of tenuousness which expressed itself in the physical trappings. None of the homemakers knew quite what a home was supposed to look like. They had no tradition of decor, the adoption of which would be anything other than arbitrary.

When our grandparents left the *shtetl*, they brought nothing with them. What, in fact, could they have brought? There was, in their villages, no 'Jewish' style of decoration, or furniture; there was no ornament, the look of what domestic artifacts there were was dictated by poverty.

There was no art in the Ashkenazi homes. And, as Jews, there were no religious trappings beyond, perhaps, a *Kaddish* cup or a menorah.

What did our immigrant grandparents bring with them? Perhaps a photograph or two, perhaps a samovar; in short, nothing. And the children of those immigrants, my parents' generation, were raised in the New World in varying degrees, again, of poverty.

Surplus income was devoted to education of the young, to help them Get Ahead. As get ahead they did. They rose to prominence, in the Jewish way, in the professions which, since the days of Egypt, had been intermittently open to them: medicine, law, negotiation, commerce, banking, entertainment.

My parents' generation was in the rabid pursuit, first, of education, and then, of success, greatly assimilationist. They were, in my experience, largely Reform; and thought themselves 'racially' but not 'religiously' Jewish. They held to the increasingly sparse practice of religious ritual with a sense, quite frankly, of foolishness, as if to say, 'I don't know why I'm doing this, and I share your ('you' being the world-at-large, which is to say, the Christian world) quite correct vision that all of this nonsense is *vastly* beside the point, and only serves to accentuate the differences between us, when we should, rightly, be concentrating on our similarities.'

What did it mean, then, to be 'racially' Jewish? It meant that among ourselves, we shared the wonderful, the warm, and the comforting codes, language, jokes, and attitudes which make up the consolations of strangers in a strange land. We shared, among ourselves, Jewish humor, a pride in each other's accomplishments, a sense of sometimes intellectual and sometimes moral superiority to the populace-at-large. For were we not, as a group, socially conscious, socially committed, socially active, and dedicated to equal rights and consideration for all races and nations? Yes. We were. For all races except our inferior own.

In Mel Brooks's film *The History of the World, Part I*, Cloris Leachman, as Mme. Defarge, harangues the canaille in a wonderfully dreadful French accent. She says, 'We have no home, we have no bread, we don't even have a *language* – all we have is ziz lousy *accent*.'

Similarly our second generation had no language. Our parents eschewed Yiddish as the slave language of poverty, and Hebrew as the dead language of meaningless ritual. Yes, it was being spoken in Israel, and one could make Aliyah and *go* there, but, as the old joke has it, 'What kind of job is that for a nice Jewish boy?'

For my generation, Jewish culture consisted of Jewish food and Jewish jokes, neither of which, probably, were very good for us.

We did not and we *do* not believe in the – let alone *excellence* – *existence* of anything which could even remotely be referred to as a 'Jewish Culture.' We American Jews have been, and remain, quite willing to have the populace-at-large consider us second-class citizens – second-class citizens to be, in many ways, envied and scorned rather than oppressed and scorned, but nonetheless . . .

We Jews consider it a matter of course, for example, that there has never even been a Jewish candidate for *Vice* President.

In our lack of self-esteem, we, as a race, are happy and proud that our country has progressed to the point that we can see a serious presidential candidate in Jesse Jackson. And this in *spite* of Mr. Jackson's rather blatant anti-Semitism.

His career awakens deep feelings of happiness that social justice is being done, and feelings of relief that the terrible racism in which we all grew up is beginning to wane. But we listen to his anti-Semitic remarks, we watch his endorsement of anti-Semitic leaders, we listen to his insulting disclaimers, and we think, 'All right – to preserve the *peace*, we will all pretend that you don't mean it,' and, singularly, in this aspect of our social life, we behave like fools.

Why then, my fellow Jews, have we never supported, or thought to support, why are we incapable of *envisioning* a serious presidential attempt by a Jew? Why does this prospect seem to us irrelevant and faintly ridiculous? As it seems to us faintly ridiculous that we might want in our cities major thoroughfares called Birnbaum or Schwartz?

We Jews know, even at the remove of Seventy Years – the span since my grandparents arrived in New York from the Pale till now – we know the warmth of camaraderie-in-exile, we know the warmth of self-depreciation. We know the warmth of the feeling of secret superiority, and of personal success against odds. But of the demand, of even the feeling of *rectitude* of the demand for absolute social equality, we know nothing very much at all.

We know that Black is Beautiful. We saw the young Jewish women of my generation *flock* to Black Studies programs at our universities, and we said, 'Yes, they are drawn, quite rightly, in the strength of a correct and revolutionary cause. God bless them'; and we supported them in their support of Black self-love at the same time we supported them in surgically re-carving their faces so that they would look less 'Jewish.'

We could not, as American Jews, feel that Jewish is Beautiful, that the sexy, vital, essential assertion of a just demand was within our power, *just* as it was and is within the power of the American Indians, or the Eskimos, or the American blacks. And *never* have we American Jews thought, let alone asserted, 'Yes, *I* am beautiful. I come from a beautiful race.' And we would say, with the irony which has been our most prized and useful possession for quite a few millennia: 'I'm not going to say *that* – too *arrogant* . . .,' i.e., 'too Jewish.'

In our support of the moral, social, and emotional rights of the oppressed, we put ourselves, the Jews, behind not only every other racial group, we put ourselves behind the seals and the *whales.* Now, funny as that is, you, gentle reader, you tell me I'm wrong.

In what do we take pride? What symbols and what models do we possess?

We can point to the odd Jewish athlete with pride. What about Jewish business leaders, professional men and women? Entertainers?

They are not sources of racial pride. Why not? Because they're simply doing what is expected of them. It is expected that we and our fellows will strive and succeed in the traditional pursuits of a landless people; in the pursuits of the mind.

But a Jewish *football* player ... that person would stand as a magnificent and welcome freak. That person is an image which gets the heart beating a bit faster with pride. As does the success of the crypto-Jew.

'You know who's Jewish ...' was a recurring phrase at my house, and in the homes of my contemporaries. That a Jew could rise to prominence, *particularly* in the entertainment industry, *without* being overtly Jewish, without playing Jewish parts, without being stereotyped, this filled us with a secret joy. Why? Because this person *had escaped*. This person had fulfilled a wild personal fantasy, they had 'passed' with no effort, and, so, with no guilt, into the greater world from the lesser. (By the way, I wonder why it has escaped general comment that when the part of an *incontrovertible* 'Jew' must be filled in the movies, it is *inevitably* filled by a non-Jew. Why? Because the Jew would look and act 'too Jewish.')

Concomitantly, someone who obviously *was* Jewish and who sought to deny it, primarily through the adoption of a Christian religion, was, in our homes, an object of wonder and scorn. This person was despised as a weakling, and we thought (1) *I* can take it, why can't *you*?; and (2) How can you be so ultimately foolish as to trade your *Jewishness* for a greater acceptance in a community of strangers which (3) you aren't going to get anyway.

Or, to distill: What would induce you to renounce the only people who love you?

Because we do love each other very much. It is, I think, notable that we have *not* noted that we tend not to love ourselves.

We have our rare ballplayers, we have our tales of Charlie Chaplin and Cary Grant, we have the menorah or we had the samovar before Dad turned it into a lamp, we have our Jewish food (disappearing with the generation of the grandmothers), and we have our self-deprecating humor. (Yes, I know that it's funny. It is the funniest humor in the world, it's how I have made my living all my life, and, it *is* self-deprecating.)

But in our homes, in that which speaks of rest, of identity, we have no symbols. We do not know how a Jewish home (finally, we do not know how a *Jew*) is supposed to look.

We see in our homes the occasional and vaguely Semitic 'quote', a Hebraised motto in English, a mosaic coffee table, a souvenir of a trip to Israel; or, in advanced cases, the display of a piece of Judaica. And that's a Jewish home to this day. The home of an outsider. We fit out our living places as if we were Yankees, we cast Laurence Olivier and Klaus Kinski as prototypical Jews. We have never known any better.

God bless those in all generations who have embraced their Jewishness. We are a beautiful people and a good people, and a magnificent and ancient history of thought and action lives in our literature *and lives in our blood*; and I am reminded of Marcus Garvey's rhetoric, in addressing the black populace: 'Up you Mighty Race, you Race of Kings, rise to your feet, you can accomplish what you will.'

We would say, 'I already knew that,' as we always have. Accomplishment has not been the problem, pride and enjoyment has.

When we let an anti-Semitic remark pass, with the silent thought, 'What a sorry and misguided person'; when we shrug in sorrow at Jesse Jackson; when we sigh at the cocktail party when a 'friend' says, 'If you have been persecuted all these thousands of years, isn't it possible that you are doing something to bring it about?'; when we espouse, support, and champion *every social cause* but our own, we contribute to anti-Semitism.

I am sick of the Passover Seders at which we invite our non-Jewish friends to engage in social colloquy, and which inevitably degenerates into fair-minded discussions of how *authentic* it is to be a Jew, how *authentic* is the state of Israel and who is to blame for historical Jewish suffering. Are we so poor that we can't even celebrate our own holidays, without using them as a social *offering* to the larger group? Because, finally, the social activism, the vast support of Liberal causes, the invitation of our non-Jewish friends to the Seder, I'm sorry, but finally, as much 'good' as it may do, it stinks of 'take this but don't hit me.'

I don't know what a Jewish home looks like.

I have never been to Israel. I wish my brothers and sisters in Israel well, as do we all. It would be fine if we could end our exile in this country, too.

A Plain Brown Wrapper

The periodic arrival of the Charles Atlas material disturbed me greatly. I was nine or ten years old, and had answered their ad in a comic book. The ad assured me that there would be no charge for information regarding the system of Dynamic Tension – the system which could and would transform the weakling into the well-proportioned strong man of the ads; the ad further assured me that the material would arrive in a plain brown wrapper.

The material did come, as advertised, in the plain wrapper. But it did not make me strong. It terrified me, because each free installment dealt with one thing and one thing only: my obligation to the Charles Atlas Company, and my progressively intransigent, incomprehensible, and criminal refusal to pay for materials received.

I dreaded the arrival of those envelopes; and when they arrived I slunk in shame and despair. I loathed myself for ever having gotten involved in this mess.

Was the whole Charles Atlas promotion geared to idiots and children? Looking back, I think it must have been. The Method of Dynamic Tension promised fairly instant strength and beauty at no cost to the consumer. And the vicious and continuous dunning letters played masterfully on the undeveloped ego of that idiot or child. I, one such child, thought, on receiving their threats: 'Of course they are disappointed in me. I am weak and ugly. How dare I have presumed to take these fine, strong people's course? How dare someone as worthless as I have aspired to possess the secrets of strength and beauty? The Charles Atlas people have, as they must, recognized my laughable unworthiness, and my only defense against them is prayer.'

For they were, of course, God – they offered me transformation in exchange for an act of sacrifice and belief. But I was unprepared to make that act.

The other religious experience of my youth was equally inconclusive and unfortunate. It was Reform Judaism: and though the God Jehovah, the God of Wrath and Strength and Righteousness spoke through the mouth of Charles Atlas, he was deemed quite out of place at the Sinai Temple.

The Rabbis were addressed by the title 'doctor,' the trumpet was blown in deference to the shofar, the ancient Hebrew chants and songs were rendered in Victorian settings, we went to Sunday School, rather than *shul*. There is nothing particularly wrong with these traducements of tradition, except this: they were all performed in an atmosphere of shame.

Untutored in any religion whatever, we youngsters were exposed to the idea of worshipper-as-revisionist. Our practices were not in-aid-of, but in-reaction-to. The constant lesson of our Sunday School was that we must be better, more rational, more up-to-date, finally, more *American* than that thing which had come before. And that thing which had come before was *Judaism*.

Judaism, at my temple in the 1950s, was seen as American Good Citizenship (of which creed we could be proud), with some Unfortunate Asiatic Overtones, which we were not going to be so craven as to *deny*. No, we were going to steadfastly bear up under the burden of our taint – our Jewishness. We were such good citizens that *although it was not our fault* that our parents and grandparents were the dread Ashkenazi, the 'superstitious scum of Eastern Europe,' we would not publicly sever our connection with them. We Reform Jews would be so stalwart, so American, so non-Jewish, in fact, as to Play the Game. We would go by the name of Jews, although every other aspect of our religious life was Unitarian. Our religion was nothing other than a corporate creed and our corporate creed was an evasion. It was this: We are Jews, and we are Proud to be Jews. We will express our Jewishness by behaving in every way possible exactly like our Christian Brethren, because what they have is better than what we have.

I found the Reform Judaism of my childhood nothing other than a desire to 'pass'; to slip unnoticed into the non-Jewish community, to do nothing which would attract the notice, and, so, the wrath of mainstream America.

Why would America's notice necessarily beget its wrath? Easy: We were Jews, and worthless. We were everything bad that was said against us, we didn't even have a religion anymore, we'd given it up to placate the non-Jewish community, to escape its wrath.

What of the Wrath of Jehovah? He, too, was better left behind if we were to cease being Jews.

What was it, then, to be Jewish? Heaven forfend that it was to be part of a race, and spare us the wretched image of dark skins, loud voices, hook noses, and hairy hands.

Was it to be part of a religion? Of what did that religion consist? Every aspect of its observance had been traduced. Which of us Reform (which meant and means, of course, *reformed*, which is to say changed for the better, and, implicitly, penitent) Jews could remember the names, let alone the meanings, of those joyless holidays we attempted to celebrate? Those occasions – sabbath, holidays, bar mitzvahs – were celebrated with sick fear and shame. Not shame that we had forsaken our heritage, but shame that we had not forsaken it sufficiently.

One could both despise and envy Kissinger, Goldwater, and others who, though they had rejected the faith of their fathers, at least had the courage of their convictions.

The lesson of my Reform Temple was that metaphysics is just superstition – that there is no God. And every Sunday we celebrated our escape from Judaism. We celebrated our autonomy, our separateness from God and from our forefathers, and so, of course, we were afraid.

My coreligionists and I, eventually, sought out the God we had been denied. We sought God in Scientology, Jews for Jesus, Eastern Studies, consciousness-raising groups – all attempts to explain the relationship between the one and the all – between our powerlessness and the strength of the Universe. We sought God through methods not unlike Dynamic Tension – in which the powerless weakling, having been instructed in the Mysteries, overcame the Bully (the Juggernaut, the World) and so restored order to the Universe.

Here is my question: What was so shameful about wanting a better physique?

Why did such information have to come in a plain brown wrapper?

Why did the Charles Atlas Company know that such an endeavour needs to be hidden?

The answer is that the desire for a better physique was not shameful, but that we, the *applicants*, were shameful, and that we were intrinsically unworthy, the idea of weaklings such as ourselves desiring strength and beauty was so laughable that, of course we would want our desires to be kept secret.

That was why the dunning letters worked. They threatened to expose not that we had not paid our bills, but that we had the audacity to want a beautiful life.

And that was also my experience, as a child, of Reform Judaism. It was religion in a plain brown wrapper, a religion the selling point of which was that it would not embarrass us.

Thirty years later, I am very angry at the Charles Atlas Company, and at the Sinai Temple. Neither one delivered what they could and should have; more important, they had no right to instill in a child a sense of shame.

Thirty years later I am not completely happy with my physique. I am very proud of being a Jew, and I have a growing sense of the reality of God. I say to that no doubt long-demised Charles Atlas Company, You should be ashamed; and to the leaders of that Reformed Temple, What were you ashamed of?

Women

A fellow called and asked me to write an article about women. My wife asked me what the call was about. I said they want me to write about women, but I don't *know* anything about women. 'I know,' said my wife. So I am writing this on a dare.

The first thing I realized about women is 'they are people too.' This came to me in my teen-age years, all of which were spent, in the vernacular, trying to get a leg over, and not having a *clue*. I was raised on James Bond and Hugh Hefner's Playboy Philosophy. Bond went through life impressing people with his gun, and Hefner went through life in a bathrobe; and the capper was that, of the two of them, Hefner was the one who actually existed.

'What were women?' I asked myself, and, one day the answer came, 'They are people too.' 'Well, then,' I thought, 'they must have thoughts and feelings too!' and I have spent the last twenty-five years trying to figure out what those thoughts and feeling *are*.

The difficulty, of course, is one *wants* something from women: notice, sex, solace, compassion, forgiveness; and that many times one wants it sufficiently desperately that it clouds one's perception of what *they* want. And, in negotiations, it is never a good idea to lose sight of what your opponent wants.

Are all exchanges with women negotiations? Yes. If this seems like an inappropriate response, it is just that I do not know a stronger one than 'yes.'

Women, it seems to me, like to know who's in charge. And if it's not going to be them, they would like it to be you. The problem is that 'in charge,' in this instance, may be defined as 'leading the two of you towards that goal which they have elected is correct.' I will, at this point, compare dealing with women to dealing with children or animals. This is not to suggest that women are, in any way, inferior, but merely that children and animals are smarter than men.

Men have a lot to learn from women. Men are the puppydogs of the universe. Men will waste their time in pursuit of the utterly useless simply because their peers are all doing it. Women will not. They are legitimately goal-oriented, and their goals, for the most part, are simple: love, security, money, prestige. These are good, direct, meaningful goals, especially as opposed to the more male objectives of glory, acceptance, and being well-liked. Women don't give a tinker's damn about being well-liked, which means they don't know how to compromise. They will occasionally surrender to someone they love, they will fight until they have won, they will avoid a confrontation they cannot win, but they won't compromise.

Compromise is a male idea, and goes back to 'being well-liked.' Compromise means, 'We're going to be meeting again in the future on some other issue, so don't you think it would be a good idea if *both* parties took something valuable away from this negotiation?' The female response is 'no.'

Which means women are not much fun to do business with.

George Lorimer, editor of the *Saturday Evening Post*, wrote, in 1903, that one should not do business with a woman; if they're losing, they'll add their sex to it; and if they're winning, they'll subtract their sex from it, and treat you harder than any man.

Well in *my* business, which is the Theater and Movies, I've found that's absolutely true. The coldest, cruelest, most arrogant behavior I have ever seen in my professional life has been – and *consistently* been – on the part of women producers in the movies and the theater. I have seen women do things that the worst man would never entertain the thought of – I do not imply that he would be stopped by conscience, but he *would* be stopped by the fear of censure, which takes us back to the inability to compromise.

The woman says, 'I'm going to win *this* battle, and I'll worry about the *next* battle at that time.'

Women have a tough time of it. Our society has fallen apart and *nobody* knows what he or she should be doing. A man usually deals with this by referring to his superiors, but he doesn't have to consider childbirth.

Is having kids an option, a necessity, a divine commandment? This has to be one of the most difficult questions in life, and it is one that half the population doesn't have to address, let alone answer.

Women, it seems to me, spend most of their childbearing years feeling guilty. When they're pursuing their career they feel, probably correctly, that they're short-changing their kids, or their own possibility of having kids. When they're having or raising kids, they feel the sands of their career-advancement clock running out on them. This is a bind I wouldn't like to be in; for a career and a home are very strong drives and desires. Popular publications inform the Modern Woman that she can have both to a completely full extent; but I never met a women who believed it.

Women *want* to believe it, but my sad report is that they cannot, and so the working woman always has a segment of the popular thought to reproach herself with, *whatever* she chooses.

This dilemma deserves male sympathy. Males cannot, however, let themselves feel sympathetic, because we are somewhat guilty about how happy we are that we don't have the problem.

Men *generally* expect more of women than we do of ourselves. We feel, based on constant evidence, that women are better, stronger, more truthful, than men. You can call this sexism, or reverse sexism, or whatever you wish, but it is my experience.

The Governor of my State, a woman, refused to send the National Guard to South America – an act of real courage and conviction. I expected it of her.

And I think men are reassured generally by the presence of women in previously all-male positions.

I feel about the woman governor, or airline pilot, or doctor, that she's less apt to be distracted than a man; I'm thankful for it. Are there *bad* women? Yes. I've already enumerated the single instance of women 'producers.' I know there are women criminals, I worked for a while in a women's prison. The inmates did a lot of crying, which seemed to me the appropriate response to the situation; and women, it seems to me, generally are more aware of what's going on than men are.

Over the years, I have come to rely completely on my wife's judgment of character; and am coming to rely on my daughter's ability to assess a situation correctly. The other day she got a splinter in her foot, and I got a tweezer and came over and stood in front of her, and she started to cry piteously. '*Why* are you crying?' I said. 'I haven't even *touched* you yet . . .' 'You're standing on my foot,' she said.

Can we broaden this conceit of women having splinters in their feet, and men, their supposed saviors, adding to the discomfort? Women are, as we know, very much second-class citizens in this country.

As with any oppressed group, gains are not *awarded*, but won, and so the sight of the female airline pilot is, I think, a salutary reproach to the male; i.e., 'I got here without you, and you can't begin to believe how hard it was. Do you think *you* could do as well?'

And to the young men in the audience who have not had the benefit of the armed James Bond or the robed Hugh Hefner, I offer the following observations.

Our Western World is devolving into a more primitive, more effective society. When that more primitive society has taken root, you or your descendants will know how to get on well with women by obeying tradition, religion, and listening to your uncle. In the meantime: (1) be direct; (2) remember that, being smarter than men, women respond to courtesy and kindness; (3) if you want to know what kind of a wife someone will make, observe her around her father and mother; (4) as to who gets out of the elevator first, I just can't help you.

The Central Park Wolf

Bicycles and dogs are not welcome on the upper track of the Central Park Reservoir. There are signs to the effect that they are not allowed, but the only sanction taken against offenders is a scowl from the passing runners to whose use the track is consecrated.

The custom of the track, for some reason, is for runners to proceed in a counterclockwise direction. At any given time the majority of runners may, in fact, be running clockwise, but they will be understood by themselves and by those they meet to be running *the wrong way*.

Prior to last Wednesday (March 28) the most provocative thing that ever happened to me while running around the reservoir was that a fellow sitting by the south pumphouse one day last spring pointed at me and for no conceivable reason, shouted 'Boola Boola' each time I ran past him. I later realized I had been wearing my cousin's Yale sweatshirt at the time.

Last Wednesday morning I was jogging counterclockwise around the track and, walking slowly towards me, there was a German shepherd dog. I wished to exercise my perquisites and looked behind him for his owner to scowl at, but there was no one there.

The dog was white and wheat-colored, bruised along his left flank, and wore no collar.

'Wouldn't it be funny,' I thought, 'if the dog were mad. Then I would have to jump up on the fence. Somebody should call the police.'

On my next lap, passing the south pumphouse and proceeding north up the Fifth Avenue side, I saw the dog again, still continuing in the same direction. A moment later various martial vehicles appeared in the bridle path below the running track.

The first were two police cars moving very quickly in reverse. They were followed by a squadroll – moving in the usual fashion, a white van, and more police cars.

I did not grow up in New York and so take great pride in understanding its quiddities. I was glad to grasp the nature of the procession at once: someone was filming a car chase. (Actually not an uncommon occurrence in and around Central Park.)

I started jogging north again when I heard the public address of one of the police cars blaring, 'Get away from the dog. Get away from the dog.' I looked back to see the cars had stopped even with the dog and the policemen were getting out of their cars.

'Great,' I thought, 'you are a rotten New Yorker. The dog is obviously the star of the sequence. He was *obviously* the object of the car chase. This must be a movie about some mad dog, or an escaped dog that knows the location of some jewels or something.'

Thinking back I could see that the dog *must* have been trained to be able to proceed so regularly around the reservoir without human control. It was a trained dog and there must have been hidden cameras filming its progress around the reservoir, I thought. Perhaps I would be in the movie.

The Police kept screaming. 'Get Away from the Dog. Get off the Reservoir. Get off the Reservoir.' I looked back to see them climbing up the bank towards the dog, along with a man and a woman carrying nooses, who had just alighted from a white sedan blazoned A.S.P.C.A.

Jogging in place at the 86th Street stairs I asked a fellow runner if she knew what was going on. 'It's a wolf,' she said.

The wolf was frightened and took off clockwise around the reservoir. The Police and the A.S.P.C.A. ran back to their vehicles and gave chase.

I continued jogging north and had a good view of the chase – the Mars lights flashing, the amplifiers blaring, 'Get away from the dog,' startled runners scowling.

The chase ended at the north pumphouse with the Police and the A.S.P.C.A. officials clustered up on the concrete apron and the passers-by and joggers relegated to the lower bridle path.

Car and van radios were humming and people on the scene were assuring others elsewhere that everything was all right.

Two very competent-looking A.S.P.C.A. Emergency Squad officers were sitting in their van. I went over to them and asked them what was going on. They told me they had caught a wolf. I asked them what was the wolf doing in Central Park. They told me it escaped from their East Side animal shelter the night before. They had been looking for it for several hours.

I asked them what was a wolf doing at their Manhattan shelter and they said its owner had brought it there.

When I told the story later to friends the most-often-held opinion was that the wolf had been bought small as a cute pet to commemorate some holiday or occasion and, like a turtle or an iguana or a baby alligator, or like a baby chick purchased for Easter, it had grown into its own and was no longer desirable as a pet.

Introduction from
A Practical Handbook For the Actor

Most acting training is based on shame and guilt. If you have studied acting, you have been asked to do exercises you didn't understand, and when you did them, as your teacher adjudged, badly, you submitted guiltily to the criticism. You have also been asked to do exercises you *did* understand, but whose application to the craft of acting escaped you, and you were ashamed to ask that their usefulness be explained.

As you did these exercises it seemed that everyone around you understood their purpose but you – so, guiltily, you learned to pretend. You learned to pretend to 'smell the coffee' when doing sensory exercises. You learned to pretend that the 'mirror exercise' was demanding, and that doing it well would somehow make you more attuned on stage. You learned to pretend to 'hear the music with your toes,' and to 'use the space.'

As you went from one class to the next and from one teacher to the next, two things happened: being human, your need to believe asserted itself. You were loath to believe your teachers were frauds, so you began to believe that you *yourself* were a fraud. This contempt for yourself became contempt for all those who did not share the particular bent of your school training.

While keeping up an outward show of perpetual study, you began to believe that no actual, practicable technique of acting existed, and this was the only possible belief supported by the evidence.

Now how do I know these things about you? I know them because I suffered them myself. I suffered them as a longtime student of acting, and as an actor. I suffer them second hand as a teacher of acting, as a director, and as a playwright.

I know that you are dedicated and eager – eager to learn, eager to *believe*, eager to find a way to bring that art that you feel in yourself to the stage. You are legitimately willing to sacrifice, and you think that the sacrifice required of you is subjugation to the will of a teacher. But a more exacting sacrifice is required. You must follow the dictates of your common sense.

It would be fine if there were many great master teachers of acting, but there are not. Most acting teachers, unfortunately, are frauds, and they rely on your complicity to survive. This not only deprives you of positive training but stifles your greatest gift as an artist: your sense of truth. It is this sense of truth, a simplicity, and feelings of wonder and reverence – all of which you possess – that will revitalize the Theater.

How do you translate them onto the Stage? The answer to this question is reducible to a simple stoic philosophy: Be what you wish to seem.

Stanislavsky once wrote that you should 'play well or badly, but play truly.' It is not up to you whether your performance will be brilliant – all that is under your control is your intention. It is not under your control whether your career will be brilliant – all that is under your control is your intention.

If you intend to manipulate, to show, to impress, you may experience mild suffering and pleasant triumphs. If you intend to follow the truth you feel in yourself – to follow your common sense, and force your will to serve you in the quest for discipline and simplicity – you will subject yourself to profound despair, loneliness, and constant self-doubt. And if you persevere, the Theater, which you are learning to serve, will grace you, now and then, with the greatest exhilaration it is possible to know.

Conventional Warfare

Sahara Hotel, Las Vegas Poolside

By seven P.M. the pool area was filled with conventioneers dressed in camouflage fatigues. It was announced that unsavory elements had taken hostages and were holed up on the third floor of the hotel. These elements, terrorists brandishing automatic weapons, appeared on the balcony and showed us the bound hostages.

Three men in black jump suits began rappelling rapidly from the hotel roof.

The cocky terrorists shouted their demands while the three men in black descended their ropes and took positions above and to the side of their balcony. A concussion grenade was lobbed into the terrorists' midst, the attacking forces swung onto the balcony, and the sound of simulated small-arms fire was heard. A woman in a violet ball gown appeared on the balcony beneath, and looked about wonderingly.

The black-suited S.W.A.T team emerged from the smoke on their floor and held their weapons high, indicating victory was theirs. The conventioneers by the pool cheered – myself included. The woman on the second floor shrugged and went back into the building. Captain Dale Dye, U.S.M.C. (Ret.), then announced that the pugil-stick contest would begin.

This interested me particularly, as I had entered my name in the lists and was a contestant in said contest.

I waited for him to call my name and wondered whether I had the capacity to stand and slug it out with men, or whether I was just another wussy Eastern Intellectual with a marvelous gift for dialogue.

What was I doing in Las Vegas? I had come to have fun, and to hang out with my friend Bagwell and his friends.

His friends were the people at *Soldier of Fortune* magazine. The magazine was running its fifth annual convention at the Sahara Hotel. Bagwell, who makes knives for a living, is the knife editor of the magazine.

Soldier of Fortune was started ten years ago by Colonel Robert

K. Brown, a veteran of the Special Forces; and the concerns of the magazine are fairly well represented by the activities at the convention. These included a three-gun (rifle, pistol, shotgun) competition with a hefty $40,000 in prize money; Operation Headhunter, a military-oriented five-mile cross-country obstacle/orienteering/endurance race; a parachute jump; a firepower demonstration; an arms show; sundry lectures; a pugil-stick competition; and a banquet.

The conventioneers were men – and a few women – interested in the history, theory, and practice of warfare – especially of unconventional or guerrilla war. They were, in the main, former and current members of the armed forces, law enforcement officers, gun aficionados, and, I suppose, a couple of people like me who were just trying to get out of the house.

I had never been to a convention of any kind before, and I was getting a kick out of wearing one of those name tags, which looked kind of silly when those other guys are wearing them but feel rather comforting when you've got one on yourself.

I found the conventioneers lovely people. I didn't agree with some of the ideas, but then I don't agree with a lot of my *own* ideas and seem powerless to rid myself of them.

One idea at the convention I found quite attractive was that of unabashed patriotism. The fellows seemed to love the idea of America in much the same way that someone else might love the idea of The Theater – that is, as a perfect institution.

The conventioneers also seemed to love the idea of Having Fun.

I was already having fun. The cab from the airport dropped me at the Sahara and the cabdriver asked me if I wanted to flip for the four-dollar fare. I said okay and reached for a coin. '*Uh uh*,' he said, 'we'll use *my* coin.' Well, okay, I thought, everybody's got to eat and he flipped his coin and he lost.

'What a great beginning to a Weekend with the Boys,' I thought, and checked into the hotel and started looking for Bagwell.

The next morning I found him at his table at the arms show. Bagwell had seventeen of his knives laid out for display. He makes the knives at an open forge out behind his house in east Texas, and when I arrived he was putting on a display with one of them. He had a twelve-inch bowie knife and was about to cut four wrapped one-inch free-hanging strands of hemp rope with one swipe. The onlookers muttered among themselves that it was impossible, but I had seen him do it many times before. I asked him if *I* could try it when he got done. He gave a look that seemed to say, 'Get away, boy, you are queering the pitch.'

He then suggested, for good measure, that a friend of his take me for a walk. The friend introduced himself as an Air Marshal, late of the R.A.F.; and so the Air Marshal and I started on a leisurely tour of the arms show. We chatted about the State of the World (both dubious) and gave much attention to the tables laden with Interesting Stuff.

There were displays of holsters, freeze-dried foods for camping, and other exotica.

The fellow with the booth next to Bagwell's was selling blowguns.

They were tubes around four feet long with a mouthpiece at one end. He had put up a saucer-sized target on a wall thirty feet away, and all day long he was putting darts into the blowgun, going *whoosht*, just like the movies, and the darts would appear in the target.

I asked him how accurate the blowgun was, and he told me that with just a little practice I could consistently hit a dinner plate at a hundred feet. I asked him if this would not involve my giving up smoking, and he told me that, on the contrary, the blowgun seemed naturally to increase one's lung capacity; and that the biggest problem his customers reported was the necessity of moving up to the next-sized shirt.

I wanted to try the blowgun, and kittenishly hung around his booth and waited for him to offer me a shot; but (and I suppose for sanitary as much as for ballistic reasons) he never did.

Both the Air Marshal and myself were entranced by a new pistol at the Beretta table (the pistol was a Teflon-finished military version of their 92SB, 'The Gun That Guards Connecticut').

The Air Marshal said he was covering the convention for another magazine, and we both thought it would be a good idea to misuse the powers of the press and suggest to the Beretta people that we, as disinterested and powerful representatives of large organs of Public Opinion, might like to actually fire this pistol out at the range.

The Beretta people, with great reserve and no visible display of ill humor whatever, said they would see what they could do.

On the other side of Bagwell's display was the booth of the Free-World Congress of Paratroopers.

This organization had, in 1983 and 1984, taken paratroopers from all over the Free World to Israel to train with and jump with the Israeli Army for ten days. The organization was represented by Mike Epstein, a homeboy from North Clark Street in Chicago. Mike had jumped that morning with a group from the Phantom Division, an independent parachutists' club. The Phantoms, Mike told me, were running a jump school that could prepare even complete neophytes to jump – after one day's instruction – from operating aircraft.

I allowed as how I might like to try that myself, and Mike told me that I was too late to sign up for the program being run during the convention, but that I might like to attend the next Israeli Congress (Spring 1985). I told him I would like nothing more, and would only have to check with my wife, or, should *she* agree, with some-one else.

Friday afternoon I attended a seminar on 'Light Machine Guns: History, Evolution, Employment.'

The seminar was given by 'Machine Gun Pete' Kokalis, small-arms editor of *Soldier of Fortune*. Pete displayed some ten types of machine guns, including the MG42, or 'Hitler's Zipper,' so named for its very high (1,200 rounds per minute) cyclic rate; the MAG (Mitrailleuse à Gaz); the famous Bren gun, which Pete proclaimed the finest magazine-fed light machine gun in the world; and the hated American M-60.

Pete excoriated the workmanship and design of the M-60 at great length – the bipod legs break and it has at least eight separate parts that can be put in backwards and, in his own words, 'Believe me, gentlemen, if they can be put in backwards they *will* be put in backwards.' (I have spent fifteen years in the professional theater and knew what he was talking about). Pete discussed kinds of fire with respect to ground, kinds of fire with respect to the target, methods of disassembly, and so on. As a sucker for technical information, I'm a cheap date *anyway*, but he was a *particularly* fascinating and concise lecturer, and when he field-stripped the MAG in about eight seconds I cheered with the rest.

Pete then told us something that made my day; he announced

that in dealing with the Bren machine gun the biggest cause of Failure to Feed (that is, failure of the gun to chamber a cartridge) is failing to load the magazine in such a way that the rim of the second cartridge comes *in front of* the rim of the previous cartridge. I have made my living all my adult life on my ability to retrieve bizarre and arcane information, and this was a gem if I had ever heard one. I cherish it still.

This is what I had done up till Friday evening, when, to get back to it, I found myself standing by the pool and waiting to be called to fight in the pugil-stick competition.

A pugil stick is about five feet long. The last foot on each end is covered with a padded sausagelike affair. The contestants wear football helmets and approach each other from opposite ends of a one-foot-wide beam. The beam is over the swimming pool.

So, Captain Dale Dye announced the Pugil-Stick Competition, and I waited for them to call my name, meanwhile trying to remember everything I knew about close personal combat.

Everything I knew about close personal combat amounted to this: (1) I once had a girlfriend who was studying aikido, and she told me that one should never look into an opponent's eyes, as one might 'see one's childhood' and be tempted to show mercy; (2) I had heard that a bloodcurdling scream can have the physiological effect of momentarily shocking an opponent into inaction; (3) I had read in *The Book of Five Rings*, a compendium of advice to the Japanese sword fighter, that an effective tactic is to thrust viciously, retire for the briefest split second, and, while your opponent is enjoying his nanosecond of peace, fall on him like the Wrath of a Just God.

Then armed, I stood at attention next to my opponent while we were given our helmets, sticks, and jockstraps.

My opponent, whose name was Kogan, or something like that, wore a bathing suit. I, knowing something about psychology, was dressed in the full suit of camouflage fatigues I had bought that morning at the show. 'Yes,' I was indicating, 'you may have some intention of getting wet, but I do not, I'll see you in hell.'

On the command we mounted opposite ends of the beam. On the first whistle we were to 'make an appropriately aggressive sound' and go into a 'ready' stance. On the second whistle we were to advance along the beam, and, in the words of Captain Dye, we were to take no prisoners, we were not to *become* a prisoner.

I did scream. I did advance, and I knocked the son of a bitch into the pool. Shocked by my own good fortune, and giddy at the roars of the crowd, I then let my pugil stick fall.

The crowd suggested this rendered my victory void, and I had to dive into the pool, retrieve my stick, and fight the battle over.

The second time through I beat him again, and in the best tradition of the Eastern Intellectual, immediately started feeling sorry for him.

I then had to stand around in my soaked fatigues and wait for the next round of the elimination.

While I waited I watched high-roller types making book on the outcome of the contest. 'Yes,' I thought, 'these folks would bet on anything, and wouldn't sue you when they lose. What a change from the World of Show Business.'

As I mused my name was called to fight my second round.

My new opponent was a *biiiiig* – not to say huge – blond athletic type. We mounted opposite ends of the beam, and I said to myself, 'Dave, *you* are going to Clean this Sucker's *Clock*.'

I stared at his midriff so as to avoid his childhood, and, on the command, I gave the most warlike yell imaginable. All of my rage at this guy for being bigger and more fit than I, I put into that yell. I screamed my head off.

And he *wilted*. Imagine my surprise. He actually lost his composure and stepped falteringly backward on the beam. Captain Dale Dye then suggested that we both start again.

So we started again, gave our screams, advanced, and that big blond guy knocked my butt into the swimming pool. I never saw the one that hit me.

Chastened and moistened, I went back to my room to change for dinner, trying to find in my memory the appropriate verse of Kipling that might render my defeat an experience from which I might profit philosophically.

'If,' of course, came immediately to mind; and then 'Let us admit it fairly, as a business people should/We have had no end of a lesson: it will do us no end of good.'

I changed out of my wet fatigues and into my Eastern Journalist Drag: blue oxford shirt, black knit tie, cunningly unconstructed cream-colored sports coat, blue jeans, and Bass Weejuns. 'Yes,' I was proclaiming, 'as you see, I am a noncombatant.'

I dined with Mr. Bagwell; the Air Marshal; Bob Gaddis, a custom-knife dealer from Solvang. California; and Bob's assistant, Chris.

We had a long and very enjoyable steak dinner. The Air Marshal talked about his experience with the Gurkha Regiments, Bill Bagwell and Bob discussed the campaigns of Genghis Khan, and I told the one about the Screenwriter and the Elf.

The next morning I went out to the Desert Sportsman's Rifle and Pistol Club, about twenty miles out of town, for a demonstration of firepower.

I found a great seat on top of the Blue Diamond Fire Truck.

John Satterwhite, representing Heckler & Koch firearms, gave a demonstration with the shotgun. He tossed a clay pigeon in the air and shot it. He tossed two; he tossed five at once and got them all. He shot behind his back, he shot over his head, he tossed three eggs into the air and shot them. The man next to me said that one of John's favorites was a Chef's Salad: egg, lettuce, carrot, and tomato; but for some reason that wasn't part of the repertoire today.

Pete Kokalis and his crew fired off the machine guns he had lectured on yesterday.

A blue and silver P-51 flew by and looked very much like America. We waited for John Donovan, explosives and demolition editor of S.O.F., who had promised to blow up part of the mountain, but his part of the demo was the victim of faulty wiring. There was a mortar demonstration, and then we were informed, 'This is what a fire fight sounds like,' and the machine guns and the mortar all fired at once and for an extended period; and I was very glad to have spent the sixties fighting the battle of Montpelier, Vermont

As the demonstration ended, the Blue Diamond Fire Truck sped off to extinguish a small brush fire that the tracers had started on the mountain, and I hitched a ride back to town with the Beretta people.

They found a convenient hillside, and, very graciously, they let me try out their new pistol. I frightened the hell out of some tin cans at sixty or seventy yards, and then, content that those cans had been amply warned, we all rode back to Vegas.

That night the concluding banquet was held, John Donovan, emcee, took some good-natured ribbing over his inability to blow up the mountain. The Colors were beautifully presented by Fox Company, 2nd Battalion, 23rd Marines, Las Vegas. Various awards were given out, anticommunist speeches were made, and we all stood to sing 'God Bless America.'

Donovan closed the banquet with a toast: 'Here's to Rape, Pillage, Plunder, and may 'Son of a Bitch' become a Household Word.'

The next morning I took a cab to the airport. The cabbie asked how long I'd been in Vegas. I told him two days. He asked me how I liked it, and I told him I considered it my second home.

Memorial Day, Cabot, Vermont

Today Vermont celebrates Memorial Day. The Country as a whole was 'let out from school' on Monday, and the Post Office was closed; but Vermont celebrates today, one day later; and, locally, it was not just another amorphous holiday, but an occasion of remembrance.

Down at Harry's Hardware – the Rialto of Cabot – we were drinking our morning coffee. Doc Caffin bemoaned the fact that most of the younger Vets, that is, the Vietnam War Vets, couldn't take off work to attend the Ceremony.

Chunk Barrett is the ex-postmaster of Cabot. He told me that when he was a child there was something called the Ladies Relief Corps, an organization originally formed to honor Veterans of the War of Independence. On Decoration Day, Chunk said, these ladies would lay a wreath at the cemetery and throw blossoms in the river off the Elm Street Bridge. 'When I came home from the Navy,' Chunk said, 'that had all stopped for some reason. So I started it up again.'

The Memorial Day Service is now under the direction of Bob Davis, who used to run the Creamery (that is, the Cabot Farmers Dairy Co-Operative).

Chunk and I were standing in front of his house when the Parade came by. Doc Caffin carried the National Colors, Bunchy Cookson, who owns the local garage, carried the flag of the American Legion. Bob Davis marched with an old M-1.

Also in the parade were an Air Force Major, four grade-school children bearing wreaths, and a troop of nine Brownies carrying lilac blossoms. They were followed by an element of the Cabot High School band.

The parade halted on the Village Green, which is right across from Chunk's house. They drew up opposite the Civil War Memorial Obelisk. The Cabot band played 'My Country 'Tis of Thee.' One of the high school students spoke on the history of the Memorial Day Observance. The Air Force Major spoke eloquently on the sacrifice made by the young men and women who, in every generation, have heeded the Call to Arms, and defended American Interests. Several of the Cabot students read poems about Flanders Fields.

Now, I thought, these young people do not know where Flanders is. They do not know that the fields were made red with blood. They do not know that, in Britain, 'Play Up and Play the Game' sentiment of the Flanders Fields poetry marked the end of an era, the end of the Martial Spirit in Britain, and the end of an Empire. They do not know that a complete generation of British men died in the First World War. They can have no idea *why* those men died – and neither can you or I. Undoubtedly one hundred years from now the causes of World War II, that 'just' war, will seem equally obscure to the schoolchildren. We think we know why our parents fought. They fought to defend themselves. They fought for their lives.

In my community and numbered among my friends are veterans of World War II, a veteran of the Luftwaffe, a member of the Dutch Resistance, and a Jewish war refugee driven out of Warsaw by the Nazi Terror. I was born in 1947, and these people are part of a historical past to me, much as the Veterans of Vietnam will be to the schoolchildren on the Cabot lawn.

All our conflicts fade into antiquity. The most furiously fought issues are reduced to captions in the history books: 'They were bitter rivals.'

In the most magnificently written speech of exhortation in the

English language, Shakespeare writes, 'Old men forget and all shall
be forgot but this they shall remember with advantage,' etc.

And who among us remembers St. Crispin's Day?

The schoolchildren know nothing of war. They are raised on the
unfortunate destructive rhetoric of confrontation, just as I was
thirty years ago. They are brought up to believe the world's divided
into *we* and *they*; and *we* are always right. And *they* are always
wrong.

The Cabot children also have a great gift: They are part of a
community that loves them. And they're present at the Memorial
Day ceremony not to honor the slain of our various wars; but to
honor their living elders who desire that the children come and
participate in this ceremony. Weighted against the tradition of Our
Gallant Dead, the children have in their midst the immediate
example of their Fathers and Grandfathers, who do not talk about
the War – those that I have met – except to wonder often what it
was that we were fighting for.

Can it be that this Luftwaffe veteran, and this veteran of the
Resistance were once sworn to kill each other? Can it be that our
ally 'Gallant Russia' is the devil incarnate and the world is only
large enough for them or us? *Why* is it that, once again, the race is
intent on self-destruction?

On the Village Green, there are four schoolchildren carrying
wreaths. At the end of the ceremony, one wreath is laid at the Civil
War Obelisk, and taps is played by two buglers from the High
School. Bob Davis announces that the parade will re-form and
proceed down to the Town Hall, then to the Bridge, and then to the
Elm Street Cemetery. That accounts for the remaining wreaths, and
I'm glad that, once again, flowers are being thrown on the river, as
they were when Chunk Barrett was young.

There is something in these same families performing these same
traditions in the same spot for over two hundred years. In this small
town, the Fourth of July and Memorial Day are observed with
speeches and songs. The community is not abashed by public
display of those things which unite it. Life in a farm community
seems to instruct the young to think what is right and then to do
what is right.

In Cabot the Thirtieth of May is flanked by the Memorial Day
Parade and a demonstration against the Federal Government.

Tonight there is a meeting at the Blue Mountain High School in Wells River, Vermont. The U.S. Department of Energy is searching for a site to dump high-level nuclear waste, and one of the proposed sites is in Spruce Mountain National Forest, about ten miles from the town of Cabot, where I live.

Down on Main Street, Cabot, the question of the week is: 'Are you going to the meeting?,' and the question is rather rhetorical, because everyone is going to the meeting.

Blue Mountain High School originally scheduled the meeting in the home economics room. Aware of the mounting local interest, they rescheduled it for the auditorium. It has now been rescheduled for the gym, and speakers have been set up outside the gym to accommodate the overflow. Buses and carpools have been arranged to transport the citizenry. In the last two days, full-page ads have appeared in the local papers saying 'tell (your representatives) that you will oppose the nuclear poisoning of Vermont with all the legal means at your disposal, *and that you expect them to do likewise.*' The ad goes on to quote General Ethan Allen in a letter to Congress, 1781: 'I am as resolutely determined to defend the independence of Vermont as Congress is that of the United States.'

I wrote the ads.

It is no longer a novel experience for me to see my words in print, or to hear them performed on stage or in the movies. But when I saw these ads in print I was shocked. 'Surely,' I thought, 'a private citizen can't just walk into a newspaper and place an ad exhorting the populace to oppose the Federal Government.' But such, it seems, is, in fact, the case.

The day is a celebration of two great American Imperatives: the necessity of Community Action and the necessity of Independent Thought. The poem 'In Flanders Fields' ends: 'If ye break faith with us who die,/We shall not sleep, though poppies grow/In Flanders fields.' The Vietnam Vets are working in the Creamery, and they can't get off work to come to the Parade. This evening they will certainly be too tired to come to the Antinuclear Meeting. Most of the older folks will be there. The strong Vermont tradition of Town Meeting has, perhaps, ingrained in them the notion that, perhaps, they *are* the government. The 'ringer' in the town is me, and I'm still amazed that the newspaper printed my ad. That such a thing is actually possible awes me.

Was this freedom worth fighting for?

Yes. It was and is worth fighting for; and if history is supposed to tell that the fighting and the freedom were not connected, those that *did* the fighting thought they were. And most of them, I am sure, went to those wars for the same reason we are going to the Antinuclear Meeting tonight: to secure the benefits of life, liberty, and the pursuit of happiness for ourselves and our posterity.

Harry's Hardware

In the back room of Harry's Hardware Store on Main Street, Cabot, Vermont, there is a framed illustration – salesman in a frock coat is speaking to a man in coveralls. The man in coveralls holds a brass-bound mahogany carpentry level in his hands. He is obviously a foreigner, of German or Scandinavian descent, and the illustration's artist has caught a mood of desire and apprehension as he looks down at the plane.

This carpenter is about to make a purchase on which his livelihood will depend. He is resolute and will not be swayed either by empty salesmanship or by his own desires. The salesman knows this. He knows the man will make up his own mind but, perhaps, he could use a bit of help. Perhaps the carpenter is unacquainted with American brands, or perhaps he has overlooked the trademark.

The salesman is making his customer a promise – he is binding his *own* reputation to that of his wares. He points to the level. His words, printed on the bottom of the poster, read: 'That's made by the Stanley Rule and Level Company.'

The illustration is a cardboard counter display from the 1920s. It hangs above a counter full of old American and English molding planes. Around the room are tables full of old chisels, drills, and rules; on the wall are displayed old saws and levels like the one in the illustration.

Chris Kaldor bought the store from Harry Foster in 1982 and Harry moved up the hill.

In the front room Chris sells hardware, clothing, ammunition, fishing tackle, farm and building supplies, and sundries.

He has hot coffee, and there is a table to imbibe at while discussing the weather and other variables.

Last month the monotony of Vermont Mud Season was broken by discussion of the Mystery Tool.

Chris bought a mixed lot of antique tools and found in it an object of this description: a curly-maple handle six inches long and flared at the lower end, a blacksmith-wrought head four inches long and looking like a cross between a logging hook and a miniature adze.

Chris wrapped a dollar bill around the handle with a rubber band and left the tool up by the cash register. The first person to identify it correctly would win the dollar.

The answer most often given was, 'I don't know, but it looks very familiar'; followed in frequency by, 'I've *seen* one before, but I forgot what it is.'

Fourth of July

The Cabot Parade draws visitors from all over New England. It is an 'Old-Fashioned' Fourth of July, with floats, a band, a barbecue, and a midway.

At the midway you can throw baskets for a quarter in hope of winning a prize, you can throw baseballs at a target in the hope of dunking a town dignitary in a tub of water. Last year ... the dignitary was the school principal. Red Bean is usually on the midway with his collection of ancient and beautifully restored gas engines, and you look at those green and red masterpieces and feel a bit of what they must have meant to a farmer in 18 , a five horse engine to drive a winch, or a conveyor belt, or a log splitter, or pull a tractor.

The Parade is usually scheduled to begin at eleven, and usually begins by twelve. It's organized by Eunice Bashaw, who drives the school bus; and Eunice rules on the acceptability of the entries – this acceptability based in the main on the application being in on time, and even this criterion is pretty elastic. I don't think she'd exclude a nice float driven by people of good will who just happened to show up at the last second. Eunice also appoints the Secret Judges and administers the Awarding of the Prizes (usually $100 for Best Float, $50 for Most Humorous, and $50 for Most Inventive). I am acquainted with these categories as I have had the honor, three times, to be one of the Secret Judges of the Parade, and am *still* smarting about some of the compromises I had to make.

The Parade is usually made up of an Honor Guard, several musical entries, home-grown statements like Ed Smith's 'Summer in Cabot' float of 1985, which featured Ed and his family swathed in woolen overgarments and huddled around a potbellied stove; various fire engines from surrounding towns, The Bread and Puppet Theater, a truck from the Creamery, and so on.

The Parade forms below the bridge on Elm Street, and marches past the town's three businesses, the Post Office, and down Main Street to the recreation field and the chicken barbecue.

Down at the Hardware Store, the community is united in discussion of the unique calendar of northern Vermont: haying, deer season, January Thaw, Mud Season, and black flies; and the universal calendar of human endeavor, wives, mothers-in-law, and why nothing seems to be as well made as it used to be.

I have been coming up to Cabot for twenty-two years, I've been shown by the local people how to cut and chop wood, how to make a hunting knife at a forge, how to ride a horse. As an outsider and a transient, I have been the recipient of that same patience and courtesy the Stanley Salesman in the poster was showing to the foreigner in the poster – a generosity founded on deep self-respect and pride.

The Mystery Tool at Harry's was identified variously as a child's miniature adze, a small picaroon, and a garden implement of some sort.

The dollar prize was finally awarded to an elder citizen who identified the tool as a wood scribe, i.e., a device for incising a line on wood.

The consensus among Harry's patrons was that the tool was *not* a scribe, but that, barring incontrovertible identification, the older fellow should claim the buck, his guess being the most likely. The tool now hangs on the wall in Harry's back room.

The Laurel Crown

Roy Jones, an American boxer, fought his way to a decisive victory over Park Si Hun, a South Korean, in the final round of the Olympics. He was then robbed of his gold medal by corrupt and partisan judges. Jones had outboxed, outfought, and outshone the other man in the ring.

American commentators described it as a walkover, and the South Korean radio, during the last round, remarked, quite rightly, that Park would need a knockout to win the gold, as he was hopelessly behind on points.

When the fight ended, Jones and his corner were proud and elated as they waited for the judges' pro forma announcement that he had won. It was then proclaimed that, 3–2, the judges had awarded the gold to Park. The referee's jaw dropped. Jones and his team were stunned, then shocked, then furious.

Jones had fought and trained for years. He had defeated his opponent, and then learned that venality, guile, and corruption are not respecters of place – that even in the most sacrosanct arena, his dedication, pain, struggle, and victory could be brazenly denied him without shame.

The highest Olympic award today is the gold medal. In the Olympic Games of antiquity, it was the laurel crown. That crown is rooted in mythology.

Apollo fell in love with the nymph Daphne and pursued her. She abhorred the thought of marriage and fled. He ran mercilessly after her. As it became clear that he would soon possess her, she prayed to her father, Peneios, to preserve her by changing that form that had so enthralled Apollo. Her prayer was answered. She was changed into a laurel tree.

The laurel crown, adorning victors in war and the Olympic Games, was understood to be an ironic reminder that victory is hollow – that most times, on achieving our goal, we find it has changed and is no longer that which we pursued – that, indeed, we ourselves have changed in the pursuit.

Many of us, I am sure, thought: 'Reject the silver medal. Don't mount the podium and glorify this vicious farce.' But Jones faced the camera and accepted the silver medal. His presence on the podium was an irrefutable indictment of his judges.

It was also a magnificent lesson – that his sportsmanship and excellence had carried him to triumph in the Games and would carry him to triumph beyond them, that the true meaning of victory is better found in the wilting laurel crown than in the seemingly incorruptible medal of gold.

The Olympics are ideally a celebration of the spirit. The Olympics have seen no greater example of it than Jones and his victory.

Some Lessons from Television

Bill Macy's Acting Class, Lincoln Center, 1988

I was watching the television show *Hill Street Blues* last night. A woman was playing the part of a transsexual; that is, a woman was playing the part of a woman who had once been a man. As I watched, I thought, 'What a brilliant characterization.' Which characterization, of course, consisted in her having the understanding and the self-control *to not do a thing*. She let the script do the work. We were told by the script that she had once been a man. And why should we disbelieve what we had been told? So we, the audience, accepted it, and the actress's correct understanding aided our enjoyment of the script. *She did not torture the audience to assuage her feeling of not having worked hard enough.*

How, by extension, would one characterize a King, a Policeman, a Doctor, a Thief? Well, by extension, one would characterize them in just the same way. By leaving the characterization in the hands of the writer, which is where it belongs, and the only place where it can be safely dealt with. Why? Because there *is* no meaning to the concept of 'a king.' *King* is not a character, it is a title; and, as the Bard reminds us in *Twelfth Night*: '*Cucullus non facit Monacum*,' the Cowl does not make the Monk, the Title does not make the Man or Woman.

But surely, you say, there is such a thing as 'regal bearing.' Yes, surely there is, and it is possessed by many not in the Royal Line, and many kings do not possess it, and, in fact, the possession of Regal Bearing by a king is nothing other than coincidence.

You and I, that is to say, the audience, will accept anything we are not given a reason to disbelieve. This is the reason the actor must study vocal and physical technique. These techniques are studied solely to render the actor sufficiently uninflected to allow the audience to accept him in a multiplicity of roles.

What else can be learned from this woman on *Hill Street Blues*? This: We judge people by first impressions. We have all had the experience of liking a girl, or boy, from afar, and having a friend say, 'Oh, he or she is a snob,' or of a potential business partner, 'He's a deadbeat,' et cetera, and it is then well-nigh impossible to separate those labels from our feelings about the person in question *irrespective of how that person acts*.

How can the actor employ this phenomenon? Well, as I have said, by understanding that the audience will accept what The Script has told them is true, and that the actor need not touch it. Also, the actor can profit in this way: By *endowing* the other actors, those with whom he plays, with the essential characteristics of the scene.

I stress the *essential*, rather than the *superficial* characteristics of the scene. That is, it is not important that one's opposite player is A King, it may be important that it is *as if* he could give you a job. It may not be important that the script characterizes someone as A Lackey, but it may be important that it is *as if* he owed you a favor.

Our minds will accept these endowments, just as the audience does, if we state them simply. It will *not* accept these suggestions if we *perform* them, but it will accept them if we *act on* them. We don't have to *believe* them (no more does the audience), we simply have to act *as if*.

We have all had the experience of an *endowment* changing our perceptions of our fellows. For example, we are told that the boss is a much-decorated hero of combat; or that the underling is a brilliant pianist; or that the Nobody at the bar is an infallible success with women; or that the apprentice is worth five million dollars. We hear and we *act* on these endowments all the time.

When we are told that the apprentice is vastly wealthy, we some-how can't quite see her the same way, *can* we?

This is the fun part of acting. This is 'playing.' It is the simple solution to a complex problem, the problem of 'characterization.' There is no such thing, for the actor, as characterization. Charac-ter, as Aristotle reminded us, is just habitual action. We know a man's or woman's character *by what they do*, and we tend to blatantly disregard what they say about themselves, particularly and especially when those things which they say about themselves are obviously designed to induce us to respond to them in some manner which will redound to their own self-interest. We are no fools. We know when someone is mouthing off in order to get in our pants, or in our pockets. We know that we will withhold judgment of someone's character until we see *how they act*. We know it when we meet them at a party, and we *also* know it when we meet them in the theater.

Characterization is taken care of by the author, and if the author knows what he is about, he *also* will avoid it like the plague, and show us *what the character does* rather than having the character's entrance greeted with 'Well, well, if it isn't my ne'er-do-well half-brother, just returned from New Zealand.'

Remember that the psychology of those in the audience is exactly the same as the psychology of those on the stage.

The simple magic of the theater rests in the nature of human perception – that we all want to hear stories. And the stories we like the best are those told the most simply.

This magic, if correctly understood, leads to happy actors and a happy audience. It is the gift given by God, and not the dull technical manipulations of some smarty-pants 'artist' with a good idea. As Stanislavsky told us: Any director who feels he has to do something 'interesting' with the text doesn't understand the text.

I was also watching *Cagney and Lacey*. Here we have Tyne Daly, surely one of our *finest* actresses, a model artist and a delight to watch in any part. In this episode, she, and her cop-olicewoman, played by Sharon Gless, go into a building which a sign identifies as a Meat-Packing Firm.

As Tyne goes into the place, she has been directed to sniff. Why? She was directed to sniff to *further* inform us that she was in a meat-packing firm. Well. We knew that already. We all saw the sign. And nobody needs to be told twice. It's like saying, 'I love you. (*Pause*) And I mean it.' If we believed 'I love you,' we certainly *don't* believe it when we get the addendum.

We saw the sign, we saw the hanging slabs of meat. We knew we were in a meat-packing firm. Why did the director feel compelled to help us along. To tell us how the place *smelled*? Why? How the placed smelled was not part of the play. How do I know? Because it wasn't part of the *action* of the play. Tyne was acting the part of a woman In Great Danger. Why would such a woman take time out to *comment* (which is what she was directed to do) on the smell of a place in which the overriding, the essential element was: *This is a place in which I might be killed.*

No. *Also*: We didn't wonder how the place smelled *until she sniffed*. And when she sniffed we *doubted* that she was in the place the sign told us she was in. Why? Because we sniff to identify a surprising and, usually, unpleasant odor. That is why we sniff. And Tyne was directed to do the opposite. *Not* to identify, but to *comment*. Here she, is, involved in trying to Apprehend a Dangerous Killer, and we see her directed to take time out to comment that 'her character' finds the smell of hanging beef unpleasant. And when she *did* that, not only did we doubt the *place*, but we doubted the *action*, even when performed by this magnificent artist.

Further, if the *place* of action is not germane to the plot (i.e., The Room in Which My Sister Secreted My Share of the Inheritance), *leave it out*, you writers. We're better off in a Dark Wood, a Light Wood, a Drawing Room. Why? Because then we'll watch the Action.

And Realism, in this day and age, is an attempt to *convince*, *not* an attempt to *express* (as it was in the time of Stanislavsky).

That is why 'realistic' acting rings so false. 'Realism' – the con cern with minutiae as revelatory of the truth – was an invention of the nineteenth century, when The Material seemed to be, and, perhaps, was, the central aspect of life. Our own time has quite understandably sickened of The Material, and needs to deal with things of *The Spirit*.

So we must, simply, lay aside our boring and fruitless pursuit of the superficial and dedicate ourselves to Action, which is to say to *Will* as the expression, as it is, of the Spirit.

We do not need to characterize. We only need, simply as possible, to *elect* and to *do* what we elect to do.

Jimmy Stewart, in accepting an Academy Award, thanked all the directors who had, over the years, broken him of his 'good intentions.'

What does this mean? Actors who want to take charge of items *not in their job description* make themselves and the audience unhappy. (Just as the director's good intention to have Tyne Daly sniff, his desire to 'help' the audience, hurt the scene.)

Actors who want to change the script, who want to correct the director, or to direct the other actors, or to criticize the audience, these people are working too hard, and to no purpose whatever. There is only so much psychic energy. Any energy devoted to one task will be subtracted from another.

Similarly, the audience only has so much energy. If they are watching the heroine navigate her Progress through a Dark Night of Danger, they are going to be paying very close attention. When we show these attentive people the heroine sniffing at the smell of meat, they are going to accept that clue as as important as the unexpected creak of a door, and they are going to be disappointed and confused when they realize that it is not a clue at all, it is merely a *comment*.

It is the strength to resist the extraneous that renders acting powerful and beautiful.

A Thank-you Note

I was recently riding on a London bus. Some one was smoking. The association of the rocking of the bus and the smell of good, non-filtered cigarettes took me back twenty-five years.

In my mind, I was, again, riding various Chicago buses to various jobs, schools, or assignations. And as I rode those beautiful buses, which felt so much like home, I smoked my Luckies and I devoured the world's literature.

I loved those bus rides and I loved those books. I was surprised and, I suppose, charmed, to see that I still associate the rocking, the diesel smell, the toasted smell of someone else's cigarettes, with those vast, long novels – especially those of the Midwesterners: Dreiser, Sherwood Anderson, Willa Cather, Sinclair Lewis. Those big, long books about the prairies that never end, about an emptiness in the stomach, about a certain felling, almost a love, of pain.

The old librarian at my high school once found me reading a paperback copy of *Lady Chatterley's Lover*, and chided me for my errant taste.

He felt he was expressing his regard for me by showing me his disappointment. He pursed his lips and said, 'Why do you read that stuff?' and even at the time I felt sad for him, and rather pitied him both as a fool missing the pleasures of literature, and as a weakling incapable of constructing a better sexual advance. What effrontery. But he had seen a lot of me. I spent all of my after-school time in the man's library, reading anything that had not been assigned.

In high school class I did read the assigned *A Tale of Two Cities*, which, apart from *A Christmas Carol*, is the only thing of Dickens I have ever been able to abide.

Call me a philistine, but I prefer the boredom and repetition of Sinclair Lewis, and the painful sincerity of Dreiser, to butchers named 'Mr. Cuttymeat,' and so on; and I say, further, what of Thackeray, or even Wilkie Collins, either of whom Dickens, in my estimation, was not fit to fetch tea for. But then I seem to always get it wrong, as the Librarian said. I think that Dostoyevsky is not fit to be mentioned in the same breath with Tolstoy, nor Henry James with Edith Wharton. I do not like the tortured, and I prefer the truth in straightforward honesty to the 'art' revealed by whatever it is that we call talent.

Well, there, I've said it. And as long as I'm *coming out*, I might as well add that I think that Mozart couldn't adjust Bach's shoe buckles an opinion which can be of interest to *no* one, and which I include solely because I have been trying to work it into cocktail conversation for many years and I have recently stopped drinking.

And I stopped smoking cigarettes long enough ago that they, when smoked by someone else, smell awfully good to me. They take me back to the days of my youth, and the beginning of my Love of Literature.

I have great gratitude to George Eliot, to Willa Cather, to the men and women beyond genius, to the simple writers to whom the only meaning of 'technique' was clarity. These people have been my great friends, my teachers, my advisers, for twenty-five years, from the time I thought Anna and Vronsky were romantic older people, to my last reading, when I was shocked to find that they were unfortunate young people.

To those writers – *how* can I feel they are dead –

Thank you for the insight that the only purpose of literature is to delight us. Thank you for your example. I am sorry that you were in pain. Thank you for your constancy.

Stanislavsky and The Bearer Bonds

Stanislavsky once asked his students to determine how to act the following scene: An accountant brings home from his office a fortune in negotiable bearer bonds, which he must catalogue. Living with him is his wife, their newborn child, and his wife's idiot brother.

He arrives home while his wife is bathing the baby. The idiot brother is seated by the fireplace staring into the fire.

The accountant wants to get started on his work before dinner so he sits down at the table, strips the wrappers off, which he throws in the fire, and starts cataloguing the bonds.

His wife calls from the next room, 'Come and see how cute the baby is.' The accountant gets up and goes into the next room. The idiot brother takes the bearer bonds and begins throwing them into the fire and laughing. The laughter draws the accountant back into the room. As he sees what is happening, he thrusts the brother out of the way, in an attempt to get the remaining bonds out of the fire before they burn. The brother hits his head on an andiron and dies. The wife comes running into the room and sees her brother dead. She then screams, 'Oh my God, the baby!' and runs back into the other room, followed by her husband, where they both discover the baby drowned in the bath.

Stanislavsky told his students that when they know how to

analyze and perform that scene, that *then* they would know how to act.

Any school of theatrical thought is short-lived. A 'school' really only exists in retrospect; the title is a post-facto assessment of the naturally occurring similarities between the works of several artists, each affected secondarily by the work of the others and, more important, by the time in which they live.

During the period of the artist's healthy production, the work of the individual artist, and of the collective unconscious expressing itself through the artistic community, is the *most effective way* for the artist to express what he or she sees; and innovations in technique (which is what the audience perceives as *style*) arise *only* to allow the artist to express more simply and forcefully what he or she knows to be the *most realistic vision of the world*. Eventually the superficial – i.e., reducible and copyable – aspects of this new technique are adopted by those *without* a vision as the 'correct' way, not, as in the case with the prime creator, to express a realistic vision of the world, but now, 'to create Art.' And while the ecstatic was becoming, in the consciousness of the nonartists, the formulaic, the true artist was moving on to a new vision, driven not by the need to be different from the imitators, but by a more basic need to explore the unexplored.

So that any 'school' of art is short-lived, and none can possess a final 'say' as to the correct technique. Technique arose out of an unrepeatable moment in the life of the world, and in the life of that one part of it which was the individual artist.

We cannot say that any technique is more correct than another, cave painting is not more 'real' or more 'beautiful' than the perspective of Caravaggio or the semi-abstract skies of Turner; all rely on conventions, and when we say that any work is an absolutely realistic depiction, we mean only that we find it beautiful – it responds to some of our *preconscious* views of the world; i.e., it reflects *what we think, but we didn't know we thought* until we saw the painting. In the words of Mr. Wilde, 'We didn't have these pea soup fogs till someone described them.'

Again, there is no 'correct' school of any artistic thought. There is, however, a fairly good test of an *incorrect*, which is to say, a *useless*, school (a useless school of artistic thought being one that does not serve the purpose of communion between the artist and the audience on this subject: the true, hidden nature of the world).

We may assume that a school of artistic thought is useless when it is universally accepted as being the only and exclusive possessor of truth.

A new artistic vision, a new school of thought, a new satisfying artistic 'reality' must coalesce around the rebel. It is not the job of the audience, not the job of the amateur, it is only the job of the true artist to, not 'supersede,' but *ignore* the obvious accepted standard of artistic excellence in favor of the vision which to him or her is real. The audience, the amateur, the critic – *their* job, in the face of this new vision of reality, is to *resist*, to the point where the determination of the artist overcomes their resistance. This is the scheme of aesthetic natural selection.

New artistic vision grows in absolute contravention of this accepted thought. This is its fetile soil. In Berlin, in the 1870s, Stanislavsky saw a traveling troupe of players whose performance was the opposite of the formalized presentation theater of the day. They were the protégés of the Duke of Saxe-Meiningen. This troupe treated each new play as a new problem in psychology; and rather than (in the accepted procedure) handing each actor only his or her lines, and assembling the cast several nights before the performance, said cast to act in support of the star around whom the performance was built, the Saxe-Meiningen troupe saw the play as an exercise in psychology. They analyzed the play in its entirety, and each individual part, to find the unifying theme, and then related that theme to congruent events in the life of the individual players, so that the actor trained to bring to the stage the message of the play, the actions of the character *as he believed it to relate to his own life.*

This was a revolutionary departure, and Stanislavsky, the son of a wealthy manufacturer, was sufficiently moved to forsake his class, adopt a foreign stage name (his family name was Alekseyev, 'Stanislavsky' was the name of a Polish vaudeville performer), and embrace a despised profession.

Stanislavsky's obsession with 'theatrical truth' grew and changed over the next forty years.

His axiom was to attempt to 'Bring to the Stage the Life of the Human Soul' and, like many other artists, his attempts became more and more formal as he tried to codify his gains in knowledge, up until the point where they started becoming more and more mystical. He started out extending the set off the stage, so that the actor would not have to be shocked by the transition from the 'real' into the 'artificial,' and, at the end of his career, he had his company sitting in a circle and endeavoring to transmit *prana*, or rays of energy, to each other.

All his work was to the one end: to bring to the stage the life of the Soul. As his vision of that life changed, he discarded the old and moved on.

The active life of even the most healthy theatrical enterprise seems to me to be, at most, ten years, and more probably, five to seven years.

The Company is an organism, and usually an organism made up of artists of at least slightly disparate ages.

The economic, social, and spiritual ties which bind a company aged twenty-five to thirty-five together will not hold those same folk at age thirty-five to forty-five. There are other reasons for the dissolution of the Company, but this one alone is sufficient.

The successful Company is only the manifestation of the successful artistic vision. When the Artist (in this case, the aggregated Artists, the Company) moves on, the dross, the 'school,' the physical plant, the administrators, the audience, stays behind, and, rightfully, demands that which they have been receiving for the last while. The Artists, however, are now constitutionally incapable of providing that same vision.

Two things may happen. The first, of course, is the disappearance of that artistic entity entirely. Equally possible and, in fact, more probable – in direct relation to the community acceptance of the Company – is the continuation of the *form* of the Company's vision with its content, and there we have the mechanics of the creation of a 'school' of theatrical design, of playwriting, of acting.

In the 1930s, representatives of the very vital Group Theatre in New York (themselves descendants and offshoots of the Yiddish Theater) went to Paris to meet with a very aged Stanislavsky and discuss his 'system' of acting. They returned to the States with an inspiration, an 'outline' of The Stanislavsky System, and, significantly, their own place in the Apostolic Succession.

Many of the members of the Group Theatre had actually studied with members of Stanislavsky's Moscow Art Theatre, with Maria

Ouspenskaya, and with Richard Boleslavsky, and others.

Boleslavsky's book '*Acting*': *The First Six Lessons* was and is a beautiful and useful anecdotal rendering of the Stanislavsky System. The true anointing of the Group, however, came with the direct Laying on of Hands by Stanislavsky in Paris.

The creators of the Group were the real possessors of theatrical insight, talent, and desire. These helped them to found a Theater; their anointing by Stanislavsky helped them to form a Gospel; and, since they had personally received wisdom from the Fount, it was they *alone* who could 'create new bishops,' who could anoint, who could bless, who might determine which work was correct and which was heresy.

The good and the bad of the Group Theatre, of any theater, is assimilated into and dies with the memory of the immediate theatrical audience.

The life of a Gospel, however, is somewhat different, and somewhat longer as there is no immediate test of its utility; the received wisdom is not being judged and changed or discarded on the basis of its ability 'to do the job,' it has become an end in itself, it becomes a *creed*. The intellectual content of a creed is not to be used to aid its members in the wider universe, but, rather, their subscription to that content is to be used as a test to enforce their loyalty.

The point was not whether or not there were Communists in the State Department, or if there were, what damage, if any, they might have done, the point was whether one was willing to subscribe to the *assertion* that there were Communists in the State Department, and having done so, to eradicate, *not* those Communists, but, rather, all those who did not share the belief in their existence. So, the more blatantly incorrect or foolish the content of a creed, the more useful it is as a test of loyalty, for we may then be assured that its subscribers have not coincidentally accepted it because of its utility.

Similarly, with the Method – the philosophy/technique/aesthetic born in the Group and nurtured in the actor's studio – generations of actors, directors, and those who aspired to join their ranks, were informed, or inferred, that theatrical wisdom was available from a single fount, and that admittance *to* that source of wisdom was available only to those who swore allegiance, *not* to the idea of

Theater (whatever the individual held that idea to be), but, rather, to the idea of the Method, as an intellectual system *so correct* that its utility was not to be gauged by traditional theatrical tests, i.e., the ability of the performer to communicate the idea of the play to the audience.

The Gospel, received by the Group from Stanislavsky, was so successful – for Stanislavsky's ideas were and are very useful – that it outlived the brilliant artistic life of the Group, and survived in its institutional form as the Actors' Studio and the Lee Strasberg Theater Institute, at both of which we see the students of the students of the students of ... to the seventh or eighth generation ... Stanislavsky reiterating a series of theatrical notions in the creation of which they had no part and the actual utility of which they have never had to test before The Audience.

What those people possess is the honest faith that the things they have been told are correct. What they have lost is interest in whether or not those things are useful.

The overwhelming excitement at the birth of any new artistic experience comes from the sense of *discovery*, the sense that one is an explorer, and that, armed with nothing but a sense of humility and a healthy arrogance, one is creating something out of nothing at all. That one's tool, subject, and material is only the *nature of things as they are*. This cannot be found through reference to an authority.

Stanislavsky was driven to observe, question, and codify his theatrical thoughts to one end only: to bring to the stage the life, as he said, 'of the Human Soul'; said life expressed not only and, perhaps, not even primarily, through the soul of the actor, but expressed through the soul *of the play*. So striving, Stanislavsky wrote, taught, and acted those things he found correct for himself and his audience, in that brief moment of time in which they lived.

Similarly, any truly creative artist living at any time and in any circumstances, is going to be moved or driven to observe the world prima facie, and draw those conclusions which will help him or her better to prosecute their Art. This observation will most probably include, but need not be limited to, nor even primarily derived from, instruction.

What is the answer to Stanislavsky's Bearer Bonds problem? Stanislavsky said that when one knew how to correctly analyze and perform the problem, one would know how to act; so, then, the question is, How Does One Act?

You start with a conundrum. You have to find the answer yourself.

A Party for Mickey Mouse

I remember Riverview. This vast amusement Park was located on Chicago's North Side. It was magnificent, dangerous, and thrilling. There were freak shows, there was the renowned BOB's roller coaster, the fastest in the world; there was the ROTOR, a room-sized cylinder in which one stood back against the wall and was spun around, while the floor dropped away; there was the PARA-CHUTE JUMP, the symbol of Riverview, and visible for a mile.

There was illicit gambling, one could die on the rides, the place reeked of sex. A trip to Riverview was more than a thrill, it was a dangerous dream adventure for the children and for their parents.

My father took me up in the Parachute Jump. We were slowly hoisted ten stories in the air, seated on a rickety board, and held in place by a frayed rope. We reached the top of the scaffold, the parachute dropped, the seat dropped out from under us, and my father said under his breath: 'Jesus Christ, we're both going to die here.'

I remember wondering why I was not terrified by his fear. I think I was proud to be sharing such a grown-up experience with him.

Black men in jump suits sat suspended over tubs of water. White men paid to throw baseballs at a target. When the target was hit, the black men were dropped into the tubs below. The black men Uncle-Tommed in thick Southern accents.

The fix was in. Everyone was getting fleeced *and* short-changed to boot at the ten-in-one. Hell, that's why we *came* here. This was a *carnival*, this wasn't a merry-go-round and cotton candy, this was a *carnival*, and we were making fun of the horror of existence, saying, 'Fuck *you*, tonight I'm going to *party*.' And this was our Family Entertainment.

Did it bring the family together? You bet it did. And thirty-five years later I prize the memories. As does every other kid who went there with his family. As does everyone who ever went there, *period*. You got the bang for your buck that you were promised. Riverview; the very *name* is magic, to a kid from those days in Chicago, as magic as the name of the first girl you ever laid, and that's the truth.

My family took me to Disneyland the first year it was opened. I was eight, the year was 1955, and it seems to me that much of the park was still under construction.

I came back with my five-year-old, thirty years later. And I remembered it all. I remembered the route from one ride to the next. I remembered where the hot-dog stands were. Nothing had changed. I was charmed to remember the Pirate menus in the restaurant, and how one punched out the ears of the menus, and could wear them as masks. I remembered the souvenirs. I went on the Dumbo Ride, and my wife took a picture of me and my kid, and it looks just like the picture of me and my mom on the same elephant.

Leaving the park, we ran into a parade on the Main Street of Disneyland. The parade was commemorative of the Sixtieth Anniversary of Mickey Mouse. The parade was a lavish panegyric, was designed to evoke feelings of fealty.

A part of the parade was musical variations of the Mickey Mouse Song: 'M-I-C – see you real soon – K-E-Y . . . why? Because we *like* you . . .' et cetera; which song I both heard and sang along with weekdays for the several years I watched *The Mickey Mouse Club* on television. I remembered Jimmy Dodd, the *compère* of the Club, singing to us viewers, rather sententiously, and I remembered being moved by his affection.

Well, here we were, kids and adults alike, smiling at that same Anthem, wishing Mickey well, thirty years later.

But I asked myself, what *actually* were we endorsing? What *was* it that we were wishing well? How, and to what end, was this warm feeling evoked?

Were we feeling 'good' about wishing Happy Birthday to a mouse? It's not a mouse, it's a character in a cartoon. Were we wishing well to a commercial enterprise? For surely Disneyland is the most commercial of enterprises. It is the *State of the Art* in crowd control; it is terrifying to reflect that one stands in line for approximately fifty-five minutes out of every hour on a moderately crowded day at the park, that a five-hour sojourn at the park contains twenty-five minutes of 'fun.' The turns and bends and sights in the waiting line are designed to create the illusion that the line is shorter than it actually is. One sets one's sights and hopes on a Crest Up Ahead, which, surely, must be entrance to the side, only to find, on reaching that crest, that yet another stretch of waiting is in store, that one must wait, further, until one passes under the arches up ahead, certainly not too long a time. But on *reaching* those arches, one finds, et cetera.

Why does no one complain? Why does everyone return? Are the rides that thrilling? No, they are enjoyable, and some are rather good, but they aren't any more thrilling than the run-of-the-mill traveling carnival rides. Is the atmosphere that enjoyable? No. I think, to the contrary, that the atmosphere is rather oppressive. It is racially and socially homogeneous, which may, to a large extent, be a function of its geographical reality. But there is, more importantly, a slight atmosphere of *oppression* in the park. There is the nagging feeling that one is being watched.

And, of course, one *is* being watched. One is being watched by those interested in crowd control, both to extract the utmost in dollars from the visitors, and, also, to ensure their safety. The atmosphere and oppression come, I think, from this: that the park's concern for extraction far outstrips the concern for safety, but the regimentation is presented, as, foremost and finally, a desire to *care for* the visitor – to protect, to guide, to soothe.

One creates for oneself the idea that things at Disneyland are being done *for one's own good*. And, far beyond obeying the rather plentiful signs forbidding one or another thing, one finds oneself wondering, 'I wonder if this is allowed here ...' 'This' being, for example, smoking, eating-in-line, et cetera.

At Disneyland one creates (with a great deal of help) the idea that Every Thing Not Required Is Forbidden. And so we see, as in any other totalitarian state, the internalization of authority, and its transformation into a Sense of Right.

We see the creation of a social Superego, which is sometimes a handy tool, but perhaps out of place at an amusement park. I.e., (1) the Id says: 'Well, hell, I'm going to Cut in Line, and get to Space

Mountain sooner'; (2) the Ego says: 'Don't *do* it. They will get you
and, in some way, punish you'; and so, to overcome the anxiety and
humiliations of being subject to a superior force, (3) the Superego is
created and says: 'No, it is not that you are *afraid* of authority, not
at all, you are just concerned with Right and Wrong, and *you* want
to go to the back of the line because it is the correct thing to do.'

And it is *this* feeling that one is celebrating, I think, in singing
paeans to Mickey Mouse, the feeling that I am a Good Person. I am
one of the good, and *happy*, people, and I would never do anything
wrong. It is this feeling that is being sold in the park. As an
amusement park, it just ain't worth the money – far from being
Riverview, it's not as much fun as a video arcade. The Mickey
Mouse phenomenon is compelling not in spite of, but because of, its
authoritarian aspect.

A cow was born on a farm near my home in Vermont. We saw its
picture in the local paper. The cow ws notable for this: On its white
side was found that conjunction of three black circles inter-
nationally recognized as the silhouette of Mickey Mouse. The
mouse silhouette was rather large, perhaps three feet across, and
was perfect. Mention was made that representatives of Disneyland
were coming to look at the cow.

I later saw a news item to the effect that the park had purchased
and was displaying this wondrous cow, and that only a fair retail
price had been paid for the creature.

My first thought was, 'Well, that's as it should be.' And then I
thought, '*Wait* a second. What is going *on* here? That blankety-
blank cow is worth a vast fortune to the Disney folks.' As of course
it *is*, and I wondered, on sober reflection (i) why in the world the
cow's owner would consider parting with the beast for less than a
vast fortune; (2) why the Disney people would find a value in
advertising that they (from another, and rather defensible point of
view) *stole* this cow; and (3) why I was going along with their plan,
and endorsing not only their purchase, but their proud announcement *of what they elected* was the 'right' thing to do.

The Disney people were telling me that in paying only a 'fair
market price,' or words to that effect, *they were protecting my
interests*. Absolutely. That's what they were doing, and that's how I
took it. How? In what possible way were my interests being protected?

The Disney people bought the freak cow for its publicity value. It was going to *create income* for their Company. *If* the cow were going to bring enjoyment to the visitors to the park (and, so, income to the Company), in what way would that enjoyment be affected by the price which the Disney Company paid for the cow? Is it not in the best interests of show business, on the contrary, to proclaim, 'Brought to You at Great Expense'?

Why was I asked to be an accomplice, finally, to a lie? What was I being sold? Not 'entertainment,' not 'amusement,' not, 'a thrill.' I was being sold the idea that I am a Good, Right-Thinking Person.

Well, I am capable of my own estimation of my own worth, and I don't need to be sold such an idea; and, difficult as it is, and it is rather difficult, I find that I have to admit that I don't like Disneyland. I think it is exceeding the job description for an amusement park to sell its product by appealing to, perhaps, even, by finally questioning, the self-esteem of the people who are paying the freight. There *is* no Mickey Mouse; and as to 'Why, because we *like* you!,' I'll be the judge of that, and thank you very much.

In the Company of Men

It is not, I think, very energy efficient to have two parts of a machine performing the same task. A mechanical, and by extension, a spiritual, union might better be described as the conjunction of dissimilar parts such that the ability of each to realize a common goal is improved.

The roof is pitched to shed the snow, the floor is flat for the convenience of the occupants: Both conduce to the comfort of the inhabitants and to the structural integrity of the house.

Well, then, let's *talk* about sexual relationships. Let's talk about men and women. Our sexual organs, as has been noted, are dissimilar. It is also widely known, though to aver it in certain circles is impolite, that our emotional make-ups are quite different; and try as one may to hew to the Correct Liberal Political Line of Equal Rights, and elaborate a moral imperative into a prescriptive psychological view (i.e., Men and Women are entitled to the same things, therefore they must *want* the same things), we know that such a view is not true. We know that men and women do *not* want the same things (as much as they may want the *rights* to want and to pursue the same things). And *why* men and women want dissimilar things is, as they say, beyond the scope of this inquiry.

As I amble, so pugnaciously, into my twilight years and into what I so dearly hope will be a time of reflection and peace, it seems to me that women want men to be men.

This is a new idea to me. In my quite misguided youth, I believed what the quite misguided women of my age said when they told me and my fellows that what was required for a Happy Union was a man who was, in all things, save plumbing, more or less a woman.

Leisurely reflection would have revealed to me and the boys that women do not, on the whole, get *along* with women, and that efforts by men to be more *like* women would give those *actual* women yet another batch of objects with which to indulge in the, forgive me, intrafemale activities of invidious comparison, secrecy, and stealth.

So there we men were as, *disons le mot*, Dagwood Bumstead, and wondering why both we and our women were vaguely discontented without being in the least starry-eyed.

Well, then, for the moment, to hell with women; and to hell with the Battle of the Sexes, and its current and least charming aspect of litigiousness.

C'est magnifique, mais ce n'est pas la guerre.

Men get together under three circumstances.

Men get together to do business. Doing business is not devoid of fun. It gives us a sense of purpose. We run around in ways the society-at-large has determined are basically harmless, and, every so often, we get a paycheck for doing so.

Men also get together to bitch. We say, 'What does she *want?*' And we piss and moan, and take comfort in the fact that our fellows will, at some point, reveal that, yes, *they* are weaklings, too, and there's no shame in it. This is the *true* masculine equivalent of 'being sensitive.' No, we are *not* sensitive to women, but we are sensitive to our own pain, and can recognize it in our fellows. What a world.

The final way in which men get together is for That Fun Which

Dare Not Speak Its Name, and which has been given the unhappy
tag 'male bonding.'

Now, let's talk turkey for a moment. Let's look at this phrase.
What does it mean? We know, first of all, that it is not a description
of a legitimate good time, and that 'male' seems to be a derogatory
modifier of an activity which in itself seems to be either an
approximation or a substitution.

For, *who*, friends, do we know, who would suggest that we all
spend a nice afternoon 'bonding.' What is 'bonding'? It means this:
it means the tentative and somewhat ludicrous reachings towards
each other of individuals who are neither prepared to stand on their
own emotional feet, nor ready, for whatever reasons, to avow their
homosexuality. And if I'm lying, I'm flying. 'Male bonding' is an
odious phrase meant to describe an odious activity.

What *ever* happened to 'hanging out'? What happened to 'spending time with the boys'? What happened to The Lodge, Hunting,
Fishing, Sports in general, Poker, Boys Night Out?

What happened to men having *fun* with each other? Because we
do, though we may have forgotten, have quite a good time with
each other, in the above-mentioned and other activities, and,
though the talk is many, and perhaps, most, times of *women*, the
meaning of the talk is: isn't it great being here together? Now,
perhaps one might think this is latent homosexuality. If so, so
what? And if you're sufficiently liberal as to hold that overt homosexuality is No Crime, then perhaps you might extend your largess
to its latent counterpart, and, perhaps, further, we might look at
our impulse to brand The Need of Men to Be Together with various
types of opprobrium and just say, It's All Right.

Because it is all right.

It's good to be in an environment where one is understood, where
one is not judged, where one is not expected to perform – because
there is room in Male Society for the novice and the expert, room
for all, in the Poker Game, the Golf Outing, the Sunday Watching
Football; and room and encouragement for all who wholeheartedly
endorse the worth of the activity. That is the true benefit of being in
the Company of Men. And the absence of this feeling of peace,
'Maybe she will think it's silly,' is one of the most disquieting and
sad things which a man can feel with a woman: It means 'Maybe
I'm no good.'

I have engaged in many male, and specifically masculine, activities – shooting, hunting, gambling, boxing, to name a few. I have sought them out and enjoy them all vastly. They are times that I cherish.

I was sitting last October, bone cold, with some old-timers in a hunting shack, and they were passing around ginger brandy to pour into the coffee, and reminiscing about the cockfights which their dads used to take them to back before World War I. Is this corny? You're goddamned right it is, and I wouldn't trade it for anything. Nor the hanging-out at Mike's Rainbow Cafe, rest in peace, with a bunch of cab-drivers and bitching about the Police; nor leaning on the ropes and watching two guys sparring while a trainer or two yells at them; nor twenty-five years of poker games, going home flush, going home clean; nor doping the form out before the first race.

I love hanging out at the gunshop and the hardware store. Am I a traitor to the Cause? I have no cause. I am a card-carrying member of the A.C.L.U. *and* the N.R.A., and I never signed up to be sensitive.

In the Company of Men, this adage seems to operate: You will be greeted on the basis of your actions: no one will inquire into your sincerity, your history, or your views, if you do not choose to share them. We, the men, are here engaged in this specific activity, and your willingness to participate in the effort of the group will admit you.

Yes, these activities *are* a form of love. And many times, over the years, I have felt, at three or four o'clock in the morning, sitting out a hand in the middle of, perhaps, a vicious game, I have felt that *beyond* the fierce competition, there was an atmosphere of *being involved* in a *communal* activity – that by *sitting there*, we, these men, were, perhaps upholding, perhaps ratifying, perhaps creating or re creating some important aspect of our community.

You may ask what it was about our passing money back and forth which was important to the community. And I am not sure that I know, but I know I felt it. And I know that it's quite different from business, and from the competition of business, which is most times prosecuted for the benefit of ourself as breadwinner, as provider, as paterfamilias, as vestigial and outmoded as you may feel those roles to be.

I was shooting partridge, and I watched the dog on point in the, yes, frosty morning, and I said to the other fellow: 'Isn't that beautiful?' and he said, 'That's what it's all about,' and it certainly was. That day's shooting was about things being beautiful. And the trainer saying, 'You got no friends in the ring,' was about things being true, like the one player who says, 'Don't call, I've got you beat,' and the other one who pushes his stack in and says, 'Well, then, I guess I'm just going to have to lose.'

Is this male companionship about the quest for grace? Yes, it is. But not the quest for a mythical grace, or for its specious limitations. This joy of male companionship is a quest for and can be an experience of *true* grace, and transcendent of the rational and, so, more approximate to the real nature of the world.

For the true nature of the world, as between men and women, is sex, and any other relationship between us is either an elaboration, or an avoidance. And the true nature of the world, as between men, is, I think, community of effort directed towards the outside world, directed to subdue, to understand, or to wonder or to withstand together, the truth of the world.

I was sitting at a bar in Chicago many years ago. It was late at night and I was drinking a drink. An old waitress came over to me and correctly guessed the root of what she correctly took to be my state of the blues. 'Look around you,' she said. 'You have more in common with any man in this room than with the women you'll ever be closest to in your life.'

Perhaps. But in any case, to be in the Company of Men is, to me, a nonelective aspect of a healthy life. I don't think your wife is going to give you anecdotal information about the nature of the Universe. And perhaps if you are getting out of the house, you may be sufficiently renewed or inspired that she will cease to wonder whether or not you are *sensitive*: perhaps she will begin to find you interesting.

Corruption

In his response to the Tower report, President Reagan said: The record *seems* to say that I traded arms for hostages, but in my heart I did not.

If we reduce this statement to meaningful English, we are left with this: 'Whatever the report says is irrevelant – far from being bound by the report's findings on my actions, I am not even to be held accountable *for the actions themselves* – I am accountable only to "my heart." ' I.e.: '*I* believe in my superiority to the public, to the law, even to the laws of logical discourse. *I* know what I was doing, and that's got to be sufficient for you below.'

This behavior is an expression of the ultimate contempt for the electorate, the ultimate corruption, the megalomania brought about by power. Political corruption in the pursuit of money is limited by the location and the amount of the money; political corruption in pursuit of a personal vision of the public good is limited by nothing at all, and ends in murder and chaos, as it did in Nazi Germany, and as it does today in Central America.

Psychologically, the corrupt leader creates, and then offers himself as the only protection against, chaos. This is a ploy which recalls and recapitulates the experience of the unhappy child – the child forced to idolize the manipulative parent.

The corrupt parent says: 'If you wish to be protected you must withhold all judgment, powers of interpretation, and individual initiative. *I* will explain to you what things mean, and how to act in every situation. There are no universal laws you are competent to divine or to understand – there is no understanding except through me.'

So, Reagan's monstrous statement that he did not trade hostages in his own heart is an appeal to the child in each of us. It is, in effect, this threat: 'If you want to remain a child, if you want to enjoy the privilege of life without fear, do not judge me. If you deign to judge me, I will withhold my protection.' The corrupted person, politician, parent, doctor, and artist offer us two choices: to accept them and their presumption of power *totally*, or to reject them *totally* and, so, realize that we have been cruelly duped and accept the humiliation, anger, and despair that realization entails.

Those of us who have been in a position of authority as parents, teachers, employers, et cetera, know that it is often difficult to abide by our contracts with those over whom we hold authority. It is sometimes hard to remember that that authority was awarded to be exercised within specific limits, and not as an expression of unthinking and eternal fealty.

Those of us who have held authority know how great the temptation is to supersede our limits, to act 'in the best interests of those under us,' to, in effect, betray them for their own good.

In a normal lifetime we may have executed or experienced this betrayal; we may have spanked children, or humiliated students, or lied to those in our care – and while we were committing those corrupt acts, may have assured ourselves that we were acting for some higher good.

But most of us have also been on the receiving end of misused authority, have been spanked, or humiliated, or lied to, and we know that there is no good, no boon to be gained, no lesson to be learned from someone who treats us with contempt, who misuses a position of power over us.

The other night I was telling a bedtime story to my young daughter, letting my mind ramble and create a fantasy. As I neared the end of the story, I found myself beginning to weave in a moral – to cajole the free fantasy into having a 'meaning' to reduce it to a motto. Later that night I thought about a phrase of Carl Jung's I had read some time before. Jung wrote that the analyst must enter into the fantasy/neurosis/dream of the patient.

I had, previously, found that phrase an expression of nice, human, common sense – a good but technically useless idea. As I reflected on my temptation to insert the moral in the fantasy, however, to make a freely told story about 'bears' become, in effect, an advertisement for 'safety,' I felt uneasy. I felt that I had, 'in my child's best interests,' stolen her time to serve the purposes of my own agenda; and this gave me a clue to Jung's real meaning.

Jung meant, I believe, this: that it is *specifically* the renunciation, on the part of the analyst, of *the desire to control* that gives to the patient *and* the doctor the self-respect and strength to participate in the therapeutic interchange.

Now, analytic technique, philosophy, and method are, of course, essential; but without the act of self-renunciation by which the analyst ratifies the patient's position, they will not get a chance to come into play.

It is the renunciation *itself*, the act of respect *by* authority for its dependents, which is the first, *and the most powerful* good to be done for the patient; for, finally, the patient must cure himself; just as, finally, the country must rule itself.

As the analyst enters into the patient's fantasy (i.e., again, relinquishes the desire to control) whatever strengths, insights, and ideas he may have are relegated to a position *secondary* to his endorsement of the needs of the patient to express, and secondary to an endorsement and ratification of their contract. The patient will feel the renunciation in direct proportion of the effort which it cost the analyst. The patient, in effect, will have witnessed an act of *courage* performed in his interest. This act, an act of self-effacement, of deference, of respect, creates order. It is the opposite of the act of corruption, which creates fear.

If the bedtime story has political content – 'and, so, the children came out of the woods, and they had learned never to disobey their grandmother' – the child may ostensibly seem reassured and comforted, but will, more deeply and importantly, feel rightly betrayed, for the parent will have misused a position of power and acted against the child's interest, and the child will take away from the story *not* the information and guidance it supposedly contains, but the more powerful idea: that the parent wishes to direct and exercise control in areas which are inappropriate; that the parent will not relinquish his or her power in favor of the child's rightful need for self-esteem. It is not important what was 'in the parent's heart,' what is important is that he or she thought the *dictates* of that heart more worthy than the legitimate interests of the child.

The bad parent says, '*I* will be the judge of what you need, not only are you going to be deprived, but I expect you to be grateful to me for my efforts to deprive you.'

It is the same mechanism as 'playing the Red Card.' The corrupt politician says: 'I, *alone*, am in possession of information heretofore unknown to you. This information is so powerful, you are in such immediate and pressing danger, that all laws and orderly methods of communication must be suspended, and *I alone* will decide what measures you must take.'

It is the demagoguery of the third-rate politician, of the third-rate doctor: Believe me and live, or doubt me and die.

The same mechanism operates in the Theater. Only when the artist renounces the desire to control the audience will he or she find true communication with the audience – not power *over* them, but power *with* them.

Just as in politics, there is, in the arts, corruption which misuses the audience's trust in order to gain money (writing 'down' to the audience) and there is corruption 'in the audience's best interest': i.e., plays, productions, performances whose intention is to *change*, to *motivate*, even to *inform*.

The desire on the part of the artist to inform, to change, to motivate, may be laudable, but it is inappropriate in the theatrical setting. The audience has come to engage in *drama*, and before they rule on the truth or utility of the artist's 'ideas,' they will be affronted and disappointed by the inability of the artists *into whose care they have voluntarily placed themselves* to subjugate their own interests to the interest of their charges, the audience.

The director may set *Macbeth* in El Salvador; the playgoer may say: 'How fascinating,' but, subconsciously he feels affronted, and feels, 'Who is this director to be teaching me a lesson and why does he see his *insight* 'the situation in El Salvador is not unlike the situation in *Macbeth*' as more important than his responsibility to me and to Shakespeare to tell the story simply?' (And if there are parallels between the situation in El Salvador and the plot of *Macbeth*, surely the viewer is as capable of perceiving them as was the director.)

The power of a person to serve is in direct proportion to the strength of his or her resistance to the urge to control. To possess or not to possess the urge to control others is not in our power – we may have it or not, it may come suddenly upon us with an increase in our 'status' or supposed 'power.' To choose whether or not to *act* on such an urge *is* within our power. The man or woman in a position of authority who forgoes the inappropriate desire to control will stand not as a *message*, but as an *example* of strength, self-denial, and love; that example has the power to make our lives easier and ourselves less fearful; that example of strength endorses our desires for both autonomy and love, and serves as a balm for our pain in the pursuit of these sometimes divergent goals.

But the person who breaks the rules we have, as individuals or as a culture, created for interpersonal dealings (therapeutic, dramatic, familial, political); the person who sets him or herself 'above the common,' who is not willing to renounce the desire to control others, who cannot rid him or herself of the idea that he or she is acting 'for the best reasons in the world,' and so can exceed the authority ceded, does great harm.

We may, indeed, idolize that parent, doctor, teacher, leader; in fact, we generally do. We frequently need to idolize those who oppress us – the alternative is to feel the constant pain of their betrayal. The tyrant strikes a silent bargain with the tyrannized: 'Identify with me, obey me unthinkingly, and I will provide for you this invaluable service: I will tell no one how worthless you are.'

We idolize these people in inverse proportion to the extent that we believe in them. We respect and love, however, those who act as part of the community, who respect and love their fellows sufficiently to abide by their commitments to us and renounce their desire to control.

That Reagan cried at Bitburg, that he cries when the Holocaust is mentioned, that his heart tells him he did not trade arms for hostages – these assertions are none of our business, and a self-respecting man would forgo sharing them with us. They are equal to the parent who beats his child and tells him, 'This hurts me more than it hurts you.'

It is always the person in the superior position who says, 'I am not laughing at you, I am laughing *with* you'; and always the inferior who knows this means, 'I am both laughing at you and lying to you.'

A Community of Groups

Since the beginning of Bob Sickenger's theater at Hull House in the early sixties, Chicago Theater has been a community not of aspirants, but of citizens. Its progress and development from beginnings at Jane Addams Center through the early days of the Body Politic, Kingston Mines, and the heyday of Lincoln Avenue, and to the present has been the progress of *groups* – of individuals dedicated to the progress of a performance group.

This has created a certain security in the individual members of the theatrical community (or at least the great possibility of such), and marks a difference between the theatrical community in Chicago and that in New York. In Chicago, the individual worker is striving to improve him or herself and perfect his or her craft in the view of and for the benefit of a small group sympathetic to his or her aims (the company), rather than a large and unsympathetic group capable of perceiving only results (the theater-going public and commercial production interests acting as their docents).

We in Chicago are, perhaps, therefore not enthralled with the question of *alienation* – of *identity*. A basic need of the worker has been met, and this enables him or her (represented by the *group*) to turn the attention outward, to concern themselves with the life of the city.

We, to a large extent, are chauvinists. We perceive the city not as an adversary, or as a random arena, but, quite accurately, as an extension of our dream-life. This is also an identifying characteristic of the Midwestern artist, who labors to explain to him or herself the *fact* of Chicago – understanding it as a manifestation of him or herself. E.g.: *The Pit, Sister Carrie, An American Tragedy, Lucy Gayheart, The Man with the Golden Arm, Herzog, Bleacher Bums, The Wonderful Ice Cream Suit, Boss, Some Kind of Life? All I Want, Sexual Perversity, Grease, Working*, etc.

As citizens – which is to say as individuals who are secure in their own worth – we have been able to direct energy outward – towards expression and *actualization*, rather than towards merchandising, consolidation, and packaging. This freedom from puerile concerns has resulted in great growth, great vitality, and much artistic creation.

The theater has been forming, and reforming, on both geographical and artistic lines. Last year's church-sheltered improvisation is next year's institution.

The last fifteen years have seen the growth of the idea of the strength and primary importance of the groups of individuals banded together with a common aesthetic aim; this idea has changed – in the general consciousness – from a nice but, realistically, impractical notion, and is now considered the necessary norm.

This is a great achievement, and creates the possibility of great achievement.

We in Chicago are proud of our theatrical workers in the same way Naples is proud of its singers or Washington State of its apples, if I may: 'Yes, we grow these here – rather nice, don't you think?'

Some Random Thoughts

Twenty-Fifth Anniversary Issue of *Backstage* (1985)

In 1960 I was bar mitzvahed. Nothing much else of importance happened to me until 1963.

In 1963 I was working backstage at *Second City* and heard Fred Willard introduce a scene by saying, 'Let's take a sleigh ride through the snow-covered forests of Entertainment.'

That was my first personal encounter with Greatness, and at that moment I knew that I owed it to myself not to become, in the tradition of my family, a labor lawyer. My first true milestone in the Professional Theater came in 1967. I had been an usher and then the house manager at The Sullivan Street Playhouse in New York. At that moment they happened to be doing *The Fantasticks*. One day the Assistant Stage Manager got sick, and I was pressed into service running the lightboard. In those pre-microchip days we had actual dimmerboards with huge dials and knobs and sticks, and some of the light changes involved plugging, turning, adjusting, replugging, etc., in sequences that were quite balletic.

My first and only night running the lightboard clipped along quite merrily until the end of the show. All the contestants on stage were reunited, El Gallo said, 'So, remember: . . .,' which was to be followed by a reprise of the song 'Try to Remember.' It was also my cue to do the most elaborate 'send 'em home smiling' light change in Greenwich Village. Ever an innovator, however, I elbowed the master switch and plunged the stage, the house, and the light booth into total darkness for a period which can only be described as a 'long, long time.'

In the eighteen ensuing years not much has happened. Once, greatly depressed, and in New Haven (but I repeat myself), I was walking up and down in front of the Yale Rep. An old woman came up to me and said, 'God bless you: You are the $avior of the American Theater, I have been to see your play six times.' I cheered up and thanked her for raising me out of my self-involved, ridiculous torpor. I told her she had given me hope and that, yes, I was going to go home and write. I thanked her again. 'Not at all, Mr. Durang,' she replied.

In 1976 Dick Clark told me that Theater was all very well and good, but that, finally, it was 'a flea on the ass of an elephant.'

That's my report.

Liberty

In Hemingway's *A Farewell to Arms*, an American soldier, fleeing from the War, is playing billiards with a European Nobleman. The Nobleman comments that America will surely win the War, and the American asks him how he can be so sure. America will win, the man responds, because she is a young nation, and the young nations always win the wars. Then how is it that those young nations fade, the American asks, and he is told that they fade because they, with the passage of time, become old.

I once saw a film which recorded the transformation of an individual from arrogance to humility in the twinkling of an eye. An investigative reporter for a Chicago television station had hidden a camera to capture the dealings of a pimp who was brutalizing the young women who worked for him.

The Chicago police force had an undercover officer pose as a prostitute wanting to be taken on by this pimp. In the film she presents herself and the pimp struts and proclaims his dominance. To emphasize a point, he strikes the policewoman in the face and she falls. Several Chicago police officers appear from their hiding places, and for several very long seconds, beat the pimp summarily. The pimp falls to the ground and is immediately hauled back to his feet. He is broken and bleeding, and his arrogance is gone. It has been replaced by the demeanor of a child. 'What has happened to me,' his eyes say. 'It's only me, whom everybody *loves* ... why are these people hurting me? Will nobody *help* me???'

Both the pimp's arrogance and its price are revealed to him in one moment. He becomes, in one moment, the perfection of the Tragic Form: he gains self-knowledge at the same moment that his state is transformed from King to Beggar – like Oedipus Rex, like Lear, like any nation which has grown old.

In our denial of asylum to Central American Refugees, we are avowing our state as an Old Nation – a nation resting on its laurels, a nation which draws its self-esteem from a bank of moral credit which, if it ever existed, was expended long ago.

'We need not *do* good,' we are saying, 'because we *are* good. Everybody *loves* us, and the things which we do are de facto good. They are good because we *do* them.'

In our name, our Government asks, 'How can we be sure these refugees are truly fleeing Political Oppression? What if they're just *hungry*? We will extend our sanctuary to the miserable to the extent they gratify our image of ourselves. As to their actual *need*, however, we do not feel we should be responsible.'

And so a young nation's love of liberty has become a love of the power to control through the awarding or withholding of liberty. A love of liberty has become a love of power.

But in Emma Lazarus's poem, 'The New Colossus,' one hundred years old, we find not a love of power, but a celebration of humility before God.

Her poem and Bartholdi's statue of *Liberty* are a celebration not of blessedness, but of thanks. It was the act of a young nation to bless the hand of a God which had given it freedom to worship, to speak, to make a living. The Nation of 1886 thanked God in word and deed, and the deed was a happy sacrifice, and the sacrifice was open immigration.

In acceptance of the Stranger, in acceptance of the wretched of the world, America, the Young Nation, grew and prospered and became, in the inevitable course of time, an Old Nation.

We see the trappings of our age around us: an economy based on waste, the moral and economic cost of maintaining a standing army, immigration policies used as a political tool. These signs are both symbol and a further cause of the fear in the midst of which we live.

We look around and ask why we can no longer win a war, balance a budget, ensure the safety of our citizens at home or abroad. 'Are we not,' we ask, 'the same good-hearted good-willed,' in effect, 'lovable people we have always been? Are we not still beloved of God?' And as we ask we are brought low by humiliation after inevitable humiliation. These blows are inevitable because, as per the laws of tragedy, our story is not yet complete. We are undergoing reversal of our situation, but we are far from recognizing it. We suffer at home and abroad because we are like the spoiled children of the Rich. We see comfort as our given state and we accept obedience from those we, on no evidence whatever, think of as our beneficiaries.

To ensure the safety of our self-image as Peacemaker, we have become a warmonger nation dedicated to the proliferation of arms: and we would, quite literally, rather die than *examine*, let alone alter, our image of ourselves as just, all-seeing, always right. So we, like the heroes of tragedy, like the pimp in the news film, have tried to appropriate to ourselves the attributes of God, and, no less than those other misguided heroes, we must and will and do suffer.

One hundred years ago, in a time of plenty of all kinds, in a time of spiritual abundance symbolized by Ms. Lazarus's poem and Mr. Bartholdi's statue, we were a different land. We were a Young Nation. Our National Conceit was not to be protector, but to be the comforter of the world. Our constituency was not the politically correct, but the politically repugnant of the world. And that office and that conceit and direction made us, for a time, a truly great nation.

In 1886, free open immigration offered America neither economic nor psychological hardship, today it would offer us both. And it would also offer us a peace and a protection not afforded by any nuclear arsenal or metal detector. Open immigration, as Ms. Lazarus pointed out, would give us something that would be both more comforting and more powerful than the strength of moral right, it would give us humility before God.

A Speech for Michael Dukakis

I am not very much of a political person. I believe most politicians are No Better Than They Should Be. But I am saddened by the decay of the American Political Process as most clearly evidenced in the absence of true free debate between the candidates.

It is not that I think we ever had an honest presentation of opposed ideas for the edification of an information-hungry electorate, no. I do not long for an apocryphal Golden Age of Symposia. I miss the political debate as a Vicious Brawl. I miss the spectacle of the candidate using wit as a bludgeon, and employing the tools of rhetoric spontaneously and with no regard for the truth, in order to gain personal advantage.

What passes for political debate is, in these days, nothing more than Trial By Ordeal. We, the electorate, score the fight on how perfectly the talking head can get through his set piece and detract points not for his inability to respond, but, on the contrary, for his inability to stick to the prepared text.

I was watching the first television debate between George Bush and Michael Dukakis. Being an American myself, I was waiting for one of the fellows to emerge as a clear underdog, so that I could root for him.

My hopes for a divertingly dramatic confrontation rose when Mr. Bush started assailing Mr. Dukakis's patriotism. 'Well,' I thought, 'aren't his keepers *bold*, but won't they be disappointed when Dukakis comes back and *starts fighting dirty* himself!' 'Yes,' I thought, 'now that Bush has "opened the Ball" we're going to have an American Showdown. Oh Good.' You, gentle reader, cannot only imagine, but probably shared my disappointment when Mr. Dukakis refused to Stand on his Hind Legs and Fight.

His pacifism offended my sense of both drama and history. Not only was it a chance for a good fight, it was a chance for a good fight in the great American Tradition of 'Waaal, I have, as you have all seen, held my peace until now. And I have evidenced forbearance in the face of provocation, but Call Me Other Than a Man if I can keep still any longer!'

This is the *true* stuff of the American Dream: a peace-loving man given *so much provocation* that the very tenets of pacifism *themselves* would be offended if he did not come out and fight. (I call your attention to two of our major documents on the subject: *Shane* and *Bad Day at Black Rock*.) But Mr. Dukakis had not been paying enough attention to our cinematic heritage, and he retired to his corner irked when he should have been out there taking names.

So I, watching the television, became offended on the part of the viewership, and wrote Mr. Dukakis a speech, which follows here.

You know, every Presidential Election, one or the other side says that 'never before have the choices been so clear, never before has the choice been so important.'

Well, I don't know. A candidate, and those working for a candidate, like to feel important, we all like to feel important, and we each like to feel that our vote is important.

I don't know that this is the 'most momentous choice you will even have to make.' But I think it is an important choice.

The election, as you see, has been hotly contested. I think it's *good* for the country. I think it's good to call things by their right name, and I see no reason not to.

Mr. Bush has implied, time and again, that I am not patriotic enough for him. Why would he say that?

He doesn't truly believe that I'm not patriotic. Why would he make such a charge?

He did it because it suited his purposes.

He doesn't believe that anyone who opposes the Pledge of Allegiance in the schools is not Patriotic. He says it because it suits his purposes.

He makes these slurs because I, as his opponent, *got in his way*, and it suits his purposes to abuse me, and to make accusations that he knows are false. He did it because he found it convenient. He has also questioned my 'passion.'

What about 'passion'?

What does a person care about?

Let me ask you a question.

Suppose you were at a party, or some social gathering. The conversation turned to the problem of the Homeless. You said, 'There are so many more homeless in our streets today than there were ten years ago. What can we do?' You and your friends discuss the problem. One says, 'Let's collect clothing,' one says, 'I wonder where we can send money or food . . .' and so on. . . . One man said 'Let's create a thousand points of light.'

What would you think about that man? He may be passionate about that *phrase*, but he's not passionate about the problem. If he were passionate about it, he would *do* something about it.

A pretty phrase created by some speechwriter is not passion. Passion is what a man or woman cares about. And you can fairly well judge what they care about by what they *do*.

What does Bush care about?

He cares about the special interests of himself and his group of cronies. He cares about them more than he cares about the Law.

He and his group subverted the Constitution, they subverted the Law of the Land, the Law they swore to uphold, when they traded arms for hostages.

For whatever reason they did it, they broke the Law, and they are unrepentant.

And you know it's true.

They aren't sorry they broke it, they don't even seem aware that what they did was wrong

Now, you may, some of you may *concur* with Bush's actions, with the actions of his little group, *but he assured, that if he broke the law in THIS instance, which you may agree with, he will break the law, and bend the law, and look the other way in other instances with which you DISAGREE, and to purposes which you find despicable, as soon as it suits his purposes.*

You may have remarked his use of the phrase, 'The Governor of Massachusetts.' And the constant references to my being from

Massachusetts, as a sort of 'code.'

His inference is that, 'You know and I know that Massachusetts is, somehow, not part of America,' or '*less* than American,' or not part of the 'America' of which you and I approve.

Does Bush believe this?

Does he actually and 'passionately' believe these snide remarks and insinuations, that one part of the country is less worthy than another?

Of course not. He's an Easterner, he spent much of his life in Massachusetts, he went to school there. That's who he is.

And what sort of a man would stoop to divide the Union of these United States through insinuation and sarcasm?

Why would he do that? He knows that Massachusetts is neither less nor more American than any of the other states.

Why would he disparage his own heritage? Why would he imply something he knows is unjust, and untrue, in addition to being destructive?

He did it because it suited his purposes.

And if he did it when it suited his purposes about *my* State, he will do it, when it suits him, about the State in which *you* live, or the Union to which you belong, or the profession which you practice.

You can listen to the voice which says, 'What do you expect from the Governor of Massachusetts,' and you can hear the same voice saying, 'What do you expect from a steelworker,' or 'from a doctor,' or 'from a Southwesterner.'

And many of you feel 'included' by his, in effect, 'winking' at you, by these coded references that seem to say 'You and I know who the good and the bad people are . . .' (Pause)

Well, we all like to feel included. I personally don't believe there are 'good and bad' people. *But I do believe there are good and bad ACTS.* And I believe it's a bad act for a public official to break the law *for WHATEVER reason*, and I believe it is a bad act for a public official to curry favor through lies, through half-truths, and through insinuation. *There is no REASON to divide this country.* And the public forum should concern itself with what *unites* us.

A lot of mystery and ceremony has become associated with this job of President.

It's an important job, and, in confusing times, we sometimes look for the person who holds this job to be all things to all people.

And, so, the election process itself has become, year by year, less of a reasoned casting of votes, and more, if you will, of a 'beauty contest.'

The man who can say the right catch phrase first, the man who can best master 'the use of the camera,' the man who is the next-to-the-last to get caught out in some mistake or inconsistency gets awarded the prize.

But the job was designed, and the job should *be*, to *preside*, to preside over legitimately opposed factions in such a way as to *represent the interests of the people as a whole.* To represent their interests, as expressed in our laws. And, especially in these moment-ous times, amidst crises of health, of foreign relations, of the environment, of human necessity, that is what the job must be.

Now, I am not a passionless man; it is not my nature. But I believe that the job of Chief Executive should be performed, and is per-formed best, by a man who is *not* a zealot; who refers his decisions to the rule of Law, always in the knowledge that he was elected *not to enact his own whims*, his own 'passions,' but to represent his constituents; and to put the rule of law, and the will of the People *as expressed in Law*, above his own will.

If elected, I swear to obey the Laws of this Country, and to tolerate *no one* in my administration who subverts those Laws.

I swear to work for *all* the people, for the people from *all* our States; for the homeless, for all minorities, for those oppressed by hardship, and by illness.

This is a remarkable time in our history.

We can look at the vast changes around us with Fear, but we do not *have* to be fearful.

We can, as a Nation, take a deep breath, and say that we are *equal* to those changes. And we *are* equal to them.

There is not a challenge, whether it is housing, or World Peace, or AIDS, or the budget, which we, *working together*, are not equal to.

We can be nostalgic for the Past, but the Past is gone, and nothing will bring it back.

This is a time of change, and, for good and ill, the Past is behind us.

With it, we have lost segregation, the oppression of Women, and of Labor, and countless other social ills. We have started to put them behind us.

We have also lost the comfort of World Peace, of a stable

economy, of a clean environment, of a country safe from the ravages of disease. But *these* things can be reclaimed.

They can absolutely be reclaimed. By a populace working together, undivided, working under the Law.

It is that populace I was raised to be a citizen of, and it is that populace of which I want to be President.

I am asking you for your vote. Thank you.

That's the speech. I sent it to his People by a mutual friend. He never used it; and if *any* of you readers might be inclined, even fleetingly, to think, 'Why, hell, if that man had just said those words, he'd be President today,' I would, of course, most humbly demur, and respond, 'Oh, hell, I was trying to even up the fight . . .'

A First-time Film Director

I started writing screenplays in 1978 (*The Postman Always Rings Twice*).

Along with most other screenwriters and Other Ranks, I quickly conceived a desire to direct movies. My agent told me that the best way to break into that job was this: write an original screenplay and hope someone wants it badly enough to bet on you as a director.

Michael Hausman, producer of *Amadeus*, *Ragtime*, *Heartland*, etc., liked the screenplay and gave me the chance to direct it, which I did. We filmed the movie the summer of 1986 in Seattle. It's called *House of Games*, it stars Lindsay Crouse and Joe Mantegna. It's a *film noir*, psychological thriller.

Here is the story:

A psychiatrist (Crouse) treats compulsive gamblers, drinkers, etc. One of her patients tells her that he is $25,000 in debt to the Mob, and if he doesn't pay within the week, he is going to be killed. The patient pleads with her to intercede. She goes to the gamblers who hold the patient's marker. She becomes involved with one of them (Mantegna).

He is, by profession, a confidence man. Crouse, fascinated by the man and his life style, starts going out on criminal escapades with him; she becomes more and more involved.

Here are some thoughts on directing my first movie.

Familiar and nonfamiliar occupations

I once had to take a specific dose of pills with me on a trip. I shook the pills out of the bottle, counted them carefully, tore a sheet of paper out of my notebook, wrote the dose and directions on the sheet, and poured the pills onto the sheet and twisted it into a spill, an action from a pharmacy of a bygone day.

As I did this, I was overcome with a sense of *déjà vu*. 'I have *absolutely* done this before,' I thought.

This was a feeling I never had while directing the film.

It seemed to me, prior to attempting the job, that film directing was like barn raising: the job was laid out, the opposing walls would be hoisted up, and the farmer would scramble up a ladder to peg the opposing walls together. If the farmer had not done his job correctly, he would be left fifty feet in the air, leaning against an unsupported wall, with the people who employed him and the people he employed standing down below and watching his shame.

I'd written for the movies before, worked with the directors, and been around a set. It was obvious to me that there were many aspects to the job, that I was good at some of them, competent at others, and at a complete loss in several of the most important. In those areas in which I have no talent and little understanding, it occurred to me, I had better have either a good plan or a good excuse.

The area of which I was completely ignorant was, unfortunately, the visual. Oh well, I thought, and went back to hit the books.

I decided that I was going to plan out the whole movie, shot by shot, according to my understanding of the theories of Sergei Eisenstein.

I found Eisenstein's theories particularly refreshing, as they didn't seem to call for any visual talent. The shot, he said, not only *need* not, but *must* not be evocative. The shot should stand as one unemotional term of a sequence, the totality of which should create in the mind of the audience a new idea, e.g. rather than the shot of a distraught woman crying, or the same woman describing to her friend over the telephone how she found out her husband was cheating on her, Eisenstein would suggest the following: (1) shot of woman reading a note; (2) shot of the note which reads, 'Honey, I'll be home late tonight. Going bowling, I love you'; (3) shot of woman putting down the note, looking down at something on the floor; (4) her point of view, shot of the bowling ball in the bowling ball bag.

In the example above, each of the shots is uninflected and unemotional and so the shots could be determined by someone without visual 'talent,' but who knew the 'meaning' of the sequence, i.e., a woman discovers her husband is cheating on her.

So I thought, Well, that's for me; I'm not going to be John Ford or Akira Kurosawa, but I *do* know the meaning of each of the sequences, having written them, and if I can reduce the meaning of each of the sequences to a series of shots, each of them clean and uninflected (i.e., not necessitating further narration), then the movie will 'work'; the audience will understand the story through the medium of pictures, and the movie will be as good or bad as the story I wrote.

That was the task I set myself in preparation: to reduce the script, a fairly verbal psychological thriller, to a *silent movie*. It seemed to be a tough, and possibly pointless, task, but I've always been more comfortable sinking while clutching a good theory than swimming with an ugly fact.

So I made out the shotlist, then I tried to sketch the shotlist in a bunch of cunning little rectangles, each representing what the shot would look like on the screen. Then I arrived in Seattle to make the movie.

Preproduction

Three people were in the production office in Seattle. Somebody went to Abercrombie & Fitch and got their deluxe Pigeon Shoot dart game. We played Pigeon Shoot for much of the first few days. We drove around and scouted locations, I wrote letters to friends back home. 'This is a breeze,' I thought. Then everybody showed up.

As a kid I did a lot of white-water canoeing. Once, up in Michigan, I was in the stern, shooting some rapids, when we hit a bad rock broadside and swamped. The canoe with me in it was pinned upside down in the white water, and the force of the water was such that I couldn't get out. 'I'd be okay,' I thought, 'if someone would just turn this thing off.' And so it was when the movie got rolling.

Our producer had to put together 'the board,' that is, the schedule of what gets shot when; the production designer had questions about the color of a wall; the costume designer wanted to go out shopping; the propmaster wanted to know how many poker chips of which color were needed; the transportation captain, et cetera. Now: this was the kind of action I was looking forward to. I like to make decisions, and I like to be at the center of things, but this was a bit too much of a good thing. Everybody said that the prime requirement for a film director was good health, and I quickly saw the reason. *Each* decision is important. *Each* decision is going to affect the film. *Each* choice presented to you is the result of work and thought and concern on the part of the person asking the question. Sloppiness won't do, and petulance won't do. Also, I *prayed* for the chance to direct a movie, nothing would do but to do the job, which I was fast realizing was, in the main, administrative.

So I got the job in hand and tried to remember to meditate twice a day, and preproduction was going along pretty well. Then we started with the Real storyboard.

The Real storyboard was going to be drawn by our professional storyboard artist, Jeff Ballsmeier. It was to be, in effect, a comic book of the entire movie, showing what the camera was to shoot, where the camera was to move.

Ballsmieier and I and our cinematographer, Juan Ruiz-Anchia started meeting to transform *my* storyboard into The storyboard.

The only trouble with my original efforts was that all my drawings looked like amoebas, and that those things they represented 'would not cut' (i.e., could not be assembled into a coherent film).

Crossing the line

And so, as Stanislavsky would say periodically to his students: 'Congratulations, you have reached the next step of your education.'

The storyboard conferences were incredibly exhausting for me. I had to force myself to think in totally new concepts. Most of these concepts were on the order of 'How many boxes are hidden in this pile?' and it was like taking a visual intelligence test for several hours every day, with the questions written in a foreign language.

In cutting film, the *axis* of the shot, I learned, has to be preserved. If the hero enters looking to his *left* at the heroine, then, in subsequent shots, he has to *continue* looking to his left. You can't cut to a close-up and see him looking to his *right*. *Unless* . . . and here followed a list of Talmudic exceptions which I could never follow, but which Jeff and Juan discussed quite a bit, while I felt *very* stupid.

One is not supposed to *cut in axis*, i.e. from a longshot of a subject to a *closer* slot of the same subject or vice versa, unless . . . et cetera.

When trying to show *passage of time*, one had better not cut from the subject to the same subject again *unless* . . .

All these rules are to this point: *Don't confuse the viewer*. I tried and tried, and the editor, Trudy Ship, showed up and said don't worry, it will become clearer when you're in the editing process. The next one will be easier. (*Insh'allah*) And so we went on making up the shotlist, the conference room was covered with diagrams, the table was covered with sketches. Juan and I and Jeff would posture and pace aorund the room saying things to each other like, 'Okay: I'm the ashtray and you're the camera,' and getting excited. It felt like the Algonquin Round Table on Speed.

My days of preproduction were like this. I would go from a costume fitting, to a storyboard conference, to a location scout, and driving back to my apartment, I hit the same tree three nights in a row. I would arrive home, thank God I hadn't fallen asleep on the way, take my foot off the brake and start out of the car, and the car, which was still in drive, would proceed into the tree.

The numbers on the days-till-shoot notice on the office wall got lower and lower. The cast showed up for rehearsal. We were all Old Cronies, and had worked together on the stage, most of us, for at least a decade, and had a happy reunion in Seattle. Rehearsals went swimmingly, and it was just about time to shoot.

Full of beans, and happy in the flush of having convinced somebody to let me direct a film, I said to myself: Think past the shooting process. Plan the film, and always think towards the *editing*. The script, for good or ill, is finished, and it's going to work; you have wonderful actors, you have a superb D.P., don't go out there on the set to 'improvise,' or even to 'create,' but, simply, *to stick to the plan*. If the plan is good and the script is good, the movie will cut together well and the audiences will enjoy the story. If the plan is *no* good, or the script is *no* good, then being brilliant or 'inventive' on the set isn't going to be to much avail. In effect, *keep it simple, stupid*.

Well, those were fine words, and very comforting to me, and I put up a great front and ate a lot of fresh Seattle salmon with the cast and crew, and preproduction went on apace.

Always a cocky lad, I had told the producer not to worry about me as a first-time director – that he would get either a good film or a sincere apology. The night before the first shot, my jollity came back to haunt me and I had a *crise de foi*. I couldn't sleep, I got the shakes, 'I can't *do* this,' I thought, 'who in the *world* am I fooling?' And I wallowed in self-pity and fear for a while, until the words of the great Dan Beard came to me: 'Just because you're lost,' he said, 'don't think your compass is broken.' And then I was, for that moment, suffused with Peace. I wasn't taxed, I saw, with having to make a masterpiece. Whether or not the movie was even any *good* was, at this point (on the night before shooting), fairly well out of my hands, all *I* had to do was stick to the plan. 'Hell I can do *that*,' I thought, 'all I've got to be is obstinate.' So I went to sleep.

The husbanding of energy in directing a movie is, I found, of as much importance as the husbanding of time: there's only so much of it, and you don't want to get into deficit spending.

Mike Hausman produced *House of Games*. His favorite axiom hangs on a sampler in a prominent position wherever his command post is. It reads: ALL MISTAKES ARE MADE IN PREPRODUCTION.

I was happy I made the amount of film decisions I did in preproduction, because when the snowball started rolling downhill I could barely remember what the movie was about, let alone try to think where to put the camera.

The shoot

We had forty-nine scenes and forty-nine days to do them in. We had to average approximately two and a half pages a day (about average). We had about twelve hours a day to get those two and a half pages.

Each day Juan and I and Christine Wilson, the script supervisor, would meet with Ned Dowd, the first assistant director (the man who ran the set), and reduce the storyboard to a list of shots, e.g., Scene Two: (1) a master of the entire action; (2) a close-up of the patient; (3) a close-up of Doctor Ford; (4) an insert of Ford's wristwatch; (5) a shot of Ford writing on a pad, etc.

We would plan to shoot in one direction as much as possible, so as not to have to relight twice, then turn the camera and shoot in the reverse direction. The average shotlist for each day was nine shots. And we would proceed in a deliberate and orderly fashion, cast and crew, from one shot to the next, and then go home and fall into what I wish I could describe as a dreamless sleep, but which comes closer to a 'night of fitful musings.' (I should point out things would proceed in an 'orderly fashion' until the end of the shoot, when I, 'smelling the barn,' as it were, began to lose it, a bit, and wish that everything could happen all at once so I could get dressed and go to the Opening.)

My job, once the shooting began, was a lot of worry, and a lot less work. Having started into the day's shotlist, I was fairly free from one shot to the next, and improved the hours by drinking tea, while our magnificent crew worked full-out dealing with the foreseen: the necessity of putting light places where it is not and taking it away from places where it is; and the unforeseen: cars that would not start, a mailbox that had to be removed, a prison elevator to which the key had been lost, a ruined costume, et cetera.

I was in constant awe of the crew, camera, light, and grips. Many friends and acquaintances had told me that a film director's life was taken up with professional intransigence of the crew and with time-wasting minutiae. My experience was completely the opposite. I felt that *these* guys were setting the example and that I was just along for the ride, and would (and did) do well to follow them. They were up all day, they were up all night, they were hanging lights on window ledges ten stories up, they spent the night in a crane in the rain.

They came over to ask me my opinion regularly, not because of any talent on my part, or because of any expertise I had demonstrated, but because the film is a hierarchy and it was my job *to do one part of it*: to provide an aesthetic overview, and to be able to express that overview in simple, practicable terms – more light on her face, *less* light on her face; the car in the background, no car in the background.

I came over to the camera once every hour or so to 'approve' a shot the D.P. set up. My 'approval' drill was this: go over to the camera, look through the lens at a brilliant clear composition which reflected the essential nature of the shot, thank the cinematographer, return to my camper.

Most of 'approving the shot' made me a bit nervous. I understood the drill of deference, I understood that *someone* had to be in charge of the movie, and that someone was me, and that I was doing it; but I *did* feel like a great big interloper looking through the camera. One part I did like was turning my hat around. I wore a beaked hat throughout the shooting, and when I walked over to the camera I would drop my glasses off my face and turn my hat around, so that I could get close to the eyepiece. That was a never-failing source of enjoyment, and I felt great and I felt I *looked* great doing it. The hat was given to me by Dorothy Jeakins, the costume designer. She designed *The Postman Always Rings Twice* (1980), which was my first experience with the movies. And she had worked with Cecil B. De Mille, and told me the hat was from some De Mille extravaganza, I have forgotten which. I also rented a pair of jodhpurs to wear on my first day as a director.

My plan was to show up on the set in jodhpurs, a monocle, and my Dorothy Jeakins hat. On the way to the set, however, this costume struck me as a tad *chudspudik*, and so I, thank goodness, refrained. (I *did* put this directing drag on after finishing the first day's shooting, and posed in it with the actors on that day, Ms. Crouse and Ms. Kohlhaas.)

Mike Hausman, the film's producer, thoughtfully scheduled one easy 1½-page scene as the first day's work. So we finished that scene and another 2-page scene written for the same location, but scheduled for the *next* day, all in three hours and I ended my first day as a director, *one day ahead of schedule* (which was, of course, Mr Hausman's secret plan) and I put on the jodhpurs and posed for a picture.

I didn't take too much of a deep breath until after the third day of shooting, when our first day's dailies came back from New York. I got drunk with my assistant, Mr. Zigler, and we poured ourselves from 'The Thirteen Coins,' a Seattle Bar and Grill, into the screening room, and there, sure enough, was the film we took on the first day. Juan's photography was beautiful, the acting was beautiful, it was going to cut together and make a movie.

There's an old joke about the belowstairs gossip on the night after the Prince and the Princess got married. 'What happened?' says the butler. 'Well,' says the chambermaid, 'the Prince comes in, the Princess says: "I offer you my honor," the Prince replies, "I honor your offer." ' 'And that's it?' says the butler. 'Yep, that's about it,' says the chambermaid, 'all night long: honor, offer, honor, offer.'

And that was about it for the shooting of the movie. Shoot, go home, shoot, go home, et cetera.

The previous September in New York, I was on a panel with Spike Lee, Alex Cox, Frank Perry, and Susan Seidelman. The topic of the panel was: Directors Discuss Independent Films. As questions were addressed to the other panelists, I listened and thought, enviously, 'Gee, I wish *I* could be a film director.' That's how it was on the set. Day by day we followed the plan. No 'light at the end of the tunnel' – just getting the day's work done. At night we went to the dailies, and Juan and Mike Hausman and I sat in the back row with Trudy Ship, the editor, and I would look at the takes I asked to have printed and tell Trudy my preference, and in what order the shots could be tacked together to make the scene.

At the beginning of shooting, I printed only two takes of each shot. As the shooting went on and I got more and more fatigued, I started to print more and more takes. One day Mike Hausman suggested politely (and correctly) that I was 'going native,' and that I only had to print one or two; and if those were not sufficient, I could always print up the out-takes. Not only was he right economically, but, I noticed, he was right artistically.

As a screenwriter, I spent a bit of time watching others direct; as the husband of a film actress I spent more time doing the same. I would frequently ask myself: '*Why* is that guy shooting so much?' And the answer occurs to me now: he's probably tired.

There is a condition called hypothermia, and it occurs when the body can't keep itself warm. Two of the symptoms are inability to think clearly, and panic; and it's no joke, it happened to me once alone in the woods in winter and I was lost and very lucky to stumble across a road before I froze to death.

A situation very like this state of mind is brought about by stress as well as cold; and if Eisenstein would have lived longer and spent more time in Hollywood, he might have talked less about the Theory of Montage, and more about healthy eating, and what to have on the Craft Service Table.

Speaking of the theory of montage, it was very easy to choose between two takes of a shot. I found it difficult to choose among three and impossible to choose among more. As my fatigue led to vague anxiety, I had to remind myself more frequently to Stick to the Plan and Keep It Simple, Stupid: to follow the shotlist and storyboard in such a way as to capture the simple, uninflected shots which would cut together to make the movie.

How successful was this stoical approach? Well, it made the editing process very straightforward, for the most part. There were scenes which were superfluous, which had to come out; a few looks which were needed and were not shot and so had to be 'stolen' from other shots or scenes, but, for the most part, the editing process, like the shooting process, was a reflection of the original plan of the storyboard.

The storyboard was, in effect, the 'script' we were going out to shoot; and it is the prejudice and observation of a writer and theatergoer that, finally, the production is only as good as the script.

Do you want to work or do you want to gamble?

What did we do for fun on the set? Well, we did a whole bunch of things, and would have done more, except I am a rotten liar, and when we had planned a gag I'd be laughing so hard I couldn't say 'Action,' and so the object of the jokes, who was almost invariably Lindsay Crouse, would get wind that something was up.

My favourite was the Spawning Salmon. Crouse did a scene on a beach overlooking an embankment overlooking Elliott Bay. She's supposed to be staring out to sea, and we sent a production assistant down below the embankment. On cue, he was to heave this ten-pound salmon up into the air, where it lands at her feet. You can see it on the Joke Reel, but Crouse is staring a few degrees off to the side, and concentrating on her acting, and she didn't actually see the salmon. Ned Dowd instructed me that good form dictated that I tell the script supervisor that we should print that take because 'there was something special at the beginning that I think I liked.'

Ned Dowd won $56,000 off of me at blackjack, and I'm just lucky that he allowed me to cut double-or-nothing One Last Time several more times. Gambling was endemic in the cast and crew. One sequence of the film is a poker game, and many of us, for the week that sequence took, spent twelve hours a day in a staged poker game and the remaining twelve in a real one.

Crouse had an actor friend dress up in a bunny suit and prepare to hop through the back of a shot on her cue, but it seems that that day I was a tad 'out of sorts,' Crouse was reluctant to make my day harder, and so the actor stayed under the table we were shooting, dressed *en lapin* for four hours. We shot one long sequence in a pool hall, and spent a lot of time between setups shooting pool and learning trick shots from the pool hustlers, and so on, and there you have it. We were a cross between a mobile army corps, an office, and a bus-and-truck company; we were a happy family.

What I remember

I remember shooting the film's last sequence on the last day of shooting. In the scene, Joe, one of the actors, is to get shot, and I remember his wife sitting behind the camera crying as she watched him do the various takes of his death scene.

I remember racing the dawn on a couple of weeks of night shooting trying to get the last shot before the sun came up, and the seagulls cawing a half-hour before dawn. I remember our wonderful soundman, who wanted to break into acting and was given the part of a hotel clerk. He had to say, 'May I help you?,' and take a pen out of a penholder and a form off of a sheaf of forms, and hand them to Crouse and Mantegna. We drilled him on the specific timing of the movement of the pen and form, and told him that the whole rhythm of the shot keyed off of his precise movement; and then, on his first shot, we glued the pen into the holder and the forms together. I remember the camaraderie on the set – the sense that we were engaged in a legitimate enterprise as part of a legitimate industry, and that hard work and dedication would ensure one a place in the profession. I remember thinking how very sad that this feeling is absent from the Theater, where *no one* is guaranteed employment from one year to the next, where this year's star writer, actor, designer, may not work again for years; and I remember feeling grateful that I could feel that camaraderie again.

What I'm going to do differently next time

We finished shooting the movie on time and under budget in mid-August. I went home happy as a clam and immediately got as sick as I've ever been in my life. I couldn't get out of bed for two weeks, didn't eat a thing, and sweated the whole time. Sidney Lumet called to welcome us back. 'How did the film go?' he asked my wife. She told him. 'How's David?' he said. 'Is he sick yet?'

Back in the editing room, Trudy Ship told me that, as I look at the film, I am going to think the following three things: I shot too much, I shot too little, I shot the wrong thing. This, basically, is what I *do* think as I look at the film. There is a lot of coverage I shot that was never used; the main cost of this is not the exposed film, or even the more serious lost setup time, but this: When capturing footage that is essential, the mood and the work on the set is, of course, more directed than when capturing footage that is protective. There is a lot I *should* have shot. There was one close-up I left out which necessitated a reshoot and wasted a lot of worker-hours. Finally, my Master Plan was not directing the movie, *I* was directing the movie, and next time out, I'll know more about what to shoot, what not to shoot, and when to deviate from the plan.

Next time I'll eat nothing but macrobiotic food, exercise every day, and, God willing, work with exactly the same people.

Film is a Collaborative Business

Working as a screenwriter I always thought that 'Film is a collaborative business' only constituted half of the actual phrase. From a screenwriter's point of view, the correct rendering should be, 'Film is a collaborative business: bend over.'

When one works as a screenwriter, one is told that the job is analogous to being a carpenter – that as much pride and concern as one takes in one's work, one is only working for hire, and the final decision must be made by the homeowner.

The analogy, I think, is not quite correct. Working as a screenwriter-for-hire, one is in the employ *not* of the eventual consumers (the audience, whose interests the honest writer must have at heart), but of speculators, whose ambition, many times, is not to please the eventual consumer, but to extort from him as much money as possible as quickly as possible. The antagonism between writer and producer is real and essential; and writers tend to deal with it by becoming enraged, leaving the business, or, by suiting up and joining in the game by exploiting the *producer* for as much money as possible.

But Man oh Manischevitz what a joy to be on a project which was *not a* 'collaboration.' In the summer of 1986, I directed a script I had written, *House of Games*.

As I write, we are in New York, at Transaudio Studio, and engaged in the last three days of the sound mix. After the sound mix, nothing remains to be done to *House of Games* except the color timing; and when I finish working on the color timing then the film will be completed, almost exactly one year to the day since the start of preproduction.

Here at the studio, the sound team and the film editors and I work from nine until six.

At six, the *House of Games* people leave, and the sound people from the *Untouchables* come in. I wrote the script for *Untouchables*.

We finished photography for *House of Games* on a Saturday in August, and *Untouchables* started shooting the following Monday. I had the fantasy of going to Chicago with a deck chair and a bottle of beer, and sitting behind Brian De Palma and watching him direct.

I didn't act on my fantasy. I flew from Seattle, where we were filming, to my home in Vermont, and got deathly sick and didn't get out of bed for two weeks.

Two very different experiences – *Untouchables* and *House of Games*: a big-budget and a low-budget movie, being the screenwriter and being the writer/director.

My experience as a screenwriter is this: a script usually gets worse from the first draft on; this may not be an immutable law of filmmaking, but in my experience it is generally true.

Untouchables may have been a bit of an exception. I met with Brian De Palma three or four times, and he and Art Linson, the film's producer, had some ideas for cuts and restructuring which definitely aided the script.

Inevitably, however, De Palma, Linson and I disagreed about several aspects of the film and, as usually happens, we got to the point where someone said to me: 'Look, we disagree, and (in effect) you are the employee, so do *you* want to make the script changes which we require, or would you like us to do them, and do them badly?'

On films in the past, this mixture of flattery and aggressiveness usually brought me around, like other screenwriters, with a sigh to make the requested changes. On *Untouchables*, however, in the final and minor instances where I disagreed with the director and producer, I said fine, *you* fuck it up. Spare me.

I said the above for a number of reasons: (1) that I have gotten to the point as a writer where I am tired of being finessed; and (2) that I was directing my *own* movie, and had no sympathy to waste on the plight of others.

It is my experience that up to a certain point, somewhere around the submission of the first draft, a filmmaker's anxiety is dedicated to the script for want of other idleness, and that that anxiety is more or less on the level of 'What am I going to wear to the prom?' Like that prom anxiety, the worry is not how to choose the correct outfit, but a handy mask for a basic feeling of unattractiveness and unworthiness.

When a film actually goes into production, however, the frantic phone calls about the script cease. In fact, once in production it is almost impossible to get a director to change a script on request from the writer – the script is a thing of the past, and the director is now worried, as he should be, about *the film*.

What *does* one worry about while directing a movie? This: 'I've forgotten something.' The time is ticking so quickly, and one is never going to get it back. The director thinks, 'There's a shot that I forgot to take; there's a piece of business which pays off in reel eleven, and I've already shot reel eleven, and I think I just forgot to shoot the setup in reel two; I haven't left room for a cutting "out" ...' et cetera. One feels the constant pressure of time and thinks, 'I've shot too much, I haven't shot enough, I've shot the wrong things.'

I am very well acquainted with Creative Panic; and, over the years, have learned to deal with it as a writer, by using the *Lawrence of Arabia* approach: 'Yes, it hurts, but the trick is not minding that it hurts.'

As a writer, I've tried to train myself to go one *achievable* step at a time: to say, for example, '*Today* I don't have to be particularly inventive, all I have to be is *careful*, and make up an outline of the actual physical things the character does in Act One.' And then, the following day to say, 'Today I don't have to be careful. I already have this careful, literal outline, and all I have to do is be a little bit inventive,' et cetera, et cetera.

Many people ask me if I write on a word processor. I write longhand, first, and then do subsequent drafts and corrections on a typewriter. I like to have all the actual physical pages that I have done in front of me: all the drafts, and all the revisions, and all the markings on them. It gives me a sense of security; i.e., 'look at all these drafts you have done, you must be a very responsible person – now all you have to do is use your good taste and refine these pages.'

When directing on stage, I would, similarly, arm myself with a detailed outline, the intentions of each character, and notes to myself on how to communicate these intentions to the actors (through means of direction) and to the audience (through manipulation of the scenic elements).

So, prior to directing *House of Games* I resolved, once again, to try to overcome my natural laziness, my natural aversion to tasks I would characterize as 'routine,' or 'uncreative,' and to apply myself to a series of detailed outlines: of the actions of the characters, of the rhythm of the movie as an expression of the proximity of the protagonist to her goal, and, finally, of the shots, shot by shot, of the entire film.

So that's what I did. Once again, I subscribed to my 'mountain climbing' theory of creative endeavor – get an absolutely firm foothold, and then make a small excursion to another absolutely firm foothold.

Armed with my outlines (prior to photography) I thought this: You've *been* creative, in the writing of the script; you've been responsible and careful in the reduction of the script to shots and directions which you can communicate to the crew and cast; now all you have to be is courageous, and *stick to the program*; and that is what I tried to do.

House of Games is a very different movie from *Untouchables*. Out budget was modest and theirs was large; *Untouchables* has big-name stars, and ours does not, and *Untouchables* was made by an ad hoc group, while *House of Games* was made up of a group of friends and colleagues of long standing.

Someone once got the better of me in an important business dealing by what I thought was fairly sharp practice. I was pitying myself in this regard one day, and the friend with whom I was talking – a high-level film producer – said, 'Forget it. Forgive and forget, you both are going to be in the business a long time, chalk it up to something, and go on.'

This seemed and seems to me good advice, and I have never been able to take it.

Like all of us, I get my feelings hurt easily, and, like most of us, I have tried to learn to deal with it. As I grow older, I have begun to learn to forgive, but have never learned to forget.

Hollywood is the city of the modern gold rush, and money calls the turn. That is the first and last rule, as we know, of Hollywood – we permit ourselves to be treated like commodities in the hope that we may, one day, be treated like *valuable* commodities.

In accepting the brashness, and discourtesy, and inevitable cruelty of a world without friendship, we promote and strengthen that world. We all do it, and we do it either in resignation, or in the hope of subsequent gain. But none of us likes it; and when we cease to notice it, there's probably not much of the creative force left in us. How can you create if you think of yourself as humiliated and venal? Not very easily, and I speak from experience.

This is not to say, of course, that all transactions between strangers in Hollywood must come to grief. But I think somewhere between 'many' and 'most' of them do. So I thought that, on my first movie as a director, and, as what seemed to me a matter of good principle, I would stack the deck, and make the movie with my friends, actors and designers with whom I had worked for many years.

Another of my friends, Art Linson, was the producer of *Untouchables*. When we'd shoot the bull over the phone, me shooting in Seattle and him in preproduction in Chicago, he would say of some production problem he was having on his large movie, 'You don't know how lucky you are . . .' But I did know.

I had worked with the five principal players an average of eleven and a half years apiece, I had worked with the two designers for ten years, and with the composer since we were kids in high school.

These people had no need to prove themselves to me, and, more important, I had no need to prove myself to them. The energy (small or large, but inevitable) that is devoted to establishing bona fides in an artistic collaboration between strangers ('How much does this other guy know? Can I trust him, is he going to hurt me?') was in our movie devoted to other things.

During the shooting of *House of Games* Art Linson flew from *Untouchables* preproduction in Chicago out to Seattle to meet with me about changes he and Brian De Palma wanted in the *Untouchables* script. I am afraid that my lack of helpfulness was tempered both by the necessary callousness of 'just not having the time to concentrate on someone else's problems,' and, if the truth be told, by at least a twinge of enjoyable cruelty; i.e., 'You guys made me intermittently miserable for a couple of months, and I "had to understand your position." Now *you* understand mine . . .'

I was probably also making Art and Brian pick up part of the tab for seven or eight years of work with producers who forgot to say 'thank you,' or used the phrase 'moral dilemma.' I was, in short, feeling my oats. I was strutting a bit after seven years on the receiving end.

There is that about film directing. The amount of deference with which one is treated is absolutely *awesome*. One is deferred to by the crew because of the legitimate necessity of the chain of command in this sort of an enterprise, and by a great deal of the outside world because of supposed and real abilities to bestow favors, contracts, jobs, orders, et cetera.

This deference was awfully refreshing after several years acquaintanceship with Hollywood in the position of a writer (where, I should point out, I was treated, if one wants to judge by local standards, exceedingly well).

One of my most treasured Hollywood interchanges follows: I made a suggestion to a producer and he responded, 'The great respect that I have for your talent doesn't permit me to sit here and listen to you spout such bullshit.'

It is nice to be treated with deference, and, I think, even nicer to be treated with courtesy; which, I think we can all say, is almost universally lacking in Hollywood transactions.

How often do we say, or think, 'Yeah, I like you, and you like me, so we don't have to go through the garbage of being 'nice,' because we have a movie to make, and our crassness is not going to make the movie any worse.' But, of course, it does make the movie worse; and even if it didn't, it makes the time spent a little less enjoyable.

Also this: I think we know that the callousness which passes for Refreshing Frankness in many Hollywood dealings doesn't exist as a direct way to expedite a difficult business – it exists, again, because we view each other as bargaining chips, and we tend to think thus: 'I can treat you anyway I like, because, *if you need something from me*, you have no recourse, and I'm letting you know it.' Correct me if I'm wrong.

The downside of all that jolly deference and courtesy one receives as a film director is, of course, that one has to *direct* the movie.

Directing is, I think, a lot like being a night watchman over something one finds personally priceless: one must be unstinting in vigilance over a very long period of time, and it *does* get draining.

When in my 'Keep printing this shot until Kodak hollers Uncle' stage I'd sit watching the dailies with ten or twenty of the cast and crew, and, as I'd printed six takes and couldn't remember the first when I'd seen the sixth, I'd ask for hands on who liked which take best ... Every time I'd ask for a vote I'd get a few giggles, a few hands, and a lot of nervousness, and then it *came* to me that *I* was the director, and that it wasn't funny. The people in the cast and crew were working hard enough at *their* job and I shouldn't, even in jest, be asking them to do mine.

That's what I learned on my summer vacation.

Film is *not* a collaboration, which implies equality – if not of contribution, at least of position. Film is produced under the most stringent and detailed conditions of hierarchy, as we know. To pretend otherwise is to insult those lower on the hierarchical scale, and to excuse those higher on it. And I found that the highest courtesy one could enjoy or perform was doing one's own job well.

Personally, I found film directing grueling, exhilarating, sobering, and addictive. I loved it.

Art Linson tells me that Brian De Palma is going to let me see *Untouchables* next week, and I can't wait. Next week, also, I will, as I said, be, except for color timing, signed off of *House of Games*, and several weeks after that, I start thinking about preproduction of my next movie with Mike Hausman, *Things Change*, which we start filming in October.

Practical Pistol Competition

Marksmanship appeals to two basic aspects of our American character: the love of skill, and the desire to hear things go boom.

I have been a backyard marksman (the more technical term is *plinker*) for years. I have a bull's-eye target set up on a stump twenty-five yards behind my back porch, and a bunch of swinging metal silhouette targets out beyond that; and, to break up an afternoon of writing or pretending to write, I periodically step out on the porch with a .22 pistol and plink away. My wife says she can 'hear me thinking.'

It is awfully enjoyable to be able to extend your reach fifty or sixty yards – to hear the metal silhouette go 'ping,' or to break the Necco wafer. To find enjoyment in handgunning, you have to be able to hit the target fairly regularly, and to do that you need to practice the basic skills. There are only two of them.

The first is correct trigger pull. It used to be said that what the shooter wanted to do was squeeze the trigger so that he would surprise himself when the gun went off. More accurately, however, what the shooter wants is this: *gradually* to take up the slack in the trigger (short of letting off the shot) while correctly aligning the shots so that when the pistol's sights are aligned in correct relation to the target, the last, least pressure on the trigger will let off the shot.

The second skill is obtaining correct sight picture. It is one of the bizarre anomalies of handgunning that one concentrates *not* on the target, but on the pistol's front sight. In shooting you are aligning the following: the target, and the pistol's front and rear sights. The rear sight is two and a half feet from your eye, the front sight is three to ten inches beyond that, and the target is seventy-five feet beyond *that*. There is no way all three can be kept in focus at once. So what the shooter does is let the rear sight *and* the target go slightly blurry, while keeping the front sight in sharp focus. When you can learn to do this, when, after long practice, you can force yourself to resist the natural impulse to look at the target, you begin, as if by magic, to hit what you are shooting at.

My eyes are terrible, but after a few days of good, correct practice, I can hit a quarter at twenty-five yards with some degree of regularity. (The quarter is actually a great target because, taped in the center of a black bull's-eye target, it offers great contrast. One of the most impressive and simplest demonstrations of marksmanship is shooting out a candle at night: it's awfully easy to line up your sights in the flame – it's the only thing you can see.)

The handgun was developed as a weapon of personal defense. Dating from the first practical multishot revolvers of Samuel Colt (1836), the handgun began to replace the saber in the cavalry i large and the cutlass in the naval boarding.

Skill with a handgun was, as we know, highly prized on the American frontier. In the twentieth century, as we Americans moved from the country to the cities, we had less need to develop skill in marksmanship; and the handgun, as one needs practice to shoot it well, ceased being regarded as an accurate weapon. General consensus was that with a pistol, 'you shouldn't shoot at it if you can't spit on it.'

The handgun began to acquire a reputation as an inaccurate weapon, useful for personal defense or offense, capable only of inflicting a terrible amount of damage at close range, and useless for any legitimate sporting purpose.

This attitude began to undergo a change after World War II, and this change was brought about by the F.B.I.

The F.B.I. observed that despite rigorous firearms training, its agents and law officers around the country were being killed and wounded in shootouts.

The F.B.I. agents, as all other police officers, and amateur handgun marksmen at the time, were being trained to shoot at bull's eye targets at fixed distances. And the F.B.I. concluded that such training did not equip the agents with the skills necessary to come out on top in the less formal but more exacting competition of a real gunfight.

A practical course was developed to teach marksmanship as it applied to gunfighting.

The agents were trained to shoot at moving targets rather than stationary ones. They were trained to shoot quickly and accurately at unknown distances and from different postures and in different lights; to make quick and accurate shoot/don't shoot decisions; to shoot from behind cover; and from unconventional postures; and while moving; to reload and clear malfunctions quickly – to do all these things under stress, not the stress of physical danger, but the stress of *competition*. Police forces around the country sent and still send members to the F.B.I. course to learn and return home to teach practical pistol skills.

In the 1950s, inter- and extradepartmental competitions developed to test these *practical* handgun skills. The handgun, viewed since the turn of the century as an inaccurate weapon of defence, became an accurate sporting arm to be used in marksmanship competition.

Various pistol sports developed: P.P.C. (Practical Pistol Competition), which stressed the basic police skills of target acquisition, quick decision-making, reloading, and marksmanship, I.P.S.C. (International Practical Shooting Confederation), which concentrated on those things in a rather more athletic way, and involves scaling obstacles, et cetera.

The bowling-pin shoot, a popular pistol event, awards the speed with which a marksman can draw and knock six bowling pins off a table at twenty-five feet. These sports stress the combination of speed and accuracy.

Silhouette shooting was imported from Mexico (*siluetas metálicas*). This sport is devoted to extracting the ultimate in pistol accuracy, and it involves knocking down metal silhouettes of animals at distances to three hundred yards.

Hunting with the handgun as an alternative to the rifle became, and is still, popular.

In the late sixties, top competitive shooters began opening schools to teach handgunning either for sport or defensive purposes. Gunsmiths around the country began custom tuning and custom building pistols and revolvers for increased accuracy and competitive utility. And prestigious and lucrative pistol competitions – the Bianci Cup, the Soldier of Fortune, the Second Chance – attracted top competitors and much spectator interest, and so improved and continue to improve the breed. It might not be too much of a stretch to compare competitive handgunning to sculling – both sports have loyal and dedicated spectators and competitors; and very few besides these competitors and spectators know the sports exist.

Much of the I.P.S.C., P.P.C., and bowling-pin competition of today is done with what is generally known as a Colt .45 Auto. This is a semiautomatic pistol in .45 caliber, and is familiar, from the movies, even to nonwarriors.

The pistol was designed by John Browning for the Colt Firearms Company, and was adopted by the United States government as a sidearm in 1911. (The pistol was recently replaced by the Beretta 92SBF 9 mm.)

The patent was given by Colt to the United States government during World War I, and the pistol was made, and still is made, by many manufacturers in addition to Colt.

I found one of those manufacturers by accident in the back of a health food store. I was buying something tasty, and heard heavy machinery noises coming from the next room. I asked and was informed that there was a gun factory in the basement. I went down and discovered the Caspian Arms Company of Hardwick, Vermont.

Caspian was making very high quality automatic pistols on contract for some highline American arms companies. They were also making a super accurate M1911 .45 pistol under their own name.

The owner showed me targets shot offhand (without support) at twenty-five yards. All the shots were in one hole. This is both remarkable shooting and a *very* accurate pistol.

Next to the target was taped a schedule for the Vermont Handgunners Association (the existence of which I had not theretofore been aware). The schedule listed a P.P.C. meet coming up in one week in a town near me. I remarked that that sounded like fun and Cal Foster, the owner of Caspian Arms, remarked, 'Why don't you go?' I told him I couldn't go as I didn't have a .45 automatic, and he suggested that I just borrow *his*, which is just what I did.

(To digress for a moment, and on the subject of Mr. Foster's generosity: Colonel Homer Wheeler, reflecting on his life on the frontier [*Buffalo Days and Ways*, 1925], wrote, 'In countries where the populace is armed, men generally tend to be more polite.')

Mr. Foster loaned me his pistol and two magazines, so that I could compete. The pistol was fairly representative of what one does to transform a stock-as-a-stove firearm into a competitive one. The barrel is lengthened by one inch. The barrel is *ported* (i.e. ventilated) on the top of the protruding portion. Recoil tends to make the muzzle of a pistol rise after each shot. Gases escaping through the porting tend to counteract this rise and keep the muzzle down – thus making for faster on-target follow-up shots. The safety is ambidextrous, so that it can be safely manipulated when shooting either with the right or left hand. The trigger is tuned for a crisp, fairly light let-off. The pistol has high-grade adjustable sights. The magazine is believed to facilitate quicker insertion of a new mag. There are several other things done to the pistol, but those listed are the major ones.

In addition to spending amounts possibly in excess of a thousand dollars on his competition pistol, a serious competitor will invest in special competition belts and holsters, and will, most probably, load his own ammunition. (The last, in addition to offering the ability to tailor the cartridge to the competition, affords a great saving. Factory .45 ammunition costs around twenty dollars for fifty. Home-loaded ammunition can be one tenth that. It makes a difference if you're going to practice as a *truly* serious competitor would – with fifty thousand rounds a year.)

I took Cal Foster's competition pistol over to my backyard range and, after a very educational week, I was able to keep most of my shots on a shoebox at twenty-five yards. (The .45 is a bit more difficult to shoot well than a .22 target pistol. It is heavier, it is heavy over the hand, rather than at the muzzle end, it is, generally, not very forgiving. *You* have to learn to shoot *it*.)

I practiced reloading, shooting with the weak (in my case, the left) hand, drawing from the *surrender* position (both hands held shoulder high). I blithely went down to the P.P.C. meet at Benson, Vermont.

The Benson meet was divided into three parts: Assault, International Rapid Fire, and Shotgun. This was the order of the assault course: The shooter starts with his pistol holstered and both hands in a surrender position. On command, the shooter draw and fires two shots at a target twenty yards out. He then runs ten yards and, leaning out from behind a barricade, fires two shots at a target ten yards out. Continuing, he must fire two shots on each of two targets fifteen yards out. He then runs ten yards, kneels behind a barricade, and shoots twice at a target at twenty-five yards. He runs another ten yards, again kneels, puts two shots on a ten-yard target, and fires at a metal plate suspended five yards from him. The sound of the plate being struck stops the clock.

The shooter is scored on his time over the course, and on his point score. The target, like a bull's-eye target, is made up of concentric circles, and hits closest to the center score highest. Unlike a bull's-eye target, however, these scoring circles cannot be seen by the shooter, who must determine his point of aim and shoot to it without external signs. The targets are torso-sized cardboard cutouts. They are flanked and partially obscured by similar torsos, which are covered with an 'X.' Hits on these 'hostages' accrue penalties to the shooter.

The man before me ran the course in 43 seconds and scored 121. He would have stopped the clock quicker, but his first shot on the metal stop plate went high. I thought, How untutored of you – *don't* you know that when shooting at targets beneath you, you must hold *low*?' My lack of charity was soon to be rewarded. I ran it in 1 minute 43, and scored 89. I couldn't find my spare magazine in my belt; I reloaded at the wrong time; I couldn't hit the stop plate at *all*, I couldn't hit the target, I finished shaking like a leaf.

I looked forward to the International Rapid Fire Course: simple timed fire at twenty-five yards. 'Here,' I thought, 'my backyard training is about to pay off.' But I made the same mistake as the F.B.I. In my backyard, I was training for an event which I was good at, but at which I wasn't going to be tested. My showing at international rapid fire was wretched.

I assembled my gear and watched a state trooper fire the assault course. He moved not at all slowly, but with complete determination. He placed his shots right around the 10 ring, and two inches apart. He reloaded at the right time. He was obviously a man who had trained as if his life depended on it, as, in his case, it did.

Driving back from the match I was a bit chagrined – not because I did badly, but because I was silly enough to think that I would do well. The essence of practical Pistol Competition is *to shoot well under pressure*, and if I wanted to develop that skill I would have to train *at that*. This thought brought me back to marksmanship as a Stoic discipline.

It is easier to teach a woman to shoot a handgun than it is to teach a man. A woman has fewer preconceptions, less at stake, and is more willing to follow the first principle of marksmanship: If you look at the front sight you hit the target; if you look at the target, you waste your shot.

One of the most respected figures in handgunning is Bill Jordan, ex-Marine marksman, ex-border patrolman, marksmanship demonstrator, gun writer.

Someone asked Mr. Jordan about the training of police officers: Isn't it impossible to *know*, they asked, what a man will do under pressure? Mr. Jordan replied that, far from impossible, it was the easiest thing in the world. 'A man will do what he's trained to do.'

This, to me, is the beauty of marksmanship: that it tests, under great pressure, those skills and principles we have developed in moments of calm.

It is possible to quickly 'go native' and start upgrading your equipment: your leather, your reloaders, your pistol, your ammunition. Generally, though, the gun always shoots better than *you* do, and you're left with the basic first principles: (1) front sight, (2) squeeze, (3) practice. Follow those principles and the shot goes where you want it. The gun *does* go boom, and that's nice; but better than that is the feeling of having done something right.

When I Was Young: A Note to Zosia and Willa

When I was young, the corner restaurant made a thing called a francheezie, which is the best thing that I ever ate. It was a hot dog sliced down the middle, filled with cheese, wrapped in bacon, and then sizzled on an open grill until it snapped.

And at the pharmacy they made a drink called a Green River, made with green syrup and carbonated water; or root beer, or any kind of soda that you wanted.

My father always had a Chocolate Phosphate, which is a thing we had in Chicago. It was made with chocolate, carbonated water, and a secret ingredient.

It was so cool and seemed dark in the drugstore, and smelled of vanilla and chocolate, and like nothing else in the world.

Even the water there was special. It was served in a white cone upside down on a cool silver base. And in the summertime how cool that marble counter was when we had been out playing.

We played Kick the Can on summer evenings. Or we'd play ball in the streets, where the first manhole was a single, the second a double, so on down the street. And someone always watched out and yelled 'Car.'

There was a row of garages back on our alley, tied together under a flat roof that ran the whole block, and sometimes we'd climb up and play football on top of the garage.

The policeman on our block was named Tex, and he wore two stag-handled guns on his belt.

Times in the street, infrequently, there'd be a horse-drawn rag truck. The ragpicker either yelled, 'Rags, Old Iron,' or else that's something I remember from the stories my mother used to tell me of her old neighborhood.

I remember that we had an organ grinder and his monkey who would come around. And I remember Gypsies, though I don't member how the Gypsies looked or what they did.

At school we'd line up, boys on one side of the building, girls on the other. When the whistle blew we would march in.

In eighth grade, I was a patrol boy. I wore a white belt and helped the crossing guard. There was a special way you learned to fold the patrol belt, and wore it clipped to your pants belt during the day. When it dropped below ten degrees in winter, they gave the patrol boys hot cocoa.

And I remember in the schoolyard every spring, the coming of the Duncan YoYo man, dressed in his Duncan YoYo costume, who would demonstrate the latest models and the latest moves, and was an artist of such skill we were not envious, but awed.

We had a School Store on the corner. Joe sold candles, pens and pencils and three-ring paper. Once he spied a shoplifter, and cursed at him, and moved his huge bulk out from where he sat behind the counter and he caught the shoplifter and shook him on the sidewalk until the candy fell out of his shirt and on the street.

On Saturdays I walked two blocks to the Theater, and, for a quarter, saw fifty cartoons and a movie, which was usually a Western, and I came back after dark.

Once they raffled off a bicycle and I think that I almost won.

I lay on my lawn in the springtime, on my back, and watched the winds blow high clean clouds over the lake.

My first friend told me that his father rode in a jeep in the War, and almost lost a foot when the jeep which they rode blew up.

Down the street a new family moved in. The man came by and borrowed money from all of the people on the block and never paid it back.

I learned to ride a bike. They say you never forget how; and I remember how it felt to learn. How it felt to be pedaling alone that first time, and I knew that it was going to hurt when I fell, and I didn't give a damn.

And we had the Park and the Beach and the Museum, and I don't remember why I wasn't killed when we would spend the day climbing around the museum caryatids thirty feet above the ground.

We lived near the railroad tracks on the South Suburban Line.

When we went downtown, we bought tickets from the old woman in the old wooden booth up on the platform.

The waiting room smelled of steam and piss and in the winter it was the warmest place on Earth.

They had black steam engines then, and when we waved at the

engineers, they always waved back.

And now I'm older than my parents were when I was young.

The best thing since then, I think, is just being here with you.

Encased by Technology

The movies find themselves in between the past and the future. Their ancestor is, of course, the Theater; which required no technology whatever, and is just a story told in a formalized manner.

The movies' progeny are the electronic media, which require the work and the conspiracy of many thousands to produce and to reclaim an image.

In a world without electronic circuitry, in a world without electricity, a world which nuclear or natural disaster may very well bring upon us, videotape will not be a medium for the transfer of information, that videotape which exists will no longer be translatable.

A radical but arguable thesis is that the progression from the acted drama and the printed word to a culture most of whose works are *erasable* is, perhaps, the cosmic reason for the existence of videotape. After The Bomb, after The Deluge, the record of our world will be erased and good riddance to bad rubbish. We see this progression at work in our daily lives already.

Microfiche, microfilm, and computer storage have virtually replaced the library as the repository of information.

Their care, operation, repair, etc., require increasingly more specialized and trained personnel. The writings, the thoughts of the culture are increasingly less accessible to the people, more prone to accidental erasure or alteration, more liable to the control, censorship, or inadvertence of both technocrats and government.

A man or woman may make a book or publish a pamphlet, may, in effect, disseminate their thoughts with little or no help or approval from the vast bureaucracies of government or industry, but the broadcasting of the electronic image, the manufacture and distribution of videotape, is in the hands of a group which grows smaller every day; and a person receiving a rejection from the networks or the distributors takes little comfort from the rejection being phrased, 'We do not think this is commercially viable,' rather than, 'This is contrary to the wishes of the State.'

The very image of videotape has been abstracted from human experience close to the point of nonrecognition, so that only the most superficial resemblances to the 'real' exist.

In a theater we have our live fellows before us, acting out stories. In film we have, wonderfully, a recreation of the very light which fell on them. In video we have that light reduced to electrons, and those electrons splayed upon a screen.

Like binomial numbers, the electrons do not handily communicate information which cannot be reduced to the statistical. They do not easily deal with the 'suggested,' with the approximate, with the ambiguous, in short, with Art.

Movies were the first new art form since the invention of painting. Acting has always been acting, and music still music whether live or recorded. Painting and drawing are essentially the same whether practiced on the stone of caves or on the stone for lithographs, or on canvas.

Movies are the first art to link the plastic and the temporal. They take place both tangibly, in the image, and continually, in the juxtaposition of those images. They find their ancestor only, perhaps, in the picture gallery, and the comic strip.

Video is another form altogether, and is linked more closely to the ticker tape. Video is the unceasing display of superficial information. (This may be why television has so rarely attained the status of an Art. It is linked not to the expression of the soul, but to the eventual and necessary regimentation of all thought. It is linked to the computer.)

But the art of Movies, as Eisenstein said, is the art of creating an image not *on the screen*, but in the mind of the beholder. (The juxtaposition of image A with image B creates in the viewer the thought C; e.g. a windlashed beach and a woman looking out of a window create the idea of apprehension.)

It is no accident that the birth of movies was coeval with the writings of Freud. At the same time Freud was saying 'I understand the significance of dreams,' Lumière et al. were beginning to put those dreams upon the screen. They were juxtaposing pictures to create an idea in the mind of the audience.

Movies represent the magnificence of the late Victorian Era, when it was thought possible for one man to 'know all things,' a phrase which embodies the magnificent misapprehension that knowledge is both finite and reducible to a technical expression, the *reductio ad absurdum* of which we see in video, where the concern for knowledge and its expression has been subsumed in the quest for technical expression devoid of content. I cite video-graphics.

The very ease of television production has hypnotized us all, as the speed of ticker-tape information accelerated the corruption of the stock market, and the speed of the auto has destroyed the commercial integrity of the American town.

These necessary, inevitable, and God-Willed accelerations which began at the turn of the century, created, in their first stage, the solace (at its best) and the morphia (at its usual worst) of the movies.

Our confusion with the accelerated world created the need of and the fact of the first new art form in fifty thousand years, the movies.

The movies stand between the past and the future, between human history and human extinction. They come into being at the beginning of the last stage of the Industrial Revolution, which is to say at the beginning of the End of the World.

In a technological age, our heroes are not the prime movers, not the creators, but the agents, the conductors who take us safely through a journey. We lionize not the explorer, but the pilot, not the statesman, but the president, not the writer, but the director, not the architect, but the 'developer'; we have elected to admire and envy that person who is encased by technology, that person whom we see as the *captain* of technology, who, rather than being crushed by the juggernaut, has, alone, mastered its controls.

These lavishly rewarded technocrats are adored for their sup- posed ability to conduct us through a dream, through an experi- ence of both the plastic and the temporal. They are believed to possess the ability to, if you will, steer us through a dream, to assemble and order the universe through the medium of tech- nology.

As a sometime movie director, I have had the experience of

standing, encased by technology, between those two worlds of the past and the future, of dealing with the most ancient art of Drama in a medium requiring the assistance and compliance of several hundred people, of being, in effect, a pilot.

On the movie set you hear the beautiful cadence of a specialized workers' language. The cameraman says, 'Lose the opal, please,' and the gaffer shows him the image with and without the filter and says, softly, 'Opal *in*, opal *out*, opal *in*, opal *out*.' Or he shines more and then less light on the subject to be photographed, and announces. 'Flooding, flooding, flooding, flooding; spotting, spotting, spotting, spotting.'

The cadences sounded familiar to me – I knew I had heard similar rhythms before, and it occurred to me that I'd read them in *Life on the Mississippi*.

The lead man stood on the prow of the steamboat and heaved the lead and shouted. 'Mark Twain, Quarter Twain, Quarter *less* Twain ... No bottom ...,' and gave information to the riverboat pilot, who was the most lionized and romantic representative of *his* time. He was elected to bend a new technology to the whim of the people, and so conduct them on a new journey.

The analogy to transportation is, I think, both curious and appropriate.

In the last one hundred fifty years, those controllers of the latest in transportation were enshrined as the heroes of the day.

Canal pilots, steamboat captains, railroad engineers, aviators, astronauts, those elected to guide the fastest, most dangerous, newest, and technologically most exacting means of transport were, until their technology was superseded, the heroes of the day.

Each group was a hermetic community defined by the exclusive and difficult and dangerous skills its members possessed.

Why do I add the movie director to this group?

Like the others, his profession is romantic (i.e., it attracts great common desire to be admitted and, once admitted, to be successful within) until its technology is superseded. The airline pilot becomes the driver with the appearance of the astronaut. The canal boater is out of a job when the railroads are built.

Motion pictures, again, stand on the cusp of the past and the future. They draw on existing arts and combine them into a legitimately new art. They are made to be shown in a theater so that members of the audience can commune *with each other*. To order the dreams of the populace so that the populace en masse, acting as 'the audience,' can celebrate itself, is the art of the movies.

The purpose of video is to hypnotize, to lull, to render 'information' superior to suggestion and celebration.

It is no accident that the hero of video is not the pilot of the 'entertainment,' the director, but the pilot of technology, the 'producer,' the promoter, the packager.

The movies are a momentary and beautiful aberration of a technological society in the last stages of decay.

Their beauty resides in this: that they are actual records of the light which shone on us. Not only were they created to represent our dreams in this most troubled of times, but they were created to have the potential to live after us.

After the tapes have been erased, after the technology to retrieve them has been lost, someone, quite a while from now, might possibly just find a strip of film and hold it up to the light.

Poll Finds

The name of Poet was almost forgotten, that of Orator was usurped by the sophists. A cloud of critics, of compilers, of commentators, darkened the face of learning, and the decline of genius was soon followed by the corruption of taste.

Edward Gibbon.

The Decline and Fall of the Roman Empire

In *The New York Times* of March 1, 1989, we find an article on Richard M. Daley's victory in the Mayoral primary. We were informed that 'the racial voting pattern was demonstrated by a *New York Times*, WBBM-TV poll of 2114 voters.' Further, we were told in a sidebar that 'in addition to sampling error, the practical difficulties of conducting any survey of voter opinion on primary election day may introduce other sources of error into the poll.'

This disclaimer is a lot of small print to have to swallow. Are we, one might ask, or are we not dealing with a sure-fire barometer of public opinion? Would it not be a cruel irony if, having discarded that method of election prescribed by the Constitution, i.e. *voting*, for a less democratic but more scientific mechanism, polling, we were to find that we have sacrificed in vain?

We know that polls are inaccurate and unjust. We are drawn to them not because of their ability to predict the future, but because of their ability to relieve us of the responsibility for individual thought.

In subscribing to the poll's power 'to do good,' we choose to be relieved of uncertainty and assert ourselves ready to make this bargain: to happily live with the results of a stupid or incorrect decision if only we can avoid the responsibility for having made it.

The prevalence of polling in all facets of our daily life is a reversion to Mob Rule.

When an individual in power bases a decision on a survey, he or she becomes a demagogue, and derives power from an appeal to the emotions of the majority, specifically, the burning desire of the individual (subsumed in the majority) to be Right.

This demagogue abjures any notion of responsible action, and exchanges honor for continued employment.

In entertainment, in marketing, in politics, in medicine, in all areas of life, it is the momentary opinion of the majority which now determines the course of action.

Well, one might say, are the wishes of the majority to be over-looked? Isn't the jury process itself, to which we entrust the life and liberty of accused citizens, a poll? Yes. But it is a poll of individuals who have sworn to put aside prejudice, and judge facts impartially so as to serve the community-at-large.

The oath is designed to transform what would be a poll of the mob into a panel of dedicated citizens.

For the most vicious aspect of a poll is that it submerges the individual's responsibility for choice. The person who administers the poll has no responsibility, he or she sees the job as a gathering of impartial facts; the person who answers the poll has no responsibility; they are asked how they feel at any given moment, and the very inducement to answer is this: you will have no responsibility for how these statistics are used: you are free, you are, in fact, *encouraged* to answer as self-interestedly as you wish: for a moment there are no restrictions on your libido.

There are movies, plays, books, television shows the meaning and the worth of which can only be gauged over time and by reflection. It would be bad enough if the individual, on having seen these entertainments, were robbed of the capacity to reflect at leisure by questioning as to: how did you like, and would you recommend, and what aspect did you like best about the work. How much more dreadful it is that this informnation is used to create, to jury-rig words of pseudo-art, demagogical works whose only purpose is to grant power to their purveyors by appealing to the lowest emotion of the Masses.

For it is very difficult to tell *what one thinks* about a work of art immediately after having experienced it. There are works which one acclaims to the sky, and has forgotten the next day; there are, and we have all had this experience, works which we, on first acquaintance, adjudged unimportant, which have stayed with us literally all our lives.

Polling of the electorate appeals to our universal love of being right, and our universal love of being pandered to.

We have, and very well *may*, on reflection, endorse that candidate who calls our attention to hard truths, who calls our attention to the fact that we have been wrong in our action or direction, and that correction, though necessary, will be painful; we are, however, not so likely to endorse that candidate *without* reflection. And, in the heat of the moment, and immediately after having been appealed to as the Omnipotent Electorate, the True, or Old-fashioned, or Right-as-Rain American Voter, we are likely to adopt the demagogue's suggestion that we laugh to scorn anyone who tells us that we could possibly be in the wrong.

As is the case with entertainment, this poll of our lowest emotions is unfortunate enough, but even more so is that fact that these polls are used to calculate policy (which policy is always increasingly bald demagoguery), and to choose candidates (such candidates being chosen as is the policy).

Further, as polling has replaced voting as the method of electing our officials, our capacity to stand alone, to think alone, *to be content while being thought in the wrong* has all but evaporated. Faced with the poll which tells us our candidate *has no chance*, it is regrettable in the extreme, but most understandable that we choose not to vote, or to vote for the 'winner'; and if the candidate is anything more than his or her television personality, if the candidate is, in fact, the platform for which he or she stands, and if, having, through reflection, chosen to endorse that platform, as it reflects our understanding of the nature of the world, our acceptance of the poll is our *rejection of our own thoughts or ideas* because to hold them in opposition to 'majority opinion' is not as important as to be thought 'right.' And there we have American Fascism, in which we become our own dictator, and have forced on ourselves the will, not of others, but of the lowest aspect of ourselves; and this slavery has been forced on us not by the threat of death or torture, but by the threat of the momentary discomfort of being thought wrong.

In newspapers a growing majority of Page One stories are headed 'poll finds' and, almost universally, the finding of the poll is either obvious, 'Poll finds mental attitude can help avert disease,' and banality passes for news; or it is a reflection, again, of the desire of the human being to have low wishes fulfilled.

The secondary cost of this newspaper polling is the desire of the Public, having expressed itself, to see its wish made fact. For example, a headline of July 11th, 1987, from *The New York Times*: POLL FINDS NORTH IS TELLING THE TRUTH.

What *can* a poll 'find'?

There are two closely allied applicable meanings of 'find.' One is 'discovers.'

What *can* a poll discover? Can it discover the truth? No, it can, of course, only discover what several people *believe* to be the truth. (If we believe in the methodology of the Pollsters, and finally, why *should* we? Would we not be wiser to presume that, as their masters have risen to power pandering to the Masses under a false flag of statistical impartiality, they will choose to thrive by bending statistics to serve the will of their masters?) A poll, again, can only discover what the polled believe *at that instant* to be true. A poll cannot discover how many wives Henry VIII had.

The difference between what many people believe to be true and what may, in fact, *be* true is often and perhaps *most* times vast. And one of the organs created by Society for bringing public mood and actual fact into alignment is the newspaper. News organs which publish polls as news are content to thrive on a construction not a whit more elegant or laudable than this: 'I dunno. A lot of people think it's true.'

A second meaning for 'finds,' hidden in the *North* headline, and, by extension, wherever one sees the phrase *Poll Finds*, is 'rules.' And this is, I think, closer to the unfortunate truth of the phrase.

For when an organ of information effectually makes a ruling – each time it publishes a statistic of mood in a situation of dispute, it not only disregards its responsibility to inform, it corrupts by example.

Colonel North is in the process of being granted a *de facto* pardon. He is being excused from trial through extraordinary means, finally, because of the Will of the People as determined by the Poll. (For, if the Administration had 'found' through perusal of polls, that public sentiment wanted North tried for the crimes of which he stands accused, he would, would he not, have stood trial in a real sense?) And here we see the poll usurping not only the function of the Executive, but of the Judiciary.

We tend to Ask All Our Friends, that is to say, we tend to rely on statistics, when we are very confused. The issue of Colonel North, like may issues in our times, is very confusing.

Unfortunately, it, *like* many issues in our time, cannot be resolved by asking other people what they think.

In a time of National Confusion, our need for *example* is great.

Examples of calm, reasoned, responsible method and judgment will do much to promote like qualities in the public. Examples of demagoguery will do the same.

Black as the Ace of Spades

They say you could take a bunch of men and put them in a room around a table with a pack of playing cards, but you can't induce them to pick up those cards unless they're betting on them. And if they're betting on them, they can sit for hours or for days.

And you can take those same men sitting at a table, but even the reward of money to be won is not enough inducement to those men to push that money back and forth for hours unless they also happen to be holding cards.

So it's not just the money and it's not just the cards. But you put the two together and a magic is created.

The game is not about money. The game is about love, and divine intervention. The money is a propitiatory gift to the Gods. It is the equivalent of Fasting and Prayer: it is to gain the God's attention, and to put the supplicant in the properly humbled frame of mind to receive any information which might be forthcoming.

For the Cards are the symbols of the universe. There are few of them, but their possible combinations are myriad.

We have favorites, and intelligence informs us that we will be rewarded not by fealty to symbols, but only by our correct understanding of combinations. And yet, we have favorites.

There are good luck cards and bad luck cards. Pushkin writes about the Queen of Spades; the Ace of Spades has been called the Death Card (I am a native of Chicago, and in that city, and in various other cities where I have played, that ace was called 'Chicago'), and in American Folklore, the Jack of Diamonds is a trouble card and is known as Jack the Bear. I have my own Good Luck cards, but I would not tax my luck by naming them.

When we are betting on the cards, we love their combinations. Their beautiful unfolding means that God Loves Us, their malevolent conjunction means that Someone is Trying to Teach Us a Lesson.

Cardplayers dream of cards. We have a saying, 'A winner can't get enough to eat, and a loser can't sleep.' I have dreamed of cards, and there are hands that I remember twenty years later – hands that I know I will never forget.

I've also had a recurring dream. I have it once or twice a year: I am playing poker and have been dealt a magnificent hand, a lead pipe cinch (which is to say 'a certain winner'). As I am about to lay down my hand and claim the pot, I discover that I have one too many cards in my hand, and that, through no fault of my own, my hand is now invalid. I finally succeed in discarding the unwanted card, and then find that I now have two too many cards in my hand, et cetera.

Such powerful symbols.

Playing cards are a survival of our less rational, more frightful, more beautiful past. They commemorate a numerology based on thirteen rather than ten; they restate the mythological hierarchy of Monarchy, of a state which recapitulates our infant understanding of the family-as-world; they suggest and are employed for gambling – one of the two forbidden or curtailed pastimes in the repressed, rational civilization. The cards may be diverting, or dangerous, or destructive. They are never neutral.

Kryptonite

A Psychological Appreciation

I was back in my childhood home of Chicago. I'd come back to celebrate Passover at my Father's House, which I hadn't done in twenty years.

I took a long walk down the Lakefront, along the various parks and beaches where I'd played as a boy. I tasted the Chicago Park District water out of the stone birdbath drinking fountains, and it tasted the same as it had those many years ago when it was not only cold and delicious, but also forbidden – we were in the midst of the Polio scare – and my mother grudgingly allowed us to go play in the park, but made us swear that we would not drink out of the fountains and so risk contagion. I ended my walk on Oak Street Beach. I sat down on the stone ledge and watched a group of boys skateboarding. They'd made a plywood ramp, and they took turns running up to it on their skateboards, and jumping over it, performing various feats while in the air.

It was quite beautiful, and as I was in a sentimental mood, it, too, took me back to my boyhood.

I remembered what it was like to be a boy, and to turn a simple, rather meaningless act into a skill through constant and endless repetition. I remembered throwing rocks at a streetlamp on summer evenings, my friends and I, for hours and hours. I remembered throwing a beachball up out of sight onto the garage roof and making the most intricate game out of judging where it would land.

I remembered bike chases, a sort of capture-the-flag/ring-a-levio, games which lasted all night.

As I sat watching the skateboards, a bicyclist passed in front of me. He had a bicyclelock, tradename *Kryptonite*, affixed to his bike.

And I thought it a nice American in-joke, that his bicyclelock was named after an artifact from the Superman comics.

I enjoyed the Superman comics as a boy.

I enjoyed their very dullness and predictability. The story never varied and, even as a child, I remembered thinking, 'What a dull fantasy.'

But I enjoyed them. And the story that I enjoyed was this: Superman is engaged in doing good. Playing on his desire to do good, the Evildoers lure him into a dangerous situation, and he is exposed by them to Kryptonite, a fragment of the now-destroyed world on which Superman was born. Kryptonite is the only substance in the world capable of harming Superman, and he now begins to die. At the last possible moment, he is rescued from the Kryptonite by some happy chance, and the cycle may now begin again.

As I mulled over the story, I thought, 'Why is the bikelock named *Kryptonite*?' It was named *Kryptonite* because it is to be thought of as strong, as invincible.

But, I thought, Kryptonite is strong only to one end: to destroy. And, as I so thought, a deeper meaning of the Superman story occurred to me.

Superman is born on the planet Krypton. Krypton is near destruction, and Superman's beloved father, Jor-El, used his last moments of life to put his son in a rocket and fire him to earth.

On Earth, the child is adopted and raised by a kindly, if somewhat distant, Ma and Pa Kent.

As their adopted son, Clark Kent, the child moves to the big city, Metropolis, where he takes a job at the *Daily Planet* newspaper. When Goodness is threatened in Metropolis, the man transforms himself from Clark Kent, who is portrayed as an innocuous and fairly unattractive man, into Superman, in which guise he wins the awe and adulation of the Populace. After righting the wrongs of Metropolis, however, he must flee from the populace, and the pleasures they might award him, and change himself back into Clark Kent. Whey must he flee? Because of the presence of Kryptonite. If his arch-enemies knew of his whereabouts, they would be free to seek him out and secretly introduce Kryptonite into his presence, and he would die.

His power is obtained, then, at the expense of any possibility of personal pleasure.

As Clark Kent, he is in love with his co-worker, the reporter Lois Lane. She finds the attentions of Kent, the milquetoast, laughable. She is in love with Superman. Superman cannot reciprocate. *He cannot tell her his secret, for to do so would imperil his life.* He can tell *no one* his secret. He can have adulation without intimacy, or he may long for intimacy with no hope of reciprocation.

Superman comics are a fable, not of strength, but of disintegration. They appeal to the preadolescent mind not because they reiterate grandiose delusions, but because they reiterate a very deep cry for help.

Superman's two personalities can be integrated only in one thing: only in death. Only Kryptonite cuts through the disguises of wimp and hero, and affects the man below the disguises.

And what is Kryptonite? Kryptonite is all that remains of his childhood home.

It is the remnants of that destroyed childhood home, and the fear of those remnants, which rule Superman's life. The possibility that the shards of that destroyed home might surface prevents him from being intimate – they prevent him from sharing the knowledge that the wimp and the hero are one. The fear of his childhood home prevents him from having pleasure.

He fears that to reveal his weakness, and confusion, is, perhaps indirectly, but certainly inevitably, to receive death from the person who received that information.

Superman fears women. All of his love interests are given the initials L.L.: Lois Lane, Lori Lemaris, Lana Lang; and it is not coincidental that his arch-enemy, the super fiend of all his most harrowing adventures, is named, similarly, Lex Luthor.

Superman fears women and withholds himself sexually. He presents to the world two false fronts: one of *impotence*, and the other of *benevolence*, both disguises created to protect him from Woman's fury – fury at *what* we cannot know, but fury it certainly is – for he says as clear as day, to Lois Lane: you would not take me when I was weak (Kent) and you cannot have me when I am strong.

Several years ago a book was done commemorating Fifty Years of Superman Comics. And I was asked, along with many other writers, to contribute a quote. I said that I admired Superman: I admire anyone who can make his living in his underwear. And the hero aspect of the fantasy: the fantasy of *omnipotence* has, indeed, echoes of the psychology of someone who spends his life in his underwear: of the psychology of the infant.

Superman is stuck in the loop of the attempt to master-through-repetition: he has put himself back in infancy, and is playing out this dream/wish. 'I do nothing but good. I ask nothing for myself. In fact, I *can take* nothing for myself . Perhaps if I do enough good my world will not be destroyed, and I will not be sent away from home.'

Far from being invulnerable, Superman is the most vulnerable of beings, because his childhood was destroyed. He can never reintegrate himself by returning to that home – it is gone. It is gone and he is living among aliens to whom he cannot even reveal his rightful name.

There is no hope for him but constant hiding, and prayer that his enemies will not learn his true identity. No amount of good works can protect him.

He has not only relinquished any claim on citizenship, he has relinquished any hope of sexual manhood, of intimacy, of peace. 'I do good but take no pleasure,' he says, 'I ask nothing for myself. I pray that my false-self attracts no notice: forget about me.'

ON DIRECTING FILM

To
MIKE HAUSMAN

They are most happy who have no story to tell.

ANTHONY TROLLOPE,
He Knew He Was Right

Acknowledgements

I would like to thank my editor, Dawn Seferian,
for her great patience; and Rachel Cline,
Scott Zigler, Catherine Shaddix, and Elaine Goodall for
their help in the construction of this book

Preface

This book is based on a series of lectures I gave at the film school of Columbia University in the fall of 1987.

The class was in Film Directing. I had just finished directing my second film, and like the pilot with two hundred hours of flying time, I was the most dangerous thing around. I had unquestionably progressed beyond the neophyte stage but was not experienced enough to realize the extent of my ignorance.

I offer the above in mitigation of a book on film directing written by a fellow with scant experience.

In support of the proposition, however, let me suggest this: that the Columbia lectures dealt with, and endeavored to explain, that theory of film directing I had concocted out of my rather more extensive experience as a screenwriter.

There was a newspaper review lately of a book about the career of a novelist who went to Hollywood and tried to succeed at writing screenplays. He was deluded, the reviewer said, in this pursuit – how could he have hoped to succeed as a screenwriter when he was nearly blind!

The reviewer exhibited a profound ignorance of the craft of screenwriting. One does not have to be able to see to write films; one has to be able to imagine.

There is a wonderful book called *The Profession of the Stage Director*, by Georgi Tovstonogov, who writes that a director may fall into one of the deepest pits by rushing immediately to visual or pictorial solutions.

The statement influenced and aided me greatly in my career as a stage director; and, subsequently, in my work as a screenwriter. If one understands *what the scene means*, and stages *that*, Mr. Tovstonogov was saying, one will be doing one's job for both the author and the viewer. If one rushes, first, into a pretty, or pictorial, or even descriptive staging, one may be hard-pressed to integrate that staging into the logical progression of the play. And, further, while so hard-pressed, and while working to include the pretty picture, one will undoubtedly become wedded to its eventual inclusion, to the detriment of the piece as a whole.

This concept was also stated by Hemingway as, 'Write the story, take out all the good lines, and see if it still works.'

My experience as a director, and as a dramatist, is this: the piece is moving in proportion to how much the author can leave out.

A good writer gets better only by learning to *cut*, to remove the ornamental, the descriptive, the narrative, and *especially* the deeply felt and meaningful. What remains? The story remains. What is the story? The story is the *essential progression of incidents* that occur to the hero in pursuit of his one goal.

The point, as Aristotle told us, is what happens to the *hero* . . . not what happens to the writer.

One does not have to be able to see to write such a story. One has to be able to think.

Screenwriting is a craft based on logic. It consists of the assiduous application of several very basic questions. What does the hero want? What hinders him from getting it? What happens if he does not get it?

If one follows the norms the application of those questions will create, one is left with a logical structure, an outline, from which outline the drama will be constructed. In a play, this outline is given to the other part of the dramatist – the ego of the structuralist hands the outline to the id, who will write the dialogue.

This conceit is analogous, I think, to the case of the structuralist screenwriter who gives the dramatic outline to the director.

I saw and see the director as that Dionysian extension of the screenwriter – who would finish the authorship in such a way that (as always should be the case) the drudgery of the technical work should be erased.

I came to film directing as a screenwriter, and saw the craft of directing as the joyful extension of screenwriting, and taught the class, and offer this book accordingly.

DAVID MAMET
Cambridge, Massachusetts
Spring 1990

Storytelling

The main questions a director must answer are: 'where do I put the camera?' and 'what do I tell the actors?'; and a subsequent question, 'what's the scene about?' There are two ways to approach this. Most American directors approach it by saying, 'let's follow the actors around,' as if the film were a record of what the protagonist did.

Now, if the film is a record of what the protagonist does, it had better be interesting. That is to say, this approach puts the director in a position of shooting the film in a novel way, an interesting way, and he or she is constantly wondering, 'what's the most interesting place to put the camera to film this love scene? what's the most interesting way I can shoot it plainly? what's the most interesting way that I can allow the actor to behave in the scene in which, for example, *she proposes to him?*'

That's the way most American films are made, as a supposed record of what real people really did. There's another way to make a movie, which is the way that Eisenstein suggested a movie should be made. This method has nothing to do with following the protagonist around but rather *is a succession of images juxtaposed so that the contrast between these images moves the story forward in the mind of the audience.* This is a fairly succinct rendition of Eisenstein's theory of montage; it is also the first thing I know about film directing, virtually the *only* thing I know about film directing.

You always want to tell the story in cuts. Which is to say, through a juxtaposition of images that are basically uninflected. Mr. Eisenstein tells us that the best image is an uninflected image. A shot of a teacup. A shot of a spoon. A shot of a fork. A shot of a door. Let the cut tell the story. Because otherwise you have not got dramatic action, you have narration. If you slip into narration, you are saying, 'you'll never guess why what I just told you is important to the story.' It's unimportant that the audience should guess why it's important to the story. It's important simply to *tell* the story. Let the audience be surprised.

The movie, finally, is much closer than the play to simple

storytelling. If you listen to the way people tell stories, you will hear that they tell them cinematically. They jump from one thing to the next, and the story is moved along by the juxtaposition of images – which is to say, by the *cut*.

People say, 'I'm standing on the corner. It's a foggy day. A bunch of people are running around crazy. Might have been the full moon. All of a sudden, a car comes up and the guy next to me says . . .'

If you think about it, that's a shot list: (1) a guy standing on the corner; (2) shot of fog; (3) a full moon shining above; (4) a man says, 'I think people get wacky this time of year'; (5) a car approaching.

This is good filmmaking, to juxtapose images. Now you're following the story. What, you wonder, is going to happen next?

The smallest unit is the shot; the largest unit is the film; and the unit with which the director most wants to concern himself is the scene.

First the shot: it's the juxtaposition of the shots that moves the film forward. The shots make up the scene. The scene is a formal essay. It is a small film. It is, one might say, a documentary.

Documentaries take basically unrelated footage and juxtapose it in order to give the viewer the idea the filmmaker wants to convey. They take footage of birds snapping a twig. They take footage of a fawn raising his head. The two shots have nothing to do with each other. They were shot days or years, and miles, apart. And the filmmaker juxtaposes the images to give the viewer the idea of *great alertness*. The shots have nothing to do with each other. They are not a record of what the protagonist did. They are not a record of how the deer reacted to the bird. They're basically uninflected images. But they give the viewer the idea of *alertness to danger* when they are juxtaposed. That's good filmmaking.

Now, directors should want to do the same thing. We should all want to be documentary filmmakers. And we will have this advantage: we can go out and stage and film exactly those uninflected images we require for our story. And then juxtapose them. In the editing room, one is constantly thinking: 'I wish I had a shot of . . .' Well, you've got all the time in the world before the film is shot: you can determine what shot you are going to require later, and go out and shoot it.

Almost no one in this country knows how to write a movie script.

Almost all movie scripts contain material that cannot be filmed.

'Nick, a young fellow in his thirties with a flair for the unusual.' You can't film it. How do you film it? 'Jodie, a brash hipster, who's been sitting on the bench for thirty hours.' How do you do that? it can't be done. Other than through narration (visual or verbal). Visual: Jodie looks at watch. Dissolve. It is now thirty hours later. Verbal: 'Well, as hip as I am, it has surely been a trial to've been sitting on this bench for the last thirty hours.' If you find that a point cannot be made without narration, it is virtually certain that the point is unimportant to the story (which is to say, to the audience): the audience requires not *information* but *drama*. Who, then, requires this *information*? This dreadful plodding narration that compromises almost all American filmscripts.

Most movie scripts were written for an audience of studio executives. Studio executives do not know how to read movie scripts. Not one of them. Not one of them knows how to read a movie script. A movie script should be a juxtaposition of uninflected shots that tell the story. To read this script and to 'see' the movie will surely require either some cinematic education or some naïveté – neither of which is going to be found in the studio executive.

The work of the director is the work of constructing the shot list from the script. The work on the set is nothing. All you have to do on the set is stay awake, follow your plans, help the actors be simple, and keep your sense of humor. The film is directed in the making of the shot list. The work on the set is simply to record what has been chosen to be recorded. It is the *plan* that makes the movie.

I don't have any experience with film schools. I suspect that they're useless, because I've had experience with drama schools, and have found them to be useless.

Most drama schools teach things that will be learned by anyone in the normal course of events, and refrain from insulting the gentleman or gentlewoman student of liberal arts by offering instructions in a demonstrable skill. I suppose that film schools do the same. What should film schools teach? An understanding of the technique of juxtaposition of uninflected images to create in the mind of the viewer the progression of the story.

The Steadicam (a hand-held camera), like many another technological miracle, has done injury; it has injured American movies, because it makes it so easy to follow the protagonist around, one no longer has to think, 'what is the shot?' or 'where should I put the camera?' One thinks, instead, 'I can shoot the whole thing in the morning.' But if you love that morning's work at dailies (screenings of the footage you're shooting on a daily basis), you'll hate it when you're in the editing room. Because what you're seeing in dailies is not for your amusement; it should not be 'little plays.' It should be uninflected, short shots that can eventually cut, one to the other, to tell the story.

Here's why the images have to be uninflected. Two guys are walking down the street. One of them says to the other guy ... Now you, reader, are listening: you are listening because you want to know *what happens next*. The shot list, and the work on the set, should be no more inflected than the cuts in the little story above. Two guys walking down the street ... one guy starts to talk to the other ...

The purpose of technique is to free the unconscious. If you follow the rules ploddingly, they will allow your unconscious to be free. That's true creativity. If not, you will be fettered by your conscious mind. Because the conscious mind always wants to be liked and wants to be interesting. The conscious mind is going to suggest the obvious, the cliché, because these things offer the security of having succeeded in the past. Only the mind that has been taken off itself and put on a task is allowed true creativity.

The mechanical working of the film is just like the mechanism of a dream; because that's what the film is really going to end up being, isn't it?

The images in a dream are vastly varied and magnificently interesting. And most of them are uninflected. It is their juxtaposition that gives the dream its strength. The terror and beauty of the dream come from the connection of previously unrelated mundanities of life. As discontinuous and as meaningless as that juxtaposition might seem on first glimpse, an enlightened analysis reveals the highest and the most simple order of organization and, so, the deepest meaning. Isn't that true?

The same should be true of a movie. The great movie can be as free of being a record of the progress of the protagonist as is a dream. I would suggest that those who are interested might want to do some reading in psycholoanalysis, which is a great storehouse of information about movies. Both studies are basically the same. The dream and the film are the juxtaposition of images in order to answer a question.

I recommend, for example. *The Interpretation of Dreams* by Sigmund Freud; *The Uses of Enchantment* by Bruno Bettelheim; *Memories, Dreams, Reflections* by Carl Jung.

All film is, finally, a 'dream sequence.' How incredibly impressionistic even the worst, most plodding, most American movie is. *Platoon* really is not any more or less realistic than *Dumbo*. Both just happen to tell the story well, each in its own way. In other words, it's all make-believe. The question is, how *good* make-believe is it going to be?

'Where Do You Put The Camera?'

Constructing a Film
(A COLLABORATION WITH STUDENTS IN THE COLUMBIA UNIVERSITY FILM SCHOOL)

MAMET: Let's make a movie out of the situation we're in now. A bunch of people are coming to a class. What's an interesting way to film this?

STUDENT: From above.

MAMET: Now, why is that interesting?

STUDENT: It's interesting because it's a novel angle and it gives a bird's eye view of everybody coming in, sort of accentuating the numbers. If there are a number of people coming in, you may want to suggest that that's significant.

MAMET: How can you tell if this is a good way to film the scene? There are any number of ways to film it. Why is 'from above' better than any other angle? How are you going to decide what's the best way to shoot it?

STUDENT: It depends what the scene is. You could say the scene is about a really tempestuous meeting and have people pacing around a lot. That would dictate a different scene than one in which the tension is underlying.

MAMET: That's exactly correct. You have to ask, 'what is this scene about?' So let's put aside the 'follow the hero around' way of making movies and ask what the scene is about. We have to say our task is *not* to follow the protagonist around. Why? Because there are an infinite number of ways to film a bunch of people in a room. So the scene is not simply about a bunch of people in a room: it's about something else. Let us suggest what the scene might be about. We know nothing about the scene other than it's a first meeting. So you're going to have to make an election as to what this scene is about. And it is this election, this choosing not 'an interesting way' to film a scene (which is an election based on novelty and basically a desire to be well-liked) but rather saying, 'I would like to make a statement based on the meaning of the scene, not the appearance of the scene,' which is the choice of the artist. So let's suggest what the scene might be about. I'll give you a hint: 'what does the protagonist want?' Because the scene ends when the protagonist gets it. What does the protagonist want? It's this journey that is going to move the story forward. What does the protagonist want? What does he or she do to get it – that's what keeps the audience in their seats. If you don't have that, you have to trick the audience into paying attention. Let's go back to the 'class' idea. Let's say it's the first meeting of a series of people. A person, in the first meeting, might be trying to get respect. How are we going to address this subject cinematically? In this scene the subject wants *to earn the instructor's respect*. Let's tell the story in pictures. Now, if you have trouble addressing this thing, and your mind draws a blank, just listen to yourself telling the story to a guy next to you in a bar. How would you tell that story?

STUDENT: 'So this guy comes into the class and the first thing he does is sit right next to the professor and he started to look at him very carefully and . . . and listen very carefully to what he's saying and when the professor dropped his prosthetic arm, he reached down and grabbed it and gave it to the professor.'

MAMET: Well, yes. This is what the writers do today, the writers and directors. But we, on the other hand, want to keep everything that's 'interesting' out of the way. If the character is not *made* to be interesting, then the character can only be interesting or uninteresting as it serves the story. It's impossible to make a character 'interesting in general.' If the story is about a man who wants to earn the respect of the instructor, it's not important that the instructor have a prosthetic arm. It's not our task to make the story interesting. The story can only be interesting because we find the progress of the protagonist interesting. It is the *objective of the protagonist* that keeps us in our seats. 'Two small children went into a dark wood . . .' Okay; somebody else? You're writing the film. The objective is *to earn the respect of the instructor.*

STUDENT: 'A guy in film class, who arrived twenty minutes early, sat at one end of the table. Then the class came in with the instructor, and he picked up his chair and moved it, trying to sit near the instructor, and the instructor sat on the other side of the room.'

MAMET: Good. Now we've got some ideas. Let's work with them a little bit. A fellow arrived twenty minutes early. Why? *To earn the respect of his instructor.* He sat at one end of the table. Now, how can we reduce this to shots?

STUDENT: Shot of him coming in, shot of the classroom, shot of him sitting, shot of the rest of the class coming in.

MAMET: Good. Anybody else?

STUDENT: A shot of a clock, a shot of the moment when he comes in, hold on this until he decides where he's going to sit, a shot of him waiting alone in the empty room, a shot of the clock, and a shot of many people coming in.

MAMET: Do you need a shot of the clock? The smallest unit with which you most want to concern yourself is the shot. The larger concept of the scene is to win the respect of the instructor. This is what the protagonist wants – it's the superobjective. Now, how can we figure out the first beat of the scene? What do we do first?

STUDENT: Establish the character

MAMET: The truth is, you never have to establish the character. In the first place, there is no such thing as character other than the habitual action, as Mr. Aristotle told us two thousand years ago. It just doesn't exist. Here or in Hollywood or otherwise. They always talk about the character out there in Hollywood,

and the fact is there is no such thing. It doesn't exist. The
character is just habitual action. 'Character' is exactly what the
person literally does in pursuit of the superobjective, the
objective of the scene. The rest doesn't count.

An example: a fellow goes to a whorehouse and comes up to
the madam and says, 'what can I get for five bucks?' She says,
'you should have been here yesterday, because . . .' Well, you,
as members of the audience, want to know why he should have
been there yesterday. That's what you want to know. Here,
however, we tell the story, full of characterization.

A fellow, trim, fit, obviously enamored of the good things of
life but not without a certain somberness, which might speak
of a disposition to contemplation, goes to a gingerbread gothic
whorehouse situated on a quiet residential street, somewhere
in a once-elegant part of town. While walking up the flagstone
steps . . .

This is one of those American movies we make. The script
and the film are always 'establishing' something.

Now, don't *you* go 'establishing' things. Make the audience
wonder what's going on *by putting them in the same position
as the protagonist.*

As long as the protagonist wants something, the audience
will want something. As long as the protagonist is clearly going
out and attempting to get that something, the audience will
wonder whether or not he's going to succeed. The moment the
protagonist, or the *auteur* of the movie, stops trying to *get*
something and starts trying to *influence* someone, the audience
will go to sleep. The movie is not about establishing a
character or a place, the way television does it.

Look at the story about the whorehouse: isn't that how most
television shows are formed? A shot of 'air,' tilt down to frame
a building. Pan down the building to a sign that says, 'Elmville
General Hospital.' The point is not 'where does the story take
place?' but 'what's it about?' That's what makes one movie
different from another.

Let's go back to our movie. Now, what's the first concept?
What is going to be a *building block that is necessary to
'achieve the respect of the instructor'?*

STUDENT: . . . The guy arrives early?

MAMET: Exactly so. The guy arrives early. Now, the way you understand whether the concept is essential or not is to attempt to tell the story without it. Take it away and see if you need it or not. If it's not eessential, you throw it out. Whether it's a scene or a shot, if it's not essential throw it out. 'The guy says to the madam . . .' Well, obviously you can't start the whorehouse scene like that. You need something before that. 'A guy goes to a whorehouse and the madam says . . .' In this example the first building block is 'a guy goes to a whorehouse.'

Here's another example: you have to walk to the elevator in order to get downstairs. In order to get down, you have to go to the elevator and get in there. That's essential to get downstairs. And if your objective is *to get the subway* and you begin in an elevated floor of the building, the first step will be 'to get downstairs.'

To *win the respect of the instructor* is the superobjective. What steps are essential?

STUDENT: First, *show up early*.

MAMET: Good. Yes. How are we going to create this idea of earliness? We don't have to worry about *respect* now. *Respect* is the overall goal. All we have to worry about now is earliness; that's the first thing. So let's create the idea of earliness by juxtaposing uninflected images.

STUDENT: He starts to sweat.

MAMET: Okay, what are the images?

STUDENT: The man sitting by himself, in a suit and tie, starting to sweat. You could watch his behavior.

MAMET: How does this give us the idea of earliness?

STUDENT: It would suggest that there's something he's anticipating.

MAMET: No, we don't have to worry about anticipating. All we have to know in this beat is that he's early. Also, we don't have to watch behavior.

STUDENT: An empty room.

MAMET: Well, there we go, that's one image.

STUDENT: A shot of a man by himself in an empty room juxtaposed with a shot of a group of people coming in from outside.

MAMET: Okay, but this doesn't give us the idea of earliness, does it? Think about it.

STUDENT: They could all be late.

MAMET: Let's express this in absolutely pristine, uninflected images requiring no additional gloss. What are the two images that are going to give us the idea of *earliness*?

STUDENT: A guy is walking down the street and the sun is rising and the street cleaners are going by and it's dawn and there's not a lot of activity on the street. And then maybe a couple of shots of some people waking up and then you see the guy, the first man, come into a room and other people are in there finishing up a job that they were doing, maybe finishing the ceiling or something like that.

MAMET: Now, this scenario gives the idea of early morning, but we've got to take a little bit of an overview. We have to let our little alarm go off once in a while, if we stray too far off the track; the alarm that says, 'Yes – it's *interesting*, but does it fulfill the objective?' We want the idea of *earliness* so that we can use it as a building block to *winning respect*. We do not absolutely require the idea *early in the morning*.

STUDENT: Outside the door you could have a sign saying 'Professor Such-and-such's class.' and giving the time. Then you could have a shot of our guy obviously sitting by himself with the clock behind him.

MAMET: Okay. Does anybody feel that it might be a good idea to stay away from a clock? Why might we feel that?

STUDENT: Cliché.

MAMET: Yeah, it's a little bit of a cliché. Not that it's necessarily bad. As Stanislavsky told us, we shouldn't shy away from things just because they are clichés. On the other hand, maybe we can do better. Maybe the clock ain't bad, but let's put it aside for a moment just because our mind, that lazy dastard, jumped to it first and, perhaps, it is trying to betray us.

STUDENT: So you have him coming up, and he's in the elevator, nervous and maybe looking at his watch.

MAMET: No, no, no, no. We don't need this in there, do we? Why don't we need that?

STUDENT: Maybe a *small* clock . . .?

MAMET: . . . He doesn't even have to look nervous. This gets down to what I tell the actors too, which we'll discuss later. You can't rely on the acting to tell the story. He doesn't have to be nervous. The audience will get the idea. The *house* has to look like a house. The *nail* doesn't have to look like a house. This beat, as we described it, had nothing to do with 'nervousness'; it is about *being early*, and that is *all* it is about. Now, what are the images here?

STUDENT: We see the guy come down the hall and he gets to the door and is trying to rush in and he finds that it's locked. So he turns and looks for a janitor in the hall. The camera stays with him.

MAMET: How do you know he's looking for a janitor? All you can do is take pictures. You can't take a picture of a guy turning. You can't take a picture of a guy turning to look for a janitor. You've got to tell that in the next shot.

STUDENT: Can you cut to a janitor?

MAMET: Now the question is, does a shot of a guy turning and a shot of a janitor give you the idea of earliness? No. It doesn't. The important thing is *always apply the criteria*. This is the secret of filmmaking.

Alice said to the Cheshire Cat, 'which road should I take?' And the Cheshire Cat said, 'where do you want to go?' And Alice said, 'I don't care.' And the Cheshire Cat said, 'then it doesn't matter which road you take.' If, on the other hand, you *do* care where you're going, it does matter which road you take. All you have to think about now is *earliness*. Take a look at the idea about the locked door. How can we use this, because it's a very good idea. It's already more exciting than a clock. Not more exciting in general, but more exciting as applied to the idea of *earliness*.

STUDENT: He comes to the door and it's locked, so he turns, he sits and waits.

MAMET: Now, what are the shots? A shot of the man coming down a hall. What's the next shot?

STUDENT: A shot of a door, he tries it, it's locked, it doesn't open.

MAMET: He sits down?

STUDENT: That's it.

MAMET: Does this give us the idea of earliness? Yes?

STUDENT: What if we combine them all. Start with the sun rising.

The second shot is of a janitor mopping in the hall, going down the hall, and as he goes down, there's someone sitting in front of the door and the guy gets up and points to the door and the janitor could look at his watch and the guy points to the door again and the janitor looks at his watch and shrugs and unlocks it.

MAMET: Which sounds cleaner? Which gives us more clarity in this instance? The toughest thing in writing and directing and editing is to give up preconceptions, and apply those tests you have elected are correct for the problem.

We do that by applying ourselves to our first principles. The first principle, in this case of the scene, being it's not a scene about guys coming into a room, it's a scene about trying to win the respect of the instructor; the second small principle being this *beat* is about *earliness*. That's all we have to worry about, *earliness*.

Now, we have two plans here. Which is simpler? Always do things the least interesting way, and you make a better movie. This is my experience. Always do things the least interesting way, the most blunt way. Because then you will not stand the risk of falling afoul of the objective in the scene by being interesting, which will always bore the audience, who are collectively much smarter than you and me and have already gotten up to the punch line. How do we keep their attention? Certainly not by giving them *more* information but, on the contrary, by *withholding* information – by withholding *all* information except that information the absence of which would make the progress of the story incomprehensible.

This is the kiss rule. K.I.S.S. Keep it simple, stupid. So we have three shots. A fellow is walking down the hall. Tries the handle of the door. Closeup of the door handle being jiggled. Then the fellow sits down.

STUDENT: I think you need one more shot if you want to show his earliness. He opens up his briefcase, pulls out a handful of pencils, and starts sharpening them.

MAMET: Okay now, you're getting ahead of yourself. We've finished our task, right? our task is done when we've established the idea of earliness.

As William of Occam told us, when we have two theories,

each of which adequately describes a phenomenon, always pick the simpler. Which is a different way of keeping it simple, stupid. Now, you don't eat a whole turkey, right? you take off the drumstick and you take a bit of the drumstick. Okay. Eventually you get the whole turkey done. It'll probably get dry before you do, unless you have an incredibly good refrigerator and a very small turkey, but that is outside the scope of this lecture.

So we've taken the drumstick off the turkey – the turkey being the scene. We've taken a bite off the drumstick, the bite being the specific beat of *earliness*.

So let us posit the identity of the second beat. We don't have to follow the protagonist around, do we? What's the next question we have to ask?

STUDENT: What's the next beat?

MAMET: Exactly so. What's the next beat? Now, we have something we can compare this next beat to, don't we?

STUDENT: The first beat.

MAMET: Something else, which will help us to figure out what it's going to be. What is it?

STUDENT: The scene?

MAMET: The *objective* of the scene: exactly. The question the answer to which will unerringly guide us is, 'what's the objective of the scene?'

STUDENT: Respect.

MAMET: *To win the respect of the instructor* is the overall objective of the scene. That being the case, if we know the first thing is *to arrive early*, what might be a second thing? A *positive* and essential second beat, having arrived early. In order to do what...?

STUDENT: To earn the respect of the instructor.

MAMET: Yes. So what might one do? Or another way to ask it is why did he arrive early? We know *to win the respect of the instructor* is the superobjective.

STUDENT: He might get out the instructor's book and brush up on the instructor's methodology.

MAMET: No. That's too abstract. You're on too high a level of abstraction. The first beat is *earliness*. So on the same level of abstraction, what might be the second beat? He was early in order to do what?

STUDENT: Prepare.

MAMET: Perhaps *in order to prepare*. Anyone else?

STUDENT: Now, don't we have to deal with the locked door? He has an obstacle: the door is locked; he has to respond to that obstacle.

MAMET: Forget about the protagonist. You have to know what the protagonist wants because that's what the film is about. But you don't have to take a picture of it. Hitchcock denigrated American films, saying they were all 'pictures of people talking' – as, indeed, most of them are.

    You tell the story. Don't let the protagonist tell the story. *You* tell the story; *you* direct it. We don't have to follow the protagonist around. We don't have to establish his 'character.' We don't need to have anybody's 'back story.' All we have to do is create an essay, just like a documentary; the subject of this particular documentary being *to win the respect of*. The first essay is on earliness; what's the second thing?

STUDENT: Could it be *to wait*?

MAMET: *To wait*? What's the difference between *to wait* and *to prepare*?

STUDENT: The protagonist is more active.

MAMET: In which?

STUDENT: The second.

MAMET: In terms of what?

STUDENT: In terms of his action. It's stronger to have the actor *do* something.

MAMET: I'll tell you a better test. *To prepare* is more active in terms of *this particular* superobjective. It's more active in terms of *to win the respect*.

    This class is about one thing: learning to ask the question 'what's it about?' The film is not about a guy. It's about *to win the respect of*. The beat is not about *a guy coming in*. It's about *earliness*. Now that we've taken care of earliness, let's say the next beat is *to prepare*. Tell the idea of *to prepare* as if you're telling it to somebody in a bar.

STUDENT: So this guy was sitting on a bench waiting, waiting, just waiting. And he pulled out of his briefcase a book written by the professor.

MAMET: Now, how do you shoot that? How do you know it's a book written by the professor?

STUDENT: We could have the name of the professor on the door, and in the same shot see the name on the book.

MAMET: But we don't know that he's preparing for the class. You don't have to put in all this literary narration – see how narration weakens the film? You *do* have to know the beat is about *preparing*. It's a very important distinction. We don't have to know it's *preparing for the class*. That's going to take care of itself. We *do have to know it's preparing*. The boat has to look like a boat – the keel does not.

We don't need waiting. Waiting is trying to reiterate. We've already got *earliness*. We took care of that. All we have to do now is *preparing*. Listen to yourselves when you describe these shots. When you use the words 'just,' 'kind of,' and 'sort of,' you're diluting the story. The shots shouldn't be just, kind of, or sort of anything. They should be straightforward, as straightforward as the first three shots in the movie.

STUDENT: He starts to comb his hair, straighten his tie.

MAMET: Does this fall under the heading of *preparing*?

STUDENT: It's like *grooming*.

MAMET: Preparing could be preparing *physically* or it could be preparing for the subject matter at hand – *to win the respect of*.

Which is going to more specific to the scene? What is going to be more specific to the overall superobjective, *to win the respect of the instructor*? To make oneself more attractive, or to prepare?

STUDENT: He pulls out his notebook, reads through it very fast, then thinks, no, then he goes back and looks at a certain page.

MAMET: Now, this falls afoul of one of the precepts we have been discussing, which is: tell the story in *cuts*. We're going to adopt this as our motto.

Obviously there are some time when you are going to need to follow the protagonist around for a bit; but only when that is the best way to tell the story; which, if we are dedicated in the happy application of these criteria, we will find is very seldom the case. See, while we have the luxury of time, here in class or at home making up the storyboard, we have the capacity to tell the story the best way. We can then go on the set and film it.

When we're on the set, we don't have this luxury. Then we *have* to follow the protagonist around, and we'd better have ourselves a Steadicam.*

So what we're trying to do is find two or more shots the juxtaposition of which will give us the idea of *preparing*.

STUDENT: How about: this guy has a three-ring binder. And he takes a little piece of white cardboard and rips off the perforated edges, folds them in half, puts them into the little plastic tabs that divide the pages in the three-ring binder.

MAMET: This is an interesting idea. Let's say it in shots: he takes his notebook, he takes out a piece of paper, which is one of those tabs. We cut to the insert (a tight shot on his hands.) He's writing something on the tab. He sticks the piece of paper in the plastic thing. Now we cut back out to the master (the main shot of the scene). He closes the notebook. This is all uninflected, isn't it? Does this give us the idea of *preparing*? I'll ask you another question: which is more interesting – if we read what he's writing on the tab or if we *don't* read what he's writing?

STUDENT: If we don't.

MAMET: Exactly so. Its much more interesting if we don't read what he's writing. Because if we read what he's writing, then the sneaky purpose of the scene becomes *to narrate*, doesn't it? It becomes to tell the audience where we are. If we don't have any sneaky purpose in the scene, then all that beat has to be about is *preparation*. What's the effect of this on the audience?

STUDENT: It arouses their curiosity.

MAMET: Exactly so, and it also wins their respect and thanks, because we have treated *them* with respect, and have not exposed them to the unessential. We want to know what he's writing. It's obvious that he was *early*. It's obvious that he is *preparing*. We want to know: early for what? preparing for what? Now we've put the audience in the same position as the

---

*The Steadicam is no more capable of aiding in the creation of a good movie than the computer is in the writing of a good novel – both are labor-saving devices, which simplify and so make more attractive the mindless aspects of a creative endeavor.

protagonist. *He's* anxious to do something and *we're* anxious for him to do something, right? So we're telling the story very well. It's a good idea. I have another idea, but I think yours is better.

My idea is that he shoots his cuffs and that he looks down at his cuff, and we cut to an insert and we see the shirt has still got the tag on it. So he rips the tag off. No, I think yours is better, because it goes more to the idea of *preparedness*. Mine was kind of cute, but yours has much more to do with preparedness. If you have the time, as we do now, you compare your idea to the objective, and as the good philosophers we are, as followers of the ways of both the Pen and the Sword, we choose the way that is closer to the objective, discarding that which is merely cute or interesting; and *certainly* discarding that which has a 'deep personal meaning' for us.

If you're out on the set, and you don't have any leisure at all, you may choose something simply because it's a cute idea. Like mine about the cuffs – in your imagination you can always go home with the prettiest girl at the party, but at the party sometimes that is not true.

Now let's go on to the third beat. What's the third beat? How do we answer that question?

STUDENT: Go back to the main objective, *to win the respect of the instructor.*

MAMET: Absolutely. Now: let's approach this differently. What's a *bad* idea for the third beat?

STUDENT: *Waiting.*

MAMET: *Waiting* is a bad idea for the third beat.

STUDENT: *Preparing* is a bad idea for the third beat.

MAMET: Yes, because we already did it. It's like climbing the stairs. We don't want to climb a stair we've already climbed. So *preparing again* is a bad idea. Why play the same beat twice? Get on with it. Everybody always says the way to make any movie better is burn the first reel, and it's true. All of us have this experience almost every time we go to the movies. Twenty minutes in, we say, '*why*, they should have started the movie *here*.' Get on with it, for the love of Mike. Get into the scene late, get out of the scene early, tell the story in the cut. It's important to remember that it is not the dramatist's task to create confrontation or chaos but, rather, to create order. *Start with the disordering event, and let the beat be about the attempt to restore order.*

We're given the situation: this fellow wants such and so – he has an objective. That's enough chaos for you right there. He has an objective. He wants *to win the respect of his teacher.* This fellow *lacks* something. He's going to go out and get it.

Entropy is a logical progression toward the simplest, the most ordered state. So is drama.* The entropy, the drama, continues until a disordered state has been brought to rest. Things have been disordered, and they must come back to rest.

The disorder is not vehement in this case, it's fairly simple: someone wants a guy's respect. We don't have to worry about creating a problem. We make a better movie if we worry about restoring order. Because if we worry about creating problems, our protagonist's going to do things that are interesting. We don't want him to do that. We want him to do things that are logical.

What's the next step? What's the next beat going to be about? We're talking in terms of our particular progression. The first beat being *to arrive early.* The second one being *preparation*, to prepare. And the third one being? (Always thinking in terms of the superobjective of the movie, which is *to gain the respect of.* That's your test. That's the litmus test: *to gain the respect of.*)

STUDENT: To introduce himself?

MAMET: Mayhap the beat is about *greeting.* Yes, what do we call that kind of greeting?

STUDENT: Acknowledgment . . . ?

STUDENT: Ingratiation . . . ?

MAMET: To ingratiate, to pay homage to, to acknowledge, to greet, to make contact. Which, of all these, is most specific to the superobjective *to gain the respect of?*

STUDENT: I think *homage.*

MAMET: All right, then. Let's make up a little photo essay about

---

*I know the dictionary defines entropy as a progression toward the most disordered state – but on this point, I take issue with that most excellent book.

homage here. The deeper you can think, the better it's going to be. Deeper in the sense of writing means 'what would it be like to me?' Not 'how might anyone pay homage?' but 'what does the idea of homage mean to *me*?' That's what makes art different from decoration.

What would be real homage?

STUDENT: The professor arrives, and our guy goes to shake his hand.

MAMET: Okay. But his is like the watch, isn't it? Earliness – *watch*. Homage – *handshake*. There's nothing wrong with it, but let's think a little bit deeper, because we might as well, now that we have the luxury of time.

What would be a lovely way to show homage, a way that really *means* something to you? Because if you want it to mean something to the audience, it should mean something to you. They are like you – they are human beings: if it don't mean something to *you*, it ain't going to mean something to *them*. The movie is a dream. The movie should be *like* a dream. So if we start thinking in terms of dreams instead of in terms of television, what might we say? We're going to have a little photo essay, a little documentary about *homage*.

STUDENT: When you say a dream, you mean it doesn't have to be believable in the sense that someone would actually do it in real life?

MAMET: No, I mean . . . I don't know how far we can stretch this theory, but let's find out, let's stretch it till it breaks. At the end of *Place in the Heart*, Robert Benton put a sequence that is one of the strongest things in an American movie in a long time. It's the sequence where we see everyone who was killed in the film is now alive again. He's created something that is like a dream in this. He is juxtaposing scenes that are discontinuous, and that juxtaposition gives us a third idea. The first scene being *everyone's dead*. The second scene being *everyone's alive*. The juxtaposition creates the idea of a *great wish*, and the audience says, 'oh my God, why can't things be that way?' That's like a dream. Like when Cocteau has the hands coming out of the wall. It's better than following the protagonist around, isn't it?

In *House of Games*, when the two guys are fighting about a gun in the doorway and we cut away to a shot of the sidekick, the professor character, looking on, *then* you hear the gunshot. That's pretty good filmmaking. It wasn't great filmmaking, maybe, but it was a lot better than television. Right? It gives us the idea. They're fighting; you cut to the guy looking. The idea is *what's going to happen* and *we can't do anything about it.*

It conveys the idea of *helplessness*, which is what the beat is about. The protagonist is helpless: we get it without following her around. We put the *protagonist* in the same position as the *audience* – through the *cut* – by making the viewer create the idea himself, in his own mind, as Eisenstein told us.

STUDENT: How about if the student presents something to the professor? Some kind of special present. Or he bows when the guy comes in, and offers him a chair?

MAMET: No, you're trying to tell it in the *shot*. We want to tell it in the cut. How about this – the first shot is at the level of feet, a tracking shot of a pair of feet walking. And the second shot is a close-up of the protagonist, seated, and he turns his head quickly. What does the juxtaposition of the two things give us?

STUDENT: Arrival.

MAMET: And?

STUDENT: Recognition.

MAMET: Yeah; it's not quite *homage*, it's attentiveness or *attention*. At least, it's two shots creating a third idea. The first shot has to contain the idea of where the feet are. The feet are a little bit distant, right? With the idea that the feet are distant and the fellow hears them anyway, what does the juxtaposition of these two things give us?

STUDENT: Awareness.

MAMET: *Awareness*; perhaps not *homage*, but *awareness* or great attention, which might just sneak up on *homage*. What about if we had the long shot of the feet coming down the corridor and then a shot of our guy standing up? It shows a little bit more homage, in that he's standing up.

STUDENT: Especially if he were to stand up in a humble way.

MAMET: He doesn't have to do it in a humble way. All we have to show is him standing up. He doesn't have to stand up any way at all; all he has to do is stand up. The juxtaposition of that and the shot of the other guy far off gives the idea of homage.

STUDENT: How about when the guy stands up he bows his head?

MAMET: It doesn't really tell any more. And it's more inflected, which is to say worse for the purpose of filmmaking. The more we 'inflect' or 'load' the shot, the less powerful the cut is going to be. Anyone else?

STUDENT: A shot over the protagonist with a notebook. He looks up, stands up, and runs out of the shot. A shot of our hallway and the door in the hallway, which has a glass window to it. Protagonist runs into the shot and opens the door just as a man walks in the other direction.

MAMET: Yes. Good. I see you like that. Two question we might ask ourselves – one question is *does that convey the idea of homage?* and the other is *do I like it?* If you ask the second question, you say, well, heck, I don't know if I like it or not. Am I a fellow with good taste? Yes. Does this have as much good taste in it as I think I have in myself? Gosh, I don't know, I'm lost.

The question you *do* want to ask is *does it convey the idea of homage?* If it does convey the idea of homage, then go on to the next step: *do I like it?* There is the inner ability Stanislavsky called the 'judge of yourself ,' which one might characterize as a certain amount of artistic good taste. That's going to function anyway because we all have good taste. It's the nature of the human being to please. We all want to please one another. Nobody doesn't want that. There's no one who doesn't want to succeed. What we're trying to do is make our subconscious work for us by making that task at which we can succeed very simple and very technical so we don't have to throw ourselves on the mercy of either our good taste or the cinema-going public.

We want to have some test that allows us to know when our job is done without relying on our good taste. That test here is *does it convey the idea of homage?* Feet way off, man stands up. I think it does. Let's go on the next beat. What's the next beat after *homage?* What's the first question we want to ask?

STUDENT What's the superobjective?

MAMET: Good. What's the answer?

STUDENT: *To win the respect of the professor.*

MAMET: So after showing homage, what's the next beat?

STUDENT: *To impress.*

MAMET: It's a tad general. It also rather reiterates the superobjective. *To impress, to win respect.* They are too similar. One part at a time. The boat has to look like a boat; the sail doesn't have to look like a boat. Make each part do its job, and the original purpose of the totality will be achieved – as if by magic. Make the beats serve the scene, and the scene will be done; make the scenes, in the same way, the building blocks of the film, and the film will be done. Don't make the beat do the service of the whole, don't try to reiterate the play in the scene. It's like 'would anyone like a cup of coffee because I'm Irish,' right? it's how most acting is done today. 'I'm so glad to see you today because, as you'll find out later, I'm a mass murderer.' Anyone? The next beat?

STUDENT: *To gain acknowledgment?*

MAMET: That's also rather general.

STUDENT: *To please?*

MAMET: You can't get more general than that.

STUDENT: *To show affection?*

MAMET: *To gain respect by showing affection?* Maybe; what else?

STUDENT: *To show self-confidence?*

MAMET: Be dynamic. See, there things you suggest really could come at more or less any point, and they will betray us into a circularity more appropriate to the epic than to the dramatic form. But what will be the *next essential thing* to come after *showing homage?*

STUDENT: *To blow your own horn?*

MAMET: Would you do that to gain someone's respect?

STUDENT: No.

MAMET: You can ask yourself the question thus: what would *I* like to do in the best of all possible worlds to earn someone's respect? It's a question of what you might do in your wildest imagination, not what you might do because you are bound by the strictures of polite behavior. We don't want our movies to be bound by that. We'd like our movies to be greatly expressive of our fantasy life.

There's another question we probably need to ask at this point. We might ask ourselves *when are we going to be done?* so we will know when the movie is done. We could go on trying *to gain respect* indefinitely. So we need a cap. Without a cap, the essential problem of the throughline, which is *to gain respect*, really can lead into a never-ending spiral, which is capped only by our good taste. So perhaps we need a throughline with a more positive, that is to say a more *definite* end than *to gain respect*.

For example, *getting a reward*. *Reward* being a simple and physically identifiable sign of respect. On this level of abstraction, the reward could be, for example, what?

STUDENT: It could be that he wants the teacher to do him a favor.

MAMET: Okay, anybody else?

STUDENT: He wants the teacher to give him a job.

MAMET: Yes, anything else?

STUDENT: The teacher gives him a pat on the back.

MAMET: That's not as specific as the first two, is it? I take it that you're speaking rhetorically. In which case *the pat on the back* is similar *to gain his respect* in this: it is deficient in that it lacks a *cap* or an objective, so that one is unsure when one is finished. It's going to make our task a lot easier if we always know both *where we're going* and *when we're finished*. If the *job* is the objective, then when that *job* is given or when that job is absolutely denied, the scene will be over.

Or perhaps we could say the *reward* the student requires is this: he wants the teacher to change a grade. Then, when the teacher changes the grade, the scene will be over; or if the teacher categorically refuses to change the grade and no hope is left, then the scene would be over. So we could say that the throughline of the scene in that case is *to get a retraction*. Then *that's* what everything in the scene would be about.

What's the first thing that's done *to get a retraction? To show up early*, right? What's the second thing? *To prepare*. The third beat is *to pay homage*. It's going to be a lot easier to find out what the fourth beat is for *to get a retraction* than *to gain his respect*, because now we have a specific test for *knowing* when the movie will be over; we know where we . have to end up, and we can find a beat that will lead us to that end. Does anybody know what a MacGuffin is?

STUDENT: It's Hitchcock's phrase for a little invented device that will carry the action.

MAMET: Yes. In a melodrama – Hitchcock's movies are

melodramatic thrillers – a MacGuffin is *that thing which the hero is chasing.* The secret documents . . . the great seal of the republic of blah-blah-blah . . . the delivery of the secret message . . . We, the audience, never really know what it is. You are never told more specifically than 'it's the secret documents.'

Why should you be? We'll fill in for ourselves, unconsciously, those secret documents which are important to us.

In *The Uses of Enchantment,* Bruno Bettelheim says of fairy tales the same thing Alfred Hitchcock said about thrillers: that the *less* the hero of the play is inflected, identified, and characterized, the more we will endow him with our own internal meaning – the more we will *identify* with him – which is to say the more we will be assured that *we* are that hero.

'The hero rode up on a white horse.' You don't say 'a short hero rode up on a white horse,' because if the listener isn't short he isn't going to identify with that hero. You don't say 'a tall hero rode up on a white horse,' because if the listener isn't tall, he won't identify with the hero. You say 'a hero,' and the audience subconsciously realize *they are* that hero.

The MacGuffin is *that thing which is important to us* – that most essential thing. The audience will supply it, each member for himself.

Just so in the objective *to get a retraction.* It's perhaps not necessary to know at this point a retraction of what.

The actor doesn't have to know it. A retraction of a grade, a retraction of a statement, a retraction of a reprimand. It's a MacGuffin at this point. The less the objective in inflected, the better off we, the audience, are. The less the hero is described to us, the better off we are.

Step four, anybody? We know where we're going, and we know who's going with us. We know who we love, but the devil knows who we'll marry. *To get a retraction.* Tally-ho, then, me hearties.

STUDENT: You have *to ask for the retraction.*

MAMET: Good. Now, wasn't that a breath of fresh air? The invigorating infusion of fresh air that this direct and blunt beat brings into this discussion is the same breath of fresh air that it will bring into the film. Now we have: *to show up early, to prepare, to pay homage,* and *to ask* as the four beats of the story *to get a retraction.*

STUDENT: Don't you think showing up early and preparing are the same as paying homage?

MAMET: You are saying that these may be subsumed under the larger beat *to pay homage?* I don't know. I have a question about *to prepare,* which we may come back to. Now you see that the process we're going through here is re-forming the large to better understand the small, and re-forming the small to better understand the large (working from the superobjective to the beats, and reworking from the beats to the superobjective, et cetera), until we come up with a design that seems to fulfill all of our requirements. Then we'll put that design into action and we will shoot it.*

Now, we may find, as I found a little bit in my first movie and to a greater extent in my second, that after we've shot it we have to refine it further – which phenomenon scientists call the Jesus Factor, a technical term meaning 'it works correctly on paper but for some reason doesn't work when we get it on its feet.'

That happens sometimes. All you can do then is try to learn from it. The answer is always there. Sometimes it requires more wisdom than we possess at that instant – but the answer is always there. Sometimes the answer is: 'I'm not smart enough to figure it out yet,' and we must remember that the man said, 'A poem is never finished – only abandoned.'

All right, enough lovemaking. We got our three beats and looked at the throughline and said, 'perhaps this throughline is

---

*The process we are going through in this room is the exploration of the dynamic between the *moment* and the *objective.* It is this dynamic that, in this discussion, in film, in the theater, gives both the moment and the entirety strength – in the beautiful drama, each moment serves the purpose of the superobjective, and each moment is beautiful in itself. If the moment only serves the superobjective, we have plodding narrative pseudodrama, good only for object-lesson or 'message' plays. If the moment only stands for itself, we have only self-indulgent or 'performance' art. The effort that the dramatic artist spends in *analysis* frees both him and the audience to enjoy the play. If this time is not spent, the theater becomes the most dreadful of marriage beds, in which one party whimpers 'love me,' and the other pouts 'convince me.'

not very good.' We reformed the throughline away from *to gain respect* and decided that it was *to get a retraction*. Now we can look back at the beats, and we may say that perhaps *preparing* is out of order. Perhaps *paying homage* is what that beat is about. I don't know. Let's forge on a little bit and see if the fourth step gives us some more clues.

STUDENT: Do we have to decide what the end result is?

MAMET: You mean does the hero get the retraction? Who's interested to know if he gets the retraction or not? Anyone?

STUDENT: I'd want to know, because then we can do something with the response of the teacher to the homage. Does the teacher know why the guy's there? Is he suspicious of –

MAMET: No, no, no, forget the teacher; let's stick with the protagonist. We stick with the protagonist, and that will tell us the story. Because the story is *his* story. We're here not to create disorder but to create order. What's the inherent disorder? 'The other guy has something I want.' What does the other guy have? The power to issue a retraction. When is the story *over*? When the hero *gets* it. The disorder is inherent in the story. What we're trying to do is create order. When the hero either gets a retraction or finds that he cannot have a retraction, order will be restored. The story will be over, and there will be no further reason to be interested. Up to that point, what we're trying to do is bring about that blessed state of bliss in which there is no story. For as Mr. Trollope told us, 'they are most happy who have no story to tell.'

Let's go on. Let's be jolly, jolly scientists and take one step at a time. The next step we've suggested is *to ask for*. What are some alternatives?

STUDENT: *To plead his case.*

MAMET: *To plead his case.* Now, as you see, we're suggesting two stories of two different lengths. Why? *To plead his case* is eventually going to have to contain *to ask*, right? And this is what determines the length of the healthy story – it is determined by the least number of steps absolutely essential to secure the hero's objective. Who likes which beat better – *to ask for* or *to plead his case*? On what basis can we determine which is better for the story?

STUDENT: On the basis of why he's asking for the retraction?

MAMET: No. We don't care why. It's a MacGuffin he's asking for. Because he needs it.

STUDENT: But we don't know anything about it.

MAMET: I don't think we need to. Anybody think we need to? What you're talking about is what the illiterate call the 'back story.' You don't need it. Remember that the model of the drama is the dirty joke. This joke begins: 'A traveling salesman stops at a farmer's door' – it does *not* begin: 'Who would think that the two most disparate occupations of agriculture and salesmanship would one day be indissolubly united in our oral literature? Agriculture, that most solitary of pursuits, engendering the qualities of self-reliance and reflection; and salesmanship, in which . . .' Does the protagonist have to explain why he wants a retraction? To whom is he going to explain it? To the audience? Does that help him *get* it? No. He must only do those things that help him *get* a retraction. All he has to do is *get a retraction*. The guy says to the girl, 'That's a lovely dress' – he does not say, 'I haven't been laid in six weeks.' Now, the question is: on what basis can we decide which is better in this beat – to *plead his case* or *to ask*? My feeling is *to plead his case* is better. Why? Because I'm having a good time and I'd like the story to go on a little bit longer. I don't think I have any better basis than that, and I think that that's all right. But I'd better check, because I know that I have a capacity for self-delusion. So the question I ask myself is, 'does it run afoul of any of the rules we've discussed to use *to plead his case* rather than *to ask* at this point?' I check my rules, and my answer is No, so I'll choose the one I like.

STUDENT: Since pleading is more inflected, isn't that an attempt to be more interesting?

MAMET: I don't think so; and I don't think it's either more or less inflected. I think it's just different. I think it's a choice. You could say *to plead his case*; you could say *to present his case*. By the way, we didn't say these beats had to be uninflected. We said that the *shots* had to be uninflected. *Paying homage* may or may not have certain inherent psychological overtones. We talked about *to plead, to ask, to plead his case, to present his case*. Each of these is going to call up associations in the actor. It is these personal, immediate associations, by the way, that

both induce the actor to act and keep him in line with the
intentions of the author. *This* is what brings the actor to the
play – not those gyrations of emotional self-abuse that hack
teachers have fobbed off as *preparation.*

STUDENT: How about *to bargain*, or *to bribe?*

MAMET: What about these ideas, in terms of the structure? Let's
talk about *to bargain*, because that's a little bit simpler.

STUDENT: The problem is that we started with a different
throughline. *Bargaining* wouldn't work with *gaining respect*,
but it might be a way to get a *retraction.*

MAMET: This is a problem you're going to run into a lot in
dramatic structure. Because if you are creating it, either
creating a film of your own or taking someone's film and trying
to find the inherent dramatic structure in it, no angel is going
to come down to you and say, 'this is the throughline.' What's
going to happen is *exactly* the process of wondering and
revising – to work every time either to create or to discern a
throughline.

We've decided now that *to get a retraction* is the throughline
of the scene. We are on the beat following *to prepare.* Perhaps
this next beat is *to present the case.* So this is now our new
beat. What a relief to get on to this new beat. What self-respect
we must feel for taking upon ourselves the onus of this task so
as to save the audience the trouble. *To present the case.*

Our task now is to find a series of uninflected shots that will
give us this idea: *to present the case.* The student wants to
present the case to the teacher. Now, where are we going to
find a clue? We have four beats. We're working on the fourth
beat. What is going to be our clue to the answer of the shots?
Some helpful hint we might find to the answer of *presenting
the case.*

STUDENT: How we *prepared?*

MAMET: Exactly so. The previous beat will provide a clue. It was *to
prepare.* The beat that we thought, in terms of the new
throughline, might possibly be dorky may, in effect, offer us
quite a hint. So let's go back and look at our shot list for *to
prepare.* It would be nice for the sake of cleanliness if we knew
whether there was something we were wasting in there. Some
extra step, which weakened *to prepare* but might strengthen *to*

present the case. Like Indians of yore, we want to use all parts of the buffalo.

STUDENT: The shot where he opens the notebook, has the little strip with the cardboard things, rips them, writes on one, puts it in the tab holder.

MAMET: Good. Now, what are the shots for *to present the case?*

STUDENT: The presentation of the notebook in some way.

MAMET: What are the actual shots? A guy comes into a room, a guy in the room approaches the desk. Our criterion is that a juxtaposition of shots will give us the idea we require in this instance, *to present the case.* We have to know what we're taking a picture of.

STUDENT: Start with a shot of a desk with nothing on it and the notebook is pushed in.

MAMET: What's the next shot?

STUDENT: The reaction from the teacher. Either approval or disapproval.

MAMET: No. All this beat has to be about is *presenting the case.* We don't need the teacher's reaction here.

STUDENT: If the first shot were a presentation of the book and the second shot the teacher looking down, wouldn't the juxtaposition of those two shots present the case to him?

MAMET: Maybe the first shot is the empty desk and a book is placed into it, and the second shot is the teacher at the desk looks down at the book and he also looks up, and we cut to a shot of the student. I think we need the student there because he *presents the case.*

STUDENT: But couldn't we recognize the notebook from scene two? We know it's the same student we saw preparing, so we don't need a shot of him.

MAMET: The book is identification enough?

STUDENT: Yeah; we know it's the student's book. The book stands for the student.

MAMET: Very good. Of course, you're right. I got caught up in the idea of following the protagonist around. Good. Now, this brings us to the application of the principle of the throughline to the plastic elements of production.

What music is playing? What time of day or night is it? What do the costumes and the sets look like? At one point you mentioned someone reading a magazine. You say a magazine: *what* magazine? I'm not overstating the case; because somebody makes these decisions, and that person is called the director. The prop person is going to say, 'what should the notebook look like?' and what are you, the director, going to say? First off, what is the untutored person going to say? 'Golly, the scene is about *to get a retraction*, so what kind of notebook does a person who wants to get a retraction carry?' If this seems dorky, if this seems overstated to you, look at American movies. Because that's the way all American movies are made. 'Hi, how are you today because I just got back from Vietnam.' In Hollywood, a committee of thugs wants to make sure that each word, moment, shot, prop, sound, et cetera, in a movie will stand for and, in effect, advertise the film. This committee is called 'producers,' and they are to the arts what the ducking stool was to jurisprudence.*

What answer do we give to the prop person who says 'what's the notebook look like?' What are you going to say?
STUDENT: Doesn't it depend on what the objective is or isn't?
MAMET: No, because you can't make a 'retraction notebook' any

---

*Natural, creative exuberance and self-confidence are wonderful things in an artist. They are inhibited from growing into arrogance not through the content but because of the process of education. Even the minimally serious artist is humbled constantly by the screaming demands of craft.

Those who style themselves 'producers' have not had the benefit of any such education, and their arrogance knows no bounds. They are like the white slave owners of old, sitting on their porches with their cooling drinks and going on about the inherent laziness of the Negro race. The 'producer,' having never had a run-in with the demands of a craft, sees all ideas as basically equal and his own as first among them, for no reason other than that he has thought of it. This notion is easier to fathom if one thinks back to the period of early adolescence and to, perhaps, the critique of an English teacher who said to our efforts: 'I don't understand' or 'it is unclear,' of which correction one thought: 'The old fool . . . *I* know what I meant.'

I have a great deal of pride and, I suppose, a large admixture of arrogant pride. I, in my generally losing contest with these self-styled 'producers,' many times console myself by thinking that after society falls apart, I will be able to eke out at least my meals and shelter by putting on plays that may make people laugh; but that these 'producers' would have to wait until I and those like me went to work before they could eat.

Yes, that is how I see 'producers.' They are 'let me take that cow to the fair for you, son.'

more than you can act what room you just came out of –
though there are, to their shame, schools of acting that purport
to teach such. What should the notebook look like – this
'retraction notebook'?

STUDENT: Put a label on the cover?

MAMET: The audience won't read it. It's like a sign. The audience
doesn't want to read a sign; they want to watch a motion
picture, in which the story is advanced through the cut.

STUDENT: They don't have to read it. It's a black folder, white
label, looks like a book report.

MAMET: Why should it look like a book report? I mean, it's not a
bad idea that it should look like a book report, but why is it a
good idea that it look like a book report? Prop person says,
'what does it look like?' What's the correct answer? What does
it do? What does the *report* do?

STUDENT: It *presents the case.*

MAMET: Right. Now, what's the shot list for presenting the case?

STUDENT: The open book on the desk.

MAMET: What's the next shot?

STUDENT: The face of the teacher.

MAMET: What is not the next shot? The face of the student, right?
So, therefore, how does the book look?

STUDENT: Prepared.

MAMET: No, you can't make the book look prepared. You can
make it look *neat*. That might be nice, but that's not the most
important thing for your answer to the prop person.* Think
about the shot list and the objective *to present the case.* To
make it prepared, to make it neat, to make it convincing, the
audience ain't going to notice. What are they going to notice?

STUDENT: That it's the same book they've seen already.

MAMET: So what's your answer to the prop person?

STUDENT: Make it recognizable.

MAMET: Exactly so! Good! *You've got to be able to recognize it.*

---

*The audience will accept anything they have not been given a reason to disbelieve.
So the report must look, minimally, neat, for if it did not, the audience might
question the sincerity of the hero's desire. The neatness of the report is an *antiseptic*
rather than a *creative* consideration.

That is the most important thing about this report. This is how you use the principle of throughline to answer questions about the set and to answer questions about the costumes. The book *in general* is not important. What's important is what it does in the scene. The most blatant thing it does in the scene is *present the case*. Since we aren't going to see a shot of the student, it's got to *present the case* for him. That shot of the uninflected book has to present the case. Since we know that it has to be uninflected, the answer cannot be 'it's a *prepared* book.' The answer cannot be 'it's a contrite book.' The answer must be 'it's got to be the same book we saw in shot two.' In choosing the book, you are telling the audience *that thing without which they cannot understand the movie.* In this case, it's the essential element of the shot. *That without which the beat will not survive* is that it's the same notebook as in the previous beat. It is essential to the telling of the story.

Every time you make a choice as a director, it must be based on whether the thing in question is essential to telling the story. If we don't need the shot of the student, then we'd better be jolly, jolly sure that they understand that it's the same book.

The audience is only going to look at the most overriding thing in the frame. You must take charge of and direct their attention. It's also the principle of magic: What is the single important thing? Make it easy for them to see it, and you're doing your job. You don't have to make it a book about *getting your retraction.* You do have to make it the same notebook. So our beats are *to show up early, to prepare, to pay homage, to present the case.* What were the shots for *to show up early*?

STUDENT: He arrives and tries the doorknob.

MAMET: No. I hope you don't think I'm being picayune, but it's very useful to think of the film in exactly the same way the audience is going to perceive the film. What they're going to see in the first shot is *a man walking down the hall.* What are the shots?

STUDENT: Man walks down hall, shot of a hand on a doorknob, same man sits down on a bench.

MAMET: Perfect. Now, why did all those Olympic skaters fall down? The only answer I know is that they hadn't practiced enough. Practice with these tools until you find them boring, then practice some more. Here is a tool – choose your shots, beats, scenes, objectives, and *always* refer to them by the names you choose.

What are the shots for *to prepare?*

STUDENT: Man takes the notebook out, rips out a tab, writes something down on a tab, puts the tab in the plastic thing, closes the tab.

MAMET: Good. *To pay homage?*

STUDENT: Shot of the man looking and getting up out of the frame. A shot of the man running to a glass door. He opens the door, a man walks through.

MAMET: Good. Next beat?

STUDENT: *To present the case.* An empty desk. The notebook put on the desk, and a shot of the man sitting at the desk, looking down at it.

MAMET: Good. Let's finish it now. How do we reach a conclusion?

STUDENT: The teacher could start considering the book.

MAMET: What is the beat we are trying to dramatize here?

STUDENT: *Judgment.*

MAMET: Okay, the idea is *judgment. Consideration* is a different way of saying it. But the teacher considering the book doesn't really have any weight of montage behind it. It's basically expository. A guy picks up evidence and looks at it and makes up his own mind. Not good storytelling, as Aristotle told us. The character shouldn't 'just get the idea.'

STUDENT: Why is the next beat *judgment*, if all the way through, the beats are about the student and the teacher? Don't you want to follow the course of the student and not the teacher?

MAMET: What's your idea?

STUDENT: I saw the beat as *taking a stand.* He's presented the case, and you cut to him standing there, and he's not going to take no for an answer. And you cut back to the teacher looking up at the kid.

MAMET: What are some other ideas for the next beat?

STUDENT: *Receipt of the retraction.*

MAMET: Yeah, that's an idea.

STUDENT: *To be denied.*

MAMET: That's not really the beat; that's the result. That's the end of some other beat. The student/protagonist has to be working toward completion.

STUDENT: At this point in the story, you are going to expect the response of the professor. The next logical beat after *presenting the case* is judgment, *judging the case.* When that beat is over, he has or hasn't gotten the retraction. We don't have to follow the student to complete the throughline, do we?

MAMET: No.

STUDENT: But it's the kid's job to get a retraction.

MAMET: Yes, it is. But it doesn't have to be a picture of the kid. We want to know what happens next in terms of the throughline, not in terms of what the protagonist does. What was our last shot in the last beat?

STUDENT: The professor looking down at the book.

MAMET: The professor's looking down. Cut to a shot of a bunch of kids in the doorway. A new kid comes, and they all look over to one side or another. We cut to their point of view of the empty classroom with the kid sitting there and the professor looking at him. To get to the idea of judgment. Now we're ready for the resolution. We see the professor in a long shot, he opens the book, he looks down to his right, we cut to the desk drawer, we see him open the desk drawer and he takes out a stamp pad. You see him stamp the book. And you cut to a shot of the kid, who is smiling, and he picks up the book, and we cut to a shot of the kid's hand closing the book, and then from the back of the classroom you see the kid go to his seat and the professor stand and call the rest of the class, and they go in, and they sit down. All right?

STUDENT: What if he *didn't get the retraction?*

MAMET: I don't know. It's our first movie. Let's make it a happy ending, what the hell. And now we're done, and that was excellent work.

Countercultural Architecture and
Dramatic Structure

I was a student in the turbulent sixties in Vermont at a countercultural college. In that time and place, there flourished something called a school of Countercultural Architecture. Some people back then thought that traditional architecture had been too stifling, and so they designed and built a lot of counterculture buildings. These buildings proved unlivable. Their design didn't begin with the idea of the building's purpose; it began with the idea of how the architect 'felt.'

As those architects looked at their countercultural buildings over the years, they may have reflected that there's a reason for traditional design. There's a reason that doors are placed in a certain way, there's a reason that sills are made a certain way.

All those countercultural buildings may have expressed the intention of the architect, but they didn't serve the purpose of the inhabitants. They all either fell down or are falling down or should be torn down. They're a blot on the landscape and they don't age gracefully and every passing year underscores the jejune folly of those countercultural architects.

I live in a house that is two hundred years old. It was built with an axe, by hand, and without nails. Barring some sort of man-made catastrophe, it will be standing in another two hundred years. It was built with an understanding of, and a respect for, wood, weather, and human domestic requirements.

It's very difficult to shore up something that has been done badly. You'd better do your planning up front, when you have the time. It's like working with glue. When it sets, you've used up your time. When it's almost set, you then have to make quick decisions under pressure. If you design a chair correctly, you can put all the time into designing it correctly and assemble it at your leisure. In fact, the ancient chairmakers – which is to say chairmakers up until about the turn of century – used to make their chairs without glue because they correctly understood not only the nature of joints but the nature of woods. They knew which woods

would shrink and which would expand with age, so that these
woods, when correctly combined, would make the chair stronger
over time.

I recognized two things in finishing up my second movie. When
you're doing the movie, after you finish with the shot list but
before you start shooting it, you have a period called 'preproduction.' In preproduction, you say, 'you know what would be a
good idea? To really make the audience understand that we're in a
garage, what about a sign that says "garage."' So you meet with
your art department and you talk a lot about signs and you make
up a lot of signs. I made two movies and I made up a lot of signs.
You never see the signs in a movie – never. You just never see
them. They are after-the-fact attempts to shore up that which was
not correctly designed. Another handy but useless 'reminder' tool
is the process of looping, or ADR (Automatic Dialogue Reading –
dialogue recorded and inserted after the movie has been shot), to
communicate to the audience information the film lacks. For
example, dubbing words into somebody's mouth when we see his
back on the screen. To wit: 'oh, look, here we go down that
staircase that we're trying to get to the bottom of.' That never
works either. Why? Because all that the audience cares about is
what is the thrust of the scene – what does the hero want? More
precisely, what is the essential aspect of the shot? They aren't
there to look at signs, and they won't look at them. You can't
force them to look at them. It is the nature of human perception
to go to the most interesting thing; and just as we know in terms
of the dirty joke, the most interesting thing is *what happens next*
in the story that you promised the audience you were going to tell
them. You can't make them stop and look at that sign. They don't
care to indulge you by listening to your looping, so you'd better
do your work beforehand.

That work is done in understanding the nature of the materials
and using that understanding in the design of the film. That's
basically what a film is; it's a design. You know, all these personally felt statements of people who try to put a lot of garbage
into the shot and pan around a bunch to show how moved they
are by their chosen subject: these are just like countercultural
architecture. They may be a personal statement, but they don't
serve the turn of the inhabitants or, in this case, the turn of the

viewers who would like to know *what happens next*. You tax the audience every time you don't move on to the next essential step of the progression as quickly as possible. You're taxing their good nature. They may indulge you for political reasons – which is what most of modern art is about. Political reasons being, 'dammit, I *like* those kinds of bad movies' or 'I *like* that kind of countercultural statement. I am one of that group, and I endorse the other members of this group, who appreciate the sort of things this fellow is trying to say.' The audience can endorse the triviality of modern art, but they can't like it. I suggest you think about the difference between the way people talk about any performance artist and the way they talk about Cary Grant. And to you lovely enthusiasts who will aver that the purpose of modern art is not to be liked, I respond, 'oh, grow up.'

The job of the film director is *to tell the story through the juxtaposition of uninflected images* – because that is the essential nature of the medium. It operates best through that juxtaposition, because that's the nature of human perception: to perceive two events, determine a progression, and want to know what happens next.

'Performance art' works, as it's the nature of human perception to order random images in favor of an overriding preconception. Another example of this is neurosis. Neurosis is the ordering of unrelated events or ideas or images in favor of an overriding preconception.

'I am,' for example, 'an unsightly person': that's the overriding preconception. Then, given any two unrelated events I can order them to make them mean *that*. 'Oh, yes, I understand. This woman came out of the hall and did not seem to notice me and rushed into the elevator and quickly pushed the button and the elevator closed because I am an unattractive person.' That's what neurosis is. It is the attempt of a disordered mind to apply the principle of cause and effect. This same attempt takes place subconsciously in the viewer of a drama.

If the lights go out and the curtain goes up, the overriding idea is 'a play is taking place'; 'someone is telling me a story.'

The human brain, understanding that, will take all of the events in the play and form them into a story just as it forms perception into neurosis. It is the nature of human perception to connect unrelated images into a story, because we need to make the world make sense.

If the overriding idea is that *a play is taking place*, then we will form the images that we see between the time the curtain goes up and the time the curtain comes down *into* a play whether or not they have been structured as one. Just so with the movie, which is why bad filmmaking can 'succeed.' It is our nature to want to make sense of these events – we can't help it. The human mind would make sense of them even if they were a random juxtaposition.

This being the nature of human perception, the smart dramatist will use it to his or her advantage and say, 'well, if the human mind is going to do all that anyway, why don't *I* do it first? Then I will be going with the flow rather than battling against the tide.'

If you aren't telling a story, moving from one image to another, the images have to be more and more 'interesting' per se. If you *are* telling a story, then the human mind, as it's working along with you, is perceiving your thrust, both consciously and, more important, subconsciously. The audience members are going to go along with that story and will require neither inducement, in the form of visual extravagance, nor explanation, in the form of narration.

They want to see what's happening next. Is the guy going to get killed? Is the girl going to kiss him? Will they find the money buried in the old mine?

When the film is correctly designed, the subconscious and the conscious are in alignment, and we *need* to hear what happens next. The audience is ordering the events just as the author did, so we are in touch with both his conscious and his unconscious mind. We have become involved in the story.

If we don't care what happens next, if the film is *not* correctly designed, we may, unconsciously, create our own story in the same way that a neurotic creates his own cause-and-effect rendition of the world around him, but we're no longer interested in the story that we're being told. 'Yes, I saw that the girl put the kettle on the fire and then a cat ran out on stage,' we might say of 'performance art.' 'Yes, I saw, but I don't quite know where it's going. I'm following it, but I am certainly not going to risk my unconscious well-being by becoming involved.'

That's when it stops being interesting. So that's where the bad author, like the countercultural architect, has to take up the slack by making each subsequent event *more* diverting than the last; to trick the audience into paying attention.

The end of this is obscenity. Let's really see their genitals, let's really endanger the actor through stunts, let's really set the building on fire. Over the course of a movie, it forces the filmmaker to get more and more bizarre. Over the course of a career, it forces a filmmaker to get more and more outré; over the course of a culture, it forces the culture to degenerate into depravity, which is what we have now.

Interest in a film comes from this: the desire to find out what happens next. The less reality conforms to the neurotic's view, the more bizarre his explanation must become, the end of which development is psychosis – 'performance art' or 'modern theater' or 'modern filmmaking.'

The structure of any dramatic form should be a syllogism – which is a logical construct of this form: If A, then B. A play or movie proceeds from a statement: '*if A*' (in which a condition of unrest is created or posited), to a conclusion: '*then B*' (at which time entropy will once again rear its corrective head, and a condition of rest will have been once again achieved).

For example, as we've seen, if a student *needs a retraction*, he will pursue a series of actions that will lead him to the retraction or to an irrevocable denial of the retraction. And then he will be at rest; a condition of entropy will have been achieved.

This *entropy* is one of the most interesting aspects of our life as a whole. We are born, certain things happen, and we die. The sexual act is a perfectly good example. Things are called into motion that did not heretofore exist and that demand some form of resolution. Something is called into existence that did not heretofore exist, and then the unrest that this new thing creates has to be resolved, and when it's resolved, the life, the sexual act, the play, is done. That's how you know when it's time to go home.

The guy solved his problem at the whorehouse. The guy lost all his money at the racetrack. The couple was reunited. The bad king died. How do we know this is the end of the story? Because *the rise to power of the bad king* was the problem that we came to see solved. How do we know that *when they kiss* it's the end of the movie? Because it's a movie about the boy not getting the girl. The solution of the problem posited at the beginning of the experience is the end of the story. That's also how we know the scene is over, isn't it?

We said that the scene is the correct unit of study. If you understand the scene, you understand the play or movie. When the problem posited by the scene is over, the scene is over. A lot of times in movies you want to get out of the scene *before* the problem is over and have it answered in the *next* scene, as a matter of fact. Why? So that the audience will follow you. They, you will remember, want to know what happens next.

To get into the scene late and to get out early is to demonstrate respect for your audience. It's very easy to manipulate an audience – to be 'better' than the audience – because you've got all the cards. 'I don't have to tell you *anything*; I can change the story in midstream! I can be whatever I want. Go to hell!' But listen to the difference between the way people talk about films by Werner Herzog and the way they talk about films by Frank Capra, for example. One of them may or may not understand something or other, but the other understands what it is to tell a story, and he *wants* to tell a story, which is the nature of the dramatic art – to tell a story. That's all it's good for. People have tried for centuries to use drama to change people's lives, to influence, to comment, to express themselves. It doesn't work. It might be nice if it worked for those things, but it doesn't. The only thing the dramatic form is good for is telling a story.

If you want to tell a story, it might be a good idea to understand a little bit about the nature of human perception. Just as, if you want to know how to build a roof, it might be a good idea to understand a little bit about the effects of gravity and the effects of precipitation.

If you go up into Vermont and you build a roof with a peak, the snow will fall off. You build a flat roof, the roof will fall down from the weight of the snow – which is what happened to a lot of the countercultural architecture of the 1960s. 'There may be a reason people have wanted to hear stories for ten million years,' the performance artist says, 'but I really don't *care*, because *I have something to say.*'

The film business is caught in a spiral of degeneracy because it's run by people who have no compass. And the only thing *you* can do in the face of this downward force is tell the truth. Anytime anyone tells the truth, that's a counterforce.

You cannot hide your objective. No one can hide. Contemporary

American films are almost universally sloppy, trivial, and obscene. If your objective is to succeed in the 'industry,' your work, and your soul, will be exposed to these destructive influences. If you desperately crave acceptance by that industry, you will likely become those things.

The actor cannot hide his or her objective, neither can the playwright, neither can the film director. If a person's objective is truly — and you don't have to do it humbly, because you'll get humble soon enough — to *understand the nature of the medium*, that objective will be communicated to the audience. How? Magically. I don't know how. Because it will. It just can't be hidden. In addition to what you will or will not learn about the medium through your desire to understand it, that desire *itself* will be manifested.

I carve wood sometimes. It's magical how the wooden object creates itself. One becomes enthralled by and very observant of the grain of the wood, and the piece tells you how to carve it.

Sometimes the piece is fighting back against you. If you're honest in making a movie, you'll find that it's often fighting back against you too. It's telling you how to write it. Just as we found in the 'got a retraction' movie.

Its very, very difficult to do these very, very simple problems. They're fighting back against you, these problems, but the mastery of them is the beginning of the mastery of the art of film.

The Tasks of the Director

What to Tell the Actors and Where to Put the Camera

I've seen directors do as many as sixty takes of a shot. Now, any director who's watched dailies knows that after the third or fourth take he can't remember the first; and on the set, when shooting the tenth take, you can't remember the purpose of the scene. And after shooting the twelfth, you can't remember why you were born. Why do directors, then, shoot this many takes? Because they don't know what they want to take a picture of. And they're frightened. If you don't know what you want, shoot it and sit down. Suppose you are directing the 'get a retraction' movie. What are you going to tell the actor who does that first beat for you? What do we refer to; what is our compass here? What is a simple tool to which we may refer to answer the question?

To give direction to the actor, you do the same thing you do when you give direction to the cameraman. You refer to *the objective of the scene*, which is this case is *to get a retraction*; and to the meaning of this beat, which here is *to arrive early*.

Based on this, you tell the actor to do those things, and only those things, he needs to do for you to shoot the beat, *to arrive early*. You tell him to go to the door, try the door, and sit down. That is literally what you tell him. Nothing more.

Just as the shot doesn't have to be inflected, the acting doesn't have to be inflected, nor should it be. The acting should be a performance of the simple physical action. Period. Go to the door, try the door, sit down. He doesn't have to walk down the hall respectfully. This is the greatest lesson anyone can ever teach you about acting. Perform the physical motions called for by the script as simply as possible. Do *not* 'help the play along.'

He doesn't have to sit down respectfully. He doesn't have to turn the door respectfully. The script is doing that work. The more the actor tries to make each physical action carry the meaning of the 'scene' or the 'play,' the more that actor is running your movie. The nail doesn't have to look like a house; it is not a house. It is a *nail*. If the house is going to stand, the nail must do the work of a nail. To do the work of the nail, it has to *look* like a nail.

The more the actor is giving him or herself over to the specific uninflected physical action, the better off your movie is, which is why we like those old-time movie stars so much. They were awfully damn simple. 'What do I do in this scene?' was their question. Walk down the hall. How? Fairly quickly. Fairly slowly. Determinedly. Listen to those simple adverbs – the choice of actions and adverbs constitutes the craft of directing actors.

What's the action? *To get a retraction*. What's the meaning of the beat? *To arrive early*. What are the specific shots? Guy walking down the hall, guy tries the doorknob, guy sits down. Good luck will be the residue of good design. When the actor says, 'how do I walk down the hall?' you say, 'I don't know ... quickly.' Why do

you say that? Because your subconscious is working on the problem. Because you've paid your dues at this point and you're entitled
to make what may seem to be an arbitrary decision but may also be
a subconscious solution to a problem; and you have honored the
subconscious by referring the problem to it long enough for it to
cough up the answer.

Just as it's in the nature of the audience to want to help the story
along, to help along good work, that is to say work which is
respectful of its inner nature, just so it's in the nature of your
subconscious to want to help this task along. A lot of decisions that
you think are going to be made arbitrarily are arrived at through
the simple and dedicated workings of your subconscious. When
you look back at them, you will say, 'well, I got lucky there, didn't
I?' and the answer will be 'yes' because you paid for it. You paid for
that subconscious help when you agonized over the structure of the
film. The shot list.

Actors will ask you a lot of questions. 'What am I thinking here?'
'What's my motivation?' Where did I just come from?' The answer
to all of these questions is *it doesn't matter*. It doesn't matter
because you can't act on those things. I defy anyone to act where he
just came from. If you can't act on it, why think about it? Instead,
your best bet is to ask the actor to do his simple physical actions as
simply as possible.

'Please walk down the hall, try the doorknob.' You don't have to
say 'try the doorknob and it's locked.' Just try the doorknob and sit
down. Movies are made out of very simple ideas. The good actor
will perform each small piece as completely and as simply as
possible.

Most actors are, unfortunately, not good actors. There are many
reasons for this, the prime reason being that theater has fallen apart
in our lifetime. When I was young, most actors, by the time they got
to be thirty, had spent ten years on the stage, earning their living.

Actors don't do that anymore, so they never get a chance to learn
how to act well. Virtually all of our actors in this country are badly
trained. They're trained to take responsibility for the scene, to be
emotional, to use each role to audition for the next. To make each
small and precious moment on the stage or screen both 'mean' the
whole play and display their wares, to act, in effect, 'sit down
because I'm the king of France.' It's not that actors are dumb

people. To the contrary, the job, in my experience, attracts folk of high intelligence, and most of them are dedicated people; bad actors and good actors are in the main dedicated and hardworking people. Unfortunately, most actors don't accomplish much, because they're badly trained, underemployed, and anxious both to advance their career and to 'do good.'

Also, most actors try to use their intellectuality to portray the idea of the movie. Well, that's not their job. Their job is to accomplish, *beat by beat*, as simply as possible, the specific action set out for them by the script and the director.

The purpose of rehearsal is to tell the actors *exactly* the actions called for, beat by beat.

When you get on the set, the good actors who took careful notes will show up, *do* those actions – not *emote*, not *discover*, but do what they're getting paid to do, which is to perform, as simply as possible, exactly the thing they rehearsed.

If you, the director, understand the theory of montage, you don't have to strive to bring the actors to a real or pretended state of frenzy or love or hate or anything emotional. It's not the actor's job to be emotional – it is the actor's job to be *direct*.

Acting and dialogue fall into the same boat. Just as with the acting, the purpose of the dialogue is not to pick up the slack in the shot list. The purpose of dialogue is not to carry information about the 'character.' They only reason people speak is to get what they want. In film or on the street, people who describe themselves to you are lying. Here is the difference: In the bad film, the fellow says, 'hello, Jack, I'm coming over to your home this evening because I need to get the money you borrowed from me.' In the good film, he says, 'where the hell were you yesterday?'

You don't have to narrate with the dialogue any more than you have to narrate with the pictures or the acting. The less you narrate, the more the audience is going to say, 'wow. What the *heck* is happening here? What the *heck* is going to happen next . . .?' Now, if you're telling the story with the pictures, then the dialogue is the sprinkles on top of the ice cream cone. It's a gloss on what's happening. The story is being carried by the shots. Basically, the perfect movie doesn't have any dialogue. So you should always be striving to make a silent movie. If you don't, what will happen to you is the same thing that happened to the American film industry.

Instead of writing the shot list, you'll have the student rise and say, 'isn't that Mr. Smith? I think I'll get a retraction from him.' Which is what happened to American films when sound came in, and they've gotten worse ever since.

If you can learn to tell a story, to break down a movie according to the shots and tell the story according to the theory of montage, then the dialogue, if it's good, will make the movie somewhat better; and if it's bad, will make the movie somewhat worse; but you'll still be telling the story *with the shots*, and they can take the brilliant dialogue out, if need be – as, in fact, they do when a film is subtitled or dubbed – and a great film, so treated, is injured hardly at all.

Now that we know what to tell the actors, we need an answer to the one question the crew will ask you again and again – 'where do we put the camera?' The answer to this question is, 'over there.'

There are some directors who are visual masters – who bring to moviemaking a great visual acuity, a brilliant visual sense. I am not one of those people. So the answer I'm giving is the only answer I know. I happen to know a certain amount about the construction of a script, so that's what I'm telling you. The question is, 'where do I put the camera?' That's the simple question, and the answer is, 'over there in that place in which it will capture the uninflected shot necessary to move the story along.'

'Yes, but,' a lot of you are saying, 'I know that the shot should be uninflected, but really since it's a scene about *respect* shouldn't we put the camera at a respectful angle?'

No; there is no such thing as 'a respectful angle.' Even if there *were*, you wouldn't want to put the camera there – if you did so, you wouldn't be letting the story *evolve*. It's like saying: 'a naked man is walking down the street copulating with a whore while going to a whorehouse.' Let him *get* to the whorehouse. Let each shot stand by itself. The answer to the question 'where do you put the camera?' is the question 'what's the shot of?'

That's my philosophy. I don't know better. If I knew a better answer to it, I would give to you. If I knew a better answer to the shot, I would give it to you, but because I don't, I have to go back to step number one, which is 'keep it simple, stupid, and don't violate those rules that you *do* know. If you don't know which rule applies, just don't muck up the more general rules.'

I know it's a shot of *a guy walking down a hall*. I'm going to put the camera *somewhere*. Is one place better than another? Probably. Do I know which place is better than another? No? then I'll let my subconscious pick one, and put the camera there.

Is there a better answer to the question? There may be, and the better answer may be this: in the storyboard for a movie or a scene, you may see a certain pattern developing, which might tell you something. Perhaps your task as a designer of shots is, after a point, that of a 'decorator,' quite frankly.

'What are the 'qualities' of the shot?' I don't happen to think that's the most important question in making a movie. I think it's an important question, but I don't think it's the most important question. When faced with the necessity of a particular election, I'm going to answer what I think is the most important question first, and then reason backward and answer the smaller question as best I can.

Where do you put the camera? We did our first movie and we had a bunch of shots with a hall here and a door there and a staircase there.

'Wouldn't it be nice,' one might say, 'if we could get this hall *here*, really around the corner from the door *there*; or to get that door *here* to *really be* the door that opens on the staircase to that door *there*? So we could just move the camera from one to the next?

It took me a great deal of effort and still takes me a great deal and will continue to take me a great deal of effort to answer the question thus: no, not only is it not important to have those objects literally contiguous, it is important to fight against this desire, because fighting it reinforces an understanding of the essential nature of film, which is that it is made of disparate shots, cut together. It's a *door*, it's a *hall*, it's a *blah-blah*. *Put* the camera 'there' and photograph, *as simply as possible*, that object. If we don't understand that we both can and *must* cut the shots together, we are sneakily falling victim to the mistaken theory of the Steadicam. It might be nice to have these objects next to each other so as to avoid having to move the crew, but you don't get any sneaky artistic good out of literally having them next to each other. *You can cut the shots together.*

This relates to what I said about acting: if you can cut different pieces, different scenes together, different lines together, you don't have to have somebody in every shot with the same 'continuous intention.' The same 'commitment to and understanding of the character.' You don't need it.

The actor has to be performing a simple physical action for the space of ten seconds. It does not have to be part of the 'performance of the film.' Actors talk about the 'arc of the film' or the 'arc of the performance.' It doesn't exist on stage. It's not there. The performance takes care of both. The 'arc of the performance,' the act of controlling, of doling out emotion here and withholding emotion there, just doesn't exist. It's like a passenger sticking his arms out of the airplane window and flapping them to make the plane more aerodynamic. This commitment to the arc of the film – it's ignorance on the part of the actor, ignorance of the essential nature of acting in film, which is that the performance will be created by the juxtaposition of simple, for the most part uninflected shots, and simple, uninflected physical actions.

The way to shoot the car crash is not to stick a guy in the middle of the street and run over him and keep the camera on. The way to shoot the car crash is to shoot the pedestrian walking across the street, shoot the shot of the onlooker whose head turns, shoot the shot of a man inside the car who looks up, shoot the shot of the guy's foot coming down on the brake pedal, and shoot the shot underneath the car with the set of legs lying at a strange angle (with thanks to Pudovkin, for the above). Cut them together, and the audience gets the idea: accident.

If that's the nature of film for the director, that's the nature of film for the actor too. Great actors understand this.

Humphrey Bogart told this story: When they were shooting *Casablanca* and S. Z. (Cuddles) Sakall or someone comes to him and says, 'they want to play the "Marseillaise," what should we do? – the Nazis are here and we shouldn't be playing the "Marseillaise,"' Humphrey Bogart just nods to the band, we cut to the band, and they start playing 'bah-bah-bah-*bah*.'

Someone asked what he did to make that beautiful scene work. He says, 'they called me in one day, Michael Curtiz, the director, said, "stand on the balcony over there, and when I say "action" take a beat and nod,"' which he did. That's great acting. Why? What more could he possibly have done? He was required to nod, he nodded. There you have it. The audience is terribly moved by his simple *restraint* in an emotional situation – and this is the essence of good theater: good theater is people doing extraordinarily moving tasks as simply as possible. Contemporary playwriting, filmmaking, and acting tend to offer us the reverse – people performing mundane and predictable actions in an overblown way. The good actor performs his tasks as simply and *as unemotionally* as possible. This lets the audience 'get the idea' – just as the juxtaposition of uninflected images in service of a third idea creates the play in the mind of the audience.

Learn this, and go out and make the movie. You'll get someone who knows how to take a picture, or *you* learn how to take a picture; you get someone who knows how to light, or *you* learn how to light. There's no magic to it. Some people will be *able* to do some tasks better than others – depending upon the degree of their technical mastery and their aptitude for the task. Just like playing the piano. Anybody can learn how to play the piano. For some people it will be very, very difficult – but they can learn it. There's almost no one who can't learn to play the piano. There's a wide range in the middle, of people who can play the piano with various degrees of skill; a very, very narrow band at the top, of people who can play brilliantly and build upon a simple technical skill to create great art. The same thing is true of cinematography and sound mixing. Just technical skills. Directing is just a technical skill. Make your shot list.

Pig – The Movie

The questions that you want to ask as a director are the same questions you want to ask as a writer, the same questions you want to ask as an actor. 'Why now?' 'What happens if I don't?' Having discovered what is essential, you then know what to cut.

Why does the story start now? Why does Oedipus have to find out who his parents are? This is a trick question. The answer is this: he doesn't have to find out who his parents are. He has to cure the plague on Thebes. He discovers he, himself, is the cause of the plague on Thebes. His simple quest for external information led him on a journey, which resulted in his discovery. Oedipus is the model of all tragedy, according to Aristotle.

Dumbo has big ears, that's *his* problem. He was born with it. The problem gets worse, people make more and more fun of him. He has to try to learn to cure it. He meets little friends along the way who come to his aid in this classic myth. (The study of myth is very useful for directors.) Dumbo learns to fly; he develops a talent that he didn't realize he had and comes to this understanding about himself: that he's not worse than his fellows. He's perhaps not better, but he's different, and he has to be himself – when he realizes this, his journey is over. The problem of his big ears has been solved not by ear reduction but by self-discovery – and the story is over.

Dumbo is an example of a perfect movie. Cartoons are very good to watch – are much better to watch, for people who want to direct, than movies.

In the old cartoons, the artists realized the essence of the theory of montage, which is that they could do whatever the heck they wanted. It wasn't any more expensive to draw it from a high angle or from a long angle. They didn't have to keep the actors late to draw a hundred people rather than one person, or send out for that very expensive Chinese vase. Everything was based on the *imagination*. The shot we see in the film is the shot the artist saw in his imagination. So if you watch cartoons, you can learn a great deal about how to choose shots, how to tell the story in pictures, and how to cut.

Question: What starts the story *now*? Because if you don't know what starts the story, what's the impetus to start the story, then you have to rely on 'back story' or history, all those dread terms that those swine out in Hollywood use to describe a process they not only do not understand but don't particularly care about. The story is not begun because the hero 'suddenly gets an idea' – it is brought into being by a concrete external event: the plague on Thebes, the big ears, the death of Charles Foster Kane.

Thus you start the story in such a way that you bring along the audience. They are there *at the birth*. So they are going to want to know what happens next. 'Once upon a time,' for example, 'there was a man who owned a farm' or 'there were once three sisters.'

Just like a dirty joke. That's how the drama is structured – and this drama, like the dirty joke, is just a specialized form of fairy tale.

The fairy tale is a great teaching tool for directors. Fairy tales are told in the simplest of images and without elaboration, without an attempt to characterize. The characterization is left up to the audience.'* In fairy tales, we see that it is simple to know when to begin and to know when to stop. And if one can apply those simple tests to the play as a whole, one can apply them to the scene, which is only a small play, and to the beat, which is only . . . et cetera.

'Once there was a farmer who wanted to sell his pig.' How do I know when I'm finished? When the pig's sold, or when the farmer discovers that he cannot sell the pig – when the end of that syllogism has come to pass.

Now, not only do I know when to start and when I want to stop, but I also know what to keep in and what to throw out. The farmer's interesting encounter with a female swineherd, which has nothing to do with selling the pig, probably shouldn't be in the movie. In plotting a film, one can also ask: 'what am I missing here?' Am I going from the beginning to the end in a logical progression? And if not, what missing term will render the progression logical?

Here's a story: 'once there was a farmer who wanted to sell a pig.' Now, how do you open the film? What are the shots? How do you make up your shot list?

STUDENT: You establish a good farm.
MAMET: Why do you have to establish a good farm? Everybody in
    Hollywood always whines, 'but we won't know where we *are*
    . . .' But I put it to you, ladies and gentlemen, how often in the
    thousands of movies that we've all seen has anyone said, 'hey,
    wait a second, I don't know where I am'? In fact, quite the
    contrary is true. You come to a movie in the middle, turn on the
    TV in the middle, look at a tape in the middle, you know exactly
    what's happening, always, immediately. You are interested in it
    because you want to know what's going on. That's what
    interests you. What would be better than an establishing shot of
    a farm? What will answer the question 'why now?'
STUDENT: The reason he has to sell his pig?

*Bettelheim, *The Uses of Enchantment.*

MAMET: The reason he has to sell his pig. What's his reason? The answer will lead us to a very specific beginning. A beginning specific to *this film* – rather than one specific to *a* film. 'Once there was a farmer who wanted to sell his pig' leads us to 'once there was a farmer who *had* to sell his pig.' You will find that the study of semantics, which is the study of how words influence thought and action, will help you immensely as a director. Notice the difference in those two beginnings: they lead you down very divergent trains of thought. They will change the words you use to tell your ideas to the actors. It's very, very important to be concise. Okay: 'once there was a farmer who had to sell his pig.'

STUDENT: A wide shot of pigs in a pasture. And then the farmer walking across the pasture. The next shot is a For Sale sign that he is hammering.

MAMET: Into his pig?

STUDENT: Into a post.

MAMET: Uh huh. Exposition in film is like exposition in any art form. If you explain the joke's punch line, the audience might understand it, but they won't laugh. The real art, the essential art in choosing the shots, is not so much to make the audience understand as to invest yourself in the clear telling of the story. You aren't smarter than *they* are. *They're* smarter than *you* are. *You* understand the story as well as you possibly can, and then they will too. Putting up a sign is an easy way out. That's not *always* bad per se, but I think we can do better. We can ask *what the character is doing*, but better to ask *what is the meaning of this scene?* (To help understand this distinction, may I recommend the 'Analysis' chapter of *A Practical Handbook for the Actor*, Bruder, Cohn, Olnek, et al.)

Literally, on the page, as it is written, the farmer has to sell his pig. What does this mean in this scene? The *essence* of having to sell one's pig could be many different things. The essence could be, a man fell on hard times. The essence could be, a man had to leave his ancestral home. A man had to take leave of his best friend.

STUDENT: A man had to do his duty.

STUDENT: A man had too many pigs.

MAMET: Well, yes. But you're thinking on a different level of abstraction. The point is not the pigs, right? The point is *what does the pig mean to the man*? A man's business, for example? What might be the meaning of that? A man's business grew too fast for him. What you want to dramatize is not the *surface*, 'a man needs to sell his pig,' but the *essence* – what selling the pig means in *this* story.

Why does he need to sell the pig? The more specifically you think about the nature of the story, the more you can think of the essence of the scene rather than the appearance of the scene, then the easier it will be to find the image. It's a lot easier to find specific images for 'a man fell on reduced circumstances' than for 'once there was a man who had to sell a pig.'

Jung wrote that one can't stand aloof from the images, the stories, of the person who's being analyzed. One has to enter into them.

If you enter into them, they'll mean something to you. If you don't enter into them, then your subconscious will never work. You'll never come up with anything that the audience couldn't have thought of better at home.

It's like the actor who goes home and figures out what the performance is supposed to mean, then shows up on the stage and does *that* performance. The audience will probably understand this actor, and his performance, but they won't care.*

---

*Stanislavsky said that there are three types of actors. The first presents a ritualized and superficial version of human behavior, the version coming from his observation of other bad actors. The actor will give the audience a stock rendition of 'love,' 'anger,' or whatever emotion seems to be called for by the text. The second actor sits with the script and comes up with his own unique and interesting version of the behaviour supposedly called for by the scene, and he comes to the set or stage to present *that*. The third, called the 'organic' actor by Stanislavsky, realizes that *no* behavior or emotion is called for by the text – that only *action* is called for by the text – and he comes to the set or stage armed only with his analysis of the scene and prepared to act moment to moment, based on what occurs in the performance . . . to deny nothing and to *invent nothing*. This last, organic actor is the artist with whom the director wants to work. He is also the artist we most admire on stage and in films. *Curiously*, he is not the artist most usually denominated the *great* actor. Over the years, I have observed that there are two subdivisions of the thespian's art: one is called Acting, and the other is called Great Acting; and that, universally, those who

'Pig for Sale.' Why? The problem starts now. The picture starts with the inception or the discovery of the problem. Most movies start thus: 'honey, is that damn pig, which we can ill afford to keep, still eating up the last groceries in the house?' The real artistry of the film director is to learn to do without the exposition; and, so, involve the audience. Let's come up with some dramatic shot lists that are going to communicate the idea 'why now?'

STUDENT: The letter from the bank arrives?

MAMET: Let's stay away from that.

STUDENT: Start in a graveyard, and the farmer is at the grave, and the next shot would be the house and it's nearly deserted and there's no food in the cupboard.

MAMET: When we see the empty cupboard, we might wonder, why don't they just kill the pig? Here's a different story: A small child is dressed in rags and playing in the yard and then a shot of the pig jumping over the fence and attacking the child. Eh? Kid playing in the yard – she sees something, starts to run away. Second shot, a pig jumps into the thing, squeak, squeak, squeak, squeak, squeak; and the third shot is the farmer walking down the road with the pig. Does that tell you a story? Yes.

But how can we do it without showing the pig mauling the child? We don't want to show the pig mauling the child, because that has one of two results. Every time you show the audience something that is 'real,' they think one of two things: (1) 'oh, dash it all, that's fake' or (2) 'oh my God, that's *real*!' Each one of these takes the audience away from the story you're telling,* and neither one is better than the other. 'Oh,

---

are known as the Great Actors, the Premier Actors of their age, fall into the second of Stanislavsky's categories. They bring to the stage and screen an intellectual pomposity. The audience calls them Great, I think, because it wants to identify with them – with the *actors*, that is, not with the characters the actors portray. The audience wants to identify with these actors because they seem empowered to behave arrogantly in a protected setting. On the other hand, look at the old character actors and comedians: Harry Carey, H. B. Warner, Edward Arnold, William Demarest; look at Thelma Ritter, Mary Astor, Celia Johnson. *Those* people could *act*.

*This is the meaning of the concept 'violating the aesthetic distance.'

he's not really copulating with her' or 'oh my God, he's really copulating with her!' Both lose the audience. If we *suggest* the idea, we can shoot it better than if we *show* it.

What about we cut from kid playing in the yard to mom's in the kitchen, she snaps around, and then she's running out, she grabs a broom, for example. Third shot is dad walking the pig out of the barn. He's on the road, we see him going on past the gate. He's obviously going to get rid of the pig.

STUDENT: But he could just shoot the pig. Don't we have to show the empty cupboard to show why he has to sell the pig?

MAMET: If you try to narrate the fact that the family is on the brink of poverty, you split your focus. You split it between (1) 'I need the money' and (2) 'the pig just attacked my daughter.' Now the guy has two reasons to sell the pig, which is not as good as one reason to sell the pig. Two reasons are equal to no reasons – it's like saying: 'I was late because the bus drivers are on strike and my aunt fell downstairs.'

And so now, what's the idea: once upon a time, *a man had to sell a dangerous pig.*

STUDENT: The first shot is the child playing in the yard.

STUDENT: The second shot is the pig eyeing her.

STUDENT: Cut to mom in the kitchen.

MAMET: She hears something, she turns, she picks up a broom and runs out of the house. Cut to a shot of the farmer leading the pig down the road. Okay.

Here's another possibility. There's an interior of a barn. It's a shot of the door. Door opens, here comes a farmer in work clothes. He comes in and lays down his hoe, picks up a lantern and lights it. Now he turns, and there's a tracking shot of him walking past a row of empty pens to one pen that has a pig in it. He puts the lantern on the ledge. He reaches down and takes out a small trough and puts it in front of the pig. Then he comes up and empties a sack of grain into the trough. He turns the sack upside down and empties it. Then cut back to the shot of the trough, and only two or three kernels fall into it. Then next day – that is, *exterior day*, which shows the audience that *time has passed.* We know the barn sequence was at night – it involved lighting a lantern. This is a shot of an exterior, and it is day. It may be picayune to suggest that a filmscript not contain the description 'the next day' – but as the audience can only determine that it *is* 'the next day' from that which they see on the screen, perhaps it would be a salutary habit only to *describe* those things that the audience is going to see on the screen. The shot of the farmer leading the pig down the road: how does that work?

STUDENT: We're not worrying about the baby anymore.

MAMET: That's right. It's a different story. One is the idea of a man *getting rid of danger*, a man *eradicating danger*. The other is a man *brought to straitened circumstances*. Yeah, you're right. I like the dangerous pig more. How do we know when that story is over?

STUDENT: He sells it or he doesn't.

MAMET: So what happens now? 'John,' the pig's owner, is walking down along the road with the pig, when he comes to a crossroads, and as we say in Chicago, he sees a prosperous-looking man walking down the road. They enter into a conversation, and John convinces the man to buy his pig. Just as the deal is about to be concluded, however, what happens?

STUDENT: The pig bites the man.

MAMET: We said the essence of the scene was the man wants to divest himself of the pig. He's offered a perfect opportunity to sell the pig. Great, we didn't expect it, we thought we were going to have to go all the darned way to town and have to take the bus home, with nothing to read. Now, out of nowhere, comes this guy, a buyer, a perfect opportunity presents itself, and what happens? The pig, the dangerous pig, bites the guy. Now, what's this beat about?

STUDENT: *Failed attempt.*

MAMET: No, let's describe the beat as a step on the road to the objective of the scene, which is to divest oneself of a dangerous commodity. You might say, *capitalizing on a golden opportunity*. That is the *active* thrust of the beat. 'Failed attempt' is just the result.

The great thing about this method is this: what did we say the film was about? *A man had to rid his house of danger. That's* what you go out to film. *It doesn't matter* that all your cinematographers and assistant directors and producers are pleading with you to show more of the farm. You'll say to

them, 'why? It's not a movie about a farm. You want to see a
movie about a farm? Great. You know? go see a travelogue.
Go look at a map. This is a movie about a man who has to rid
his house of danger. Let's make *this* movie. The audience
knows what a farm looks like or they don't. That's their
lookout. Let's respect their privacy.' So, *a man tries to
capitalize on a golden opportunity.*

STUDENT: Well, we could start with him walking with the pig, and
on the roadside, fixing a broken cart wheel, he sees another
farmer. And he goes over and takes the initiative to talk to that
man.

MAMET: Stay with the shots; our guy walking down the road. He
stops because he sees something. Come to his point of view, a
cart with a broken wheel, two pigs in the back, and a
prosperous farmer is fixing the cart wheel. Now, what would
we like to include?

To keep the idea of *capitalize*, what about if he does
something with the pig?

STUDENT: He might walk differently, knowing he was going to sell
the pig.

MAMET: The idea is *capitalize*. The verb is not *to make a sale* but *to
capitalize*.

STUDENT: He can spruce up the pig.

MAMET: The shot is: he takes out a handkerchief and wipes off the
pig's face. He wants to sell the pig.

STUDENT: He might take the handkerchief and put it around the
pig's neck.

MAMET: I like this handkerchief. Let's think of something else.
How else could he capitalize? He wipes the pig's face off and
he ties the thing around the pig and he walks over to the guy.
What's going to happen now?

STUDENT: Maybe he would help the guy fix the cart wheel. That
way he would get into his confidence.

MAMET: He could do that. That would help him capitalize. Good.

STUDENT: When he helps the guy, that would make his sale easier.

MAMET: Yes. We got the shot of him sprucing up the pig, now a
shot of him as he leads the pig over to the farmer, who's just
pulling the cart out, maybe helps him push the cart the last
inch up the road, and the shot of these two guys talking for a

couple of seconds. The new farmer looks down at the pig, looks up at the guy, they talk, the new guy reaches in his pocket, gives our guy some money. It doesn't have to be more intricate than that. Does that tell the story?

Or else you don't have him putting the hand in the pocket. You have the two guys talking, blah-blah-blah . . .

STUDENT: . . . and the shot of that pig, with the same look he had before he attacked the little girl.

MAMET: Exactly so. We have the two guys talking, and they shake hands. Now we have a shot of the new farmer picking the old pig up and putting the pig inside his cart. It's an open cart, so we can have a shot of the pig in the cart, extreme close-up of the pig. We cut to the pig's point of view, through the bars, of two guys talking. While the new farmer puts his hand in his pocket for money, we cut to the shot of . . .

STUDENT: . . . the pig jumping out of the cart, and the next shot is *our* farmer walking down the road with the pig.

MAMET: Great. Now we are really telling the story of 'once there was a farmer who tried everything he could to sell a dangerous pig.'

So now our guy is back to walking down the road with the pig. What's the next interchange going to be? Where's he going to go? Anybody? Let's make sure we follow the rule against circularity. Don't do the same thing twice. This *circularity*, or repetition of the same incident in different guises, is antithetical to the dramatic form. It is the signature of both the *epic* and the *autobiography*, and the reason both are adapted into drama with much difficulty and little success.

STUDENT: The slaughterhouse.

MAMET: We're going to go to the slaughterhouse next. All right. But before we get there, we want to move the story along. Why was it a golden opportunity when he saw the farmer on the road?

STUDENT: Because he didn't have to travel.

MAMET: So because he blew that golden opportunity, *now* what?

STUDENT: He has to go all the way into town, after all.

MAMET: And with what time-honored convention of cinema do we dramatize that?

STUDENT: It's night, and it used to be day . . . ?

MAMET: It's night, and we are at the slaughterhouse. The dark,
inky, Egyptian blackness of night has fallen as only it knows
how to fall. Unencumbered by the roseate glow of the mercury
vapor lamps of the city streets, reflected by the trapped smog of
the inversion layer caused by those internal combustion
engines so favored by today's urban men and women as a
means of powering those machines designed and appointed for
their conveyance. Night, I say again, *night* has fallen. One half
of that circularity, in sum, that never-ending round of day-and-
night. Night: for some a time of sleep, while for others a time
of wakefulness, as in the case of our farmer. Night has fallen.
    Now, our farmer walks into town, walks wearily into town,
it being night, and walks up to the slaughterhouse. Anybody?
STUDENT: What if it's locked?
MAMET: The slaughterhouse is locked, and then what? Do it in
shots.
STUDENT: Shot of the road at night with the farmer and pig.
Another shot of the slaughterhouse. Takes the pig over there.
Shot of the farmer at the slaughterhouse door, which is locked.
MAMET: Yes. What idea do we seem to be dramatizing here?
STUDENT: Last chance to sell the pig?
MAMET: Let's call this beat *the end of the weary quest*. It's not that
it's his last chance; it's that the story is over. Now we're getting
good luck as the residue of good design, we're getting some
extra mileage out of having been assiduous and following the
form. What's the extra mileage? It's night because it took him
a long time to get to the slaughterhouse. It took him a long
time because he didn't get a ride on the truck. He didn't get a
ride because the pig bit the driver. That same dangerous pig
about whom we are now composing a story – so that even the
night is a function of the throughline. The extra mileage is that
the slaughterhouse is locked. Now we have a raking shot from
around the corner of the front of the slaughterhouse, and we
see that the light is on, and we see in the office, the little office,
we see the light go off. A guy comes out the office door, turns
the key, and walks off screen left, as the farmer comes up from
the right and tries the door. So it's *the end of the weary quest*.
STUDENT: How do we know it's a slaughterhouse?
MAMET: How do we know it's a slaughterhouse? There's a big pen

full of pigs behind it. We don't have to know it's a slaughterhouse. We have to know it's *where he wants to go.* It's the end of the quest. There's a building with a pen with a lot of pigs in it, and he's walking toward it.

'The end of the quest' does not, however, mean the end of the story. *End of the weary quest* is only the title of this *beat.* Every turn takes us to the next. That's why it's a good story. Oedipus wants to end the plague. He finds that this plague hit because somebody killed his father, and he finds that he's the guy. Any good drama takes us deeper and deeper to a resolution that is both surprising and inevitable. It's like Turkish taffy; it always tastes good and it always sticks to your teeth.

STUDENT: Do you need the guy leaving the slaughterhouse?

MAMET: I think so. But it's the same question as 'where do you put the camera?' At some point, you, the director, are going to make some decisions, which may seem arbitrary but which in fact may be based on a continually emerging aesthetic understanding of the story. My answer to your question is: 'I think so,' *End of the weary quest.*

What tool are we going to use to help us determine what happens next?

STUDENT: The *throughline.*

MAMET: And we know the throughline is he wants *to rid himself of a dangerous pig.*

STUDENT: So he sits down and waits.

MAMET: He could sit down and wait at the slaughterhouse.

STUDENT: He could tie up the pig at the slaughterhouse and go down the block to the bar. Sits down and has a drink, and the farmer from before comes in and starts a fight. We come back to the pig, he's tugging on the rope and he breaks free and runs into the bar and saves our guy.

MAMET: Now we get a little bit of extra bang for our buck! We got interested in our story and the quiddities and oddities of the story; and what suggested itself was a possible ending to our story. And the reason that we laugh at our ending is it contains the two essential elements that we learned of from Aristotle, *surprise* and *inevitability.*

Aristotle uses rather different words, as he's talking about tragedy rather than drama: he calls the two fear and pity. Pity because of the fate of the poor guy who got himself in such a jam; and fear because, in identifying with the hero, we see that it could also happen to us.

The reason we identify is that the writer left out the narration. We only saw the story.

We can identify with the pursuit of a goal. It's much easier to identify with that than with 'character traits.'

Most movies are written, 'he's the wacky kind of guy who . . .' But then we can't identify with that person. We don't see ourselves in him because we aren't being shown his struggle but instead are shown those idiosyncrasies that *divide* us from him. His 'knowledge of karate,' his wacky habit of yodeling to call his dogs, his peculiar partiality to antique cars . . . how interesting. It's a good thing that the people in Hollywood have no souls, so that they don't have to suffer through the lives they lead. Who would like to suggest another ending?

STUDENT: I was just thinking that perhaps the pig has to fight one more person.

MAMET: As Leadbelly says about the blues, he says in the first verse use a knife to cut bread, and in the second verse use a knife to shave, and in the third verse use it to kill your unfaithful girlfriend. It's the same knife, but the stakes change, which is exactly the way a play or movie is structured. You don't want to use the knife in the first verse to cut bread and in the second verse use it to cut cheese. We already know it can cut bread. What *else* can it do?

STUDENT: But shouldn't we elaborate on the pig's danger somehow, at this point, to raise the stakes?

MAMET: We don't have to get him in trouble. We've got to get him *out* of trouble. Remember, our task is not to create chaos but rather to create order out of a situation that has become chaotic. We don't have to worry about making it interesting; all we have to worry about is getting rid of the pig.

Let's complete this story in a happy, peppy manner that is both surprising and inevitable or, at the very least, pleasing, or, at the very, *very* least, internally consistent. We're sitting on the steps with the pig. It's nighttime. The slaughterhouse is locked.

STUDENT: Well, the next shot is it's daylight and there's a guy walking up the steps to open up the front door of the slaughterhouse and can you guess what's going to happen then? He's going to sell the pig.

MAMET: And then the movie's over. Okay.

STUDENT: How about: it's morning, he wakes up, he thinks something is missing or he feels for his wallet and it's gone. Then we cut to the pig sitting there peacefully and then another shot, a guy lying there dead with our guy's wallet in his hand. The pig saved his wallet.

MAMET: So the pig redeems himself and he can set the pig free. *Setting the pig free* fulfills his original purpose, doesn't it? If the original purpose is to rid himself of danger.

STUDENT: Why didn't he set the pig free before?

MAMET: All right. Good. You have found a very important logical *lacuna* in our film. He is trying, throughout, *to rid himself of danger.* After the first sequence, when the pig attacks the little girl, we, as you point out, need a *second* sequence, which we might call 'the easy solution to a difficult problem.' In this sequence, the farmer is leading the pig away. Shot of the pig, abandoned, on a hillside. Shot, pig's point of view, of the farmer walking away.

Shot of the farmer approaching his house. The farmer stops. Shot, his point of view, of the pig, back in his appointed stall. And then we resume the story, and the next sequence, after 'The Easy Solution,' is 'Capitalizing on a Golden Opportunity.'

Good. I think this discovery makes it a better movie. By the way, I have always found that these piddling points inevitably reveal most important information when they are explored. They are, I think, like the minor or half-forgotten points in dreams. One is tempted to brush past them and think of them as unimportant. But *no* step in the logical progression is unimportant. And I know, from my own experience, that persistence in these 'small' points will be rewarded.

Here's another possible ending. It's dawn. Your sound department is torturing you to okay the inclusion of the sound of birds chirping, ladies and gentlemen. Oh, well. You see the same guy from the office open up the slaughterhouse and see the pig. He opens up and leads the pig into the pen. Our guy wakes up, there's no pig. He goes in, he wants his pig. The owner says, 'how am I going to know what pig is yours, bobbity, bobbity, bobbity.' Our man is obstreperous. The owner of the slaughterhouse gets in a fight with our farmer and is going to brain him to get him to stop bothering him about the pig. We cut to a shot of the pig, our proverbial pig shot, looking back through the fence at our guy. We know it's *our* pig because it's wearing the handkerchief it acquired in the 'golden opportunity' beat, *hein*? Next we have a shot of the slaughterhouse owner turning, and then a shot of our guy, walking back down along the road with the pig. Close-up: our guy stops, turns.

Angle: the pig, who is looking back down the road. Hold on this. The farmer starts walking the pig back in the direction the pig is looking.

Cut to our proverbial pig shot, our pig looking at something. Shot of our farmer paying some money to the slaughterhouse owner. Back to the pig shot, back to the slaughterhouse owner taking the money, slaughterhouse owner moving gingerly past our pig.

Our pig looking through the bars. Shot, his point of view: the slaughterhouse owner entering a pen in which is one single pig. He starts to lead this pig out.

Now. Final sequence. Our farmer walking down the road with *two* pigs. Shot of the farmhouse. The wife comes out. Shot, her point of view: our farmer leading home the two pigs. Shot of the barnyard fence. The gate is swung open, the two pigs enter. Shot of the farmer looking on. Shot of the two pigs kissing. Fade out, fade in. Shot of a pig suckling many little piglets. Shot of 'our' pig, with the handkerchief around his neck, riding the little girl around on his back. Shot of our farmer looking on. What a pig. That's the movie, perhaps. He solved his problem. He didn't get rid of the pig, he got rid of the danger. Now, you can look back over the shot list and ask, 'what have I left out?' As you have devoted yourself consciously, honestly, and gently to the story, you will have created a certificate of deposit, if you will, in your subconscious, on which you can draw for simple answers to

the question of 'where shall I put the camera?' – such questions
also being aided by your reference to your list of objectives: a
man tries to rid himself of danger, a man takes the easy
solution to a difficult problem, a man tries to capitalize on a
golden opportunity, a man comes to the end of a long quest, a
man tries to regain possession, a man rewards a good deed.
That is the story the director must tell – the internal story of
the hero's persistence in a difficult world. Anybody with a
Brownie can take a picture of a 'pig.'

Conclusion

It's always up to you to decide whether you are going to tell the
story through a juxtaposition of shots or whether you are not. It's
not always up to you to decide whether or not that process is going
to be interesting. Any real technique is going to be based on things
within your control. Anything that is not based on things within
your control is not a real technique. We would like to learn a
technique of directing and analyzing as concrete as that of the
shoemaker. The shoemaker will not say when the harness breaks,
'golly, you know, I did it in the most interesting way I knew how!'
Stanislavsky was once having dinner with a steamboat captain on
the Volga River and Stanislavsky said, 'how is it that among all the
major and minor paths of the Volga River, which are so many and
so dangerous, you manage to always steer the boat safely?' And the
captain said, 'I stick to the channel; it's marked.' And the same
thing is true here.

How is it that, given the many, many ways one might direct a
movie, one might always be able, with economy, and perhaps a
certain amount of grace, to tell the story? The answer is: 'stick to
the channel; it's marked.' The channel is the superobjective of the
hero, and the marker buoys are the small objectives of each scene
and the smaller objectives of each beat, and the smallest unit of all,
which is the shot.

The shots are all you have. That's it. Your choice of the shots is all you have. It's what the movie is going to be made up of. *You can't make it more interesting when you get to the editing room.* And also you can't rely on the actors to take up the slack. You can't rely on them to 'make it more interesting.' That's not their job either. You want them to be as simple as you are in your choice of the shots.

If you're correct in the small things, the smallest of which in this case is the choice of a single uninflected shot, then you will be correct in the larger things. And then your film will be as correct and as ordered and as well-intentioned as *you* are. It can never be more so, but it can be less so if you desire to manipulate the material, or hope that God will intervene and save you, which is what most people mean when they talk about 'talent.'

You might want the shoemakers' elves to save you, but how wonderful it is not to *need* the elves to save you. Especially under conditions of great stress, you have to know your trade. And there is a trade to screenwriting and there is a trade to directing a movie. They're very much the same trade. If you pay the price, you can learn that trade. If you persevere, that analytical method of think-ing will become easier for you. The problems of the individual films will not get easier – they only get easier for hacks. The task is always the same. Stick with it until you solve it. It's not your job to make it pretty. It will be as pretty or unpretty as God intended. It's your job to make it correct according to your first principles.

We, just like the protagonists in our movies, have a task. In completing the task, we have to go from one thing to the next as logically as possible. Our work is like mountain climbing. It's frightening sometimes and it's usually arduous, but we don't have to climb the whole mountain all at once. All we have to do is make a foothold here, figure out what that beat is or what that shot is or what that scene is; and when we're completely secure here, *reach* until we get the next foothold that is absolutely secure. Dramatic analysis is a bit like plotting out a compass course over rough territory. When we get lost, or get confused, terrified, tired, fright-ened, all of which will happen to you if you do get the chance to direct a movie, all we have to do is refer to our map and compass. The analysis is not the movie, any more than the map is the terrain – but the right compass and analysis will enable you to navigate both.

The more time you have invested, and the more of yourself you have invested in the plan, the more secure you will feel in the face of terror, loneliness, or the unfeeling or ignorant comments of those from whom you are asking a whole bunch of money or indulgence.

Someone once asked Daniel Boone if he had ever been lost. He replied, 'I was never lost, but I was once a mite bewildered for three days.'

It's good, as the Stoics tell us, to have tools that are simple to understand and of a very limited number – so that we may locate and employ them on a moment's notice. I think the essential tools in any worthwhile endeavor are incredibly simple. And very difficult to master. The task of any artist is not to learn many, many techniques but to learn the most simple technique perfectly. In doing so, Stanislavsky told us, the difficult will become easy and the easy habitual, so that the habitual may become beautiful.

It is the pursuit of an *ideal* that is important. This pursuit will lead to a greater possibility of the unconscious asserting itself, which is to say, the greater possibility of beauty in your work. The Navahos, I am told, used to weave flaws into their blankets to let the devils out.

Some contemporary artist said, 'well, we don't have to weave in the flaws. We can try to weave perfectly. God will see that there's enough flaws in them anyway; that's human nature.'

The application of these principles, in my experience, will help you to weave as perfectly as is humanly possible – which is to say not very perfectly at all.

Keep giving yourself over to the simple task. This dedication will give you great satisfaction. The very fact that you have forsworn the Cult of Self for a little while – the cult of how interesting you and your consciousness are – will communicate itself to the audience. And they will be appreciative in the extreme and give you the benefit of every doubt.

Is it possible to 'do everything right' and still come up with a bad movie? To 'do everything right' means to progress according to philosophically correct principles step by step such that your evaluation of your own effort is honest and you are happy that you have fulfilled the specific task at hand. Is it possible to do that and come up with a bad movie? What's the answer to that? Well, it depends on your definition of bad. Once again, a tool that the Stoics would advise us to use is this: if, before going into battle, you asked an omen of the gods and they told you that you were about to lose, would you not be bound to fight in any case?

It's not up to you to say whether the movie is going to be 'good' or 'bad'; it's only up to you to do your job as well as you can, and when you're done, then you can go home. This is exactly the same principle as the *throughline*. Understand your specific task, work until it's done, and then stop.